ECONOMIC GROWTH OF MIZORAM

About the Author

K.C. Kabra is a senior faculty in Commerce at the North-Eastern Hill University, Shillong. He did his M.Com. and Ph.D. from J.R. Nagar Rajasthan Vidyapeeth University, Udaipur. He was awarded UGC-JRF and IFCI-RF in 1991. Dr. Kabra has published research papers in various journals of repute, and participated in a number of seminars and conferences.

ECONOMIC GROWTH OF MIZORAM

ROLE OF BUSINESS AND INDUSTRY

Dr. K.C. Kabra
Faculty Member
Department of Commerce
North-Eastern Hill University
Shillong (Meghalaya) - 793022

CONCEPT PUBLISHING COMPANY, NEW DELHI-110059

Cataloging in Publication Data--DK
Courtesy: D.K. Agencies (P) Ltd. <docinfo@dkagencies.com>

Kabra, K. C.

Economic growth of Mizoram : role of business and industry / K.C. Kabra.
p. cm.
Includes bibliographical references (p.)
Includes index.
ISBN 13: 9788180695186
ISBN 10: 8180695182

1. Industrial policy--India--Mizoram--History. 2.Mizoram (India)--Commerce--History. 3. Industrialization--India--Mizoram--History. 4. Mizoram (India)--Economic policy. 5. Mizoram (India)--Economic conditions. I. Title.

DDC 338.954 166 22

ISBN-13: 978-81-8069-518-6
ISBN-10: 81-8069-518-2

First Published 2008

Published and Printed by
Ashok Kumar Mittal
Concept Publishing Company
A/15-16, Commercial Block, Mohan Garden
New Delhi-110059 (INDIA)

Phones : 25351460, 25351794
Fax : 091-11-25357103
Email : publishing@conceptpub.com

PREFACE

Business and industry constitute one of the most important sources of livelihood from non-agricultural activity in modern times. Business and industry remain inter-linked as growth in one leads to growth in other. The term 'business' in its widest sense include 'industry' also. In common parlance business is understood as 'trade' and 'aids to trade'. In crude sense of the term 'business' is 'trade'. Business and industry take inputs from society and together render an important service to society by way of manufacturing, providing and distributing products and services that are needed for consumption may be for luxury or for daily needs or for capital goods. The state of advancement of business and industry is reflective of the state of economy of an area/region as the economic development and growth in business and industry go hand in hand.

However, the practices of business and industry vary from place to place, region to region and country to country. These depend upon factors such as availability of resources, skilled manpower, attitude of society, level of education, propensity to consume, readiness to use/import of technology, stage of entrepreneurial development, etc.

Mizoram is a small hilly state carved out of Assam on ethnic grounds located far from main heartland sandwiched between two international boundaries and connected through a narrow road with rest of the country. It has a recorded history of just 100 years. In the process of transforming itself from primitive tribal homeland to Indian statehood, it has seen many interesting developments during short span of time. The studies done so far on Mizoram have emphasis upon political, ethnic and historical and to very little extent on economic aspects.

The present book is an outcome of research undertaken by the author. The study has striven to explore and highlight how business and industry have emerged in this small and distinct State over the last 125 years through various phases such as pre and post British era, pre and post independence, pre and post statehood, etc. and to put these developments systematically in chronological order. For centuries people of the region were not subject to sophisticated provisions of civilized life and even now to an extent they are immune from the coverage of 'central laws and taxation'. The people of the State constitute totally different culture and life style.

Under such a backdrop an attempt has been made to analyze and document how they took to business and industry, what role the government played as a promoter, regulator and participant in business and industry, the role played by State PSUs, the aspect of entrepreneurial development, spread of modern means of credit, etc. The study is an important effort in the direction of presenting the historical developments and present status in a systematic order.

It may appear little out of place for readers especially in view of the advancement that has taken place in the field of research and in the areas of field study across the globe but the author is confident of the value of his endeavour, so far as it is an unique work in the area in as much as no similar study is available in the State. It has opened an area that shall provide a very useful background on which researchers in future can further develop.

The work is submitted in all humility for the readers to evaluate and benefit.

K.C. Kabra

ACKNOWLEDGEMENTS

Words often fail to express one's feeling and indebtedness. It is a matter of great pleasure for me to express my indebtedness to a number of individuals and organizations for their help, tireless guidance, co-operation, continuous encouragement, comments and criticism during the course of this book. It has been a stimulating experience to write the book under meticulous attention, scholarly criticisms, affectionate reprimands and perceptive suggestions without which the book would not have been possible. It is a matter of great pleasure for me to place on record my deepest sense of gratitude for their valuable opinions and healthy criticism, which have gone a long way enabling me giving the book the present shape and completing it successfully. The individuals whom my sincere thanks is due are Dr. K.R. Sharma, Professor and Ex-Head, Department of Commerce, Mizoram University, Aizawl, Dr. N.K. Pandya, Professor & Head, Department of Accounting, M.L.V. Shramjeevi College, J.R. Nagar Rajasthan Vidyapeeth University, Udaipur, Dr. Brajesh Kumar, Lecturer, Department of Commerce, Assam University, Silchar, Dr. R.K.P.G. Singha, Head, Department of Commerce, P.U. College, Aizawl, Dr. Bhartendu Singh, Lecturer, Department of Commerce, P.U. College. I am thankful to executives and staff members of Department of Finance, Department of Law & Judicial Matters, Directorate of Economics & Statistics, Directorate of Industries, Directorate of Trade & Commerce, Directorate of Taxation, MCAB, MRB, MUCO, SBI, SIDBI, UCO, VB, MAMCO, MIFCO, ZENICS, ZIDCO, ZOHANDCO, MIZOFED, MULCO, NECON, SISI who helped me in providing the required data, facts and figures at an appropriate time.

Last but not the least, I am pleased to place on record my thanks to M/s. Concept Publishing Company, New Delhi without which this book would not have seen the light of the day.

At the end, I am alone responsible for all the shortcomings in the book, if any.

Shillong

Dated: 31st March 2007

K.C. Kabra

CONTENTS

1

INTRODUCTION

Business and Industry in Mizoram: An Overview

The Northeastern region, one of the least developed and most problematic part of India consists of eight small states, namely Arunachal Pradesh, Assam, Manipur, Meghalaya, Mizoram, Nagaland, Tripura and Sikkim. It is geographically isolated from the rest of the country and is linked through a narrow stretch of land near Siliguri in West Bengal.

The Northeastern region at the same time is the most densely administered region of the country today. Most of the states were carved out of Assam to fulfil certain ethnic aspirations. Financial and economic viability was not a consideration. It was presumed that the Central Government would bear a substantial burden of governance. As a result, out of the ten special category states of the country receiving most liberal funding from the Central Government, eight states are from this region.

All the states except Assam are small. Tripura is smallest in area and Mizoram is lowest in population. Population is scattered and people live mainly on hilltops. This makes connectivity, in terms of roads, communication, water supply and electricity very expensive. Construction of a kilometre of road in the Northeastern hills costs almost twice as much as in plains. The linkage this region had with rest of India till pre-partition was lost in post-partition, and unfortunately, till today, could not be built-up again to replace the system completely. Therefore, anything brought from elsewhere in India to the region costs more, and at the same time, anything produced in the region costs more to sell anywhere in India.

Constitution of India provides certain reliefs to the hill areas and hill states pertaining to land, tax and funding from Centre. Land in these areas cannot be sold to non-tribals and because of the land mortgage problem, banking sector finds difficult lending to small and medium enterprises (SMEs). These states receive in the form of budgetary support about 90 per cent grants and 10 per cent loan from the Centre, whereas other states receive only 30 per cent grants and 70 per cent loan from that source. Tribals residing in the tribal areas declared as exempted areas from paying income tax. Only the non-tribals working and engaged in business in these tribal areas are subject to tax. Except for Assam, agriculture is not subject to tax in these states.

Incomewise, Northeastern states have not done well. Their per capita Net State Domestic Products (NSDPs) are lower than the all India average. While, India's GDP was growing at an average rate of over six per cent in real terms, Northeastern states' economies were growing at a lesser rate. Barring Assam, manufacturing sector is very small. In the secondary sector, higher growth noticed in few states in some years was mostly due to higher construction activity (mainly roads and government buildings) financed by the Central Government in certain years. The largest contributor to the national income of these states is the tertiary sector, which is mainly composed of public administration and other services. Further, the income from these sources does not come under the purview of tax. Owing to the above factors, the tax base of the Northeastern states is small.

The Northeastern states are no exception to the problem of fiscal profligacy in varying degree. Their revenue resources are not enough to pay for salaries, pension and debt servicing. Growth in their revenue does not commensurate with their expenditure. Financial resources have to be diverted to control insurgency. Besides, there are frequent natural calamities in the form of flood, landslides, etc. In case of rural development, the Central Government funds 75 per cent of the cost of programme and the states have to bear 25 per cent only. However, most of these states cannot even mobilize this 25 per cent of the funds and as a result, much of the rural development funds remain unutilized.

During 1998-99 to 2000-01, in spite of being special category State, Mizoram had continuously high gross fiscal deficit at 11.6 per cent, 13.2 per cent and 12.1 per cent of NSDP respectively as against 1.6 per cent, 6.4 per cent and 7.1 per cent in Assam, 4.6 per cent, 25.7 per cent and 8.3 per cent in Manipur, 5.8 per cent, 7.4 per cent and 8.7 per cent in Meghalaya and 3.4 per cent, 7.6 per cent and 10.2 per cent in Tripura respectively. This reflects not only lack of efforts to raise revenue resources but also imprudent management of public resources[1].

In spite of most liberal funding from the Centre, the benefits of development have not percolated to the lowermost strata of the society in these states. These states have failed to deliver as they have developed oversized administrative machinery, which consumed most of the resources in payment of salary, perks and pension. Practically, meagre fund was left for development works. Leakage of resources and wasteful expenditures continues unabated. Serious efforts have not been made towards mobilization of resources locally. Non-plan and revenue expenditure swelled; plan and capital expenditure dwindled[2].

The development scenario in the Northeastern states brings into sharp focus that dense administration cannot ensure increased capacity to govern. No amount of liberal funding can ensure development unless there is efficient productive investment with clear vision, professional morality and combined will of political elite and bureaucrats to bring the change.

Mizoram—The Locus

Mizoram (previously known as *Lushai* Hills), the land of highlanders, an extension of the Himalayas consisted of unformed young rocks with steep, rugged hills with an average height of about 900 metres, very little flat land and plateau, profusely lacerated and flushed by six major rivers that are largely non-navigable. It is an elongated diamond/tongue shaped mountainous region situated in the southern part of North-East India and is sandwiched between the Chin Hills of Myanmar on the east and south, Chittagong Hill Tracts of Bangladesh and Tripura on the west, with its northern frontier touching Cachar (Assam) and Manipur. Among the Indian States, Mizoram is a small and new State set up in 1987. It consists of seven long north-south traversing parallel ranges with intervening valleys, which form a panoramic physiographic feature of hogs back. Nearly 72 per cent of its boundary forms international border with Bangladesh (318 km.) and Myanmar (404 km.). Its diagonals are of about 250 km. north-south and 125 km. east-west, covering an area of 21,087 sq. km. with a population of 8,91,058 (2001 census). The entire region falls under the direct influence of southwest monsoon with an average annual rainfall of about 254 centimetres. It is not only endowed with natural resources of diverse range of mountainous ecosystem, but also is rich in pristine natural green thick forests occupied by variety of flora and fauna. Mizoram has a mild and pleasant climate of 11°C to 21°C in winter and 20°C to 30°C in summer. The State is divided into eight districts with its capital at Aizawl. The languages in use are Mizo (*Zotawng*), English and Hindi.

Of 21,087 sq. km. area of the State, about 83 per cent is covered by forests of which 7,127 sq. km. is reserved forest, 3,568 sq. km. is protected under control of District/Village Councils, and 5,240 sq. km. is unclassified state forest[3]. Firewood, bamboo, timber, orchids, and medicinal plants are found in abundance. But, the steepness of the ranges and transport bottlenecks are main constraints in the way of scientific forestry. Bamboo grows in abundance all over the State. In time to come, if properly harnessed, it can form a useful resource for industrialization. There has been no trace of any minerals of commercial value in the State. According to the Survey and Planning Report on Industrial Development in Mizo Hills District (Mizoram) 1963, coalmines were reported in Chawngte, Bairabi and Bilkhawthlir. Salt springs were also in existence for many years in eastern, western and northern side of the State. However, in the absence of minerals of any specific value, people have to depend upon agriculture and its allied activities like, pisci-culture and weaving.

The Blackwood's expedition (1844), the Lister's expedition (1850), the *Lushai* Expedition (1871), and the *Chin Lushai* Expedition (1889-90) launched by the British were punitive in nature to teach a lesson to the marauding *Lushai* (Mizo) that they must remain peaceful and abjure violence. Punishment to the guilty participators in the raids, deliverance of British subjects carried away into captivity and necessity for establishing security of the frontiers were the main considerations. The British deliberately followed the policy of "Kick and Kiss" towards Mizo. As the East India Company was a financial institution, money was the most important consideration in administration. It would not have put money in the hills of Assam, if the investment yielded no result. The expedition to check Mizo Chiefs' raids on their tea gardens, rubber plantations, etc., was also financial in nature, as the raids caused damage to their properties. Because of this consideration, the British introduced the Inner Line Regulation, 1873, which put blanket ban on entry into the *Lushai* Hills[4]. It was thought that the sophisticated laws of the civilized society would disturb the social and political harmony of the people and complexities of sophisticated civilized life would harm them. Their customary laws were better suited to them. These simple hill men were to be kept confined to their environs free from outside interference. Lewin enunciated it as: *"Let us not govern these hills ourselves; but administer the country for the well-being and happiness of the people dwelling there in... their mode of government may be described as a democracy tampered by despotism"*[5]. With this in view, Indian Penal Code, 1860 was not made applicable to Mizo. The *Lushai* Hills District Regulation, 1889 drafted by Shri B.C. Carey, the then Political Officer of Chin Hills, permitted the Chiefdom to continue and prohibited operation of Indian laws into the

Lushai Hills. The Assam Legislature also had no jurisdiction over the *Lushai* Hills and there were no representatives of Mizo in Assam Legislature owing to the provision of Government of India Act, 1919 declaring the district as 'Backward Tract'. This provision disabled the Assam Legislature from making laws for the *Lushai*. Only one Governor, Robert Reid, visited *Lushai* Hills and took some interest in it. Similarly, the Government of India Act, 1935 declared *Lushai* Hills District as an 'Excluded Area' debarring Mizo of sending their representatives to the Assam Legislature and enabling the Governor of Assam to discharge his functions according to his discretion. This provision deliberately debarred the Mizo from participating in the government[6]. Thus, the *Lushai* Hills District was ruled directly by the Superintendent of the district and Chiefs according to the established *Lushai* customs known as 'Mizo Hnam Dan' under the nominal supervision of the Governor of Assam.

The government also did not like the entry of lawyers to Mizo Hills' District. Any rebellion of any kind was ruthlessly suppressed. Being cut off from rest of India, Mizo lived in 'cage of' economic stagnation. The economic development of Mizo Hills was neglected totally. It seems that they (British) wanted to keep the people of these areas as primitive as possible[7]. The foreign Christian Missionaries, who were the only advisors of the Superintendent, disfavoured the economic upliftment of the Hillmen as the conversion was not complete and the economic development was fraught with the dangers of coming of plains' people to the hills. The Chiefs paid insignificant revenue to the Government and the administration also spent very little for the economic upliftment of Mizo. It was A.G. McCall, the Superintendent of *Lushai* Hills (1939-40) who at first realized the danger of economic neglect of Mizo and was sorry to see the abject poverty, he demanded more funds, advocated change in *jhum* cultivation, setting up of cottage industries and use of electricity. He liberalized timber trade with plains of Chittagong and Cachar, allowed the tradesmen from the plains to come and settle at Aijal, Lunglei and Demagiri, and advocated improvement of road communication[8]. His wife helped in organizing social welfare activities among Mizo women. Thus, the *Lushai* Hills District, though placed under the British influence since 1871 and in direct control since 1890, was ruled through the Chiefs and virtually no attempt was made to improve its economy.

British annexed Mizoram in 1871-72 after military expedition. It was made part of the then Assam *vide* Government of India Notification No. 591-E.B. Dated 1st April 1898.[9] During Pre-British time, the inhabitants of the State had limited trade relations with outside world through their market centres. After annexation, due to exigencies of the State, currency was introduced and gradually the trade developed. Till the separation of Myanmar and Bangladesh from India, it had well-established trade linkages with Arakan hills of Myanmar and Chittagong hills of Bangladesh, even when barter system of exchange was in vogue.

The independence of India in 1947 introduced democracy in this primarily tribal region. Gradually the interior areas were opened and road construction was undertaken. However, the people at large could not benefit much from the national planning and development. For a long period, it remained cut off from the mainstream of Indian Union. It was connected with rest of India by one single road and that to still remain blocked during rainy season owing to landslides. Situation gradually changed with Mizoram becoming a Union Territory in 1972 and finally, the 23rd State on 20th February 1987. This journey from a tribal homeland to full membership of Indian Union is very interesting and full of events. After the attainment of statehood, putting its history back, Mizoram has tried hard to change its economy, and education has played a significant role in this process. Leaving other 27 states behind, it has emerged as the second most literate State (88.49 per cent literacy) in India after Kerala (2001 census).

Mizo "children of the hills" is the generic name and includes nearly 300 clans and sub-clans, viz. *Biate*, *Chawngthu*, *Chawte*, *Hmar*, *Khawlring*, *Khiangte*, *Lai*, *Lushai*, *Mara*, *Ngente*, *Paite*, *Pautu*, *Pawi*, *Ralte*, *Rawite*, *Renthlei*, *Sailo*, *Zote*, etc. of the analogous hill tribes living in the *Lushai* Hills (now Mizoram). These clans bear the name of their ancestral father. The Mizo are of Tibeto-Mongoloid stock and their homeland had been Shan State in Burma after they left Chhinlung in Central China. Mizo were formerly head hunting savages with a pagan faith. Now, they are Christians. The founder of the *Lushai* clan was the tribal Chief Zahmuaka. Mizo migrated from the Chin Hills of Myanmar probably in the middle of the 16th century.[10] Mizo led a simple life with minimum requirement. They were known to be honest, simple, sincere, courteous, considerate, unselfish, outspoken, sturdy, courageous, industrious and helpful to others even in times of inconvenience.[11] The primitive Mizo society was an ethnic group closely knitted by blood relationship and so they were bound to have a deep sense of feeling for others who were also their kith and kin. Because of this, Mizo beggars are not found even this day. They are a close-knit homogeneous society with no class distinction from social, religious and economic point of view and no discrimination on grounds of caste, sex, and status.[12] Whatever distinctions exist is functional only.

Though, the society, in the past, was more or less homogeneous, yet, there was lack of entrepreneurship. The *Lushai*, like other hill tribes of the North East, are by nature averse to physical labour. The abundance of nature made them so. The *Lushai* aristocracy took pride in warfare, raids and hunting but was averse to labour. During 1890, there was emphasis on road making, but, labour was the problem and hence, it could not be taken up at desired level. The labour force has always been either from the neighbouring Cachar district of Assam or from upper India. Among the people, there is a great love for white-collar jobs. Mizos are quite intelligent, capable of learning but lagging on specialization in the field of their work. Majority of the people in Mizoram do not have saving habit. People love to spend money till they can spend. This resulted in low level of capital formation and consequently investment and with this, rapid development cannot be expected.

The absence of authoritarian rule and egalitarian relationship among people gave Mizo society a sense of cohesion and equality. Land distribution by the Chiefs in the past and by the Village Councils since the abolition of Chieftainship under the Assam *Lushai* Hills District (Acquisition of Chief's Rights) Act, 1954 has been largely need-based. This acted as a check on privatization of land as property. Land being the basic resource of livelihood the community collectively owns it in Mizoram. Due to low pressure of population and consequently high land-man ratio with low level of technology, the economy has remained almost self-contained. However, there exist some influential families who possess large land area in the name of gardens and plantations under special garden pass 'Huan pass'.

The backbone of Mizo economy has been agriculture through *Jhuming*, which made the Mizo till recent past a migrating tribe. They shifted from one village to another at regular intervals and this practice led them to possess very little property.[13] Whatever they had was simple to replace and could be carried easily without the help of transport facility.

Owing to scarcity of food, hunting played a vital role in Mizo life. In Mizo economy elephant tusks were the medium of exchange and its bones and skins were valuable articles of commerce. These items had a very good market in the neighbouring plains.[14] Hunting led them to possess flintlock guns[15] (mostly old muskets) imported from Myanmar and Chittagong during later half of 19th century.

Scarcity of cultivable land and food coupled with lust of wealth made Mizo raiding the enemies' villages in the neighbouring territories to carry off slaves or captives and loot as much as possible.[16] They considered raids as wars and a matter of prestige. They knew the art of war, use of iron implements, and molding of brass pipes.[17] Even, they knew the skill and art of systematic construction of buildings and towns before they settled in present Mizoram. Mizo Hills remained unexplored till 1800.[18]

With the increase in the number of marts, Mizo became dependent more and more on the produce of the plains for their necessities of life. They also got accustomed to peaceful trading, which brought a tremendous change in their political and social outlook. Barter trade gradually died out and coins came into circulation.

Business and Industry

Business and industry form the backbone of an economy. Countries with strong economies have well developed business and industry and *vice versa*. Business and industry generate products and services, which go into consumption of people. The surplus generated goes into investment and sustains the development process. Employment generation also takes place in business and industry, which provides livelihood to people. The government also receives revenue in the form of taxes, levies, fees, duties etc. that may be utilized for meeting expenditure on government services and also for carrying out developmental programmes.

The traditional economies, however, heavily depend upon agriculture. Land is the main resource in these economies and agricultural produce is the source of livelihood. Most of the people in such economies are dependent on agriculture directly or indirectly. The nature and scope of business and industry also depend upon the state of agriculture in such economies. The small scale and cottage industries using farm and forest produce as inputs have been a special feature of these economies. The shift from agrarian economy to industrial economy marks the beginning of the process of development. This transformation is a slow process and takes place over a period of time through sustained efforts.

The concept of business has undergone a tremendous change across the globe during last two decades. With globalization, the boundaries of business have widened. Manufacturing and marketing of products and services are not limited within the geo-political limits of a country. The whole globe becoming one market-village has made business a boundary less activity. Recognizing the strengths, weaknesses, opportunities, and threats, resource utilization for production of goods and services is made to obtain better quality products at competitive prices. This focuses attention on strengths and opportunities, doing away with the weaknesses and threats. The concept has assumed increased inter-dependence among the countries of the world and has led to emergence of multinational companies (MNCs). The genesis lies in a country specializing in production of few goods; exporting the goods that provide it comparative cost advantage in exchange for what others can produce at a lower cost. Gradually, countries are removing restrictions (barriers and hurdles) on foreign trade. In such a situation, no country can remain in isolation for a long period of time. It has to join the mainstream across the globe. Liberalization, Privatization, and Globalization (LPG) processes are the result of the above-mentioned developments in the world's economy.

To ensure free flow of goods and services in a regulated manner, the World Trade Organization (WTO) has emerged as a nodal agency. The WTO is a large multilateral trade forum with 144 member countries. It holds the key in directing the policies and trends of world trade. With India becoming a WTO member from 1st January 1995, there has been an increasing pressure from both the developed and developing countries to open up Indian economy for foreign goods and services.

It is high time for Indian entrepreneurs in general and the people and the state government in immediate vicinity of foreign countries in particular to equip themselves to face the challenges, of global market. There has been a plea for creation of a 'Bay of Bengal Growth Triangle' to have joint studies and coordinated investment plans to tap natural resources of the region comprising the Northeastern States of India, Bangladesh, Nepal, Bhutan, and Myanmar. Though, it appears very difficult to achieve because of complexities involved, recently some studies have suggested creation of a growth quadrangle involving Northeastern states of India, Myanmar, Southwest China, Northern Thailand and Bangladesh. The idea is to have coordinated market development that may remove many of the problems arising out of small sized markets and pave the way for rapid development of trade and commerce. Declaration of certain areas as free trade zones has also been suggested.

Following the above, the BIMST-EC (Bangladesh–India–Myanmar—Sri Lanka–Thailand Economic Cooperation) Agreement was signed. The Indo-Myanmar border trade formally opened on 12th April 1995,[19] as a follow up measure of the Border Trade Agreement (BTA) signed between the two countries on 21st January 1994, at New Delhi. The Government of India and the Government of Myanmar have agreed to open the border trade between the two countries in three sectors, viz., Moreh (Manipur), Champhai (Mizoram) and Lungwa (Nagaland) in India as against Tamu (Sagaing Division), Hri (Chin Division) and Paletwa (Rakhine State) in Myanmar respectively. Of these, presently Moreh centre is facilitating border trade officially and Champhai has been just opened. The bilateral agreement had identified 22 items of trade that are to be traded on head-load basis under barter system of exchange besides other usual items of trade under Export-Import (Exim) policies of the two countries.[20] This augurs well for the future.

During pre-British time, Mizo had limited trade relations with outside world through their market centre. For the first time, regular markets in *Lushai* Hills (Mizoram) were established in 1871-72 to handle the volume of rubber trade.[21] Trade was carried on through trade marts established on the confluence of navigable rivers like the Tipaimukh Bazaar on Barak River, Sonai Bazaar (*Lushai* hat) on Sonai (*Tuirial*) River, Chengsil (*Jhalancherra*) Bazaar on Dhaleshwari (*Tlawng*) River, Pakwamukh Bazaar at south of Bhairabi at the junction of Pakwa and Gutur rivers. On Bangladesh side, Bepari Bazaar on the Sylhet border and Kasalang Bazaar (half way between Demagiri and Rangmati) on the Chittagong border were well-known trade marts.[22] Through these marts, the Pawis, Maras and *Lushai* had been selling rubber to the Chittagong traders. On Myanmar side, the markets were Yazagyo, Kalemyo, Indin, Sihaung, Myintha, and Gangaw. There was also small trade in metal bells, silver beads, and other ornaments of Indian manufacture,[23] which found their way through the Mizo Hills from Chittagong to Akyab. Before independence the exchange that took place with the markets outside the State was a sort of exchange for production for use and sustenance. It did not appear to have brought a transformation from production for use to production for exchange. This may be as a result of inadequacy of transport, communication and capital. The former restricted the scope of exchange and the later the growth of surplus. Thus, the production of material basis of the economy was halted or strangulated, and this in turn resulted in thwarting the development of the productive power. Transformation of natural resources into products of higher order through improved technology was not possible in this situation. This provided hardly any opportunity to the people to own property. Absence of private property made the society less stratified.

The situation changed significantly after the separation of Myanmar from British India and Indian independence in 1947. The age-old ethnic and historical relationship changed overnight and people were forced to search for new trade relationship with people of lower Assam. Gradually, Silchar and Guwahati in Assam and Kolkata emerged as major trading centres for Mizoram, the routes became longer and goods became costlier in the process. During early phase, business was in the hands of Bengali traders and Marwari businessmen, which was gradually taken over by locals.

There existed no industry worth the name in Mizoram before independence. During early phase of planning; industrialization could not be emphasized upon, as there was neither a resource base nor the necessary infrastructure. Industrialization started initially with cottage, tiny and village industries in the urban areas. Lately, some modern small-scale industries were set up in Aizawl and some large district towns.

The survey of existing literature leads to the conclusion that most of the earlier works related mainly to history, culture, social system, and customs of Mizo. Recently there have been some research works and publications covering various aspects of economy of Mizoram. However, no work dealing with Business and Industry in Mizoram has come to the knowledge of the author. Most of the works are based on the information drawn from plan documents and government publications. Business, particularly the private sector has remained completely out of focus. Whatever factual information is available about business from diverse sources is scanty and scattered. No work has covered the border trade. Some works discussed the location and government's developmental activities for industry. But, the aspects like organization, policy, roll of incentives, entrepreneurship, etc. have not been discussed. There has been no study covering the development and functioning of public sector enterprises in the State. Banking including commercial banks and cooperative banks has been mostly the recent development. The activity of these institutions is limited to district towns. Moreover, except for the general banking facility, other developmental and promotional activities have not been emphasized. There has been no study examining the activities of financial institutions in the State. Taxation has a limited role in the State's economy. Central taxes like income tax, excise duty, etc. are not levied on tribals in the State. The scope of state taxes is limited to state sales tax (now VAT), profession tax, entertainment tax, land revenue, registration fee and stamp duty. No study of the role significance and contribution of taxation have been done.

The book covers the following aspects:

- Trace the growth of business, development of business related infrastructure and allied services, border trade and examine the role of government in promotion and regulation of business in Mizoram.

- Trace the growth of industry, industrial infrastructure, determine the developments in industrial structure and entrepreneurship, its present status and appraise the role of government in promotion and regulation of industry in Mizoram.
- Assess the role of financial institutions including development banks, commercial banks, cooperative banks, direct financing by State in the growth of business and industry in Mizoram.
- Survey the policy and measures of taxation, their present status, contribution to State revenue and implications for business and industry in Mizoram.
- Identify the problems of business and industry in Mizoram and suggest remedial measures.

NOTES

1. CMIE—Public Finance 2002 and Economic Survey 2001.
2. Editorial Perspective, *India's North-East*, Dialogue, Vol. 4, No. 1, July-September 2002, p. 7.
3. Northeastern Council, *Basic Statistics of NER*, 2002, p. 45.
4. Acharya, N.N., *Modernisation of Mizoram*, Proceedings of the NEHA, Aizawl, 1984, p. 222.
5. Chartterjee, Dr. Suhash, *Mizoram: Encyclopedia*, Vol. III, 1990, pp. 568-71.
6. Roy, A., *Mizoram: Dynamics of Change*, pp. 45-47.
7. Constituent Assembly Debates, September 6 ,1949, Vol. X, No.27, p. 1015.
8. Allen, B.C., *Assam District Gazetteers*, Vol. X, Part III, Lushai Hills District, p. 38.
9. A.S., For A., May 1898, Nos. 13-46. Quoted in Lalrinmawia's *Mizoram: History* and *Cultural Identity*, Spectrum Publications, Guwahati, 1995, p. 56.
10. Soppitt, C.A., *A Short Account of the Kuki-Lushai Tribes,* Tribal Research Instituted Aizawl, 1976, (Reprinted) p. 7. Quoted in Lalrimawia's *Mizoram—History and Cultural Identity*, Spectrum Publications, Guwahati, 1995, p. 14.
11. Parry, *N.E.: A Monograph on Lushai Customs and Ceremonies*, Firma KLM P. Ltd., Kolkata, 1976, p. 19.
12. Lianzela: *Economic Development of Mizoram*, Spectrum Publications, Guwahati, 1994, p. 6.
13. Heerion Lloyd, *On Every High Hill*, Liverpool, p. 17. Quoted in Lalrimawia's: '*Mizoram: History and Cultural Identity*', Spectrum Publications, Guwahati, 1995, p. 3.
14. BJP, April 12, 1855, No. 95; Verner, Superintendent of Cachar to the Secretary, Government of Bengal. Quoted in Lalrinmawia's: *Mizoram: History and Cultural Identity*, Spectrum Publications, Guwahati, 1995, p. 3.

15. Quoted in Lalrinmawia's: *Mizoram: History and Cultural Identity*, Spectrum Publications, Guwahati, 1995, p. 3.
16. Lalrinmawia, *Mizoram: History and Cultural Identity*, Spectrum Publications, Guwahati, 1995, p. 5.
17. Hranglien Songate, *Hmar History*, Hmar Chanchin, Imphal, 1956, p. 7.
18. Lalrinmawia, *op. cit*, p. 8.
19. Editorial, Indo-Myanmar Border Trade, *Northeast Trade Line*, Vol. I, No. III, February 2003, p. 5.
20. Reserve Bank of India, A.P. (DIR Series) Circular No. 17, October 18, 2000.
21. ——; *The Lushai: 1878-1889*, Firms KLM P. Ltd., Kolkata, for Tribal Research Institute, Aizawl, Reprint 1978, p. 41.
22. A. Machenzie, *The North East Frontier of India*, Mittal Publications, New Delhi, Reprint 1999, p. 363.
23. Bertam S. Carey and H. N. Tuck, *The Chin Hills*, Tribal Research Institute, Aizawl, 1976, p. 215.

2

BUSINESS IN MIZORAM

Introduction

Business implies doing something or attending to a thing, or being busy at occupation, profession, trade, work etc[1]. It includes buying and selling, commerce, and trade[2]. Business also includes activities of commercial producers of goods and services. These producers range from small shops owned by single person to large organizations owned by thousands of shareholders. The word business is sometimes used to refer to producers of products and services such as clothing business, entertainment business, or insurance business. An individual enterprise may also be called a business.

The word 'business' thus in its widest sense refers to all those activities, which are connected with production, purchase of goods and services to sell them at profit. It includes activities connected with manufacturing, trading, transportation, insurance, warehousing, banking, and finance. It is not concerned with non-economic activities of people. A business essentially has characteristics such as sale or transfer for value, dealing in goods and services, recurrence of dealings, profit motive, and risk. Broadly speaking, business comprises industry, commerce including trade, and related services. The components of business are shown in Figure 2.1.

Commerce is buying and selling in large amounts between different places, business, and trade. It refers to exchange and distribution of goods[3]. The process of buying and selling and all those activities that facilitate trade such as transportation, insurance, storage, finance, grading, packaging etc. are known as commerce. Thus, commerce includes trade and aids to trade. For conducting trade, many hindrances have to be removed. The hindrances may be as regards place, time, finance, and knowledge. Hindrance of place is due to difficulties in transfer of goods from the places of production to the places of consumption. These hindrances are removed with the aids like transportation, insurance and packaging. Hindrance of time is due to long interval between the time of production and the time of consumption. This hindrance is removed by warehousing. Hindrance of finance arises due to inadequate funds in the hands of businesspersons. Many potential businesspersons failed in their careers because of inadequate finance. Lack of finance, a big hindrance, is removed by banking. The hindrance of knowledge refers to problems of sale by producers. This is removed with the help of advertising and publicity.

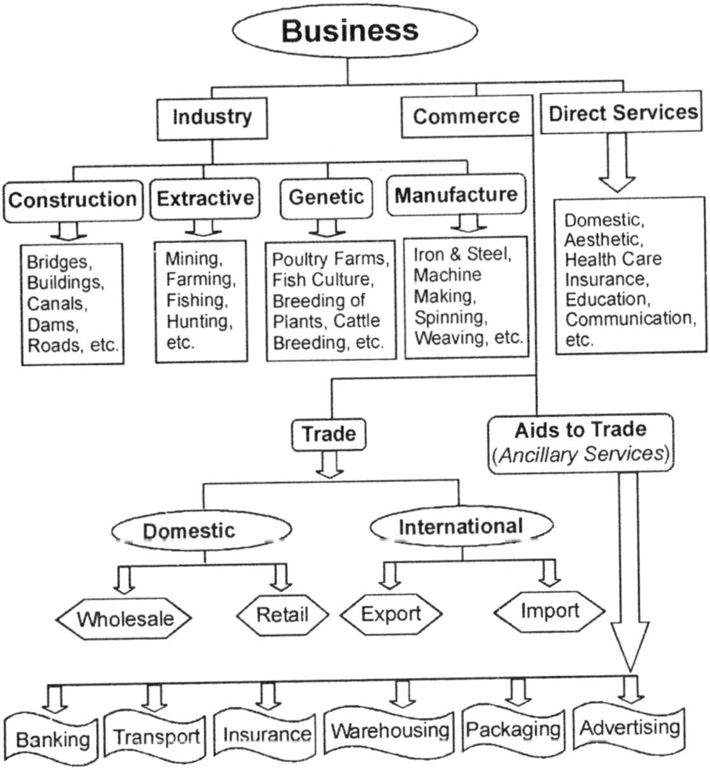

Fig. 2.1: Components of Business

Trade is a branch of commerce and is concerned with exchange of commodities. Trade is commonly understood as an act or process of buying and selling, exchange of goods, and services, etc. It is a kind of task that requires skilled mechanical work[4]. Trade occurs because people need and want things that others produce or services others perform. It does not include aids to trade like transportation, insurance, banking, finance, etc. Trade may be either wholesale or retail, depending on the quantities dealt with. Trade can also be classified as local trade, regional trade, internal trade, and foreign trade, depending upon the scope of area under operation.

Trade has contributed greatly to the advancement of civilization. As merchants travelled from region to region, they helped spread civilized way of life. These traders carried the ideas and inventions of various cultures over the routes of commerce.

Business affects nearly every aspect of life. It provides almost all the goods and services that people use daily from orange juice to air travel. It also generates most of the jobs and incomes that enable people to buy those goods and services. The world of business includes a tremendous variety of products and services, some of which one may never see. For example, many people think of a car as the product of an assembly line in a plant. However, the assembly line is only the final stage of a long process involving many companies. These companies include producers of batteries, glass, steel, tyres, and upholstery. Manufacturing a car requires the service of people such as draughtsman, engineers, and tool and die makers. Business also includes advertising, selling, and other marketing activities. Business plays a dominant role in countries that have economies based on free enterprise. In a free enterprise system, the managers of businesses decide what goods and services should be produced and what their prices should be.

Evolution and Growth of Business in Mizoram

The development of business in Mizoram may be rightly seen as a product of forces operating in the region over the last two hundred years, the period during which Mizo migrated and settled in the region. It may be interesting to trace its origin and growth over this period.

Pre-British Era (Before 1871)

The history of business in Mizoram is not very old. Mizo lived in spending isolation, and in sylvan glory. They had very few wants and had no commerce worth the name. They were a self-sufficient lot. As they could procure all their requirements simply by hunting and *Jhuming*, they remained involved in these two activities. However, with the passage of time, the children of the hills multiplied resulting into multiplicity of wants. To satisfy their wants they used to move down to the plains of Chittagong, Sylhet, Cachar and Manipur with their articles of commerce. Mizo, before they got exposed to British, were head hunting savage people accustomed with the use of gun, sulphur, flint glass, medicine, tobacco and cloth. Before British annexation of the region, Mizo did not know the modern practices of selling and buying. However, they did barter goods from time immemorial. As their weights and measures were relative and not absolute and accurate, the standard measurement of quantity, especially of rice, was number of buckets varied in shape, size and length such as *Fawng* (U-shaped), *Dawrawn* (long), *Tam em* (big) and *Empai* (medium size). But, *large quantities* were measured in number of loads[5]. Records show that in the primitive Mizo economy, forest products (mithuns and elephant teeth) were the medium of exchange. The forests of *Lushai* (Mizo) Hills were the abode of elephants. Elephant hide, and bones had a good demand among the merchants of Sylhet during Mughal period. Elephant hide was used to manufacture shields for infantry and cavalry of Mughals and native princes. The bones of elephants were used to make butts of sword and to prepare fancy goods for nobility. Elephant tusks were in great demand for manufacturing luxury articles and ornaments. The Sylhet and Chittagong merchants collected elephant teeth from Mizo Hills. The tusks were not only medium of exchange; ivory reserve served the purpose of gold reserve among the Chiefs of *Lushai* (Mizo) Hills. The standard price of standard size elephant tusk was twenty rupees in the fifties of 19th Century. During the famine of 1882, the price of a pair of tusk was Rs. 25 to Rs. 30, which according to the then price index was reasonable.

Mizo (Kukie clan of Lalchukla Cheif) for the first time came in contact with the Bengali petty traders dealing in consumer goods like rice, salt, rubber, sulphur, flint glass etc., around 1838[6] on the border of British district of Sylhet. The extension of tea plantations in south Cachar and east Sylhet encroached upon the natural hunting grounds of elephants. Besides, in 1861, the East India Company started setting up their own 'Khedas' to hunt elephants and came in competition with the Mizo/Kukie[7]. This affected Mizo adversely, but, they needed consumer goods of daily use from the plains and the only source was 'the raid'. In Mizo economy raids had a secured place. There was scarcity of food, specially rice and salt, and Mizo had to depend upon the Bengali traders of Cachar, Sylhet and Chittagong. Later, to sell their hill produce such as rubber, ginger, elephant tusks, bones, etc. and to purchase rice, salt, flint glass, sulphur, tobacco, clothes, etc., they used to go to Silchar and other trade marts of Cachar.

Bepari Bazaar on Sylhet border and Kassalong (half way between Demagiri and Rangmati) on Chittagong border were well-known trade marts for the Mizo[8]. They used to come down every winter with their commodities and sold *Jhum* products, big fishes and forest products including elephant hydes, tusks and crude rubber to Bengali traders of Sylhet and Cachar. The Mizo Chiefs welcomed the traders as friends by providing security, as they used to get their supplies of sulphur, salt, gun, clothes, tobacco, rice, and flint glass from them[9]. Traders from Cachar and Chittagong became a source of permanent income by way of rent, preferably in kind, for security provided to them by Mizo Chiefs[10]. Captain Lewin, Political Officer of Chittagong Hill Tracts, had encouraged the establishment of trade marts at different places such as, Kassalong etc.[11]

Like Malaysia, Singapore, Thailand and Myanmar there had been natural forests of rubber in the region. Owing to their contiguity, the Chin Hills of Myanmar and the Lushai Hills had been original habitat of rubber plantation. The heavy rainfall and salubrity of soil of Lushai (Mizo) Hills helped the vegetation of rubber species. Mizo although aboriginal tribes lived away from the civilization, knew very well that civilized people had use of rubber. They exploited it, as they knew how to tap rubber from the trees. It was a very important article of commerce and had good market in Cachar, Sylhet and Chittagong. The East India Company exported a large quantity of it from India to London, and a large part of it was collected from Chittagong and Sylhet. Local industries also used rubber increasingly and the commodity had good demand. To handle the volume of rubber trade, the first temporary 'government market' was established in 1868 and regular markets in 1871-72 at British outposts in the interior of the Lushai Hills. In fact Sir John Edgar, the then Deputy Commissioner of Cachar, initiated a proposal before the authorities in Calcutta that trade marts should be opened in the Mizo hills for the benefit of Mizo people. He thought that the Bengali traders from Hailakandi and Cachar and Manipuri traders might be allowed to sell their merchandise and produce in those bazaars. To exploit the sentiment of Mizo, he encouraged annual fairs (*Melas*) at Silchar and Rangamati. Dancing, singing, magic shows, sports, games, and marketing were part of these *Melas*. The Assam Government had organized one such *Mela* in 1869 at Silchar.

These bazaars not only provided regular revenue to the Chiefs, but also enabled them in general to acquire most of their requirements at very low cost and trouble. Mizo also collected and sold bees-wax, seeds of tea plants, raw rubber, bamboo, cane, reeds and other hill products.

On the Myanmar side, the favourite market was Yazagyo, which was frequented by the Thados, Kanhows, Kalemyos, Siyins, Indins, Sihaungs, Tashons, Myinthas, Gangaws, Hakas and other southern tribes. The principal articles of import trade were salt, iron, and luxuries, such as cattle, especially buffaloes, gongs, brass, iron pots, beads, ornaments of various kinds both of brass and white-metal, silk thread, coloured cotton yarn, yaw plaids, and in times of scarcity rice.[12] There was also a small trade in metal bells, silver beads, and other ornaments of Indian manufacture, which found their way through the Mizo Hills from Chittagong to Akyab.[13]

The internal trade, however, was not large[14], and consisted for most part in exchange of beads for live-stock, which gradually filtered towards British posts, where the demand for fresh meat exceeded the available supply, and in conversion of guns, gongs and similar valuables into grains when the crop of a particular village failed. There had been a continual movement of petty trade between villages say blankets from Laizo, salt and bee-wax from Zahautract, new weapons and implements from Haka village of Venha and pots from Lente and Tashon going in all directions. The principal products flowing from west to east were blankets, metal pots, pigs, fowls, mats and lac to Falam and salt, rice, iron for hoes, cotton thread to Laizo.[15]

In addition, the bazaars, which flourished at British posts, supplied Mizo with beads, buttons, English cloth, sticks, tobacco, and sugar, all of which were readily purchased. Circulation of coin, internal peace and cessation of raids between Myanmarese and Mizo, gave impetus to trade, and provided a ready market for grain, which existed at British posts. The love for money gradually induced Mizo to sell their surplus grain rather than putting it into liquor pots, as was the practice. Among Mizo, the Myanmaree Tashons were keenest traders. This enabled Chiefs to affect monopoly of trade, as they were able to undersell all other traders. To ensure that there was no competition, they would put every obstacle in the way of other villagers going to the plains. Their plans were successful, as all procured their supply from them. For instance, in the open season of 1892-93, not less than 100,000 lbs. of salt was purchased at Indin and Sihaung, and passed through the hands of the Chiefs, who took it as their chief source of wealth.[16] Until April 1876, Mizo had not learnt the value of articles, which they were so eager to barter in exchange for the traders' goods. Though they were alive to their own interests, they were not born traders like the Myanmarese. Before British occupation, the staple trade of the Hills was barter of bees-wax for salt, guns, gongs, iron and other luxury items they desired. Money earned by carrying loads for the Commissariat, labour on public works, and exports in kind like bees-wax, husk of Indian-corn, cane mats, horns of buffalo; deer, and other animals gradually took the place of slaves and plunder. Of these, the most valuable were tusks and horns of rhinoceros, the later having a ready sale for use as medicine. The price of a fair-sized horn was as much as Rs. 100/-.[17]

British Era (1872 – 1947)

After the expedition of 1871-72, which resulted in annexation of the *Lushai* Hills by British, the Government established some bazaars inside the Mizo Hills, beyond the British territory. The traders of Cachar supplied merchandise to these bazaars. The most important among these Bazaars were Tipaimukh, Sonaimukh, Sairang ghat and Changsil in the north. In south, on Chittagong side important trade marts at Demagiri, Kassalong, Barkhal and Rangamati were established on the advice of T.H. Lewin in pursuance of the policy of conciliation. Lewin knew very well that to maintain friendly relationship with the *Lushai* they must be supplied with the necessaries, i.e., the consumer goods. The Cotton Estates (*Kapas Mahals*) of Chittagong Hill Tracts were established in these areas and *Lushai* of these areas gave up their primitive way of life and gradually got mixed up with the modern society. Generally, the traders from Sylhet and the Chakmas of Chittagong were the investors in these markets. Some Bengali tradesmen also penetrated into the *Jampui* Hills. Some Sylhet and Chittagong businesspersons also entered deep into the Mizo hills to sell their commodities.[18] With the increase in the number of marts, the *Lushai* became increasingly dependent on the produce of the plains for their necessities of life. They also became accustomed to peaceful trading, which brought a tremendous change in their political and social outlook. Barter trade gradually died out and coins came into circulation. During the winter season every year, Mizo came down in large numbers to purchase cattles in exchange of cash which they obtained from the sale of rubber. It was estimated that from December 1874 to 1878, there had been annual trade of salt, iron, brass, and copper utensils, tobacco etc., of the value of £ 48,402 (Rs. 4,84,025) in the bazaars of Cachar border[19] alone in exchange for rubber, ivory, etc. Mizo Chiefs in south Mizoram used to take help of '*Karbari*' (Men of Business) while dealing with foreigners in matters of trade and other political and social transactions. *'Karbari'* were usually clever, knew jungle routes, customs of different clans, and were well versed in Bengali, the link language.

The Chiefs enjoyed some special economic privileges, such as receiving tribute from their subjects, getting best land for cultivation, good rates of revenue, etc. The Chiefs could sell slave (*Bawi*) like pigs or goats and their price was determined according to their utility which was usually six years free labour or Rs. 40/- when Sir Archdale Earl was the Governor of Assam (1911). According to the Lushai system, the hills belonged to the Chiefs and the rubber plants were the property of the Chiefs. The common Mizo could tap the rubber with the permission of the Chiefs. The Chiefs being migratory in nature never took care of the rubber plants, as was done by the Malaysians. The shifting cultivation was also responsible for the destruction of rubber plants. Mizo considered them as gift of nature and never endeavoured to plant them again. During the Mizo famine of 1881-82, there had been over-tapping of the rubber plants by Mizo and they sold huge quantity of rubber to merchants in Kassalong and Changsil bazaars. This resulted into loss of valuable rubber forests. The *Lushai* Chiefs also sold considerable amount of tusks and exhausted their ivory reserve. The British government, though distributed famine relief to Mizo through these bazaars, did not attempt to revive the resource by replanting rubber trees, even after having received a report from Mr. Knox Wight, the then District Commissioner Cachar in 1884, who emphasized on the need of an urgent revival. In 1891, Mr. J.F. Kennedy, the then District Commissioner Cachar lamented the loss of rubber trade in the *Lushai* Hills district. According to Shri Hari Charan Sharma, the E.A.C. in charge of Relief in the North *Lushai* Hills, altogether 20,000 maunds of rice were imported to the Mizo Hills during 1882, while 1,000 maunds of rubber worth Rs. 40,000/- and 4,25,000 bamboos were purchased from the Mizo through these markets. The value of import was Rs. 61,800/- and of export Rs. 42,700/- on Cachar side alone[20]. The Pawi, Mara and Lushai sold similar quantity of rubber to the Chittagong traders in the South Lushai Hills. On Chittagong side, the Bengal Government supplied 22,500 maunds of rice during the lean months of 1882 to famine affected Mizo. The Government provided Rs. 50,000/- as famine relief to the Mizo through Chengsil Bazaar[21]. The markets gradually increased in size and importance, but their growth was somewhat checked by the exactions imposed on the traders by the Chiefs. The details of various trade marts that existed in Mizoram during 1870—89 are given in Table 2.1.

Table 2.1: Trade Marts in Mizoram During 1870 to 1889

Point of Time	*Tipaimukh Bazaar*	*Sonai Bazaar*	*Changsil Bazaar*
Opened / Established	*Near Expedition of 1871-72*	*Before Expedition of 1871-72*	*1870*[2]
	Not known[1]	*August 1874*[1]	*Before 1871*[1]
1873	—	—	Closed (June)
1874	—	—	13 shops
1875	3 shops (May) and 35 shops[1]	2 shops (April)	18 shops
1876	6 shops (April)	6 shops (April)	13 shops (April)
1877	5 shops (January), 111 maunds	8 shops (January)	6 shops (February), 60 maunds
1877	Closed[1]	—	—
1878	Reopened[1]	6 shops (April)	8 shops (April)
	—	—	Looted (November) Loss of goods and Cash worth Rs.3000 and ultimately closed
1879	—	—	Reopened (April)
1881	—	7 shops (January)	—
1881	—	2 shops (May)	—
1883	Closed (January) owing to heavy rent, looting and personal danger[1]	—	—
1883	4 shops (June) – No Trade	—	—
1883	2 shops (November)	—	—
1884	Reopened but could not be made functional[1]	Looted and Closed (January)	—
1884	2 shops (June)	—	Traders quit the market as the trade had ceased[1]
1885	Reopened (April-May)	—	—
1887	Closed (September)	—	Closed (January)
1887	Made operational	—	—
1887-88	3 shops	—	—
1888	Abandoned (August)	—	—
1889	—	Reopened (January)	—
1889	—	Closed (February)	—
Commodities Traded	Raw Rubber, Salt, Tusk, Rice, Tobacco	Rubber, Salt, Wax, Cotton, Tusk, Rice, Mithun, Brass Utensils, Lead and Steel through smuggling	Rubber, Bamboo, Cotton, Salt, Tobacco, Cloths, Cane, Ivory, Utensils, Wax, Rice, Hill Products
Mizo Products	Rubber, Tusk	Rubber, Wax, Tusk	Rubber, Bamboo, Can, Ivory, Hill Products

Source: 1. Verghese, C. G. and Thanzawna, R. L., *A History of Mizoram*, Vol. - I, Vikas Publishing House P. Ltd.

2. Chatterjee, Dr. Suhas, *Mizoram –Encyclopaedia*, Jaico Publishing House, Mumbai, 1990.

3. *The Lushai 1878 – 1889*, Tribal Research Institute, Aizawl (Mizoram).

Gradually consumption of tobacco became common among Mizo, from children to old. As per one estimate in 1898, Mizo consumed tobacco worth £10,000. Similarly, there had been brisk sale of ivory by Mizo throughout the second half of the nineteenth century. Formerly, Mizo collected salt from the salt springs, but after the establishment of bazaars at different point since 1872 salt springs lost their importance and Mizo purchased common salt worth thousands of rupees annually from these bazaars.[22]

Essentially all the bazaars in Mizoram were at the confluence of rivers owing to their navigability. In 19th Century and in the early part of 20th Century a major portion of the *Lushai* trade was carried out through rivers. In the north, the main centres of trade were the Tipaimukh bazaar at the confluence of Barak and Tuivai Rivers, Sonai Bazaar (Lushai Hat) on Sonai (*Tuirial*) River and Changsil (Jhalanchera) bazaar on the Dhaleshwari (*Tlawng*) River and Pakwamukh bazaar at south of Bhairabi at the junction of Pakwa and Gutur rivers. The Bengali traders had their shops at these places. It was estimated that salt, iron, brass and copper utensils, tobacco etc., were sold in exchange of rubber, ivory etc. Changsil and Turial bazaars were within the territory of Suakpuilala, while Tipaimukh bazaar was within the territory of Pawibawia. Suakpuilala used to levy tax at the rate of Rs. 15/- per shop per year. The Bengali traders considered this too much and consequently it became one of the subjects of talk between Mr. O.G.R. McWilliam, the then officiating Deputy Commissioner, Cachar, and Suakpuilala, held on 28th May 1874 at Changsil. Following the agreement reached between them, Suakpuilala reduced the tax to Rs. 10/- per shop.[23] By the end of 1875 there were 18 shops at Changsil, 2 at Tuirial and 3 at Tipaimukh. Similarly, as Kolodyne was the most important river in south, all the trade marts in south were set up on its banks. Kolodyne valley was very fertile and the villages on its banks had commercial traditions.

Chittagong, a big town and a seaport, was nearer to south Mizo Hills. The trade connection between Mizo and Bengali was brisk in this part of Mizoram. Chakma of Chittagong Hill Tracts and South Mizoram were more exposed than Mizo and they acted as intermediary in Mizo commerce. They had the educational heritage. As Buddhists, some of them were well versed in Buddhist scripture and medicine[24]. They were not only good cotton growers but also expert in riverine and surface trade. Mizo had traditional trade relationship with Chin Hills of Myanmar and with Chittagong Hill Tracts. According to Shri L.C. Roy, before partition Mizo produced rice, cotton, *til*, oranges and chillies in large quantities in their *Jhums* for trade in Chittagong Hill Tracts. Forest produce like bamboo, timber, and cane were also exported[25]. Mizo got in exchange consumption articles like food items other than rice and vegetables, clothing, kerosene, betel nut, agricultural implements, utensils, medicines and stationery. Mizo were talented, clever, and shrewd. No other tribal community was so advanced in business as Mizo were[26].

During British time Mizo inhabiting in the eastern part of the District had trade relations with villages of western Myanmar and Naga Hills. In this respect Mr. B.C. Allen had observed, "a certain amount of wax was sold to the shopkeepers, and itinerant dealers of Myanmar, Manipur, and the Naga Hills. Forest produce was exported from Mizoram but the business was in the hands of plainsmen who sent their sawyers into hills."[27]

The first regular Bazaar was started at *Dawrpui*, Aizawl, in 1910 by H.W.G. Cole, the then Superintendent of Mizoram. This bazaar was meant for selling vegetables and other local products and was held every Saturday. The people of surrounding villages were ordered by the Superintendent to come and sell whatever commodity they could find. Naturally, at that time, buyers were few and things brought for sale were those, which were easily and commonly available, and the supply was often far in excess of the demand. As an encouragement, the Superintendent himself bought whatever was left over. Very soon, people started coming to the bazaar of their own accord and *Dawrpui* became the biggest business centre in Mizoram.

After the abolition of Changsil Bazaar, the commercial importance of Aizawl (Aijal) bazaar began to grow gradually. A large number of Bengali traders like M.K. Guha and Sons, Marwari business houses like the Khandelwals, the Sardas, and the Bhuras established their shops and godowns at Bara Bazaar in Aizawl. Chotelal Seth and M.K. Guha were pioneer traders at Aizawl with large investment. Mizo business houses like Pachhungas and Lalminthangas established themselves as leading businesspersons and flourished within a short time. In 1902-03 trade in Aizawl was chiefly in the hands of Hindu shopkeepers from Sylhet, Arrah and elsewhere. There were 17 shops at Aizawl and 16 at Lunglei and Demagiri, which sold goods to the tune of Rs. 53,375/- (about Rs. 300/- per shop per month)[28]. Within a few years, there had been a marked improvement in trade owing to extensive use of imported and manufactured articles by the Lushai. Weekly bazaars had been started both at Aizawl and Lunglei, which were well attended by Lushai even from distant villages. Mizo businesspersons played an important role in it. A noticeable feature of 1921-22 was increase in the number of Mizo shops. As a result, the volume and variety of trade increased and included cotton and woollen yarns, brass, enamel, aluminium utensils, iron pans, *daos*, tobacco, cigarettes, matches, soaps, clothes, umbrellas, piece goods, shoes, fancy goods and foodstuffs. Export comprised bees wax, cotton, chillies, ginger, oranges and forest products[29]. The Government gave protection to locals to ensure that the plains people do not monopolize the trade in Mizoram. M/s. Pachhunga and Sons and M/s. Zangena and Bros. handled a considerable business of controlled goods like, petrol, kerosene oil, etc. Yet, the supply position depended on Silchar as commodities had to be brought from there. It became the base of trading operations in Mizoram. It is like a funnel for Mizoram.

During this period, the villages in the southern and the western parts of Mizoram had trade with Bengal and Myanmar, taking out cane, bamboo, timber, cotton, and Tobacco from the Mizo Hills for articles of consumption. The articles traded were mainly salt, mithun, cotton and slaves. Salt was a necessity Mizo had to purchase. They could get this in sufficient quantity by selling wax gathered in the jungle or a maund of cotton. Mizo kept *mithun* (wild oxen) in domesticated state in all villages for trading, festivals and for milk. The price of a full-grown mithun varied from Rs. 40/-to Rs. 80/-. Among Mizo, the value of a person's property was often spoken of as so many mithuns[30]. Cotton was grown in the Mizo hills to a small extent and in Chakma area in south Mizoram known as '*Kapas Mahal*'. It was sent out through river Koladyne towards the Arakan and through river Dhaleswari towards Chittagong. The price per maund (unclean cotton) varied from Rs. 4/- to Rs. 5/-. Mizo obtained weapons from the tribes on Myanmar border, giving slaves in exchange. A strong male slave was considered equivalent to two guns.

Post-Independence

With partition of India, the East Pakistan authorities did not allow Mizo to trade freely with Chittagong and Sylhet and artificially separated the interdependent Mizo economy. This caused serious depression in trade and commerce in south Mizoram, adversely affected its economy more especially in southwest part of the district[31]. The fiscal regulations of Pakistani authorities at the beginning were not very strict, but it became very rigid in late fifties. The prices of imported commodities went up and the prices of local produce fell considerably. The economy of south and west Mizoram suffered a severe setback because of loss of market for goods produced there. The trade ties with Myanmar were already snapped in 1935 when Myanmar was separated from British India and as with East Pakistan smuggling continued there freely[32]. The Government of Assam also did not come forward to improve road linkage between Cachar and south Mizo Hills to help trade and commerce. The communication between Aizawl, the headquarters of Mizoram, and Silchar the nearest trade centre in the plains was often snapped by landslides during rainy season. Until the completion of blacktopping of this road in 1970, the vehicular traffic took about a week's time to cover the distance of about 180 km from Aizawl to Silchar. The prices of commodities shot up beyond the reach of common man in Mizoram.

After 1966, the villages were regrouped into bigger units along Silchar-Aizawl-Lunglei road on economic viability, on recommendation of the Planning Commission. For this, the habitants were supplied with building materials and ration free of cost till the time of next harvest. This regrouping cost at Rs. 2 crore to the Government and affected 65 per cent of total population in general and 80 per cent of the rural population in particular could offer an advantage of location and other facilities[33].

After independence the control of trade passed on to the District Council set up in 1952, which under the Lushai Hills (Trading by non-Tribals) Regulation, 1953 regulated it and issued trade licences to the traders. There were two kinds of licences—one, permanent and the other, temporary. A permanent trade licence holder in Aizawl and Lunglei Sub-divisions, had to pay Rs. 10/- per year as tax in case of non-tribal and Rs. 5/- per year in case of tribal.

Union Territory Period (1972–1986)

To mitigate the feeling of alienation this isolated district of Assam was declared a Union Territory on 21st January 1972. This raised the political status of the region and the people. Aizawl, which was formerly a district headquarters, became the seat of power. With the budgetary support from Central Government a number of measures were taken up to usher an era of development, but the situation remained more or less disturbed. The establishment of urban centres after the Mizo insurgency (1966-1986), made the Mizo conscious about the usefulness of town life. There was a rush to live in Aizawl. Within two decades Aizawl developed into a city.

The position regarding the number of firms and the number of people engaged in business (trading activity) of different commodities in Aizawl as on 1st September 1974 is given in Table 2.2.

Table 2.2: Commodity-wise Break-up of Number of Firms and Employees in Aizawl (As on 1st September 1974)

Commodity	*Number of Firms*	*Number of Employees*
Beverages	33	42
Books and Magazines	11	17
Buildings	14	25
Cloths/Textiles	80	99
Food Articles	96	111
Foot Wear	37	42
Fuel (Oil and Lubricants)	13	77
Industrial Materials	7	8
Machineries	24	55
Meat	10	10
Milk	11	14
Miscellaneous	192	256
Pulses	36	41
Ready-made Cloths	30	82
Stationery Articles	28	57
Tobacco and Cigarettes	12	17
Tools and implements	9	16
Transport Equipments	13	35
Utensils	17	19
Vegetable (Fruits)	13	14
Total	686	1037

Source: *Statistical Handbook of Mizoram*, 1974, p. 284.

After their conversion to Christianity at *en masse*, the Mizo adopted the Western mode of living. The village life was not conducive to the Western mode of living. The pumping of huge amount of funds in Mizoram since the seventies made the Mizo money conscious. There has been large accumulation of money among the Mizo. The Pawi, the Lakher, the Chakma and the Nepali, however, could not derive the benefit of this easy flow of money. During this period, Cachar supplied about 80 per cent of the consumer goods to Mizoram.

In respect of trade and commerce measures were taken to create the basic infrastructure for its development. Though the State Bank of India had set up its branch earlier on 29th December 1971, it started expanding its activities. The United Commercial Bank had set up a branch on 16th September 1976 and Vijaya Bank soon after on 23rd September 1977 both at Aizawl. Mizoram Industrial Development Corporation (MIDC) now known as Zoram Industrial Development Corporation Ltd. (ZIDCO) was set up in 1978. In the cooperative sector Mizoram Cooperative Apex Bank (MCAB) was set up on 5th December 1978 but became functional on 31st July 1982 and Mizoram State Cooperative Marketing and

Consumers' Federation Ltd. (MIZOFED) was set up on 9th December 1981. This provided a great fillip and support to trade and commerce in general and to the cooperative sector in particular. The Mizoram Rural Bank (MRB) was established on 23rd September 1983, which paved way for rural credit.

Notification of the Mizoram Trading by Non-Tribals (Regulation) Act, 1974 on 17th January 1975 was yet another measure to promote business and industry in the territory. Rules in this respect were made applicable from 1977 for a period of 10 years. This provided for granting of licence to non-tribals for a definite period with further provision of renewal which created a potential for growth of business, as local persons till then were not adequately equipped to take up business entrepreneurship.

Even four years after the Union Territory status promotion and expansion of trade and commerce remained neglected in the economy of Mizoram. This was manifested by the fact that no department under the government was established to look after their problems, to implement programmes for promotion and development, and to suggest ways and means conducive to a speedier development in this direction. Trade in its accepted parlance was limited to purchase of goods for cash from neighbouring states and reselling the same to consumers in Mizoram. The entire territory depended for the supply of almost all conceivable items from the most sophisticated machines to the simplest items like chalk and pencils and from the most essential items like rice to the least essential items like beer from the outside the state.

In the regional economy, the trade and commerce of Mizoram occupied little importance, as compared to the adjoining Cachar District and other Districts of Assam, and Meghalaya. The volume of trade carried out in the territory continues to be small. The main commodities of trade with other districts were oranges, ginger, timber, and bamboo. Most of the essential goods including food items were imported from other parts of India.

Post-Statehood

Union Territory status though ushered in an era of administrative and development activity could not meet the aspirations of people and bring peace to the region. Finally, the peace accord was signed between the Government of India and Mizo National Front led by Mr. Laldenga on 30th June 1986. As a consequence, the Union Territory was elevated to statehood and Mizoram became 23rd state of the Indian Union on

20th February 1987. In spite of small size of its territory and population and meagre financial and other resources, this provided an opportunity for the development of the region. For the promotion of trade and commerce a variety of measures were initiated including the administrative mechanism for promotion and regulation of business.

Promotion and Regulation of Business

Government has played an important role in the promotion and regulation of business in Mizoram. Various measures undertaken by the government in this respect are discussed here.

Directorate of Trade and Commerce

The Directorate of Trade and Commerce was created on 20th February 1987. It was given the responsibility under the Government of Mizoram (Allocation of Business) Rules 1987 to deal with promotion and regulation of trade, agricultural marketing, regulation of markets, establishment of market yards and trade centres, border trade, trade by non-tribals and inter-state trade. It was also required to prepare rules relating to the task given to it. The responsibility of repair, renovation and improvement of various market buildings was vested with it. In view of its functions, its infrastructure could not be confined in state capital alone, as in addition to existing three districts five new districts were created. Other activities of the Directorate were as under:

1. Agricultural Marketing

Administration and management of agricultural marketing was handed over by the Central Government to the State Government from 1st April 1992. The Government of Mizoram incorporated the Mizoram Agricultural Marketing Corporation Ltd. (MAMCO) in 1993 to take up marketing of marketable surplus of agricultural products outside the State. Its initial share capital was Rs. 10 crore. The Government of Mizoram assists it through Directorate of Trade and Commerce for which Rs. 300 lakh were provided in Tenth Plan for the purpose under "Assistance to Public Sector Undertakings".

2. Promotion and Regulation of Markets

With the Mizoram State Agricultural Produce Marketing (Regulation) Act, 1996 and the Rules made thereunder came into existence, the management of markets was shifted from different agencies like Land Revenue and Settlement Department, Local Administration Department and the Village Councils in their respective jurisdictions to the Directorate of Trade and Commerce. Besides, Agriculture Department constructed market sheds along the roadside of National Highway. To remove this duplicity, management and administration of markets was placed under the Directorate of Trade and Commerce as per the Government of Mizoram (Allocation of Business) Rules, 1987. It was also planned to have a Regional Office at Vairengte for better promotion and efficient regulation of trading in Mizoram.

3. Development of Market Yards

The growth of business and industry depends upon simultaneous growth in infrastructure including development of markets. In an effort to develop markets in various parts of the State, the State Government with equal participation from the Central Government has undertaken from time to time a Mini Mission-III of Technology Mission through Mizoram Agricultural Marketing Corporation Ltd. (MAMCO). Some wholesale markets and rural primary market sheds were constructed since 2001-02. The district-wise information regarding market sheds constructed along with their respective cost is given in Table 2.3.

Table 2.3: Market Sheds Constructed and Cost thereon in Mizoram (From 2001-02 to 2004-05)

(*Rs. in lakh*)

District	*2001-02*				*2002-03*				*2004-05*			
	WSM		*RPM*		*WSM*		*RPM*		*WSM*		*RPM*	
	No.	*Cost*	*No.*	*Cost*	*No.*	*Cost*	*No.*	*Cost*	*No.*	*Cost*	*No.*	*Cost*
Aizawl	Nil	Nil	5	37.5	2	200	11	165	3	N.A.	11	N.A.
Champhai	1	50	3	22.5	Nil	Nil	7	105	1	N.A.	8	N.A.
Kolasib	2	100	2	15.0	Nil	Nil	1	15	Nil	Nil	Nil	Nil
Lawngtlai	Nil	Nil	1	7.5	Nil	Nil	1	15	Nil	Nil	3	N.A.
Lunglei	Nil	Nil	2	15.0	Nil	Nil	4	60	Nil	Nil	8	N.A.
Mamit	1	50	2	15.0	Nil	Nil	3	45	Nil	Nil	1	N.A.
Saiha	Nil	Nil	1	7.5	Nil	Nil	2	30	Nil	Nil	1	N.A.
Serchhip	Nil	Nil	2	15.0	Nil	Nil	3	45	Nil	Nil	2	N.A.
Total	4	200	18	135.0	2	200	32	480	4	N.A.	34	N.A.

Legend: WSM = Wholesale Market, RPM = Rural Primary Market, and NA. = Not available.

Source: Mizoram Agricultural Marketing Corporation Ltd. Aizawl.

The Table 2.3 reveals that during 2001-02 to 2004-05, in all 10 wholesale market sheds were constructed though all these were confined to Aizawl (5), Champhai (2), Kolasib (2) and Mamit (1) districts only. At the same time in all 84 rural primary markets were constructed. These though concentrated in Aizawl district, covered the entire state. The funds allocated for construction of market sheds (per unit) in 2002-03 were just double than that of 2001-02. It may be concluded that Aizawl being the state capital and Aizawl district were given more weightage.

4. Inter-State Trade in Essential Commodities

The Directorate of Supply and Transport was formed on 17th May 1972, for procurement and distribution of food grains and other essential commodities, building material, cement, G.I. sheets, etc. through public distribution system and cooperation. Earlier, this work was under the Deputy Commissioner. Goods were carried by rail from Kolkata to Silchar by Deputy Director of Supply-*cum*-Liaison Officer. Food grains were transported by road from Silchar to FCI godown at Aizawl and then distributed through fair price shops.

Later, the Directorate was bifurcated into two separate directorates, one for public transport and the other for food and civil supplies. The Directorate of Transport undertakes the registration of motor vehicles, regulation of transport and also runs a fleet of buses for inter-city, inter-district, and inter state transportation. The Directorate of Food and Civil Supplies is responsible for procuring essential commodities and their distribution through a distribution network which comprises MIZOFED, gas agencies and petrol pumps for liquid petroleum gas (LPG), petrol and diesel and fair price shops for food and other consumable items.

The Table 2.4 show the quantity of foodstuffs and petroleum products brought into Mizoram under PDS during 1971-72 to 2001-02.

It may be observed from Table 2.4 that while the quantity procured and distributed by the Directorate had grown many fold over the period there have been year to year fluctuations in consideration of the local demand and local production. This gives a clear indication of the increasing volume of inter-state trade in Mizoram under state regulation. Apart from the above the inter-state trade is undertaken by private business enterprises, which is significantly larger in proportion in respect of commodities as well as volume as is revealed by Table 2.5.

Table 2.4: Quantity of Foodstuffs and Petroleum Products Brought to Mizoram under PDS (from 1971-72 to 2001-02)

Year	Rice (MT)	Atta (MT)	Sugar (MT)	HSD (KL)	Petrol (KL)	K. Oil (KL)
1971-72	12753	N.A.	50	N.A.	N.A.	N.A.
1972-73	16845	8210	229	N.A.	N.A.	N.A.
1973-74	20536	2201	1129	N.A.	1677	427
1974-75	23500	3600	1226	N.A.	1321	723
1975-76	27000	1850	N.A.	N.A.	1400	1922
1976-77	22420	1160	N.A.	N.A.	1992	3045
1977-78	16380	600	N.A.	N.A.	N.A.	780
1978-79	N.A.	N.A.	N.A.	N.A.	N.A.	N.A.
1979-80	N.A.	N.A.	N.A.	N.A.	N.A.	N.A.
1980-81	34149	2700	N.A.	N.A.	N.A.	N.A.
1981-82	50076	2137	N.A.	N.A.	N.A.	N.A.
1982-83	37678	2314	N.A.	2760	2171	232
1983-84	59203	5342	N.A.	2124	1800	2424
1984-85	54977	3611	N.A.	3834	2032	2791
1985-86	66289	2443	N.A.	2187	1717	1940
1986-87	71241	1762	N.A.	2071	2071	3187
1987	78628	7644	N.A.	N.A.	N.A.	N.A.
1988	81462	7644	N.A.	N.A.	N.A.	N.A.
1989	88293	12720	3445	5376	5533	7889
1990	93175	13447	3226	5394	6244	7133
1991	86855	13931	3374	4657	5837	5628
1992	101256	11321	3457	4794	4724	6448
1993	93502	13813	3622	6091	4738	5969
1994	86632	15229	3571	6160	6296	7461
1995-96	100107	24022	3929	N.A.	N.A.	11000
1996-97	95997	23500	3975	N.A.	N.A.	7644
1997-98	112444	16980	3935	N.A.	N.A.	7872
1998-99	138479	22218	3842	N.A.	N.A.	7874
1999-00	77201	14080	4048	N.A.	N.A.	7933
2000-01	36715	1714	7932	N.A.	N.A.	7972
2001-02	18934	9090	8234	N.A.	N.A.	8664

Source: 1. Directorate of Supply and Transport (Transport Wing), Mizoram. 1977.
2. Compiled from various Statistical Handbooks, Mizoram.

It is distressing to note that the movement of merchandise to Mizoram has been one way. The trucks move back empty from Mizoram down to Silchar and other places after unloading the items they had carried. The only exception has been some loads of raw ginger being supplied from Mizoram to Silchar, for which full credit may be accorded to diligent cultivators in the fields. In addition, some forest products like bamboo and cane are exported from Mizoram, but in small quantity. This created an adverse balance of inter-state trade anc increased the transportation

Table 2.5: Essential Commodities brought to Mizoram other than PDS During 1998

Commodity	*Quantity*	*Unit*	*Value (Rs. in Lakh)*
Rice	22748	Quintal	235.05
Edible Oil	46417	Tin	532.47
Chana (Gram)	6963	Quintal	124.92
Potato	38314	Bag	287.00
Flour	3615	Quintal	31.74
Tea leaves	159053	Kilogram	191.45
Onion	7738	Bag	208.00
Garlic	1054	Quintal	38.00
Sugar	25462	Quintal	468.24
Salt	25437	Bag	16.39
Eggs	13640	Box	47.19
Pulses	14608	Quintal	358.69
Milk powder	301533	Kilogram	334.72
Fish	727672	Kilogram	423.28
Fish	60229	Tin	26.00
Total			3323.14

Source: Statistical Handbook of Mizoram, 2000, Directorate of Economics & Statistics, pp. 36-37.

cost for the items procured, and resulted in significant out flow of funds from Mizoram to other states, affecting its economy adversely and depriving it of the multiplier effect.

Trading by Non-Tribals

During pre-British period the non-tribals had limited trade contacts with people of Mizoram with the permission of tribal Chiefs during market days at border posts. Non-tribals were introduced deep into Mizoram during early British period to support the activities of the British Government, as there existed no formal framework of business in the region. Till independence, they continued with their trading activities at the pleasure of British authorities. After independence, their activities were regulated by the District Council under the Lushai Hills District (Trading by Non-Tribals) Regulation Act, 1953 as the Schedule Sixth of the Constitution declared Mizo district, an autonomous district, which empowered it to make regulations for the conduct and control of money lending as well as trading by non-tribals. These regulations provided that no non-tribal except the holder of a licence shall be allowed to engage in any trade or money lending in the district. Further, these regulations provided for two types of licence; one, permanent licence to those non-tribals who were engaged in trading or money lending before the enactment of the regulations of 1953 but not to new persons and two, one year temporary licence to those who apply with fee and complies with the terms and conditions. The renewal of licence was totally vested in executive committee of the District Council with no right of appeal under any clause of regulations. Apparently, these rules were highly discriminatory and resulted in low investment by non-tribals in the State. Thus, there existed, in past, no proper trading regulations except for Lushai Hills District (Trading by Non-Tribals) Regulation Act, 1953 and Rules 1954 of Mizo District Council.

On being upgraded to Union Territory status, Mizoram Trading by Non-Tribal (Regulation) Act, 1974 and the Rules, 1977 were formulated in respect of trading by non-tribals in Mizoram for next 10 years. Under section 2(b) of the Act the government appointed Deputy Commissioners of Aizawl and Lunglei districts and executive committees of the autonomous district councils of Chakma, Lakher and Pawi as licensing authority for the areas falling within their respective jurisdiction with effect from 7th May 1977. The Act provided for issue of licence to any non-tribal on application and payment of prescribed fee. However, the licence was to be granted initially for one year with a provision of renewal on expiry, until and unless revoked by the authority. The Act further provided that no application for licence was to be rejected without being given an opportunity of being heard in the matter and for the reasons to be recorded in writing. The aggrieved persons were given a right of appeal to Appellate Authority in case not satisfied. Thus, some of the discriminatory provisions of the earlier Act and Rules were set right.

On expiry of aforesaid period and after Mizoram attained statehood, the Mizoram Trading (Regulation) Bill 1991 was drafted and after vetting by the Law and Judicial Department was legislated by the State Legislative Assembly, assented by the Governor was published in the Mizoram Gazette the same year. As it was necessary to obtain 'prior' sanction of the President of India, as required under Article 304(b) of the Constitution, the approval of the President was obtained in the form of Mizoram Trading (Regulation) Ordinance, 1995 in 1997, which on promulgation by the State Governor notified in the Mizoram Gazette on 9th April 1997. However, the Ordinance was subject to approval and enactment by the State Legislative Assembly. It was, therefore, introduced in the State Assembly, but, unfortunately withdrawn after a brief discussion, as it was felt necessary to re-frame the provisions with common consensus of the then three major political parties of Mizoram.

Later, with the consensus of the then three major political parties, the Mizoram Trading (Regulation) Bill, 1998 was framed and submitted to the Ministry of Home Affairs, Government of India for examination and observations within a period of six weeks. The Ministry of Social Justice and Empowerment, Ministry of Commerce and its State cell made certain observations in return, which were communicated to Government of Mizoram through the Directorate of Trade and Commerce. The matter was discussed several times by the Hon'ble Minister, Trade and Commerce with the representatives of Law Department, Chamber of Commerce, Advisor to C.M. and the department concerned, but final decision could not be made till date. It appears from the observations of the Government of India that the Mizoram Trading (Regulation) Bill, 1998 framed with the consensus of the then three major political parties, is not likely to be approved as such. It seems that the Government of Mizoram intends to prohibit non-Mizo from trading within the State in the name of protecting the interest of locals, which cannot be permitted for an 'infinite' time under Constitution of India. It would be violative of fundamental rights granted to a citizen under Article 19(1)(g) of Constitution of India. As a promotional measure, it may be adopted for a 'fix' time frame, but, not for infinite time. Perhaps, this may be the reason, why the Government of India has not assent the bill. To benefit from the non-tribals in the development process, it is advisable to rescue the Mizoram Trading (Regulation) Ordinance, 1995 as notified in 1997. It is unfortunate that Mizoram is the only state in India where no rules governing trade exist.

Border Trade of Mizoram

Border trade refers to exchange of goods and services among different countries at border points. The borders have their own natural and human environment, which influences trade. The human groups living in border areas and their economy govern border trade. Economic linkages develop naturally between people on the borders, for they have spatial proximity and are far from mainland of their respective countries[34]. The border people, owing to difficult terrain, isolation, and lack of infrastructure, face insurmountable problems in selling their products, especially the perishable agro-horticultural products. The surplus products are bartered with each other for their survival. Such a trade is necessary where borders are in different topographic units or ecosystem, e.g., hills and plains. Borders occupied by more or less similar people, on either side often find people crossing over freely for carrying out trading activity. Sometimes, there is no physical barrier on the border, either in the form of border fencing or border roads or stricter vigilance by security forces. A sizeable number of individuals on either side of border cross over the border to sell their produce in weekly and daily markets and return home purchasing necessary goods out of their sale proceeds in these markets. These individuals hardly bring back any currency from these markets. There is also an informal trade in the form of services[35]. Perhaps, keeping this in view, the governments had permitted exchange of goods under barter system among the residents within 40 kilometres on both sides along the Indo-Myanmar border[36]. The details of Commodities are given in Table 2.6.

Border trade has a special significance for Mizoram, as it is in immediate vicinity of Myanmar and Bangladesh and is far from the main land. Its 72 per cent of boundary (1,006 km) forms international border with these countries. Owing to topography, poor infrastructural facilities, absence of mineral wealth coupled with other problems, the State has not been able to attract industries, virtually making it dependent upon the neighbouring states and countries. Further, the physical distance, the prevailing road conditions, and poor communication facilities put barriers in quick supply of goods and services from neighbouring states resulting into higher cost. Besides, the practice of charging higher profit margin by traders makes these goods and services almost unaffordable. On the contrary, the trade centres of neighbouring countries being nearer offered ease to traders in transportation, costing less. The affinity of the people with these countries owing to their similarity in ethnicity, life styles, habits, culture, and religion also facilitated trade and commerce.

Historically, Rih Dil (lake) on Myanmar side of border has a strong significance in the history and culture of Mizoram. Mizo have sentimental attachment for the lake due to its cultural significance. Both the governments have agreed to develop Rih Dil (lake) as a Cultural Tourist Centre with a facility of trading across the border.[37] Besides others, a large number of Mizo visit the place annually, which generates revenue and helps in tourism development. Construction of road by Government of India up to Myanmar territory is a commendable gesture. Mizoram-Myanmar border trade under barter system has been in existence since time immemorial in one form or other, even before the currency came into circulation and formal channels of trade were established. There was a small trade in metal bells, silver beads and other ornaments of

Indian manufacture, which found their way through the Mizo hills from Chittagong to Akyab.[38] There had been a continual movement of trade in items like blankets, salt, bee wax from Zahautract, new weapons and implements and pots from Myanmar. The principal products flowing from west to east were blankets, metal pots, pigs, fowls, mats, lac, salt, rice, iron for hoes, and cotton thread to Myanmar.[39]

The trade between Mizoram and the neighbouring countries may conveniently be classified into two types, formal and informal (illegal). The share of informal trade is much more than that of formal trade due to transaction cost and difference between levels of education on two sides. It is believed that unless the environment of formal trade improves significantly, informal trade will continue to co-exist with formal trade, even if free trade is established. The volume of formal trade as it flows through the customs check posts along the international border is recorded and the related data are available easily. However, in case of informal trade, it is very difficult to quantify the exact volume. The border trade in Mizoram has been carried on informally on regular basis, as no formal trade points are operating. Big operators from Aizawl, Silchar, Guwahati and Shillong worked through local agents at Champhai, Vaiphai, Khazwal etc., along the border. According to one survey, people in public life, administration, educated unemployed youth, common men, women and children are involved in such cross-border trade[40].

Table 2.6: Items of Barter Trade listed in Border Trade Agreement (BTA) with Myanmar

List of 22 items initially included under BTA	*List of Additional 10 items agreed during 2001*
1. Mustard/Rape Seed, 2. Pulses and Beans, 3. Fresh Vegetables, 4. Fruits, 5. Garlic, 6. Onion, 7. Chillies, 8. Spices (excluding Nut Meg, Mace, Cloves, Cassia and Cinnamon), 9. Betel Nuts and Leaves 10. Food Items for Local Consumption, 11. Roasted Sunflower Seeds, 12. Minor Forest Produce (excluding Teak), 13. Bamboo, 14. Tomato, 15. Reed Broom, 16. Coriander Seeds, 17. Resin, 18. Ginger, 19. Sesame, 20. Tobacco, 21. Katha, and 22. Soyabean.	1. Teak, 2. Natural Resin, 3. Gum Resin and Oleo Resins, 4. Ground Nut Seeds/Oil/Peanuts, 5. Rice*, 6. Bamboo based Household Products and Bamboo Caps, 7. Pepper, 8. Agarwood Subject to Provisions of CITES, 9. Animal Skin and Hides, and 10. Raw Cotton and Mats.

* Import of Rice is restricted to 50,000 M.T. in a financial year.

Source: North–East Trade Line, February 2003, p. 5.

Smuggled foreign goods are re-smuggled into Mizoram through borders. A single visit to various markets in Mizoram would make it clear that a large number of foreign items are available. These items are other than those agro-forest based products listed in Border Trade Agreement (BTA) given in Table 2.6, which both the governments had agreed to exchange.

Consumer products made in Japan, China, Korea, Thailand, etc., ranging from scrubber, soap, tooth brush, tooth paste, textiles, hosiery, pottery, crockery, mobile cupboard, interior fixtures, and electronic goods to industrial goods like tools, cutters, small machines, etc., are sold in markets of Mizoram. Obviously illegal border trade exists not only in drugs and narcotics but also in consumer goods of daily use. This does not benefit consumers, rather they are exploited, and only a handful of intermediaries gain. The consumer oriented marketing concept is a distant dream in such trading. It may be observed from Table 2.7 that average annual custom seizures in Mizoram from 1993-94 to 2002-03 was Rs. 127 lakh. This also indicated that the volume of such trade has increased 5.3 times over the decade and registered an annual growth of 6.87 per cent. Assuming that the average annual seizure was 5 per cent of actual illegal trade, the actual volume of such trade should be roughly Rs. 25 crore annually.

Table 2.7: Seizures by Customs Department, Government of India in Mizoram (From 1993-94 to 2002-03)

(*Rs. in Lakh*)

Year	*Seizure Value*	*Indices (%) 1993-94 = 100*	*Revenue*	*Indices (%) 1994-95 = 100*	*Main items seized*
1993-94	33	100	—	—	VCD, Inverters, Battery,
1994-95	105	318	12	100	Precious Stones,
1995-96	232	708	32	267	Blankets, Shoes,
1996-97	138	418	21	175	Chapples, Edibles,
1997-98	151	458	20	167	Myanmar currency, Cloth
1998-99	103	312	13	108	Carpet, Detergents,
1999-00	97	294	16	133	Soap, Readymade
2000-01	99	300	18	150	Garments, Heroine
2001-02	132	400	18	150	Powder, Narcotic Drugs (Ephedrine, Ampheta-
2002-03	176	533	110	917	mine tabs, etc.), etc
Growth (%)	127	6.87	29	11.64	

Source: Customs Preventive Division Office, Government of India, Aizawl.

Status of Border Trade with Myanmar

India and Myanmar had signed two trade agreements, one, in 1941 during British rule, which provided margin of preference in favour of Myanmar in respect of certain specified products, and second, on 27th March 1970, which provided *inter alia* for according the Most Favoured Nation (MFN) status under GATT and UNCTAD by both the countries to each other.[41] However, there exists no regular Joint Trade Committee between India and Myanmar at present to monitor the progress.

To legalize the trade, which had been going on for centuries by local residents along the border, the two countries had signed BTA on 21st January 1994, which came in force from 12th April 1995. The agreement provided for border trade initially through two points, i.e. Moreh (Manipur) and Champhai (Mizoram), and subsequently through other points to be mutually identified. Currently, the border trade with Myanmar is functional only through Moreh. Considering the advantages the Indian industry welcomed the formalization of border trade between Myanmar and India.[42] The potential for Indo-Myanmar border trade estimated at Rs. 2,200 crore annually[43], of which Moreh-Tamu sector may contribute Rs. 1,600 crore annually, Mizoram sector via Champhai-Rhi Rs. 500 crore annually and remaining Rs.100 crore can flow through Lungwa in Nagaland.

India's exports to Myanmar mainly consisted of primary and semi-finished iron and steel, cement, bicycles and their parts, tyres, tubes, drugs, pharmaceuticals, auto parts and accessories, wheat-flour, cotton yarn, bleaching powder, fenugreek seeds, ani seeds, cumin seeds, soyabari, dry chillies, agarbatti, suman rose powder, pea, garlic, stainless steel, textiles and food items and may broadly be classified into 7 categories. The respective shares of these categories are given in Table 2.8.

It is important to mention that except for the first category, i.e. miscellaneous processed items none of the above-referred items can be produced in Mizoram at competitive cost advantage. Mizoram has a scope for exporting processed food items only. Further, the relative share of miscellaneous processed items in total exports has increased three fold over the period from 1993-94 to 1996-97.

India ranked 3rd in Myanmar's total foreign trade, and accounted for 23 per cent of its total exports, which again constituted 10 per cent of its total trade volume. Main items entering India are synthetic blankets, electronic goods, betel nuts, rice, turmeric, red kidney (*rajma*), kuth roots, gram, pulses, resin, reed-brooms, teak, groundnut, iron and brass scrap, gold, silver, ruby and jade.

Table 2.8: Composition of India's Exports to Myanmar from 1993-94 to 1996-97

(Figures in percentage)

Category	*1993-94*	*1995-96*	*1996-97*
Miscellaneous processed items	7	16	22
Engineering goods	14	16	10
Iron and steel bars/rods etc.	14	6	10
Primary and semi-finished iron and steel items	31	28	36
Glass, glassware, paints ceramic, enamels, varnishes, cement, etc.	13	6	2
Chemicals, cosmetics, drugs, pharmaceuticals, etc.	14	6	4
Other commodities	7	22	16
Total	100	100	100

Source: *DGCIS, 1996-97* available with Confederation of Indian Industry.

There is no person in Mizoram actively engaged in export-import business with Myanmar under Exim policy; as such transactions are required to be settled through letter of credit (LC) only. For this appropriate banking arrangements, though announced yet do not exist.

According to United Nations' Economic and Social Commission for Asia and Pacific (UN–ESCAP) study the exports to Myanmar via Mizoram consisted of mainly medicines, diamonds, paint, rice milling machines and consumer goods including branded food products. The UN-ESCAP study estimated the average annual informal export from India to Myanmar via Mizoram border at Rs. 15.34 crore.

On the other hand, the imports consisted of alcohol products, gold, cigarettes, stones and pearls, cattle, carpets, electronic items, tools, textiles, cosmetics, blankets, meat, etc.[44] It may be noted that since 1997 Mizoram has been a dry state and import of liquor is not permitted. The UN-ESCAP study estimated the average annual informal import of India from Myanmar via Mizoram border amounted to Rs. 28.52 crore.

To facilitate increasing trade between India and Myanmar, one of the important steps taken is the construction of a 'Bailey bridge' over River Tiau at Zokhawthar. In addition to the above, the State Government is pursuing the following proposals[45]:

- Construction of a blacktop road of 350 km approximately from River Tiau to Falam–Tiddim–Kalemeo on Myanmar side. For this, both the governments had agreed at the Tenth Sector Level Meeting held in Myanmar in September 2001. Government of

Mizoram is putting its best efforts to convince Government of India to speed up the process and expedite the matter for strong economic ties.

- Air service through helicopter in the area is proposed, as suggested by Mr. Nipendra Mishra former Additional Secretary, Ministry of Commerce, Government of India, during his visit to Khawnuam on 19th November 1999. This proposal was discussed at the meeting and both the governments have given their consent to coordinate the international trade activities. The Government of Mizoram has acquired a suitable site for helipad construction near Khawnuam Border Trade Township, which is just 8 km away from international border on Indian side.
- In early days, Kolodyne River in south Mizoram was used as trade route owing to its navigability. This river connects south Mizoram with Arakan hills of Myanmar. After its navigability through Techno-Economic Feasibility survey is established, it is expected to serve as a river route and will facilitate border trade. Considering this, Government of India had commissioned Rail India Technical and Economic Service (RITES) to undertake Techno-Economic Feasibility Survey of the same as well as land route along the river.
- For speedy processing of transactions and reducing delay and halt on the road side near customs check gates, it has been planned to have a Composite Land Customs Station (LCS) at Zokhawthar at a projected cost of Rs. 7 crore. For this the Ministry of Commerce, Government of India had sanctioned Rs. 2 crore to the Border Road Organization (BRO) under Critical Infrastructure Balance (CIB) scheme. Government of Mizoram had made available 18.40 *bigha* land. The foundation stone was laid on 5th December 2001. The BRO had designed the plan layout of the proposed site in March 2002, and had started the work to be finished within three years. This is expected to boost the economy of the North-East in general and Mizoram in particular.
- Khawnuam Township has been declared as Border Trade Township owing to its proximity to Myanmar, climate, and security reasons and is being developed at an additional investment of Rs. 1,402.17 lakh. Government of Mizoram had acquired 127 acres of land, which is needed for the development of border trade infrastructural facilities. As a follow up measure,

the State Government had approved the Zokhawthar LCS township plan. The Customs Department and Trade and Commerce Department have set up their check gates at Khawnuam for monitoring/regulating the border trade. In X Plan the State Government had moved before the Northeastern Council (NEC), Shillong a proposal for Planning Commission for declaring Khawnuam area as "Special Economic Zone".

Status of Border Trade with Bangladesh

Bangladesh is an important trade partner for India. During 1997-98, it ranked at 11th in India's total exports[46]. The land border between Bangladesh and the Northeastern states is more accessible and cost effective than with other neighbouring countries. Trade between India and Bangladesh is carried out as per the Indo-Bangladesh Trade Agreement, which provided for "Most Favoured Nation" treatment to goods and services of each other country.

India's exports to Bangladesh mainly consist of cotton yarn, fabrics, glass, glassware, ceramics, primary and semi-finished iron and steel, drugs, dyes and intermediates, pharmaceuticals, electronic goods, paper, wood products, plastic, linoleum products and chemicals. The exports from Northeastern states to Bangladesh mainly consist of minerals like coal, limestone and horticultural products like ginger, oranges, citrus fruits, garlic, pears, etc. Category-wise composition of India's exports to Bangladesh with their respective share is given in Table 2.9.

Table 2.9: Composition of India's Exports to Bangladesh (From 1991-92 to 1997-98)

(Figures in per cent)

Category	*1991-92*	*1994-95*	*1996-97*	*1997-98*
Agricultural and Allied Products	17.39	8.49	11.58	16.07
Ores and Minerals	3.38	5.82	5.03	4.66
Manufactured Goods	78.13	81.86	80.92	76.52
Other Commodities	1.25	3.82	2.48	2.75
Total	100.00	100.00	100.00	100.00

Source: CMIE, Foreign Trade, August 1998.

At present, there is no formal agreement on border trade with Bangladesh. The formal trade between India and Bangladesh during 1995-97, amounted to Rs. 3,400 crore annually[47]. According to United Nations' Economic and Social Commission for Asia and Pacific (UN-ESCAP) study, the exports to Bangladesh via Mizoram consisted of mainly horticultural products including raw cotton. The study estimated the average annual informal exports to Bangladesh through Mizoram at Rs. 9.31 crore. Mizoram has good scope of exporting horticultural products like orange, lemon and agricultural products like raw-cotton.

Main items entering India from Bangladesh are manufactured goods, food items, and fuels. According to the UN-ESCAP study, imports from Bangladesh via Mizoram consisted of mainly clothes and electronic goods. The study estimated the average annual imports from Bangladesh through Mizoram at Rs. 1.14 crore. It is encouraging to note that the estimate of Mizoram's exports to Bangladesh is nine times of imports from Bangladesh.

For promoting inter-regional trade in South Asia, Bangladesh has agreed to allow the movement of goods from one part of India to other through its territory on the condition that Bangladeshi importer-*cum*-re-exporter must ensures 10 per cent value addition for such passage under back-to-back letter of credit. India can also make a similar offer to Bangladeshi entrepreneurs for providing access to Myanmar and Chinese markets through Northeastern states.

Establishment of water link between Mizoram and Bangladesh will provide access to the landlocked State to use the Chittagong port. During his visit to Bangladesh, Mr. Zoramthanga, the Chief Minister of Mizoram had emphasized on water link between Mizoram and Bangladesh through Karnaphuli River via Lake Kaptai and desired to buy natural gas from Bangladesh. He expressed that Bangladesh could be the main gateway to international market for Mizoram.

To facilitate Mizoram-Bangladesh border trade, some of the important steps taken are as under[48] :

- A land site measuring 3,01,000 square metre at Kawrpuichhuah, needed for developing border trade infrastructure near Tlabung (Demagiri) has been acquired by Government of Mizoram under CIB scheme at a total cost of Rs. 5 crore, of which Ministry of Commerce had approved Rs. 2.48 crore. The State Government has submitted a projcct to the Central Government for clearance from concerned ministries.
- Government of Mizoram has requested Government of India and Government of Bangladesh to open up the old river Karnaphuli (Demageri-Chittagong) route and allow free movement of goods, as was before partition. Recognizing the

traditional trade linkage of the people of this area with the people of former Bengal, this proposal has received a positive response from Begum Hasina Sheik, the former Prime Minister of Bangladesh in March 1999.

- A team of 31 delegates from the Federation of Bangladesh Chamber of Commerce and Industry (FBCCI), Dhaka had visited Mizoram in October 1999 and a Memorandum of Understanding (MOU) was signed between FBCCI and Mizoram Chamber of Commerce.
- A four member delegation led by Joint Director, Directorate of Trade and Commerce, Government of Mizoram had gone to Bangladesh during June/July 2001 for looking into the possibilities of exporting from Mizoram agricultural and horticultural products like ginger, chillies, chow-chow, fruits, etc. The matter was discussed with Chambers of Commerce in Bangladesh and a MOU was signed between Sylhet Chamber of Commerce and Industry and Mizoram Chamber of Industry and a 'Letter of Intent' for export of ginger was signed with M/s. Crystal Corporation, Chittagong.
- The Chief Minister and Minister of Trade and Commerce, Government of Mizoram need to plan a visit to Bangladesh to discuss with their counterparts for exploring the possibilities of enhanced cooperation for opening of Indo-Bangladesh border trade.
- Mr. A.R. Kohli, the Governor of Mizoram in his address to the State assembly had pointed out that the Ministry of External Affairs, Government of India, New Delhi is trying to convince Bangladesh authorities to open trade centres inside their territory.

Potential for Development of Border Trade

According to Mr. Zoramthanga, the Chief Minister of Mizoram, the present border trade arrangements are not in tune with the spirit of Mizoram Peace Accord. To him, border trade means sale of locally produced commodities to the neighbouring countries. However, at present mainly manufactured goods of other countries are smuggled. People in Mizoram do not benefit from it; rather the traders on both sides are beneficiaries. These goods just pass through Mizoram. It is neither exchange of Myanmar products nor exchange of Mizoram products. If Myanmar is in a position to sell certain products to Mizoram and Mizo sell their products to Myanmar through these roads, then alone it will be beneficial for Mizoram[49].

Considering the prevailing situation, it is high time to accord legal status to border trade with proper safeguards to check adverse side effects. Development of border trade will lead to reduced cost of goods from the markets of Southeast and even Far-east Asian countries. This will provide an opportunity to boost the economy of these resource poor states. Manipur had opened up its border trade with Myanmar in 1995. Though, due to certain constraints it has not been able to exploit the benefits of border trade fully. Nevertheless, Mizoram is a peaceful state in the North-East and can tap the benefits of border trade with neighbouring countries in order to improve the economic condition of its people. The consumers will also reap the benefits of border trade as also the local entrepreneurs, thereby reducing unemployment to a certain extent.

The border trade with Bangladesh should also be resumed, as this had been the lifeline of the economy of Mizoram for centuries. The economic lot of the State suffered when the traditional access to Chittagong port was closed by Pakistan in 1947. There is a need to explore areas where bilateral cooperation may be strengthened.

Myanmar's strategic location *vis-à-vis* India's cost competitiveness, educated work force, abundance of natural resources like minerals, energy and forestry among others, offers this country a potential to become a dynamic economy in medium term. As Myanmar has joined BIMST-EC, it can be a potential regional partner in India's access to South East Asian countries.[50]

Identification of potential items for increased border trade with Myanmar may be done with reference to the strengths and weaknesses of Mizoram in terms of its location, resource-base and status of infrastructure on the one hand, and demand for various items in Myanmar on the other. The Mizoram border touching Myanmar routes through Hnahlan, Champhai, Vaiphai/Rarkawn, Thingsai/Ngharchhip, Vawmbuk, Lungbun, Thaipang and Sangau sector has been identified as crucial for border trade. Mizoram is predominantly an agricultural economy with rich forest resources including cane and bamboo. Teak plantations have come up in the forests, which may be commercially used after 5-10 years. The State government provides cotton and woollen yarn to artisans engaged in production of handloom products. Mizoram depends heavily on trade through Champhai for a number of agricultural products. Considering the high volume of imports of gems, precious and semi-precious stones into India through the border, cutting and polishing of gems and manufacture of jewellery for export could be undertaken in the State. The required skill for manufacture of gold jewellery and diamond-studded jewellery is available in Champhai and Aizawl[51]. The products that have been identified for export promotion from the State include processed fruits, medicinal plants and herbs, handloom products, silk, etc. Potential areas for investment on Indo-Myanmar (Mizoram) border are[52]: teak processing, handicrafts, cutting and polishing of precious and semi-precious stones, stainless steel and aluminium utensils, cutting and polishing of granites, distillery, safety matches, polishing and milling of oil seeds, food processing, etc.

In view of the strict import regulations, low level of foreign exchange reserves and a relatively narrow manufacturing base in Myanmar, it may be suggested that Indian companies could consider investment for increasing trading opportunities by setting up joint ventures or wholly-owned subsidiaries in Myanmar. With the initiation of the programme for computerization and office automation in different sectors, there is a scope for software exports to Myanmar. Indian software companies can set up software training institutes/centres in Myanmar to train local work force in computer systems and operations[53]. Young Mizo who are trained and have acquired expertise in this field can take advantage of the opportunity. They will be best suited in Myanmar because of their proximity. Mizoram can supply trained work force to help Myanmar in restructuring banking. There may be scope for export of services including engineering, marketing, insurance, auditing and accounting. Mizoram has technically qualified unemployed engineers who may benefit from this opportunity.

The following areas may be taken up for detailed investigation to determine the feasibility and economic viability in long run from the view point of Mizoram:

(i) *Teak Processing*: Myanmar's area near the Indo-Myanmar border has abundant growth of teak. High transportation cost to Yangoon and Mandalay prohibit carrying it for processing to these centres. This disadvantage can be exploited by Mizoram by setting up processing centres in the border area of Champhai.

(ii) *Cutting and Polishing of Precious Stones*: As Myanmar does not possess expertise in cutting and polishing for its large deposits of precious stones; this can be undertaken in the border area of Champhai.

(iii) *Stainless Steel and Aluminium Utensils*: There is substantial demand for stainless steel utensils in Myanmar. As there is no local production, demand is met by imports, especially from

Thailand. The SSI units at Aizawl (Mizoram) can take advantage of this situation and make aluminium and steel utensils for export to Myanmar.

(iv) *Cutting and Polishing of Granite*: Myanmar has large deposits of raw granite. Cutting and polishing facility is not available and there is lack of capital and expertise. This facility can be developed in border area. Training in cutting and polishing of granite may be imparted at the Industrial Training Institutes (ITI) in Mizoram to Mizo to take advantage of this opportunity.

(v) *Safety Matches*: Units for making safety matches can be set up in the border areas of Mizoram, utilizing the forest resources available on Mizoram-Myanmar border.

Public Sector in Business

As discussed earlier the Mizo were not equipped to participate in large-scale business, and there was diffidence in the Government to permit trade by non-tribals, it became necessary for the public sector to take initiative in the field of business and industry. The Government came forward establishing Mizoram Agricultural Marketing Corporation Ltd. (MAMCO) to undertake agricultural marketing, Mizoram State Cooperative Marketing and Consumer Federation Ltd. (MIZOFED) for procuring and distribution of essential commodities, etc. Later, Zoram Electronics Development Corporation Ltd. (ZENICS) was set up for procurement and distribution of electronic items etc. For the purpose of knowing whether the PSUs achieved their objectives of incorporation, financial statement analysis is undertaken on the assumption that activities, working, performances, etc. of Corporations, are well reflected to a great extent in figures as shown in their respective annual reports.

Mizoram Agricultural Marketing Corporation Ltd. (MAMCO)

Agricultural Marketing plays an important role in the post harvest technology of agricultural products. Unless remunerative prices are assured to the farmers/producers, production in the field of agriculture may be adversely affected. There was no regulated market in Mizoram like '*Krishi Upaj Mandi*' and the existing market channel set up do not function effectively. Due to this, traders continued to exploit the farmers. Keeping this in view, the Government of Mizoram had set up Mizoram Agricultural Marketing Corporation Ltd. (MAMCO) on 21st February 1993,[54] with an authorized share capital of Rs.10 crore, for development of agriculture and horticulture crops in the State and to safeguard the economic interest of State's poor farmers who are totally dependent upon agriculture for their livelihood. Its objectives are[55]: to prevent unnecessary exploitation of ignorant farmers by unscrupulous traders, to ensure remunerative returns to farmers on their respective produce, to act as a module between farmers and traders ensuring healthy marketing system, to provide pre- and post-harvest management technology, to provide basic marketing infrastructure facilities, and to provide, to intervene, to finance procurement and marketing of surplus agricultural produce at the time of market slugging.

Its main activities comprise of procurement as well as marketing of surplus products of certain agricultural produce viz., ginger, chillies, sesame, tung oil etc. 'Price Support' and 'Transport Subsidies' are also given to growers/farmers. Besides subscribing share capital of Rs. 441.10 lakh, the Government of Mizoram also extended budgetary support to it in the form of 'Grants-in-Aid' from time to time, which amounted to Rs. 795.50 lakh upto 2002-03. MAMCO started with procurement and sale of agriculture produce like ginger, chillies, etc. Now it has stopped this activity. Mizoram is the only state in India, where tung trees are grown. It was estimated that not less than 50 lakh full grown tung trees existed in Mizoram. Keeping in view the feasibility of growing and the high demand of tung oil in laminates and paint industry at the national and international level, the State Government had entrusted the Corporation marketing of tung oil. Therefore, a tung oil extraction plant with capacity to store 10 MT was established. But, the Corporation is facing serious problem of marketing tung oil due to its inability to sell the produce at competitive price. On conceiving the importance of post harvest infrastructure facilities and keeping in mind the remoteness of the State, it has made a plan to create post harvest management facilities like ginger dehydration plant, contract farming, standardization, quality control, efficient market chains, establishment of proper storage godowns, and establishment of efficient market intelligence and information system.

The analysis of annual accounts of MAMCO for a decade from 1993-94 to 2002-03 is given in Table 2.10, which revealed the following:

1. The average return on investment of MAMCO at (–) 42 per cent and the average net profit after tax to operating revenue at (-) 655 per cent showed heavy loss. The average percentage of personnel cost to operating revenue at 452 per cent and administrative expenses to operating revenue at 462 per cent for the period showed that the expenditure on personal and administration were main causes of huge loss, besides sizable price support to farmers during 1994-95 to 1996-97.

Table 2.10: Abridged Annual Accounts and Financial Ratios of Mizoram Agricultural Marketing Corporation Ltd (MAMCO) From 1993-94 to 2002-03

(Rs. in lakh)

Sl. No.	Balance Sheet	Balances as on 31st March										
	Year	1994	1995	1996	1997	1998	1999	2000	2001	2002	2003	Growth (%)
	Sources of Funds :											
1.	Share Capital	Nil	Nil	Nil	Nil	Nil	Nil	Nil	Nil	Nil	Nil	
2.	Share Capital Contribution	100.00	100.00	100.00	129.00	229.00	304.00	354.00	393.00	441.10	441.10	22.81
3.	Reserves & Surplus	2.31	2.59	2.59	2.59	Nil	Nil	Nil	Nil	Nil	Nil	
4.	Deferred Govt. Grants	0.00	182.98	238.51	166.24	72.07	47.97	44.41	41.21	216.28	165.50	
5.	Miscellaneous Expenses	3.08	3.08	2.77	2.47	24.33	63.12	127.23	206.03	205.72	205.41	85.02
6.	Retained Earnings (3+4-5)	-0.01	1.82	2.38	1.66	0.48	-0.15	-0.83	-1.65	0.11	-0.40	
7.	Owner's Equity (1+2+6)	99.23	282.48	338.32	295.36	276.74	288.85	271.18	228.18	451.66	401.19	8.64
8.	Capital Employed	99.23	282.48	338.32	295.36	276.74	288.85	271.18	228.18	451.66	401.19	8.64
	Application of Funds :											
9.	Fixed Assets	11.96	117.98	129.59	137.39	136.37	108.03	114.45	126.08	165.10	200.72	17.65
10.	Depreciation	1.24	5.58	18.95	31.92	42.49	40.81	48.71	56.74	65.25	75.18	44.63
11.	Net Block (9-10)	10.72	112.40	110.64	105.47	93.88	67.22	65.74	69.34	99.86	125.55	11.00
12.	Capital Work in Process	Nil	Nil	16.02	68.66	79.45	79.45	79.45	79.45	Nil	Nil	
13.	Pre-Operative Expenses	3.75	3.75	3.75	3.75	3.75	3.75	3.75	3.75	Nil	Nil	
14.	Total Fixed Assets (11+12+13)	14.47	116.15	130.42	177.89	177.08	150.43	148.94	152.55	99.86	125.55	11.85
15.	Cash & Bank Balances	146.84	104.18	142.02	45.89	38.48	79.96	58.16	2.97	284.11	206.17	
16.	Sundry Debtors	5.46	3.38	3.38	3.38	5.27	5.27	5.27	5.27	5.27	5.27	
17.	Other Current Assets	2.90	5.94	2.05	2.05	2.05	1.05	1.39	1.39	2.00	2.00	
18.	Liquid Assets (15+16+17)	155.20	113.50	147.44	51.31	45.80	86.28	64.83	9.63	291.39	213.45	-1.71
19.	Loans & Advances	52.01	53.03	60.66	66.66	54.96	57.14	71.92	72.27	68.37	69.65	
20.	Current Assets (18+19)	207.21	166.53	208.10	117.98	100.76	143.42	136.75	81.90	359.76	283.09	2.66
21.	Current Liabilities	122.45	0.20	0.20	0.50	1.10	5.00	14.50	6.26	7.96	7.45	19.53
22.	Working Capital (20-21)	84.75	166.33	207.90	117.48	99.66	138.42	122.25	75.64	351.80	275.64	7.06
23.	Total Funds Employed (14+22)	99.23	282.48	338.32	295.36	276.74	288.85	271.18	228.18	451.66	401.19	8.64

(Contd.)

Sl. No.	*Income Statement*	*Figures for the year ended on 31st March*										
	Year	*1994*	*1995*	*1996*	*1997*	*1998*	*1999*	*2000*	*2001*	*2002*	*2003*	*Growth*
1.	Turnover	25.98	30.62	Nil	10.08	40.55	Nil	Nil	Nil	Nil	Nil	
2.	Interest	8.31	8.12	10.06	5.09	1.83	2.18	3.28	2.66	4.20	7.45	-7.79
3.	Total Operating Revenue (1+2)	34.30	38.74	10.06	15.17	42.37	2.18	3.28	2.66	4.20	7.45	-23.17
4.	Cost of Materials Sold	25.75	106.14	Nil	120.42	435.99	Nil	Nil	30.00	Nil	Nil	
5.	Packing Material Consumed	0.60	2.09	Nil	Nil	Nil	Nil	Nil	Nil	Nil	Nil	
6.	Other Direct Charges	2.42	3.77	Nil	Nil	Nil	Nil	Nil	Nil	Nil	Nil	
7.	Personnel Cost	1.18	3.50	6.11	10.90	20.22	18.42	29.70	40.51	26.45	31.63	40.52
8.	Admin., Selling & Dist. Cost	5.68	7.66	10.12	12.63	27.24	15.92	32.07	37.66	28.14	40.08	24.02
9.	Price Support	Nil	8.88	1.12	9.26	Nil	Nil	Nil	Nil	Nil	Nil	
10.	*OPBD 3-[4+5+6+7+8+9])*	*-1.32*	*-93.31*	*-7.29*	*-138.04*	*-441.08*	*-32.16*	*-58.49*	*-105.51*	*-50.39*	*-64.26*	*2.99*
11.	Depreciation	1.24	4.34	13.37	12.97	12.20	9.28	7.90	4.83	5.58	7.25	6.78
12.	*Operating Profit (OP) (10-11)*	-2.56	-97.66	-20.66	-151.01	-453.28	-41.44	-66.39	-110.34	-55.97	-71.51	3.00
13.	Other Income	4.87	97.93	20.97	151.32	434.43	5.85	4.58	31.54	106.41	71.82	7.57
14.	Profit (+)/Loss (-) on sale of F. A.	Nil	Nil	Nil	Nil	0.31	Nil	Nil	Nil	-50.12	Nil	
15.	Preliminary Expenses	Nil	Nil	0.31	0.31	0.31	0.31	0.31	0.31	0.31	0.31	
16.	PBIT/PBT/PAT (12+13+14-15)	2.31	0.28	0.00	0.00	-18.85	-35.91	-62.11	-79.11	Nil	Nil	-15.10
17.	Accumulated Profits of P.Y.	Nil	2.31	2.59	2.59	2.59	-22.17	-61.28	-125.69	-204.80	-204.80	
18.	Prior Period Expenses	Nil	Nil	Nil	Nil	5.92	3.19	2.30	Nil	Nil	Nil	
19.	*Accumulated Losses (16+17-18)*	2.31	2.59	2.59	2.59	-22.17	-61.28	-125.69	-204.80	-204.80	-204.80	-50.24

(*Contd.*)

Sl. No.	Important Financial Ratios / Year	1994	1995	1996	1997	1998	1999	2000	2001	2002	2003	Growtl
1.	Return on Investment	N.A.	-51	-7	-48	-158	-15	-24	-44	-16	-17	-42
2.	Personnel Cost to Operating to Revenue	3	9	61	72	48	846	904	1523	630	425	452
3.	Administrative Expenses to Operating Revenue	17	20	101	83	64	731	977	1416	670	538	462
4.	Operating Profit to Operating Revenue	-7	-252	-205	-996	-1070	-1903	-2022	-4147	-1332	-960	-1289
5.	Net Profit (PAT) to Operating Revenue	7	1	0	0	-44	-1649	-1892	-2973	0	0	-655
6.	Capital Turnover	N.A.	0.20	0.03	0.05	0.15	0.01	0.01	0.01	0.01	0.02	0.05
7.	Fixed Assets Turnover Ratio	3.20	0.34	0.09	0.14	0.45	0.03	0.05	0.04	0.04	0.06	0.45
8.	Working Capital Turnover Ratio	0.40	0.23	0.05	0.13	0.43	0.02	0.03	0.04	0.01	0.03	0.14
9.	Current Ratio	2	833	1041	236	92	29	9	13	45	38	234
10.	Acid Test Ratio	1	567	737	103	42	17	4	2	37	29	154
11.	Super Quick Ratio	1	521	710	92	35	16	4	0	36	28	144
12.	Fixed Assets to Net Tangible Worth	0.15	0.41	0.39	0.60	0.64	0.52	0.55	0.67	0.22	0.31	0.45

Legend: OPBD = Operating Profit before Depreciation, OP = Operating Profit, PBIT = Profit before Interest and Tax, PBT = Profit before Tax, PAT =Profit after Tax

Source: Compiled from Annual Accounts of Mizoram Agricultural Marketing Corporation Ltd. from 1994 to 2003.

2. Purchases not only exceeded but were disproportionately high than the value of sale for the entire period of study. As the commodities dealt with were perishable in nature, the Corporation hardly had any stocks which resulted in huge loss throughout the period, except for 1993-94.
3. It was distressing to note that the average operating revenue to capital employed during the period at 0.05 times, the average operating revenue to fixed assets at 0.45 times and average operating revenue to working capital at 0.14 times were very low. This showed low efficiency in the utilization of resources by the Corporation. The operating revenue for the period indicated that during later half, there was a sharp decline as the turnover became 'nil', the operating revenue consisted of interest earning only, all other activities of the Corporation came to a halt and the only activity that remained was fixing floor prices for agricultural produce.
4. There is a possibility of loans and advances turning non-performing as it had been stagnant throughout the period. Auditors have confirmed the same time and again in their reports[56]. It was revealed by officials during interview that the Corporation was neither giving fresh loans nor rotating the old loans by realizing the same. The increase was due to increase in outstanding interest. No attempt seems to have been made to realize the principal and interest.
5. The liquidity position of the Corporation as depicted by average current ratio at 234:1, average acid test ratio at 154:1 and average super quick ratio at 144:1 had been high. Large cash and bank balances were maintained by the Corporation, apparently due to no activity.
6. The value of fixed assets continuously increased from Rs. 14.47 lakh in 1993-94 to Rs. 125.55 lakh in 2002-03. It was highest at Rs. 177.08 lakh in 1997-98. A sharp decline in fixed assets was noticed in 2001-02 owing to disposal of fixed assets worth Rs. 50.67 lakh at a price of Rs. 55000 incurring a loss of Rs. 50.12 lakh. This clearly showed that the book value was inflated and not real.
7. Overheads during the entire period of study showed a sharp and constant increase, except for 1998-99, resulting in average operating cost at 13.90 times of operating revenue. Operating cost was 107 per cent of operating revenue in 1993-94, increased

to 4247 per cent in 2000-01 and settle down to 1060 per cent in 2002-03. This was partly due to employees' pay revision as per the Vth Pay Commission's recommendations. The employees had a mindset of government department and were not willing to accept the existence of Corporation. Due to this the Government of Mizoram had to subsidize the growing deficit by providing subsidies, grants, etc.

8. The Corporation being a public sector organization, it is not possible for the management to control the cost of personnel and administrative expenses. Hence, the only option available is to raise the operating revenue whatever way it may be possible.
9. To auditors, the Corporation though was not covered by Sick Industries Companies Act, 1985[57], because of a regular flow of capital. Being a Government of Mizoram public sector enterprise, the losses incurred by it were met out of deferred government grants from time to time.
10. Important points raised by the auditors in their report on the accounts of MAMCO during the period of study are summarized below:

    (a) *Management Related Points*: (i) This is the only company in Mizoram, which has completed more than 10 years of incorporation without issuing a single share till date. (ii) The share capital contribution was credited to Share Capital Contribution Account, as Share Capital Account was not opened in the books of the Corporation. (iii) No physical verification of cash balance, stock and fixed assets was done by the management at any point of time. Even no stock records were maintained. (iv) Annual General Meeting Book was not maintained. (v) Directors' register was also not maintained.

    (b) *Accounting Related Points*: (i) Fixed assets register was not maintained properly. (ii) Classifying entire loan and advances as secured and good was wrong and did not represent true picture as the Reserve Bank of India required them to be classified into standard, sub-standard and doubtful.[58] (iii) Advances for expenses remained pending for adjustment for a long time and were doubtful of recovery. (iv) No provision was made for various fines and penalties for statutory defaults under different Acts and Statutes.

> (v) Bills and vouchers relating to purchases were not available. (vi) Incomplete records were maintained in respect of purchases, sales and closing stocks. (vi) Grant-in-Aid received, to the extent of loss, recognized as profit. (vii) Bank transferred the interest on Corporation's deposit to somebody else who was not concerned with the Corporation and on being pointed out by auditors the recovery of the same was pending and was doubtful of recovery. (viii) Interest income shown was doubtful of recovery. (ix) Shortage of quantitative stock was sometimes shown as vague sales on credit and consequently sundry debtors were over stated. (x) Debtors out of short billing and long outstanding were doubtful of recovery, but no provision was made. (xi) Incomplete customers' record as regards to their address etc.

It can be summarized from the above that MAMCO decided floor prices of seasonal agricultural produces, a job of few hours in a season that can be done by officers of the government with specialization in agriculture. Such officers may be available with the government in Agriculture Department, Horticulture Department, and Directorate of Trade and Commerce. It would be better, if the government disburses cash subsidy to farmers in Mizoram equal to the amount of annual loss sustained by MAMCO. The farmers would receive greater relief than what they are getting from MAMCO.

Zoram Electronics Development Corporation Ltd. (ZENICS)

The Zoram Electronics Development Corporation Ltd. (ZENICS) was incorporated on 20th March 1991[59] with an authorized share capital of Rs. 5 crore, of which the State Government had subscribed towards paid-up capital Rs. 4.599 crore on 31st March 2004[60]. The State government also gave promotional and other grants from time to time. Its objectives included: (i) to promote and to develop IT Industry, IT Products, IT Software, and IT Services within the State of Mizoram, (ii) to undertake and assist research and development in core techniques of IT and applications for improvement of productivity and efficiency in Government and Industry, (iii) to facilitate development of IT applications for social sectors for improvement of the quality of life of common man, (iv) to develop entrepreneurship through software development, software training and software services, (v) to provide and manage internet gateway operation for providing internet connectivity, (vi) to manage, maintain and support large-scale data processing, data warehousing and data mining facilities for e-Governance of the State, and (vii) to establish professional and academic training centre so as to build up synergies between IT education and IT industry.

To achieve the aforesaid objectives, the functions and activities of ZENICS are cable TV operation, Test and Repairing Centre (TRC), component bank, ZENICS Computer Learning Academy (Computer Training Centre), Consumer Electronics Training Centre (CETC), entrepreneurs development programme for educated and unemployed youth on IT, electors' photo identity cards (EPIC), Multimedia Content Creation Centre, Sales Emporium, and supply of computers to government offices[61].

The undertaking has incurred loss every year because of drawbacks like inadequate technical support and lack of managerial skills, improper organizational structure, and lack of well thought plan of action. Piecemeal addition of share capital of Rs. 35.00 lakh per annum by the State Government, adversely affected implementation of various projects undertaken by ZENICS. Also, insufficient allocation of fund from the State Government for promotion of communication and information technology industry in Mizoram, which was approximately 0.002 per cent of the State Annual Plan Budget, was responsible for such a situation.

In view of the growing importance of information communication technology (ICT) and to provide high value added consultancy support to Government Departments, the Corporation has taken up projects[62] like (i) Software Development Centre, (ii) International Internet Gateway at Aizawl, (iii) Centre for Excellency in IT Education, (iv) Test and Repairing Centre for Personal Computer (TRC-PC), and Test and Repairing Centre for Consumer Electronics (TRC-CE) in every district headquarters, and (v) launched job oriented training programme of 12 months duration "IT Entrepreneurs Development Programme for Educated Unemployed Youths of Mizoram".

The financial statements of ZENICS for the period from 1991-92 to 2003-04 have been compiled, analyzed and are given in Table 2.11.

The analysis of Table 2.11 revealed the following:

1. Leaving the year 2003-04, the Corporation had a negative return on investment (ROI) for the period ranging from 15.28 per cent in 1992-93 to 61.35 per cent in 2002-03. On the average the Corporation lost Rs. 28.67 for every Rs. 100/- invested as capital employed, as it suffered from operating loss from 1991-92 to

Table 2.11: Abridged Annual Accounts and Important Financial Ratios of the Zoram Electronics Development Corporation Ltd. (ZENICS) from 1991-92 to 2003-04

Sl. No.	Balance Sheet		Balances as on 31st March													
	Year		*1992*	*1993*	*1994*	*1995*	*1996*	*1997*	*1998*	*1999*	*2000*	*2001*	*2002*	*2003*	*2004*	*Growth (%)*
	Sources of Funds:															
1.	Share Capital		46.75	114.75	145.75	175.75	207.20	241.20	275.20	302.40	302.40	337.36	337.36	372.36	372.36	14.49
2.	Share Capital Contribution		28.50	Nil	Nil	24.05	17.00	17.00	Nil	Nil	34.96	15.04	52.54	70.04	87.54	10.56
3.	Reserves and Surplus		0.86	0.76	0.67	0.57	0.47	0.38	0.29	0.19	0.10	Nil	Nil	Nil	Nil	-21.92
4.	Miscellaneous Expenses		2.06	12.72	29.38	51.92	94.12	119.25	141.81	168.60	213.19	259.94	308.98	358.88	354.51	41.99
5.	Retained Earnings	(3-4)	-1.20	-11.96	-28.71	-51.35	-93.65	-118.87	-141.52	-168.41	-213.09	-259.94	-308.98	-358.88	-354.51	-39.37
6.	Owner's Equity	(1+2+5)	74.05	102.79	117.04	148.45	130.55	139.33	133.68	133.99	124.27	92.46	80.92	83.52	105.39	-1.07
7.	Debt		Nil	Nil	Nil	Nil	Nil	Nil	Nil	Nil	Nil	Nil	Nil	Nil	Nil	
8.	*Capital Employed*	*(6+7)*	*74.05*	*102.79*	*117.04*	*148.45*	*130.55*	*139.33*	*133.68*	*133.99*	*124.27*	*92.46*	*80.92*	*83.52*	*105.39*	*-1.07*
	Application of Funds:															
9.	Fixed Assets		27.16	45.36	52.33	75.13	46.13	48.74	50.32	97.00	112.75	115.20	119.83	130.13	132.55	12.76
10.	Depreciation		1.03	6.31	13.38	22.00	15.48	21.11	24.04	26.69	33.71	41.90	49.83	57.28	64.63	27.94
11.	Net Block	(9-10)	26.13	39.05	38.95	53.13	30.65	27.63	26.28	70.31	79.04	73.30	70.00	72.85	67.92	8.58
12.	Capital Work in Process		5.43	15.13	12.15	13.41	48.05	48.99	48.99	8.05	8.05	8.05	8.05	8.05	8.05	-5.01
13.	Total Fixed Assets	(11+12)	31.56	54.18	51.10	66.54	78.70	76.62	75.27	78.36	87.09	81.35	78.05	80.90	75.97	5.53
14.	Cash and Bank Balances		33.33	37.82	109.24	93.20	47.28	54.74	46.75	48.05	26.95	1.34	3.44	9.86	118.02	-13.76
15.	Sundry Debtors		0.57	1.94	6.85	3.43	3.13	2.47	2.45	2.48	0.77	0.67	0.68	5.54	13.51	4.09
16.	Loans and Advances		8.10	7.38	16.88	5.56	0.45	1.86	1.90	1.84	1.01	0.49	0.32	0.30	1.50	-23.05
17.	Other Current Assets		Nil	2.33	4.86	9.18	3.71	6.12	8.09	3.18	1.32	1.62	1.16	11.75	25.45	3.59
18.	Liquid Assets	(14+15+16+17)	42.00	49.47	137.83	111.37	54.57	65.19	59.19	55.55	30.05	4.12	5.60	27.45	158.48	-9.93
19.	Inventories		2.25	2.50	10.48	8.42	10.31	12.37	10.93	11.87	11.46	11.24	11.15	9.48	9.45	9.53
20.	Current Assets	(18+19)	44.25	51.97	148.31	119.79	64.88	77.56	70.12	67.42	41.51	15.36	16.75	36.93	167.93	-5.15
21.	Current Liabilities		1.76	3.36	82.37	37.88	13.03	14.85	11.71	11.79	4.33	4.25	13.88	34.31	138.51	12.66
22.	Working Capital	(20-21)	42.49	48.61	65.94	81.91	51.85	62.71	58.41	55.63	37.18	11.11	2.87	2.62	29.42	-18.00
23.	*Total Funds Employed*	*(13+22)*	*74.05*	*102.79*	*117.04*	*148.45*	*130.55*	*139.33*	*133.68*	*133.99*	*124.27*	*92.46*	*80.92*	*83.52*	*105.39*	*-1.07*

(*Contd.*)

Sl. No.	Income Statement		Figures for the year ended 31st March													
	Year		*1992*	*1993*	*1994*	*1995*	*1996*	*1997*	*1998*	*1999*	*2000*	*2001*	*2002*	*2003*	*2004*	*Growth*
1.	Turnover		1.92	8.08	15.73	10.41	6.48	4.86	8.40	4.87	5.15	8.27	6.48	37.56	98.99	15.77
2.	Raw Materials Purchased		3.49	5.18	16.64	0.75	4.05	5.11	1.04	Nil	Nil	Nil	Nil	10.73	19.55	10.87
3.	Decrease(+)/Increase(-) in Stocks		-2.25	-0.25	-7.98	1.64	-2.96	-2.06	1.44	-0.94	0.41	0.22	0.08	-5.31	7.01	16.60
4.	Raw Materials Consumed	(2+3)	1.24	4.93	8.66	2.39	1.09	3.05	2.48	-0.94	0.41	0.22	0.08	5.42	26.56	-1.80
5.	Personnel Cost		0.60	5.98	10.09	13.36	18.93	21.38	22.12	24.13	34.22	38.60	40.53	64.01	51.85	30.65
6.	Admn., Selling & Distribution Exp.		0.89	5.39	10.69	15.17	10.18	9.50	7.35	7.69	9.73	8.65	6.36	11.12	13.03	8.99
7.	*OPBD*	*[1-(4+5+6)]*	*-0.81*	*-8.22*	*-13.71*	*-20.51*	*-23.72*	*-29.07*	*-23.55*	*-26.01*	*-39.21*	*-39.20*	*-40.49*	*-42.99*	*7.55*	*-27.25*
8.	Depreciation		0.71	5.29	7.06	8.62	6.36	5.63	4.95	5.14	7.02	8.19	7.93	7.45	7.35	9.28
9.	*Operating Profit (OP)*	*(7-8)*	*-1.52*	*-13.51*	*-20.77*	*-29.13*	*-30.08*	*-34.70*	*-28.50*	*-31.15*	*-46.23*	*-47.39*	*-48.42*	*-50.44*	*0.20*	*-28.23*
10.	Other Income (Bank Intt. Recd.)		0.32	2.76	4.40	6.49	5.29	9.47	5.41	4.36	1.55	0.55	0.09	0.58	5.37	-8.95
11.	Profit (+) / Loss (-) on Sale of F. A.		Nil	Nil	Nil	Nil	-17.50	Nil	0.44	0.10	Nil	Nil	Nil	Nil	Nil	-
12.	*PBIT*	*(9+10+11)*	*-1.20*	*-10.75*	*-16.37*	*-22.64*	*-42.29*	*-25.23*	*-22.65*	*-26.69*	*-44.68*	*-46.84*	*-48.33*	*-49.86*	*5.57*	*-28.20*
13.	Interest		Nil	Nil	Nil	Nil	Nil	Nil	Nil	Nil	Nil	Nil	Nil	Nil	Nil	-
14.	*Profit Before Tax (PBT)*	*(12-13)*	*-1.20*	*-10.75*	*-16.37*	*-22.64*	*-42.29*	*-25.23*	*-22.65*	*-26.69*	*-44.68*	*-46.84*	*-48.33*	*-49.86*	*5.57*	*-28.20*
15.	Corporate Tax		Nil	Nil	Nil	Nil	Nil	Nil	Nil	Nil	Nil	Nil	Nil	Nil	0.36	-
16.	*Profit After Tax (PAT)*	*(14-15)*	*-1.20*	*-10.75*	*-16.37*	*-22.64*	*-42.29*	*-25.23*	*-22.65*	*-26.69*	*-44.68*	*-46.84*	*-48.33*	*-49.86*	*5.21*	*-28.22*
17.	Accumulated Losses of P.Y.		Nil	1.20	11.95	28.71	51.35	93.64	118.87	141.52	168.41	213.09	259.94	308.98	358.88	-
18.	Prior Period Expenses		Nil	Nil	0.39	Nil	Nil	Nil	Nil	0.20	Nil	0.01	0.71	0.04	0.84	-
19.	*Accumulated Losses*	*(16-17-18)*	*1.20*	*11.95*	*28.71*	*51.35*	*93.64*	*118.87*	*141.52*	*168.41*	*213.09*	*259.94*	*308.98*	*358.88*	*354.51*	*39.37*

(Contd.)

Important Indices and Ratios and Z - Scores														
Year	*1992*	*1993*	*1994*	*1995*	*1996*	*1997*	*1998*	*1999*	*2000*	*2001*	*2002*	*2003*	*2004*	*Mean*
Return on Investment (ROI)		-15.28	-18.90	-21.94	-21.56	-25.72	-20.88	-23.27	-35.80	-43.73	-55.85	-61.35	0.21	-28.67
Raw Material Consumed to Turnover	65.00	61.00	55.00	23.00	17.00	63.00	30.00	-19.00	8.00	3.00	1.00	14.00	27.00	27.00
Personnel Cost to Turnover	31.00	74.00	64.00	128.00	292.00	440.00	263.00	495.00	664.00	467.00	625.00	170.00	52.00	290.00
Admn, Selling & Distribution Exp. to Turnover	46.00	67.00	68.00	146.00	157.00	195.00	88.00	158.00	189.00	105.00	98.00	30.00	13.00	105.00
Operating Profit to Turnover	-79.00	-167.00	-132.00	-280.00	-464.00	-714.00	-339.00	-640.00	-898.00	-573.00	-747.00	-134.00	0.00	-397.00
Net Profit Ratio (PAT to Turnover)	-63.00	-133.00	-104.00	-217.00	-653.00	-519.00	-270.00	-548.00	-868.00	-566.00	-746.00	-133.00	5.00	-370.00
Capital Turnover Ratio		0.09	0.14	0.08	0.05	0.04	0.06	0.04	0.04	0.08	0.07	0.46	1.05	0.18
Fixed Assets Turnover Ratio	0.07	0.21	0.40	0.20	0.21	0.18	0.32	0.07	0.07	0.11	0.09	0.52	1.46	0.30
Working Capital Turnover Ratio	0.05	0.17	0.24	0.13	0.12	0.08	0.14	0.09	0.14	0.74	2.26	14.34	3.36	1.68
Debtors Turnover Ratio		6.44	3.58	2.03	1.98	1.74	3.41	1.98	3.17	11.49	9.60	12.08	10.39	5.66
Inventory Turnover Ratio		3.40	2.42	1.10	0.69	0.43	0.72	0.43	0.44	0.73	0.58	3.64	10.46	2.09
Current Ratio	25.14	15.47	1.80	3.16	4.98	5.22	5.99	5.72	9.59	3.61	1.21	1.08	1.21	6.48
Acid Test Ratio .	23.86	14.72	1.67	2.94	4.19	4.39	5.05	4.71	6.94	0.97	0.40	0.80	1.14	5.52
Super Quick Ratio	18.94	11.26	1.33	2.46	3.63	3.69	3.99	4.08	6.22	0.32	0.25	0.29	0.85	4.41
Average Collection Period (days)		57.00	102.00	180.00	185.00	210.00	107.00	185.00	115.00	32.00	38.00	30.00	35.00	106.00
Inventory Holding Period (days)		107.00	151.00	331.00	528.00	852.00	506.00	854.00	827.00	501.00	631.00	100.00	35.00	452.00
Fixed Assets to Net Tangible Worth	42.62	52.71	43.66	44.82	60.28	54.99	56.31	58.48	70.08	87.98	96.45	96.86	72.08	64.41

Legend: OPBD = Operating Profit before Depreciation, OP = Operating Profit, PBIT = Profit before Interest and Tax, PBT = Profit before Tax, PAT =Profit after Tax

Source: Compiled from Annual Accounts of Zoram Electronics Development Corporation Ltd from 1991-92 to 2003-04.

2002-03. In the year 2003-04, it earned a small operating profit of Rs. 20,000/-. The average cost of raw material though fluctuated widely in the range of 1 per cent in 2001-02 to 65 per cent in 1991-92, averaged at 27 per cent of sales. This means the Corporation on the average was left with gross margin of nearly 73 per cent, which was quite high as compared to any other business. However, there was heavy incidence of overheads resulting in negative net margin.

2. The average operating revenue to capital employed at 0.18 times and operating revenue to fixed assets at 0.30 times was exceptionally low, and cannot be regarded satisfactory. Of course, both the ratios have improved a little bit in the year 2003-04. This showed that there was no linkage between capital employed, investment in fixed assets and revenue generation, which cannot be accepted. Further operating revenue to inventory was low, sometimes even at 0.43 times. This indicated that either there was no demand for the products/components/commodities, etc., sold by the Corporation or there was sluggish demand. On the average inventory remained in stock for 452 days. The average collection period increased from year to year up to 1996-97 and thereafter declined gradually reflecting slight improvement in receivables management.

3. The average cost of personnel was high at 290 per cent, which was lowest at 31 per cent in 1991-92 and reached the peak of 664 per cent in 1999-2000. Similarly, administrative, selling and distribution expenses on the average at 105 per cent were also high all times, except for 2003-04 when it stood at 13 per cent. These are the only two components, which were basically responsible for continuous operating loss.

Corporation's turnover has jumped sizeably from 2002-03 and onwards because it got for the first time in Mizoram one big contract of making voters' photo identity cards. But this is not going to be a regular feature, which may lucratively turn the whole financial position of the firm from loss to profit. Again the Corporation being a public sector enterprise it is not possible for the management to control the cost of personnel and administrative expenses. Hence, the only option available is to look for similar big projects/contracts of job works.

5. The short-term liquidity position as reflected by the average current ratio, acid test ratio, and super quick ratio at 6.48:1,

5.52:1 and 4.41:1 respectively, showed Corporation's inability to use working capital profitably and productively. During 2001-02 to 2003-04 the current ratio was poor and below the normal standard of 2:1 with no corresponding decline in other two ratios. This showed that the Corporation had tried to get rid of stocks.

6. The funds employed in the Corporation over the period have grown 1.42 times. However, the same could not be utilized properly for the growth of turnover. In this situation, employment of more and more funds in fixed assets and capital work in progress appear to be unjustified.
7. The organization did not borrow funds. Thus, it did not benefit from trading on equity.
8. In nutshell, the main failure of the management may be regarded as inability to generate revenue and control operating cost. The management could not utilize its human resources properly so as to promote the software business and IT industry to a large extent. No efforts were made to increase operating revenue (sales) within the State as there was no expenditure on advertising and publicity of its products and services. Economy of the scale could not be derived. The employees had a mindset of government department and are not willing to accept the existence of Corporation. The concept of accountability was far away.
9. One of the objectives of ZENICS is to give entrepreneurship training and motivation to new entrants in ICT industry. But, in view of the meagre operating revenues through out the period except for 2003-04 and its high investment in inventory as compared to sales over the last thirteen years, it failed to be as role model for private entrepreneurs in motivating them for setting up electronics industry in the State. So, in order to increase its turnover to a satisfactory level, at least to attain break-even in its operations, it is advisable that ZENICS should launch marketing promotion and brand creation exercise at least within the State.
10. The auditors had opined that, "it is a potentially sick industrial company"[63]. The Corporation was, however, not covered by Sick Industries Companies Act, 1985, because the additional share capital contribution made by the Government of Mizoram on regular basis was sufficient enough to cover its annual losses.
11. The management contended that piecemeal subscription of share capital by the State government had adversely affected

implementation of various projects undertaken by the Corporation. It also contended that insufficient allocation of fund approximately 0.002 per cent of the total State Plan Budget for promotion of ICT in Mizoram was responsible for such a situation. But, the point here is that it could borrow from financial institutions like ZIDCO or commercial banks rather than depending wholly on the State government. At the same time, the State Level Bankers' Committee for Mizoram observed[64], "at present, government corporations are not availing any bank finance. With increased scale of operations, bank credit may be required." This clearly shows that the banks in Mizoram were ready to finance any viable project of any of the State Govternment owned Corporations and the respective management could ensure timely completion of their respective projects rather than delaying and causing cost overruns. But, no such proposal was moved by ZENICS.

12. Several points were raised in auditors' report on the accounts of ZENICS from 1991-92 to 2003-04. Some of them are summarized below:

(a) *Management Related Points*: (i) Though inventory valuation was done for the first time in 1998-99, physical verification of cash balance was never done by the management at any point of time. (ii) There was no regular system to work out unserviceable/damaged stores. (iii) Adequate internal control system and internal audit system did not exist. (iv) Annual General Meeting book, Directors' register, and other statutory registers were not maintained properly.

(b) *Accounting Related Points* : (i) Physical verification of fixed assets was done for the first time in 1998-99. Fixed assets register not maintained properly. (ii) Stocks' lying at sales emporia not reflected in annual accounts, as the value was unknown. (iii) In some years, cash book and ledgers were balanced by pencil and not by ink which is against the standard practice of accounting. (iv) Cashbook was not maintained up to date. Huge cash and bank balances were allowed to accumulate with no specific purpose. Cash resources were handled recklessly and even transacted on post dated vouchers/bills/receipts. Misappropriation of cash was frequent. Misappropriated cash was not reflected in

books of accounts and even in some cases it was continued to be shown as current assets though its recovery was doubtful. (v) No provisions were made. Provision for statutory dues, various fines and penalties for statutory defaults under different Acts and Statutes were not made. Contingent liability and statutory audit fee were not provided in some years. (vi) Bills and vouchers relating to some of the fixed assets created or purchased were not available. (vii) Capital work in progress of electronic items/ components standing for very long time and their value was continuously slashing, but, no provision was made. Some of the fixed assets and capital work in progress (Cable TV network) sold/disposed of to private parties but no profit/ loss on sale was worked out rather continued to be shown in balance sheet on assets side. (viii) Grant-in-Aid received from Government of India has been shown as current liability. Advance for expenses and advance to suppliers was pending for adjustment for a long time and was doubtful of recovery. Sundry debtors were not properly classified to the requirement of Schedule-VI.

Cooperatives in Business

Article 10 of the National Cooperative Policy Resolution emphasized upon strengthening the consumer cooperatives to facilitate public distribution system as well as an instrument of price stability. In Mizoram, distribution of essential commodities in rural areas was undertaken by village level service cooperative societies. In urban areas, Mizoram Cooperative Super Markets and Mizoram Wholesale Cooperative Stores performed this function. The cooperative societies opened a network of branches to bring down the general price level in the market. The main difficulty faced in this regard by the village level societies was irregular supply of articles by the state level societies, which have also found difficult to cope with increasing volume of business, because of their weak financial base. Thus, in order to gear up these state level societies, enabling them to undertake public distribution effectively, and to strengthen the financial base of the Mizoram Cooperative, Super Market Ltd. and The Mizoram Wholesale Cooperative Stores Ltd., financial assistance was provided in the form of share capital, managerial subsidy, transport subsidy, and business loan.

The cooperatives had taken up trading in Mizoram in 1949. The progress and the achievements up to 1967 had been rather slow and unsatisfactory. During 1966-67, the Cachar-Mizo Wholesale Cooperative Stores Ltd. had three branches in the region and there were 80 primary cooperative societies including 23 consumer cooperatives with 1,229 members engaged in trading and their total paid up capital, assets and liabilities were Rs. 5,240/-, Rs. 33,426/-, and Rs. 30,898/- respectively. In 1973-74, there were 188 primary cooperative societies (27 industrial, 21 trading and marketing, 7 multipurpose, 6 dairy, 8 handlooms, 71 service, 12 consumer, 3 fishery and 33 others) with a total membership of 8,544 and their total share capital and working capital were Rs. 3.27 lakh and Rs. 18.88 lakh respectively.

There were 11 state level societies as on 1st April 2002. Mizoram State Cooperative Marketing and Consumer Federation Ltd. (MIZOFED) established in 1981 had 11 branches with paid up share capital of Rs.531.4 lakh as against the capital employed Rs. 211.53 lakh only as on 31st March 2004. Mizoram Multi Commodity Producers' Cooperative Union Ltd. (MULCO) engaged in dairy products having 25 member societies working as branches had a paid up capital of Rs. 7.43 lakh and capital employed Rs. 126.41 lakh as on 31st March 2004. Mizoram Cooperative Apex Bank Ltd. (MCAB) formed in 1978 became operational in 1982 had 10 branches with 752 members, engaged in banking business with paid up share capital of Rs. 217.77 lakh and disbursed loans to the tune of Rs. 2753.06 lakh against a total investment of Rs. 801.33 lakh as on 31st March 2002. Mizoram State Cooperative Union Ltd. (MSCU) with 207 members had 3 branches with an investment of Rs. 36.72 lakh as on 31st March 2002. Mizoram State Cooperative Fruit, Forestry and Vegetables Growers Federation Ltd. (MAFF) had a paid up capital of Rs. 9.89 lakh as against total investment of Rs. 28.07 lakh with one branch and 39-member societies as on 31st March 2002. Mizoram Apex Handloom and Handicraft Cooperative Society Ltd. (MAHCO) had a membership of 120 primary societies with total investment of Rs. 60.99 lakh including paid up share capital of Rs. 38.46 lakh as on 31st March 2002. Mizoram State Pig Producers' Federation Ltd. (PIGFED) with 75 member societies working as branches had a paid up share capital of Rs. 4.01 lakh, against its total investment of Rs. 8.65 lakh as on 31st March 2002. Mizoram State Women Federation (WOMENFED) with 38 member societies working as branches had a paid up capital of Rs. 5.5 lakh, against total investment was Rs. 2.23 lakh only. Mizoram Cooperative Fish Farming Marketing and Federation Ltd. (ZOFISHED) with 14 member societies working as branches had a paid up capital of Rs. 2.71 lakh against total investment of Rs. 1.21 lakh. Mizoram Apex Sericulture Cooperative Society Ltd. (MASCOS) with 5 member societies existed with a paid up capital of Rs. 5000/- as on 31st March 2002. Mizoram State Cooperative Housing Finance Federation Ltd. (HOUSEFED) with 25 member societies working as branches had a paid up capital of Rs. 13.26 lakh against a total investment of Rs. 0.71 lakh as on 31st March 2002.

The position regarding number of primary cooperative societies from 1973-74 to 2001-02 is shown in Table 2.12.

From Table 2.12, it may be observed that the annual growth in the number of primary societies of different categories in the state was 29 per cent in consumer societies, 20 per cent in farming societies, 14 per cent in fishery societies, 10 per cent in handloom societies, 14 per cent in housing societies, 13 per cent in livestock societies, and 12 per cent in multipurpose societies which was higher than the overall growth at 9 per cent p.a. during the period from 1973-74 to 2001-02. On the other hand, annual growth in industrial societies at 8 per cent, trading and marketing societies at 7 per cent, and others was lower than the average. However, service cooperative societies and labour cooperative societies marked negative growth over the period. It is a happy feature of cooperative movement in Mizoram that all these societies have remained actively involved in the activity undertaken by them. Perhaps one of the supporting features has been the provision of subsidy by the Government towards their administrative and other overheads.

Mizoram State Cooperative Marketing and Consumers' Federation Ltd. (MIZOFED)

Mizoram State Cooperative Marketing and Consumers' Federation Ltd. (MIZOFED) was formed in 1981 with an authorized share capital of Rs.10 crore, covered the whole of Mizoram including Cachar District (Assam) within its ambit of operations, has 121 members including state government, engaged in trading with a network of 11 branches, 8 petrol pump retail outlets—one each at Aizawl, Lunglei, Vairengte, Kolasib, Champhai, Serchhip, Hnahthial and Lawngtlai, 15 kerosene oil points at Aibawk, W. Phaileng, Thingdawl, Darlawn, Ratu, Khawzawl, Thingsulthliah and Zawlnuam, 6 liquid petroleum gas (LPG) distributorships—one each at Aizawl, Mamit, Kolasib, Champhai, Serchhip, and Saiha and 51 extended LPG points as on 31st March 2004 has diversified in length and breadth from 1981-82 to 2003-04. It has 135 employees 83 males and 52 females. It has a branch office at Silchar

Table 2.12: Number of Different Types of Primary Cooperative Societies in Mizoram (from 1973-74 to 2001-02)

Year	Industrial	Trading & Marketing	Multi-purpose	Dairy	Processing	Canteen	Handloom	Service	Consumer	Housing	Fishery	Labour	Lamps	Livestock	Farming	Others	Total
1973-74	27	21	7	6	N.A.	N.A.	8	71	12	N.A.	3	N.A.	N.A.	N.A.	N.A.	33	188
1975-76	29	3	12	9	N.A.	2	11	107	N.A.	N.A.	4	N.A.	N.A.	16	4	2	199
1977-78	41	1	18	8	N.A.	5	21	145	6	N.A.	1	N.A.	N.A.	20	6	2	274
1980-81	76	N.A.	46	17	1	9	45	192	N.A.	N.A.	14	14	4	63	20	2	503
1981-82	88	2	53	20	1	9	52	195	N.A.	N.A.	16	24	8	70	22	2	562
1982-83	92	3	61	30	1	10	59	197	N.A.	N.A.	21	31	11	77	24	2	619
1983-84	31	2	7	N.A.	N.A.	3	13	74	2	N.A.	10	6	5	33	8	2	196
1984-85	31	2	7	N.A.	N.A.	3	13	73	N.A.	N.A.	10	6	5	33	8	N.A.	191
1985-86	90	4	71	28	N.A.	N.A.	53	206	N.A.	N.A.	26	42	12	76	27	N.A.	635
1986-87	92	4	74	33	N.A.	N.A.	53	210	4	N.A.	28	42	12	70	27	N.A.	649
1987-88	92	4	72	33	N.A.	14	41	210	4	1	28	42	14	70	27	N.A.	652
1988-89	95	4	72	38	N.A.	N.A.	54	205	6	7	30	40	14	95	50	N.A.	710
1989-90	102	5	72	35	N.A.	N.A.	57	196	8	7	32	34	14	106	74	N.A.	742
1990-91	180	14	84	42	6	16	123	138	115	16	48	18	16	227	191	N.A.	1234
1991-92	182	14	89	43	6	15	126	139	119	17	49	23	16	218	190	N.A.	1246
1992-93	221	14	103	53	7	16	151	142	124	19	52	23	15	260	201	N.A.	1401
1993-94	237	15	115	70	7	19	174	138	129	22	57	19	15	295	212	N.A.	1524
1994-95	251	15	138	76	7	19	211	136	137	23	60	19	15	325	235	N.A.	1667
1995-96	259	15	189	49	7	18	245	133	143	24	56	17	15	325	234	14	1743
1996-97	221	10	189	54	7	16	169	124	132	23	59	16	13	324	229	19	1605
1997-98	213	8	205	43	1	15	165	101	123	19	53	9	8	262	191	10	1426
1998-99	178	4	192	43	4	17	170	96	138	20	55	10	12	296	251	13	1499
1999-00	162	4	211	51	4	16	145	105	134	19	61	10	12	252	227	24	1437
2001-02	119	4	185	68	12	16	160	112	141	17	77	11	12	283	239	31	1487
Growth %	8	7	12	4			10	-0.4	29	14	14	-3	3	13	20		9

Source: 1. Statistical Handbook of Mizoram, 1974 p. 54, 1976 pp. 226-27, 1983 pp.204-215, and 1985 pp. 145-159 and
2. Socio-Economic Review of Mizoram, Directorate of Economics & Statistics, Government of Mizoram, 2000-01, Table 14 in Appendixes.

for liaisoning with Indian Oil Corporation Ltd. Its paid up share capital was Rs. 531.36 lakh, of which the Government of Mizoram has subscribed Rs. 528.38 lakh and the rest by different member societies, as on 31st March 2004.

The analysis of annual reports of MIZOFED for the period of 23 years from 1981-82 to 2003-04 is given in Table 2.13 which reveals the following:

1. MIZOFED is basically a trading organization under cooperatives where profit earning is not a prime motive but is not expected to incur loss. However, the organization is expected to attain high trading volume and the margin cannot be expected to be high.
2. The Return on Investment over the period from 1981-82 to 2003-04 had been fluctuated widely ranging between (–) 48.94 per cent in 2002-03 to 10.95 per cent in 1990-91. The average return on investment at (–) 11.83 per cent p.a. showed poor operational results.
3. The average cost of goods sold at 93.56 per cent ranged between 88.42 per cent in 1983-84 to 98.22 per cent in 1995-96. The average gross margin at 6.5 per cent seems to be reasonable. However, as in some years, the cost of goods sold had been high the Federation incurred loss.
4. The average annual cost on personnel at 3.28 per cent of turnover appear to be high and so also other costs like general administration charges at 1.01 per cent and distribution cost at 1.40 per cent. Though over the years the general administration cost and distribution cost has come down yet there is a scope for further reduction.
5. The activity ratios such as capital turnover, fixed assets turnover, working capital turnover, inventory turnover, debtors' turnover, average collection period, and average inventory holding period conveyed improvement in the operations.
6. Average annual growth in sales over 23 years at 13.92 per cent as against the growth in capital employed at 2.94 per cent may be regarded as satisfactory, but, there is scope for further improvement.
7. Over the years, certain expenses were subsidized by the Government of Mizoram in the form of subsidy, which is deemed to be the other income of the Federation. But, as the other costs are increasing continuously, there are losses which is a cause of

Table 2.13: Abridged Annual Accounts and Important Financial Ratios of Mizoram State Cooperative Marketing and Consumers' Federation Ltd (MIZOFED) from 1981-82 to 2003-04

(Rs. in lakh)

Sl. No.	Position Statement		*for the year ended on 30th June*									*on 31st March*		
	Year		*1982*	*1983*	*1984*	*1985*	*1986*	*1987*	*1988*	*1989*	*1990*	*1991*	*1992*	*1993*
	Sources of Funds													
1.	Share Capital		35.17	37.64	37.64	37.64	37.64	61.64	65.71	71.87	98.87	116.97	149.59	166.08
2.	Reserves & Surplus		0.01	0.01	0.01	0.01	0.01	0.01	0.01	0.01	0.01	0.01	0.01	0.01
3.	Various Grants		9.35	9.35	9.35	9.35	9.35	11.59	Nil	27.00	Nil	Nil	Nil	Nil
4.	Miscellaneous Expenses		26.85	30.28	32.13	23.47	19.21	31.70	207.21	215.17	214.81	212.71	210.57	214.22
5.	Retained Earnings	(2+3-4)	-17.50	-20.92	-22.77	-14.11	-9.85	-20.11	-207.20	-188.16	-214.79	-212.70	-210.56	-214.21
6.	Owner's Equity	(1+5)	17.68	16.71	14.86	23.52	27.78	41.53	-141.48	-116.29	-115.92	-95.73	-60.97	-48.13
7.	Debt		146.63	166.94	188.67	217.94	184.36	178.71	196.05	201.49	244.22	269.65	319.84	286.41
8.	*Capital Employed*	*(6+7)*	*164.31*	*183.65*	*203.53*	*241.47*	*212.14*	*220.24*	*54.57*	*85.20*	*128.30*	*173.92*	*258.88*	*238.28*
	Application of Funds													
9.	Fixed Assets		9.39	9.58	11.31	10.70	10.17	8.53	17.76	27.28	49.62	65.19	61.27	69.22
10.	Depreciation		0.75	0.66	1.62	1.76	1.55	0.47	0.42	0.98	3.00	5.23	7.77	9.73
11.	Net Block	(9-10)	8.34	8.93	9.69	8.93	8.62	8.06	17.33	26.29	46.62	59.96	53.50	59.48
12.	Investments		0.15	0.15	0.16	0.26	1.41	1.41	1.41	1.41	1.61	1.61	2.13	3.13
13.	Cash & Bank Balance		4.53	8.11	13.06	9.80	10.65	9.73	23.97	7.68	6.57	15.91	17.42	26.61
14.	Accounts Receivable		105.42	119.24	104.60	149.23	130.92	151.77	28.18	47.15	42.99	39.55	40.76	91.29
15.	Other Current Assets		25.70	42.19	60.54	78.99	58.84	62.33	3.71	5.22	37.42	73.54	113.91	23.97
16.	Liquid Assets	(13+14+15)	135.65	169.54	178.20	238.03	200.41	223.83	55.86	60.05	86.98	129.00	172.09	141.87
17.	Inventories		32.52	21.73	38.27	42.49	68.54	80.30	53.02	72.08	68.61	60.95	117.38	131.13
18.	Current Assets	(16+17)	168.17	191.27	216.47	280.51	268.95	304.13	108.88	132.13	155.60	189.95	289.47	273.00
19.	Quick Liabilities		12.58	16.19	19.99	47.73	22.50	43.66	24.81	18.64	12.05	8.36	8.61	8.25
20.	Other Liabilities		0.37	0.50	2.81	0.51	44.33	49.69	48.24	55.99	63.48	69.24	77.60	89.08
21.	Current Liabilities	(19+20)	12.95	16.69	22.79	48.24	66.83	93.35	73.05	74.63	75.53	77.60	86.22	97.33
22.	Working Capital	(18-21)	155.22	174.58	193.68	232.28	202.12	210.77	35.83	57.50	80.07	112.36	203.25	175.66
23.	*Total Funds Employed*	*(11+12+22)*	*164.31*	*183.65*	*203.53*	*241.47*	*212.14*	*220.24*	*54.57*	*85.20*	*128.30*	*173.92*	*258.88*	*238.28*

(Contd.)

Sl. No.	Position Statement	for the year ended on 31st March											
	Year	1994	1995	1996	1997	1998	1999	2000	2001	2002	2003	2004	Growth (%)
	Sources of Funds												
1.	Share Capital	190.08	228.08	228.08	228.08	230.64	236.12	239.30	239.80	239.83	239.87	531.40	12.13
2.	Reserves & Surplus	0.01	0.01	0.01	0.01	0.01	0.02	0.02	0.02	0.03	0.03	0.03	
3.	Various Grants	Nil	Nil	6.75	10.25	6.75	6.75	6.75	6.75	6.75	Nil	Nil	
4.	Miscellaneous Expenses	206.01	218.12	332.16	370.35	331.17	335.57	339.98	354.96	363.47	478.49	480.96	15.18
5.	Retained Earnings (2+3-4)	-206.00	-218.11	-325.40	-360.09	-324.40	-328.80	-333.21	-348.18	-356.70	-478.46	-480.93	-14.69
6.	Owner's Equity (1+5)	-15.93	9.97	-97.32	-132.00	-93.77	-92.68	-93.91	-108.39	-116.87	-238.59	50.46	-6.80
7.	Debt	286.03	296.72	307.93	313.19	363.34	379.06	388.56	402.23	466.42	476.60	161.06	4.02
8.	*Capital Employed (6+7)*	*270.11*	*306.69*	*210.62*	*181.19*	*269.57*	*286.38*	*294.64*	*293.84*	*349.55*	*238.01*	*211.53*	2.94
	Application of Funds												
9.	Fixed Assets	65.73	76.15	85.65	75.79	78.45	76.71	71.99	85.41	71.01	72.32	68.94	12.07
10.	Depreciation	11.57	10.42	8.19	10.31	6.15	8.28	2.57	5.55	4.45	3.81	5.54	11.07
11.	Net Block (9-10)	54.16	65.72	77.46	65.48	72.30	68.44	69.42	79.85	66.56	68.51	63.41	12.23
12.	Investments	3.13	3.14	3.14	3.14	1.54	7.13	8.49	4.09	4.34	3.96	6.24	16.64
13.	Cash & Bank Balance	59.73	58.85	41.72	46.73	56.06	79.46	60.70	63.33	136.66	40.62	30.53	12.46
14.	Accounts Receivable	51.53	49.69	27.09	27.09	34.13	55.58	66.27	78.69	64.77	21.29	27.90	-5.20
15.	Other Current Assets	118.88	170.77	151.56	195.16	158.14	208.71	258.23	402.48	421.07	512.17	512.97	15.42
16.	Liquid Assets (13+14+15)	230.14	279.31	220.37	268.98	248.33	343.75	385.21	544.50	622.51	574.08	571.40	7.28
17.	Inventories	136.41	155.35	153.81	110.40	115.59	102.41	112.84	156.51	138.32	97.13	127.13	6.84
18.	Current Assets (16+17)	366.56	434.66	374.18	379.37	363.92	446.16	498.04	701.01	760.82	671.20	698.53	6.98
19.	Quick Liabilities	143.10	175.99	211.03	225.55	155.79	195.02	234.90	397.89	408.60	433.75	472.53	32.12
20.	Other Liabilities	10.63	20.84	33.13	41.25	12.40	40.33	46.41	93.22	73.57	71.92	84.12	6.35
21.	Current Liabilities (19+20)	153.74	196.83	244.16	266.80	168.19	235.35	281.30	491.12	482.17	505.67	556.65	16.25
22.	Working Capital (18-21)	212.82	237.83	130.02	112.57	195.73	210.81	216.74	209.89	278.65	165.54	141.88	1.55
23.	*Total Funds Employed (11+12+22)*	*270.11*	*306.69*	*210.62*	*181.19*	*269.57*	*286.38*	*294.64*	*293.84*	*349.55*	*238.01*	*211.53*	2.94

(Contd.)

Sl. No.	Income Statement	for the year ended on 30th June										on 31st March	
	Year	1982	1983	1984	1985	1986	1987	1988	1989	1990	1991	1992	1993
1.	Turnover	271.14	267.00	294.87	441.54	507.37	615.87	713.47	957.15	1011.58	1419.11	1173.55	1721.24
2.	Goods Purchased	222.85	235.75	276.55	395.91	474.60	606.14	671.13	936.14	950.95	1327.54	1160.62	1606.66
3.	Decrease(+)/Increase(-) in Stocks	21.33	10.79	-15.82	-4.20	-25.05	-11.02	26.55	-19.06	3.46	7.66	-56.43	-13.75
4.	Cost of Goods Sold (2+3)	244.18	246.54	260.73	391.71	449.56	595.11	697.68	917.07	954.42	1335.20	1104.19	1592.91
5.	Porterage, Wages & Trade Exp.	1.09	0.75	0.81	2.23	4.25	2.09	2.31	0.70	2.40	4.24	2.33	7.38
6.	Inward Freight	5.11	3.14	-0.34	-0.75	1.05	13.43	8.81	-0.48	-3.49	-19.72	-19.99	5.34
7.	Personnel Cost	5.53	6.56	12.45	15.59	17.62	19.25	27.41	28.04	34.57	34.72	32.56	48.24
8.	Rent	2.46	5.30	4.29	6.56	5.23	6.79	6.54	6.11	7.98	8.24	6.83	8.57
9.	General Administration Charges	2.83	3.25	4.51	4.51	5.40	9.33	4.77	6.02	8.38	10.17	10.91	19.70
10.	Sales Tax	1.54	0.18	0.21	2.60	2.80	Nil	Nil	0.77	0.50	Nil	11.14	Nil
11.	Distribution Expenses	5.80	4.78	7.38	8.15	9.02	14.28	9.82	10.41	12.54	24.47	22.28	22.59
12.	*OPBD (1-[4+5+6+7+8+9+10+11])*	*2.61*	*-3.49*	*4.84*	*10.95*	*12.44*	*-44.41*	*-43.88*	*-11.49*	*-5.72*	*21.77*	*3.29*	*16.51*
13.	Depreciation	0.75	0.66	1.62	1.76	1.55	0.47	0.42	0.98	3.00	5.23	7.77	9.73
14.	Operating Profit (OP) (12-13)	1.86	-4.14	3.22	9.18	10.89	-44.88	-44.30	-12.47	-8.72	16.54	-4.48	6.77
15.	Other Income	4.66	6.23	0.21	2.08	2.60	41.49	14.25	16.85	19.90	0.61	23.29	9.30
16.	Loss on damage of Stock	1.29	0.56	Nil	Nil	Nil	Nil	Nil	Nil	Nil	0.79	Nil	Nil
17.	Profit(+)/Loss(-) on Sale of F. A.	Nil	Nil	0.11	0.30	Nil	2.98	0.03	Nil	Nil	Nil	Nil	1.79
18.	*PBIT (14 +15+17)*	*5.23*	*1.52*	*3.55*	*11.56*	*13.49*	*-0.40*	*-30.02*	*4.37*	*11.18*	*16.36*	*18.81*	*17.86*
19.	Interest	2.24	4.94	5.40	5.11	7.54	12.83	12.68	12.34	12.85	14.26	16.66	21.51
20.	Profit Before Tax (PBT) (18-19)	2.99	-3.43	-1.85	6.45	5.95	-13.23	-42.70	-7.97	-1.67	2.10	2.14	-3.65
21.	Income Tax	Nil	Nil	Nil	Nil	Nil	Nil	Nil	Nil	Nil	Nil	Nil	Nil
22.	*Profit After Tax (PAT) (20-21)*	*2.99*	*-3.43*	*-1.85*	*6.45*	*5.95*	*-13.23*	*-42.70*	*-7.97*	*-1.67*	*2.10*	*2.14*	*-3.65*
23.	Accumulated Profits of P.Y.	-32.36	-25.17	-28.60	-30.45	-21.79	-16.80	-30.02	-72.73	-80.69	-82.36	-80.27	-78.13
24.	Prior Period Receipts / Expenses	4.20	Nil	Nil	2.21	-0.95	Nil	Nil	Nil	Nil	Nil	Nil	Nil
25.	*Accumulated Profits (22+23+24)*	*-25.17*	*-28.60*	*-30.45*	*-21.79*	*-16.80*	*-30.02*	*-72.73*	*-80.69*	*-82.36*	*-80.27*	*-78.13*	*-81.78*

(*Contd.*)

Sl. No.	Income Statement	for the year ended on 31st March											
	Year	1994	1995	1996	1997	1998	1999	2000	2001	2002	2003	2004	Growth
1.	Turnover	1697.59	1830.53	2174.99	2755.51	2797.27	2781.45	3370.80	4007.68	3635.31	3283.63	4143.86	13.92
2.	Goods Purchased	1558.43	1715.48	2134.71	2597.41	2659.45	2635.73	3157.18	3783.72	3355.07	3105.00	3955.97	
3.	Decrease(+)/Increase(-) in Stocks	-5.28	-18.94	1.54	43.41	-5.19	13.18	-10.43	-43.67	18.19	41.19	-30.00	
4.	Cost of Goods Sold (2+3)	1553.14	1696.55	2136.25	2640.82	2654.26	2648.90	3146.75	3740.05	3373.27	3146.19	3925.97	14.14
5.	Porterage, Wages & Trade Exp.	2.25	3.16	4.06	3.20	3.07	3.08	3.10	4.30	1.88	1.29	1.04	
6.	Inward Freight	-11.42	-20.44	-9.74	-15.66	28.31	-5.44	3.76	9.32	-5.00	56.82	8.86	
7.	Personnel Cost	53.69	61.63	74.87	80.40	76.59	90.21	128.19	166.06	164.24	138.62	119.93	15.17
8.	Rent	11.80	14.31	14.40	16.42	23.30	18.14	15.90	18.33	19.09	20.39	18.27	8.72
9.	General Administration Charges	23.95	24.17	21.00	29.38	22.14	24.03	24.98	58.41	31.94	22.37	30.74	12.52
10.	Sales Tax	1.51	Nil	9.57	9.14	22.53	20.26	26.56	54.83	50.43	13.14	32.71	
11.	Distribution Expenses	28.39	26.24	25.95	31.20	34.07	29.82	39.63	23.69	16.68	24.75	17.23	7.40
12.	*OPBD(1-[4+5+6+7+8+9+10+11])*	*34.27*	*24.91*	*-101.36*	*-39.38*	*-67.01*	*-47.56*	*-18.07*	*-67.31*	*-17.21*	*-139.96*	*-10.88*	*-6.23*
13.	Depreciation	11.57	10.42	8.19	10.31	6.15	8.28	2.57	5.55	4.45	3.81	5.54	11.07
14.	*Operating Profit (OP) (12-13)*	*22.70*	*14.48*	*-109.56*	*-49.69*	*-73.16*	*-55.83*	*-20.64*	*-72.86*	*-21.67*	*-143.77*	*-16.42*	*-6.49*
15.	Other Income	0.69	8.29	26.06	16.77	149.00	65.10	33.43	76.98	38.46	44.92	48.13	16.65
16.	Loss on damage of Stock	Nil	Nil	Nil	Nil	Nil	Nil	Nil	Nil	Nil	Nil	Nil	
17.	Profit(+)/Loss(-) on Sale of F. A.	0.55	0.08	Nil	Nil	Nil	Nil	Nil	Nil	Nil	7.46	Nil	
18.	*PBIT (14+15+17)*	*23.94*	*22.85*	*-83.49*	*-32.93*	*75.84*	*9.27*	*12.79*	*4.12*	*16.79*	*-91.40*	*31.71*	*-4.42*
19.	Interest	15.73	32.96	26.55	5.26	34.82	13.67	17.20	19.10	25.31	23.62	34.18	8.40
20.	Profit Before Tax (PBT) (18-19)	8.21	-10.11	-110.04	-38.19	41.03	-4.40	-4.42	-14.97	-8.52	-115.01	-2.48	-5.43
21.	Income Tax	Nil	2.00	4.00	Nil	Nil	Nil	Nil	Nil	Nil	Nil	Nil	
22.	*Profit After Tax (PAT) (20-21)*	*8.21*	*-12.11*	*-114.04*	*-38.19*	*41.03*	*-4.40*	*-4.42*	*-14.97*	*-8.52*	*-115.01*	*-2.48*	*-5.74*
23.	Accumulated Profits of P.Y.	-81.78	-73.57	-85.68	-199.72	-237.91	-331.17	-335.57	-339.98	-354.96	-363.47	-478.49	
24.	Prior Period Receipts/Expenses	Nil	Nil	Nil	Nil	-134.29	Nil	Nil	Nil	Nil	Nil	Nil	
25.	*Accumulated Profits(22+23+24)*	*-73.57*	*-85.68*	*-199.72*	*-237.91*	*-331.17*	*-335.57*	*-339.98*	*-354.96*	*-363.47*	*-478.49*	*-480.96*	*-14.75*

(Contd.)

Sl. No.	Important Ratios / Year	1982	1983	1984	1985	1986	1987	1988	1989	1990	1991	1992	1993
1.	Return on Investment (ROI)	N.A.	-2.38	1.66	4.13	4.80	-20.76	-32.24	-17.85	-8.17	10.95	-2.07	2.72
2.	Cost of Goods Sold to Turnover	90.05	92.33	88.42	88.71	88.60	96.63	97.79	95.81	94.35	94.09	94.09	92.54
3.	Personnel Cost to Turnover	2.04	2.46	4.22	3.53	3.47	3.13	3.84	2.93	3.42	2.45	2.77	2.80
4.	Gen. Admn. Charges to Turnover	1.04	1.22	1.53	1.02	1.06	1.51	0.67	0.63	0.83	0.72	0.93	1.14
5.	Distribution Cost to Turnover	2.14	1.79	2.50	1.85	1.78	2.32	1.38	1.09	1.24	1.72	1.90	1.31
6.	Operating Profit to Turnover	0.68	-1.55	1.09	2.08	2.15	-7.29	-6.21	-1.30	-0.86	1.17	-0.38	0.39
7.	Net Profit to Turnover	1.10	-1.28	-0.63	1.46	1.17	-2.15	-5.99	-0.83	-0.17	0.15	0.18	-0.21
8.	Capital Turnover Ratio	N.A.	1.53	1.52	1.98	2.24	2.85	5.19	13.70	9.48	9.39	5.42	6.92
9.	Fixed Assets Turnover Ratio	30.33	29.91	30.42	49.43	58.88	76.39	41.16	36.40	21.70	23.67	21.94	28.94
10.	Working Capital Turnover Ratio	1.75	1.53	1.52	1.90	2.51	2.92	19.92	16.65	12.63	12.63	5.77	9.80
11.	Debtors Turnover Ratio	N.A.	2.38	2.63	3.48	3.62	4.36	7.93	25.41	22.44	34.38	29.23	26.07
12.	Inventory Turnover Ratio	N.A.	9.84	9.83	10.93	9.14	8.28	10.70	15.30	14.38	21.91	13.16	13.85
13.	Current Ratio	12.99	11.46	9.50	5.82	4.02	3.26	1.49	1.77	2.06	2.45	3.36	2.80
14.	Acid Test Ratio	10.78	10.47	8.92	4.99	8.91	5.13	2.25	3.22	7.22	15.43	19.98	17.19
15.	Super Quick Ratio	0.36	0.50	0.65	0.21	0.47	0.22	0.97	0.41	0.55	1.90	2.02	3.22
16.	Inventory Holding Period (days)	N.A.	37.07	37.13	33.38	39.94	44.11	34.10	23.85	25.38	16.66	27.73	26.35
17.	Average Collection Period (days)	N.A.	153.56	138.53	104.92	100.77	83.77	46.03	14.36	16.26	10.62	12.49	14.00
18.	Interest Coverage Ratio	2.33	0.31	0.66	2.26	1.79	-0.03	-2.37	0.35	0.87	1.15	1.13	0.83
19.	Debt Equity Ratio	0.89	0.91	0.93	0.90	0.87	0.81	3.59	2.36	1.90	1.55	1.24	1.20
20.	Fixed Assets to Net Tangible Worth	50.57	53.42	65.23	37.98	31.02	19.41	-12.25	-22.61	-40.22	-62.63	-87.74	-123.59

Legend: OPBD = Operating Profit before Depreciation, OP = Operating Profit, PBIT = Profit before Interest and Tax, PBT = Profit before Tax, PAT = Profit after Tax.

Source: Compiled from Annual Accounts of Mizoram State Cooperative Marketing and Consumers' Federation Ltd. from 1981-82 to 2003-04.

(*Contd.*)

Sl. No.	Important Ratios / *Year*	*1994*	*1995*	*1996*	*1997*	*1998*	*1999*	*2000*	*2001*	*2002*	*2003*	*2004*	*Average*
1.	Return on Investment (ROI)	8.93	5.02	-42.36	-25.36	-32.46	-20.09	-7.10	-24.76	-6.74	-48.94	-7.31	-11.83
2.	Cost of Goods Sold to Turnover	91.49	92.68	98.22	95.84	94.89	95.23	93.35	93.32	92.79	95.81	94.74	93.56
3.	Personnel Cost to Turnover	3.16	3.37	3.44	2.92	2.74	3.24	3.80	4.14	4.52	4.22	2.89	3.28
4.	Gen. Admn. Charges to Turnover	1.41	1.32	0.97	1.07	0.79	0.86	0.74	1.46	0.88	0.68	0.74	1.01
5.	Distribution Cost to Turnover	1.67	1.43	1.19	1.13	1.22	1.07	1.18	0.59	0.46	0.75	0.42	1.40
6.	Operating Profit to Turnover	1.34	0.79	-5.04	-1.80	-2.62	-2.01	-0.61	-1.82	-0.60	-4.38	-0.40	-1.18
7.	Net Profit to Turnover	0.48	-0.55	-5.06	-1.39	1.47	-0.16	-0.13	-0.37	-0.23	-3.50	-0.06	-0.73
8.	Capital Turnover Ratio	6.68	6.35	8.41	14.07	12.41	10.01	11.60	13.62	11.30	11.18	18.44	8.38
9.	Fixed Assets Turnover Ratio	31.34	27.85	28.08	42.08	38.69	40.64	48.56	50.19	54.62	47.93	65.35	40.20
10.	Working Capital Turnover Ratio	7.98	7.70	16.73	24.48	14.29	13.19	15.55	19.09	13.05	19.84	29.21	11.77
11.	Debtors Turnover Ratio	23.77	36.17	56.66	101.72	91.38	62.01	55.33	55.29	50.68	76.31	168.48	42.71
12.	Inventory Turnover Ratio	12.69	12.55	14.07	20.86	24.76	25.52	31.32	29.76	24.66	27.89	36.96	18.11
13.	Current Ratio	2.38	2.21	1.53	1.42	2.16	1.90	1.77	1.43	1.58	1.33	1.25	3.48
14.	Acid Test Ratio	21.64	13.40	6.65	6.52	20.03	8.52	8.30	5.84	8.46	7.98	6.79	9.94
15.	Super Quick Ratio	5.62	2.82	1.26	1.13	4.52	1.97	1.31	0.68	1.86	0.56	0.36	1.46
16.	Inventory Holding Period (days)	28.76	29.09	25.94	17.50	14.74	14.30	11.65	12.27	14.80	13.09	9.88	24.44
17.	Average Collection Period	15.35	10.09	6.44	3.59	3.99	5.89	6.60	6.60	7.20	4.78	2.17	34.91
18.	Interest Coverage Ratio	1.52	0.69	-3.14	-6.26	2.18	0.68	0.74	0.22	0.66	-3.87	0.93	0.16
19.	Debt Equity Ratio	1.06	0.97	1.46	1.73	1.35	1.32	1.32	1.37	1.33	2.00	0.76	1.38
20.	Fixed Assets to Net Tangible Worth	-340.08	659.31	-79.60	-49.61	-77.10	-73.84	-73.92	-73.67	-56.95	-28.71	125.65	-6.95

worry. The only alternative for the federation in reaching at the break-even point is to keep its overheads under control.

8. The ratios reflecting short-term solvency position, i.e., the average current ratio at 2.38:1, the acid test ratio at 21.64:1 and the super quick ratio at 5.62:1 indicated good health of Federation. Though, these ratios have declined over the period, but, are still above the generally accepted norms.
9. The long-term solvency as indicated by the debt-equity ratio at 1.38:1 was near the general norm of 2:1, except for the period 1987-89. The interest coverage ratio at 0.16 times was low and over the years, has deteriorated. It needs to be improved.
10. A typical feature noticed in the functioning of MIZOFED was showing loss in annual accounts every time just for claiming more subsidies from the State Government. Whenever the Federation's annual accounts showed profit in a year, certain expenses jumped in the following years.
11. Some of the points raised in the auditors' report on the accounts of MIZOFED during the period of study have been summarized below:
    (a) *Management Related Points*: (i) No periodic physical verification of cash balance, and stock was done by the management. Among cash and bank balances, cash in hand accumulated all the time and remained idle. Theft cases were very common. (ii) No cost records were maintained. (iii) Quantitative and qualitative details of stocks were lagging. Loose inventory management existed as regards to receipts and issues. No minimum and maximum stock levels were fixed. No adequate system of identifying and disposal of non-moving, obsolete and damaged goods were found. Stock records wherever maintained were maintained on the basis of sales value. Valuation of stock was not in tune with the well-accepted norms. It was done at 8 per cent less than the market value. (iv) Purchasing irregularities were found. No uniform policy was followed as regards to purchase of different items. Purchase board was formed but remained inactive. (v) Private carriers made 6 to 7 rounds in a month but own fleet made 4 rounds only. (vi) Some retail outlets were found economically non-viable and were even unable to meet corresponding rent but continued. Branch management was often in the hands of new untrained

recruitees. (vii) The Federation obtained some private loans of huge amount without any approval from the Board of Directors. Faulty repayment of term loans. (viii) Accounting work was assigned to unqualified persons. (ix) Internal control system was poor. (x) Internal audit system was absent.

(b) *Accounting related points*: (i) Fixed assets register was not maintained properly. Periodic physical verification of fixed assets was not done. (ii) Adequate books of accounts were not maintained. Cashbook was not recorded from day-to-day. It was maintained improperly even at head office level. (iii) Unrecorded and unauthorized bank withdrawals were common. (iv) POL/LPG outlets often lent unrecorded and unsanctioned cash against small chits. (v) Cash shortage was regarded as expenses and no efforts were made to recover the same from the employee concerned. (vi) Shortage of stock was not adjusted. Embezzlement of stock was reported by retail outlets. (vii) Some issues from POL depot were completely missing from the stock register of retail outlets. Shortfall of POL products was treated as evaporation or short supply. However, no standards were fixed for evaporation. This may cause leakage of revenue owing to unbilled sales at POL outlets. (viii) Income from commercial vehicle was even less than 20 per cent of their maintenance cost. Consumption of petrol, oil, and lubricants on non-commercial vehicles was in excess of prescribed limit of 4.74 per cent per vehicle per month. Reimbursement of some vehicle maintenance expenses were claimed twice in two different heads. Profit/loss on sale of vehicle, if any, could not be determined as records relating to vehicles were not maintained properly. This showed the absence of proper control on petrol, oil and lubricants expenses, vehicle maintenance, telephone, rent, stationery, salary, etc. (ix) Classifying entire sundry debtors, loans and advances as secured and good was wrong and did not represent true picture. (x) Customers' records were incomplete as regards to their address, etc. (xi) No proper collection policy existed as regards to receivables caused poor recovery from debtors that resulted in large accumulation of receivables and were doubtful of recovery. Provision for bad and doubtful debts was not made. In some cases, loan recovery was not recorded in books of accounts. (xii) Advances for expenses remained pending for adjustment for a long time and was doubtful of recovery. (xiii) Grant-in-Aid received to the extent of expenses is recognized as revenue/other income. (xiv) Periodic reconciliation between inter-office accounts and bank accounts was not done. Preparation of trial balance was not in practice.

Business Centres in Mizoram

With growth of business certain large towns of Mizoram have grown into business centres. Aizawl, Lunglei, Lawngtlai, Champhai, Sairang, Mamit, Serchhip, Demagiri, and Kolasib are the important market places of the State. However, only retail trading is carried on at these centres. In most of the villages, there are small grocery shops, tea stalls, and vegetable and fruit vendors apart from village craftsmen.

Aizawl: Aizawl is the capital city of the State since the formation of Mizoram as a Union territory. However, it did not exist in 1871-72 and came up after some other places like Kolasib, Demagiri, and Lunglei. The disorderly conduct of Khalkom, a Mizo Chief, had compelled the British government to establish an outpost at Aizawl, in 1889-90. Till, it became headquarters of Mizo Hills District in 1898, it was a small town with a population not exceeding 10,000 persons. In 1892-95, Aizawl was made accessible from Silchar by fair weather road under the supervision of Major Loch and after the Second World War, an all weather road was constructed. With this the trade connection between Silchar-Kolasib-Aizawl became closer. However, until 1966, Aizawl continued to be a large village. The regrouping of villages suddenly urbanized Mizo and Aizawl become a big town and soon a city. This rapid urbanization within a short time created many new problems. It disturbed the socio-economic balance. Normally, urbanization follows industrial economy, but, it is strange to note that industrialization is almost absent in Mizoram while the urbanization is at its full pace[65]. Aizawl has become the centre of road network, connecting northern, southern and eastern hills of Mizoram. It has one mini industrial estate and one industrial growth centre.

After the abolition of Changsil Bazaar, about 37 miles off Aizawl[66], the commercial importance of Aizawl began to grow and it developed into a busy trade centre. It may be said that the Changsil Bazaar and its adjoining territories of British time are now Aizawl.[67] Its dependence on

Silchar and Guwahati remains due to economic reasons, but, Aizawl has grown into a big market where goods from Myanmar, Bangladesh, Thailand, China, and Hong Kong are sold in large quantity. Large stock of food and other materials reach Aizawl market daily from Silchar, and Guwahati. Aizawl also caters to the need of smaller towns like Lunglei, Champhai, and other district headquarters. The growth of Aizawl market has been phenomenal in recent times. It is a peculiarity of Aizawl market that amongst the trade centres in the North East, Aizawl is the only market that is controlled by local people. It is not so in Shillong, Guwahati, Dibrugarh, Imphal, and Silchar. Presently, it is perhaps the largest hill town in the North-East, with the exception of Shillong. More than 25 per cent of the State's population lives in Aizawl (2,29,714 out of total 8,91,058 people as per 2001 Census).

Champhai: Champhai being situated near international border with Myanmar at an altitude of 1678 metres has strategic importance. It was headquarter of Lalburha Sailo, a Chief against whom the British expedition of 1871-72 was directed. It was accorded the status of fort during British period. It is well connected with Aizawl by a black topped road. Near the town, at lower altitude, the famous 'Champhai Valley' exists, which is known for the best quality of rice production and large quantity of State's rice consumption is met from this area. It is a beautiful place with pine trees having scope for tourism development. There exist famous monuments of Mangkhaia and Vanhnuailiana. Presently, it is a district headquarters of the State. This has been the entry point for foreign goods from Myanmar. Government of Mizoram is now trying to develop it as a border trade centre. Large part of border trade is carried through this part of the State. State Bank of India, Champhai branch is designated by the Reserve Bank of India to undertake foreign currency transactions arising out of continual border trade. A mini industrial estate is being developed here.

Demagiri (Tlabung): Demagiri located on Karnaphuli River is situated on western border 55 miles away from Lunglei district headquarters. It had become a flourishing trade centre during 1860-70 when the Mizo in north and south had little knowledge of modern commerce. It has strategic importance for import of goods from Bangladesh through Chittagong. It has an old fort constructed during British time. It was established on Chittagong frontier on the advice of T.H. Lewin, in pursuance of policy of conciliation. Now, this centre serves the people of Chimtuipui district.

Durtlang: Durtlang is an old village at a distance of 8 kilometres from Aizawl on its northern side. It is the gateway and a suburb of Aizawl city. Majority of the people are Mizo, but there are some indigenous Nepalis and some immigrant Bengali shopkeepers also. Durtlang enjoys many urban facilities. Because of good communication, it is a fast growing business centre. Durtlang is a major supplier of milk for Aizawl. Nepalis have expertise in milk production. Enterprising villagers have set up small shops and womenfolk resorted to weaving and sewing to supplement family income. Mizo women are very hardy and helpful in running business. They go up to Manipur, Tripura and even Myanmar to purchase goods they sell. Foreign goods are available in plenty. The cottage industry has flourished at Durtlang. The Synod Hospital (run by Christian Missionary) is famous for good medical facilities.[68]

Kolasib: Kolasib is a district headquarters on Silchar-Aizawl road, inhabited by Lushai and Nepali. Some Bengalis have also settled there. It is famous for ginger and vegetables. There exists a mini industrial estate.

Lawngtlai: Lawngtlai is presently a district headquarter of Mizoram and also a seat of Pawi District Council. It has become a commercial centre mainly because of its ideal location. It is situated in south at a distance of 88 km from Lunglei.

Lunglei: Lunglei is much older town than Aizawl. Presently, it is a district headquarters and second largest town in the State, located at the terminus of Silchar-Lunglei road. From the military and commercial points of view Lunglei's importance did not dwindle till the partition of India. Lunglei in fact was more advanced than Aizawl educationally and politically. The proximity of Chittagong, a big city, made Lunglei the commercial and educational centre. It has a fort constructed during British regime. It is well connected with Demagiri, Kassalong, Rangamati and Chittagong. It has one mini industrial estate.

Mamit: Mamit, a district headquarters of Mizoram emerged out of re-grouping of villages, is a commercial trade centre. It is known as 'orange garden' of Mizoram. Bulk of merchandise is brought to this place from Cachar district of Assam through Tut River, which flows at the foothills of this place. Mamit has good prospect of development, as it is provided with modern Airport and one small scale industry engaged in ply manufacturing at an investment of Rs. 160 lakh under direct financing from IDBI. Further, export promotion industrial park of Mizoram is coming up in Mamit district at Pukpuii near Lengpui airport.

Sairang: Sairang is at 28 km from Aizawl, situated on the bank of Tlawng River (the only navigable river of north -western Mizoram). From early days it has been an important trade centre of Mizoram. During early days owing to navigability, goods were carried from Silchar to Sairang through boats and then transported to Aizawl by road. This place is known as 'sand basin' for Aizawl as it provides large quantity of sand everyday to meet the demand for construction works in Aizawl. Cement hollow bricks are also manufactured here. Large quantities of vegetables are also supplied from this place to Aizawl. MIFCO has set up two production units, viz. Ginger Oil and Oleoresin Plant and Food Processing Plant. A mini industrial estate is being developed there.

Serchhip: Serchhip emerged out of re-grouping of villages is a district headquarters of Mizoram. It regularly supplies large quantities of rice and vegetables to Aizawl, which are grown in nearby Mat river valley.

Tamdil: Tamdil is at 64 km distance from Aizawl on eastern side between Saitual and Tualbung. In Mizo dialect "Tam" stands for 'Antam' which means a 'Mustard plant' and "Dil" means 'lake'. 'Tamdil' the lake of mustard plants signifies that mustard is grown on large scale in the area. This lake is also known as 'city of prawns', since there were many prawns in it. Presently, it is being developed as fish farming belt, as a part of promotion programme for pisci-culture development.

Business Centres around Mizoram

Mizoram has its trade with a number of centers located around the State. A brief description of these business centres is given here:

Guwahati: Guwahati is known as the gateway of Northeast and is most important city. Over the years it has grown into a big trade and industrial center. The Mizo riot dated 7th June 1979 at Silchar and also disturbance of 1994 interrupted trade relations between Silchar and Aizawl, Mizo began laying greater emphasis upon direct trade with Guwahati. Nevertheless, the cost of transportation has been a major obstacle.

Silchar: Silchar headquarter of Cachar district of Assam, is the largest commercial center in southern Assam. When Sylhet became part of Pakistan, Silchar became the headquarters of Cachar-Mizo division of Assam. This arrangement continued till the creation of Union Territory of Mizoram in 1972. Supply of eighty per cent of the consumer goods to Mizoram comes from Silchar. Every big business house in Mizoram maintains a commercial establishment at Silchar. Formerly, Silchar was the principal market for Mizo. Even now many shops in Silchar call themselves, "Mizo Dawr". A large number of buses and sumos carry goods and passengers to Mizoram from Silchar every day. The shortage of labour in Mizoram is also met from Silchar.

Special Features of Business in Mizoram

Arising from what has been discussed above and on the basis of the survey conducted on business enterprises the following are important features of business in Mizoram:

1. *Organization of Business*: The organization of business in Mizoram is still primitive. All business firms are single proprietorship concerns. Women have an important role in business and about 20 per cent of the enterprises are owned and managed by the females. Only 22 per cent of the enterprises have been in existence for 20 years or more and about 3/4th of the enterprises are owned and managed by first generation entrepreneurs.

   Most people engaged in business in Mizoram have some back ground of education. Happily about 2/3rd of the entrepreneurs in business are graduates. On the average 5.4 persons are engaged in a firm, 1.4 persons from entrepreneur's family and 4 are paid employees. Accounting records are maintained by the owner of the enterprise.

   Retail trade was the order of the day. The overwhelming majority of traders were retailers and only a handful of dealers functioned as wholesale distributors. The chain stores and multiplex department stores are yet to come up. In rural areas, hawkers carrying their wares on the back are still playing a dominant role in the trading activity. The Village Councils have set up small market centres under a single roof where the vendors of fruits and vegetables and small retailers sell their produce. The State Government has also set up some such centres.

   There existed one loose association of businessmen called Mizoram Chamber of Commerce with headquarters in Aizawl. This association aimed at safeguarding the common interests of business community and to aid and advice the government in matters of trade and commerce.

2. *Increase of Business Class*: In the five-year plans of Assam State separate allocation of funds was made for the Mizo Hills District. The Amount Allocated was: First Plan Rs. 0.63 crore, Second Plan Rs. 2.11 crore, Third Plan Rs. 4.11 crore and Fourth Plan Rs. 14.12 crore. In the Fifth, Sixth, Seventh, Eighth and Ninth Plans Rs. 47.57 crore, Rs. 159.09 crore, Rs. 363.56 crore, Rs. 1064.45 crore and Rs. 1719.96 crore respectively were allocated. There were additional outlays, and separate allocations through central schemes, centrally approved/ sponsored schemes, NEC plans, and border road programmes. This abrupt circulation of large sum of money in Mizoram created a moneyed class. The contractors, the permit holders, the order suppliers and the transport carriers amassed large fortune. Further, as the Mizo were immune from central taxes, no question of black money could be raised.[69] However, they are subject to Wealth-Tax but no body is paying wealth-tax in Mizoram in spite of accumulating wealth in crores. As Mizo are exempted from central taxes, they enjoy certain economic privileges over plains people; this provision enabled them becoming wealthier quickly than their counterparts. The number of rich Mizo is larger as compared to rich Khasis or Manipuries[70]. Construction and real-estate business grew at 14.4 per cent and 17.81 per cent of NSDP and it was entirely in the hands of Mizo. Unlike other Northeastern tribes, the Mizo proved good businesspersons. They invested their capital profitably in trading, though not in industry, not only in Mizoram but also in Assam, Tripura, Manipur, Meghalaya, and Tamilnadu. M/s. Pachhunga and Sons and Lalminthanga and Company had few equals in the whole Northeast including Assam.
3. *Procurement and Transportation*: Silchar is the main centre for procuring most of the items for traders in Mizoram. Guwahati and Kolakata are the other important markets. Some items are also procured from Delhi, Mumbai, Shillong, Shivkasi, Faridabad, Dehradoon. Foreign items are procured from Kolkata, Siligury, Moreh and Champhai (Rih-Dil). As per the information gathered through survey, only 11 per cent of businessmen deal in imported/foreign goods. About, one-third businessmen procure goods on credit owing to their long standing association with up-market suppliers. However, th term of credit ranges from

45 days to 4 months. Others buy goods for cash or by sending bank draft in advance.

Most goods are procured through land route. Silchar-Aizawl highway is the main trading route. Food grains reach up to Bhairabi by train and then lifted by trucks from rail head. Costly items are brought by air link from Kolkata and Guwahati. The freight paid is very high as most of the vehicles return empty. To make it reasonable some buyers and sellers share the freight roughly fifty-fifty. Some manufacturing companies make reimbursement of freight charges to dealers such as Indian Oil Corporation Ltd. In view of the distance and cost involved, some items are procured once in a year for whole year's requirement.

4. *Marketing*: Except for the big business firms in Aizawl all other business persons in Mizoram cater to the local demand. Mostly the goods are sold for cash. Nearly 25 per cent enterprises including wholesalers sell goods on credit. About 5 per cent traders offer free home delivery facility in case of bulk purchase. Around Christmas, about 11 per cent shopkeepers offer discount on the items purchased. Generally after sales service and replacement facility is not given. However, 15 per cent traders claimed that they provide after sales service and 22 per cent claimed that they extend replacement facility.
5. *High Profit Margin*: High to very high profit margin is charged by entrepreneurs in Mizoram, as normally out of ignorance or simplicity. Mizo do not ask for price of the items before they buy. Even they do not see the maximum retail price (MRP) and also do not bargain. This provides an opportunity to traders to maintain high profit margin on items of daily use and even on MRP products like tooth paste, 2T oil pouch, auto parts, hardware, etc. Looking to this, non-tribal traders are attracted to Mizoram. Perhaps, this may be the reason for the spread of cooperative movement in trade in Mizoram, particularly for the distribution of items under Public Distribution System. Commercial banking services are available in all the towns of Mizoram now and about 78 per cent firms claimed that they were using this facility.
6. *Benami Trade*: It was observed that many non-tribals are engaged in trade in Mizoram in the name of a local Mizo, as presently no trading rules exist. They made investment, bear full risk and manages the affairs of their venture but show themselves as an employee of the local person in whose name they do business.

The person giving his/her name provides place for trading, security cover against likely extortion and threat, and permission under inner line regulations for big periodic payment. This amount may vary with location of shop, individual, and time of agreement. The non-tribal agrees to pay periodically a big amount because of inner line regulations, non-applicability of Indian Partnership Act and no rules for trading activity in Mizoram. The income from such business though actually belongs to non-tribal goes totally untaxed as Mizo are not subject to central taxes. Non-tribals are attracted for trading in Mizoram due to high profit margin prevailing and saving of income tax owing to this technicality. Some non-tribals engaged in supply business with long standing, reported that in government offices, they just pay 3 per cent of gross bill amount of government supply to local persons in whose name they operate and save the whole of profit margin tax free.

7. *New Business—Computer Institutes and Cyber Cafe*: In the recent past, a new business growing especially in urban and semi-urban areas in private sector is computer training/teaching and cyber café. The computer Institutes offer 2 to 6 months diploma or 15 days certificate courses. A number of such institutes have come up all over the State. This business may be run successfully with an investment between Rs. 3 lakh to Rs. 5 lakh and with one or two resource persons having exposure in computer and family members of the owner. Fee structure include tuition fee Rs. 500/- to Rs. 650/- per month besides registration fee of Rs. 50/- and admission fee Rs. 100/- for one hour class. The medium of instruction is Mizo. On the average, they take 15 to 20 students in each batch and run the institute from 6.00 A.M. to 6.00 P.M. The response from local people is good as the State Government is going ahead with e-governance. However, the problem of power cut disturbs the schedule of practical classes most of the time.

8. *Cyber Café*: Cyber café is a small business with an investment ranging from Rs. 2 lakh to Rs. 4 lakh offering a monthly return between Rs. 7,000/- to Rs. 13,000/-. Cyber cafés started functioning in Aizawl in October 1999 and crossed the number 40 in 2000-01 and then the number declined to 30 in 2002. Presently, there are 20 such cafés working in Aizawl. Hourly rate for using cyber café is Rs. 30, while earlier it was higher.

The irregular power supply (frequent power cuts), low speed of internet connection, spare parts for computer, damage of computer parts owing to ignorance of user, less number of users, demand of credit by users, easy accessible location of cyber café, and inefficient management are some of the problems faced.

9. *Trades Yet to Grow in Mizoram*: Certain business are yet to grow in Mizoram such as tent houses, catering service, farm machinery, fertilizers, pesticides and insecticides, dealers of heavy and medium vehicles, Zero-B water supply in 20 litre pack, credit card, private banks like ICICI Bank, UTI Bank, IDBI Bank, HDFC Bank, valuation services, tax practicing, Finance companies, etc. Of course, sweet shops are now coming up and courier business is flourishing.

NOTES

1. IBM World Book, *Encyclopedia*, 1997.
2. Horn By, A. S., *Oxford Advanced Learner's Dictionary of Current English*, 9th Edn. p. 114.
3. *Ibid.*
4. IBM World Book, *op. cit.*
5. Lalrinmawia, *Mizoram: History & Cultural Identity*, Spectrum Publications, Guwahati, 1995, p. 8.
6. Chatterjee, Dr. Suhash, *Mizoram: Encyclopedia*, Vol. I, Jaico Publishing House, Mumbai, 1990, p. 129.
7. *Ibid.*, pp. 436-37.
8. Machenzie, A., *The North East Frontier of India*, Mittal Publications, New Delhi, 1999, p. 363.
9. Lalrimawia, *op. cit.*, p. 3.
10. *Ibid*, p. 4.
11. *Ibid*, p. 4.
12. Carey, Bertram S. and Tuck, H.N., *The Chin Hills*, Firma Klm P. Ltd., Kolkata for Tribal Research Institute, 1976, p. 215.
13. *Ibid*, p. 215.
14. *Ibid.*
15. Chatterjee, Dr. Suhas, *A History of Mizo Economy*, Vol. I, Printwell Publishers Distributors, Jaipur, 1999, p. 164.
16. Carey, Bertram S. and Tuck, H. N., *op. cit.*, p. 215.
17. *Ibid*, p. 214.
18. Chatterjee, Dr. Suhash, *Mizoram: Encyclopedia*, Vol. I, *op. cit.*, p. 21.
19. Hunter, W.W., *Statistical Account of Assam*, Vol. II, 1879, p. 392.
20. Chatterjee, Dr. Suhas, *Mizoram: Encyclopedia*, Vol. II, Jaico Publishing House, Mumbai, 1990, p. 253.

21. *Ibid*, p. 130.
22. Chatterjee, Dr. Suhas, *Mizoram: Encyclopedia*, Vol. I, *op. cit.*, p. 253.
23. Report on Frontier Tribes of Assam in 1873-74.
24. Chatterjee, Dr. Suhash, *Mizoram: Encyclopedia*, Vol. II, *op. cit.*, 1990, p. 375.
25. Roy, Animesh, *Mizoram: Dynamics of Change*, p. 187.
26. Chatterjee, Dr. Suhas, *Mizoram: Encyclopaedia*, Vol. I, *op. cit.*, p. 28.
27. Allen, B.C., *op. cit.*, p. 38.
28. A.S., Home B., 1903, August, Nos. 351-79; *Administration Report* for the year 1902-03. Quoted in Lalrinmawia's *Mizoram: History & Cultural Identity*, Spectrum Publications, Guwahati, 1995, p. 4.
29. Lalrimawia, *op. cit.*, p. 4.
30. Chatterjee, Dr. Suhash, *Mizoram: Encyclopedia*, Vol. II, *op. cit.*, pp. 233-36.
31. Roy, Animesh, *Mizoram: Dynamics of Change*, p. 187.
32. Chatterjee, Dr. Suhash, *Mizoram: Encyclopedia*, Vol. I, *op. cit.*, 1990, p. 18.
33. Chatterjee, Dr. Suhash, *Mizoram: Encyclopedia*, Vol. II, *op. cit.*, pp. 355-58.
34. Zahid Hussain, The Nature of Border and Border Trade of Northeast India, in Das, Gurudas and Purkayastha, R.K. edited "*Border Trade—North East India and Neighbouring Countries*", Akansha Publishing House, New Delhi, 2000, p. 141.
35. Srinath Baruah, Certain Observation on Informal Border Trade with Neighbouring Countries and Economic Prospects of Northeastern Region, *Ibid*, p. 59.
36. Editorial, Indo-Myanmar Border Trade, *Northeast Trade Line*, Vol. I, No. III, February 2003, p. 5.
37. Directorate of Trade and Commerce, *Current Status Note on Border-Trade with Bangladesh and Myanmar*, Government of Mizoram, Aizawl, December 2001, p. 3.
38. Carey, Bertam S. and Tuck, H.N., *op. cit.*, p. 215.
39. Chatterjee, Dr. Suhash, *A History of Mizo Economy*, Vol. I, *op. cit.*, p. 164.
40. Gurudas Das, Trade between the Northeastern Region and Neighbouring Countries: Structures & Implications for Development, in Das, Gurudas & Purkayastha, R.K. edited *"Border Trade: North East India and Neighbouring Countries*," Akansha Publishing House, New Delhi, 2000, p. 41.
41. MIZZIMA News Group, *Research on Indo-Myanmar Bilateral Trade*, July 1999.
42. *Ibid.*
43. Indian Institute of Foreign Trade (IIFT), Study on Promotion of Border Trade between India and Myanmar, New Delhi, November 1995.
44. Research and Information System for Non-Aligned and Developing Countries, UN-ESCAP, Study on India's Border Trade with Select Neighbouring Countries; New Delhi, 1996. Quoted in Gurudas Das, and

Purkayastha R.K., *Border Trade—North-East India & Neighbouring Countries*, Akansha Publishing House, New Delhi, 2000, p. 81.
45. *Current Status Note on Border-Trade with Bangladesh and Myanmar*, Directorate of Trade and Commerce, Aizawl, December 2001, p. 3.
46. Gurudas Das, Trade between the Northeastern Region & Neighbouring Countries: Structures & Implications for Development, in Gurudas Das, and Purkayastha, R.K., *Border Trade—North-East India & Neighbouring Countries*, Akansha Publishing House, New Delhi, 2000, p. 41.
47. CMIE, *Foreign Trade*, August 1998.
48. Directorate of Trade and Commerce, *op. cit.*, pp. 1-2.
49. MIZZIMA News Group, *op. cit.*, May 1999.
50. EXIM Bank, *op. cit.*
51. IIFT, *Study on Promotion of Border Trade between India and Myanmar*, *op. cit.*
52. *Ibid.*
53. EXIM Bank, *Study on Scope to Increase Trade and Investment in Myanmar*, *op. cit.*
54. Memorandum to the Twelfth Finance Commission, Government of Mizoram, February 2004, p. 31.
55. State Presentation to the Twelfth Finance Commission, Government of Mizoram, 1 June 2004, pp. 31-32.
56. Third Annual Report, Mizoram Agricultural Marketing Corporation Ltd., Aizawl 1995-96.
57. Auditors' Report, *Ibid.*, p. 7.
58. Reserve Bank of India circular No. FIC-No. 841/01-02-00/93-94 dated 28.3.1994.
59. Memorandum to the Twelfth Finance Commission, *op. cit.*, p. 31.
60. Notes on Various Topics submitted to Twelfth Finance Commission, Government of Mizoram, March 2004, pp. 79-81.
61. *Ibid*, p. 80.
62. State Presentation to the Twelfth Finance Commission, *op. cit.*, pp. 21-24.
63. Auditors' Report on Annual Accounts of ZENICS, 1998-99, p. 5.
64. Report of the Sub-Committee of State Level Bankers' Committee for Mizoram on Credit-Deposit Ratio dated 15th November 1996, *op. cit.*, p. 5.
65. Chatterjee, Dr. Suhash, *Mizoram: Encyclopaedia*, Vol. II, *op. cit.*, p. 360.
66. Chatterjee, Dr. Suhash, *Mizoram under British Rules*, p. 93.
67. Chatterjee, Dr. Suhash, *Mizoram: Encyclopaedia*, Vol. II, *op. cit.*, 1990, p. 52.
68. Chatterjee, Dr. Suhash, *Mizoram: Encyclopaedia*, Vol. II, *op. cit.*, pp. 233-36.
69. Chatterjee, Dr. Suhash, *Mizoram: Encyclopaedia*, Vol. I, *op. cit.*, p. 25.
70. *Ibid*, p. 60.

3

INDUSTRY IN MIZORAM

Introduction

Industry refers to systematic work or labour; continual employment in some useful work with steady efforts. It is a group of businesses that produce a similar product or provide a similar service. Industry may be taken to mean the quality of being hard working, being always employed usefully[1]. There may be a variety of industries. Some industries change raw materials into useful products. For example, the steel industry turns iron ore into steel. Other industries, such as shipping and haulage, move goods from one place to another. In this sense, industry provides items such as clothing, food, shelter, and other basic needs. Industry helps making lives healthier and happier by providing entertainment, labour saving appliances, medicines, and many other things. Although industry enriches the quality of life, it may also have some harmful side effects. Factories pollute soil, air and water and so endanger health. Traffic jams delay people in getting from one place to another. Machines make noise that is often unpleasant and may even damage hearing. The rapid growth of industry may ultimately use up the world's supply of petroleum and natural gas.

The item or service that an industry produces is known as output. The output could be a bolt, a piece of cloth, or a refrigerator. To produce an output, industry uses inputs such as machinery and raw materials. The value and the quality of output depend on the value and the quality of inputs and on how efficiently a producer uses them. Inputs are also called productive resources. Basic inputs industry requires for production are five viz., natural resources, capital, labour, management, and technology.

Natural resources include forests, mineral deposits, soil, sun, water, and wildlife. Two types of capital (funds) is required by industry, that a firm needs to hire workers, buy supplies, and pay bills, known as working capital and that required for capital goods such as, buildings, machinery, tools, and other items that provide productive service over a period. Labour is the work, human beings do to produce goods and services. Management is a special kind of labour that facilitates business decisions. Managers decide what to produce, how much to produce, which markets to serve, how much to advertise, and what prices to charge, etc. They also decide how to raise capital and make choice of input-mix. Technology refers to a society's knowledge of machines, materials, techniques, and tools.

Global Differences in Industry

Industry differs greatly between developed and developing countries. Industry in developed countries produces more goods and services per person than it do in developing countries. The lower production in developing countries is due to shortages of machinery and other capital goods and due to less advanced technology. The developing countries also lack sufficient human capital, including engineers, managers, and skilled workers needed for industrial growth.

In developing countries rapid population growth prevents accumulation of capital, as more resources have to be used for food and other consumer goods and there are hardly any savings for investment. In developed countries, many industries produce leisure products and luxuries of various kinds. Many countries produce only one or two raw materials, which they exchange with the rest of the world.

Industry operates under different economic systems in different countries. The economic system of a country where most of the industries are privately owned is called capitalism. Where the government owns most of the industries, the economic system is known as Communism. Most countries, now, have some form of mixed economy where the government may own key industries such as steel, railways, etc. and other industries may be owned privately.

Classification of Industries

Different classification systems are used to organize information about industry. One common system used in economic research is the International Standard Industrial Classification (ISIC). Considering the items produced, industries may be classified as those manufacturing durable goods, such as appliances and furniture, and those producing non-durable goods, such as clothing and food. Likewise industries can be divided into those producing consumer goods for sale to individuals and those making capital goods for sale to business firms. Based on stage of production, industries such as agriculture, fishing, forestry, and mining belonging to the first stage of production consuming natural resources are called primary or extractive industries. The chemical, textile, and other manufacturing industries handling the second stage of production turning raw materials into finished goods are called secondary or fabricating industries. The third stage involving movement of goods from producers to consumers, the industries such as haulage firms are known as tertiary or distributive industries.

Challenges of Industrialization

Modern industry faces many problems and challenges such as environmental pollution, energy supply, unemployment, government regulation, etc. Environmental Pollution is a side effect of industrial process. Factories pour smoke and other pollutants into the air and dump waste products into lakes and rivers. Pollution harms environment and endangers health of living beings. There are laws that require industries to stop, or reduce many activities that cause pollution. Nevertheless, fighting pollution uses resources, just as producing goods and services does. Pollution control devices and new processes that reduce pollution require capital, labour, technology, and other inputs resulting in higher prices for consumers and lower profits for industry.

An Industry requires energy to run machines and to provide heat for manufacturing processes. The cost and availability of energy plays a major role in the choice of industrial location and other business decisions. Most energy today is generated from natural resources such as coal, natural gas, and petroleum. The rapid growth of industry threatens to exhaust the world's supply of easily accessible and reasonably priced petroleum and natural gas.

Unemployment results in lost income for the jobless, reduced markets for industry, and lost production for society as a whole. High unemployment occurs during economic slumps, when many businesses reduce production and lay-off workers. It results from developing new products or change in consumers' taste causing some industries to decline. It also occurs if, workers lack the skills needed for jobs even when jobs are available. Many individuals do not find work, and many businesses do not find skilled workers.

Generally government agencies control prices, standards of service, and some other aspects of business in regulated economies. In capitalist countries, government often regulates industries such as radio and television, public utilities e.g., electricity, gas, telephone companies etc. Sometimes, public utility companies have monopoly on a service within a given area, the government permitting such monopolies regulates their activities and the prices they charge.

Certain general regulations such as regulations enforcing safety and health standards at the workplace, laws covering the conditions of employment and wage levels, the purity of food, safety and effectiveness of drugs, etc. apply to all industries. Consumer goods are subject to safety regulations. Laws prohibit monopolies, prevent unfair business practices and restrict firms to protect consumers from environmental pollution, unsafe products, and unfair advertising and trade practices. However, regulations may harm consumers also say, lack of competition may cause companies to become inefficient and neglect product improvement.

Industrial Development in India

Industrialization is generally considered synonymous with economic progress and hence the developing countries give high priority to industrial development. India made advances in the industrialization during post-independence period only. A diversified industrial base has been created, making the country self-reliant in many basic industries and nearly self-reliant in a wide range of manufactures. Industrial growth averaging 1.5 to 2 per cent in the first half of the century accelerated to 5 to 6 per cent on the average during planning era. Under the impact of technological changes and liberalization of policy since 1980s, industrial output grew at 8.5 per cent in the later half of the eighties—higher than the Seventh Plan target of 8 per cent per annum. Industry, however, operated within a complex system of controls and regulations virtually sheltering the country from external competition until the mid-eighties, when industry, trade and fiscal policies were realigned to make Indian goods more competitive, both internally and internationally. The liberalization measures, freeing the industry from fetters and shackles, thus, came as a welcome change.

In India, by and large industrial locations have been influenced either by the availability of raw materials or political considerations. Pure economic considerations were seldom given weightage in the location of industry in the public sector. The industrial development in the country has remained concentrated in a few states like Maharashtra, Gujarat, West

Bengal and Tamilnadu[2]. The Northeastern region despite its vast natural resources is one of the industrially backward regions of the country.

Location and growth of industries are largely the result of a long process of historical evolution of market forces and deliberate public policies. These coupled with the lack of investment climate, absence of alert entrepreneurship, and strong pressure group to lobby for various forms of government interventions have left the resource rich North-East region industrially backward. Further, the regional industrial scene is heavily influenced by tea and petroleum industry with almost absence of engineering industry. There are few paper mills, cement plants, plywood factories, spinning mills, jute mills, rubber units, plastics units, *khandsari* and sugar mills, chemical units and miscellaneous industries, etc., of large and medium size in the region. Majority of these units are located in Assam. Large and medium industries in other states are completely absent. Mizoram and other states of the region are at nascent stage of industrialization. The medium and large industries in the region operate much below the average productivity level of the industry in the country[3]. This, points towards the attention needed to improve productivity levels in existing industrial units along with setting up new industrial units in the region. Although the number of SSI units has increased considerably in the region but majority of them are local resource based, produce locally required products and lack diversification. Further, higher relative sickness of these units is retarding their progress.

Industrial Development in Mizoram

Like other states in North-East, industrialization is at nascent stage in Mizoram. Except for some small-scale and cottage industries, there is not much worth mentioning. However, the history of growth of industries in this small tribal state is interesting.

Pre-British Era (Before 1871)

The early Mizo society was migratory having little urge to amass household possessions. Agriculture was their principal means of livelihood. Due to lack of intercourse with the neighbouring areas, the tribes living in this hilly region had to produce all that they needed for their day-to-day use. It was their own requirement that inspired the tribal people to apply their skill in arts and crafts. This fact had an important bearing on the later Mizo, who witnessed a gradual decay of cottage industries, which outlived their utility. The age-old industries, which played a vital role in economy of the territory like basket making, weaving, pottery, metalworking, lacquering, and smithy declined[4]. Most of the cottage industries were part-time occupations of the villagers and were run by members of the family without assistance from outside.

The products of Lushai Hills for export during pre-British period were confined to cane and bamboo mats, and baskets. These were made chiefly by the inhabitants on the slopes of ranges bordering Myanmar. For local use, spears, *daos*, axe-heads, hoes, and knives were manufactured. Iron was procured from Myanmar. Blacksmiths were found throughout the hills. Wunhla, a village in the Southern Chin Hills, was famous for ironwork. The blacksmith's forge consisted of two bamboo bellows made out of two large bamboos standing upright with the pistons made of bamboo and cock's feathers and worked by hand. Charcoal was used for furnace, and the anvil consisted of a block of stone or a log of wood covered with a sheet of iron. The weapons were neatly made, but the science of tempering metal was unknown. Native blacksmiths could make every portion of a flintlock gun except the barrel. Although the springs, which they made, were weak, and often snapped, they nevertheless were often found in the gunlocks. The melting of brass and telegraph wires was universally practiced. Armlets and bangles were made by pouring the molten metal into moulds made of a mixture of paddy-husks and clay. The telegraph-insulator, which was made of steel, was fashioned into knife blade. Both men and women wore ivory (*saingho*) as earrings (*bengbeh*) and necklaces (*thihna*). They also kept long hair and used hairpins (*thimkual*) and hair-sticks (*dawhkilh*) generally made of bamboo. Combs made of bamboo were also used. Men on important occasion wore a headdress like Vakiria made and composed of parrots' feathers and porcupine quills inserted into a bamboo ring.

In the Southern Hills, for wife of the Chief a brass and bead headdress was made for wearing on important occasions. Its construction displayed the neatness and accuracy with which Chins bore metal with a rough drill. The manufacture of brass hairpins, earrings, bangles, armlets, and metal beads was carried on chiefly in the villages far south of Haka in Myanmar that were on the border of Lushai region.

Earthen pots were made everywhere for holding water and liquor. The pots were dried in the sun and baked. Pottery was the work of women. Raincoats and rain hats were made everywhere. However, Rawvan in the south was most noted for this industry and superior class of articles. The coat was made out of bark of a tree and the hat was made of bamboo, bark, and date-palm leaves.

Thus, the industries were carried on to meet the bare minimum domestic needs and no attempt was made to sell the products. The Mizo lost their zest to develop anything on commercial lines when expansion of trade and commerce provided them with an easy and frugal method of obtaining articles of daily use[5]. However, the cottage industries, which formed an important part of tribal life, suffered a gradual decadence.

British Era (1872-1947)

Though, the interest of British Government was limited to its administration just by safeguarding its own economic interests, still it showed interest in the revival of cottage crafts. Government assistance for the development of cottage industries in Mizoram dates back to 1939 when the District Superintendent, made some endeavour to inject commercial bias in handloom cotton weaving industry. Some funds were raised for this purpose with personal contributions and loans from the Government. Some Mizo were sent to Kolkata to undergo training in synthetic dyeing. Sir Robert Reid, the then Governor of Assam gave the organization a building called "Reid House" for the purpose. The Government assisted through grants which was equal to staff charges for a period of three years. However, not much could be done in this respect and Mizo district remained industrially the most backward district of Assam during pre-independence times.

It is interesting to note that during 1910-11, the first industrial unit, (a printing press) 'Synod Press Printing and Publishing' was setup in Aizawl, which provided employment to 20 people with an investment of Rs.0.70 lakh. Among workers, 12 were skilled and the rest unskilled. Further, 14 were male and 6 female. This enterprise is owned by Christian Missionary of the Presbyterian Church.

Post-Independence (After 1947)

After independence the purview of the Assam State Cottage Industries Department was extended to the erstwhile Mizo District for the development of small scale and cottage industries. There existed one Government Weaving Training Centre at Lunglei in 1949 for imparting training to the weavers. Subsequently, five more training centres in different crafts were opened in Lunglei Sub-Division of which four were at the Lunglei block headquarters, viz., Soap Making Training-*cum*-Production Centre (1959), Dyeing Training-*cum*-Production Centre (1959), Woodworks Training-*cum*-Production Centre (1961), Cane works

Training-*cum*-Production Centre (1961). The other (fifth one), a Handloom Weaving Training Class was opened at Demagiri in 1960. However, *Khadi* weaving was not recommended for Mizo district, the two schemes of *Khadi* i.e. spinning in Ambar Charkha and Oil Ghanis that were taken up by the *Khadi* Board.

The Government of Assam took up a Rural Industries Project in Mizoram under centrally sponsored scheme at the instance of the Planning Commission, Government of India. The project office was established at Aizawl in December 1962, which became functional in January 1963[6] with the objective to bring cooperative agro-industrial bias in the rural economy. For implementation of project schemes committees were setup at Centre, State and Project level. Execution of the schemes started in January 1964. The Project provided for training programme, common service facilities, other development programmes, schemes for sericulture, weaving, etc.

Under the Training Programme, one Clustered Type Training Centre at Aizawl, one Tailoring, Knitting, and Embroidery Training Centre at Kolasib, training inside and outside the State, study tours, and seminars for village artisans were arranged. Under the common service facilities scheme, Service Engineering Workshop, purchase and demonstration on use of improved tools, raw materials-*cum*-sales depot, etc., were established. Under other development schemes, experiments on local raw materials were carried out, besides supplying improved tools at subsidized rates and constructing subsidized factory sheds. Industrial exhibitions were organized at times and in deserving cases industrial loans were given. Under the scheme for sericulture and weaving, establishment of a Handloom Demonstration Party and concentration centres for rearing of mulberry silk worms and cultivation of mulberry trees were taken up. The weaving party made demonstrations to convert the old and outmoded loin looms into modern ones.

Under new district level setup, the Rural Industries Project was converted into District Industries Centre (DIC) under centrally sponsored scheme with a view to provide services to cottage and small-scale industries under a single roof. Under this scheme, Mizoram got two DICs, one at Aizawl and the other at Lunglei. The District Industries Centre undertook economic investigation on potential for the development of the district including provision of raw materials and other resources, supply of machinery and equipment, effective arrangement for credit facilities, marketing assistance, quality control, research, extension and entrepreneurial training.

As Mizoram was part of Assam, there was no separate organization to look after the industrial development activities. The Assistant Director of Industries, Silchar was responsible for carrying out industrial development programmes. Practically, there was no industrial development programme for small, medium, or large scale industries to boost up the pace of development in the region. Obviously Mizoram remained a 'No Industry District' under category 'A' during this period. The factors responsible were lack of funds, lack of organizational structure coupled with lack of infrastructural facilities. The industrial activity was restricted mainly to traditional cottage and small-scale industries like carpentry, weaving, handicrafts, etc. with only 0.28 per cent of total industrial units run on electricity in 1961[7].

In 1971, Lalkhama Committee was formed to promote industrial development in the region. According to the report of the Committee, though there were 119 units under Rural Industries Project, Aizawl, except for a handful of them, these could not be called industries in real sense of the term. The Lalkhama Committee suggested certain industries, which could be conveniently developed in the Mizo Hills. These included agro-industries such as manufacture of sugar, fruit preservation, tapioca starch making, oil expelling, bamboo pulp and board, saw mill, and processing of maize, banana, chilly and ginger and other small industries like tyre retreading, radio repairing, manufacturing of plastic articles, foot wear, hosiery goods, ready made garments, aluminium utensils etc.[8]

Table 3.1 projects the position regarding industries in Mizoram from 1952 to 1962, a period from adoption of planned economic development at national level till the outburst of disturbance in Mizoram.

Table 3.1 reveals that in 1952, one new printing press in Aizawl with an investment of Rs. 0.30 lakh came up engaging 7 persons (5 males and 2 females), among them 3 skilled and 4 unskilled. In 1954, two more units, one of furniture manufacturing in Durtlang with an investment of Rs. 0.05 lakh, and one printing press "J. Buana's Press" in Lunglei with an investment of Rs. 0.10 lakh, were set up. Each of these units had engaged 6 persons. In 1959, the first automobile workshop was set up in Aizawl with an investment of Rs. 0.25 lakh, engaging 12 persons, of them 5 were skilled. In 1960, one more press was established in Aizawl with an investment of Rs. 0.20 lakh, which offered jobs to 6 persons, 2 skilled and 4 unskilled. In 1961, 2 new units came up in Aizawl, one an automobile workshop and other fabrication unit. They together offered 18 new jobs with an investment of Rs. 0.05 lakh and Rs. 0.06 lakh respectively. In 1962 also, one automobile workshop was established in

Aizawl with an investment of Rs. 0.10 lakh, which engaged 12 persons. In brief, by the end of 1962, there were 9 SSI units in Mizoram, of which one was in Lunglei and rest in Aizawl district. From 1962 to 1971 owing to disturbance in Mizo district no industrial activity worth mentioning took place.

Table 3.1: Industries in Mizoram during 1952 to 1962
(As on 31st December)

Year	*District-wise Number of Registered SSIs*					*No. of Persons Employed*	*Investment in Fixed Assets (Rs. in lakhs)*
	Aizawl	*Lunglei*	*Chhim-tuipui*	*Total SSIs*	*Cumulative Total*		
Till 1951	1	Nil	Nil	1	1	20	0.70
1952	1	Nil	Nil	1	2	27	1.00
1954	1	1	Nil	2	4	39	1.15
1959	1	Nil	Nil	1	5	51	1.40
1960	1	Nil	Nil	1	6	57	1.60
1961	2	Nil	Nil	2	8	75	1.71
1962	1	Nil	Nil	1	9	87	1.81
Total	8	1	Nil	Nil	9	87	1.81

Source: Census Report of Assam on Mizo District, 1961.

Union Territory Period (1972-1986)

To channelize the industrial development activity in proper direction, the Directorate of Industries along with Administrative Department was created in 1972, when the Mizo Hills District was elevated to Union Territory status. As only two years of the Fourth Five Year Plan were left, there seemed little scope for the Directorate of Industries to take up planned programmes. However, schemes like industrial estate, handloom and handicrafts, and sericulture were initiated. A Craft Centre at Saiha, a Handicraft Training-*cum*-Production Centre at Lunglei and a Weaving Training Centre were established. The Rural Industries Project maintained Rural Service Workshop (Common Facilities Centre), Raw Material Depot, Carpentry Training-*cum*-Production Centre, and Knitting and Tailoring Training Centre. During 1972-73 and 1973-74 the expenditure incurred on industrial sector was Rs. 15.29 lakh and Rs. 19.73 lakh respectively.

Fifth Five Year Plan (1974-79): The Fifth Five Year Plan aimed at over all growth of small-scale, village, cottage, medium and large-scale industries. A total sum of Rs. 344 lakh was spent on industrial sector during the plan.

Under the large and medium sector, schemes like paper mill, plywood factory were initiated. A paper mill project for 200 MT capacity was prepared and a study for setting up of mini sugar plant was conducted. Preliminary study for setting up a ginger oil and oleoresin plant was conducted by the Central Food Technology Research Institute, Mysore (CFTRI). Under Village & Small Industries sector 2125 artisans were assisted with grant-in-aid and 601 small-scale entrepreneurs/ artisans were assisted with small loans[9]. Preliminary work for setting up Industrial Estates at Aizawl and Kolasib was completed. Under the *Khadi* and Village Industries scheme, apiary farms (bee keeping) were established in Aizawl, Lunglei and Chhimtuipui district. Under the handloom scheme, fly shuttle looms were introduced amongst the weavers and about 225 weavers were given looms with accessories at subsidized rate, and Weavers Service Centre was established. Under the scheme of handicrafts, a Cane and Bamboo Craft Production Centre was opened at Luangmual (Aizawl) and a Craft Centre in Knitting and Tailoring was established at Saitual. Attempts were made to identify viable industries of Aizawl district by conducting industrial potential survey engaging the Small Industries Extension Training Institute, Hyderabad. The Mizoram Small Industries Development Corporation Ltd. (MSIDC) [later renamed in 1984-85 as Zoram Industrial Development Corporation Ltd. (ZIDCO)] was setup on 27th February 1978 to advance industrial loans to entrepreneurs and build a base for marketing of industrial products through emporiums. Its authorized share capital was Rs. 50 lakh, which was increased to Rs. 5 crore in 1984,[10] in which the Government of Mizoram had contributed Rs. 95 lakh. During 1984, the Corporation sanctioned loans of Rs. 190.16 lakh to 59 industrial units and 15 small road transport operators[11]. For the development of industries, a consultancy bureau was opened at Aizawl, which strengthened the Directorate of Industries.

Thus, the industrial development remained confined mostly to small scale, cottage, and tiny sectors through loan facility to entrepreneurs as short-term measure. Training programmes remained mainly restricted to handloom and handicrafts. Under village and small industries sector, schemes like Industrial Estate, Handloom development, Handicraft development, *Khadi* & Village Industries, grants-in-aid, industrial loan etc., were initiated, apart from intensifying the sericulture development activity in Mizoram. A modest beginning was made for industrial development in Mizoram.

Sixth Five Year Plan (1980-85): During the Sixth Five Year Plan, the Industries Department initiated schemes for balanced development of large, medium, village, and cottage industries. Under the large and medium sector, projects like Mini Paper Plant, Plywood Factory, etc. were perused further. Saw Mill-*cum*-Timber Seasoning Plant, Corrugated Roofing Sheets, Plant, and Mini Sugar Plant under NEC Plan were taken up. Preliminary studies for departmental projects were made. After detailed techno-economic feasibility studies, projects like Ginger Oil and Oleoresin Plant at Sairang, Ginger Dehydration Plant at Sairang and Fruit Preservation Factory at Vairengte were taken up for implementation. Mineral Exploration for industrial utilization was launched and a sum of Rs. 55.74 lakh was spent in the plan.

Under Village & Small Industries sector, schemes like Entrepreneurial Development and Training, Interest Subsidy, Power Subsidy, Transport Subsidy, Industrial Information Centre, Co-operation, etc. were initiated. Land measuring 250 acres at Zuangtui (Aizawl), and 65 acres at Sairang were acquired for Industrial Estates. Four sheds were constructed at Industrial Estate, Kolasib.

Mizoram *Khadi* & Village Industries Board was established in 1982. Under handloom development 271 weavers were trained in fly shuttle loom weaving in Thenzawl. Under handicraft development 85 persons were given training. Training-*cum*-Production Centres comprising of Knitting, Tailoring, and Cane and Bamboo trades were opened at Ngopa, Chawngte, and Champhai. Craft Museum was opened at Aizawl. Grant-in-aid was given to 1970 village artisans. Departmental loans were given to 217 SSI units. Under entrepreneurial development programme 169 prospective entrepreneurs were given training. Managerial subsidy was given to 30 industrial cooperatives. Steps were taken to establish Multi-Disciplinary Training-*cum*-Common Facility Centre in Aizawl. Rs. 19.19 lakh were spent on Mines and Minerals.

For sericulture a separate Directorate was created, which became functional in 1985. The small-scale units dominated industrial development in the State with low productivity, inadequacy of capital and management expertise. During the Plan a sum of Rs. 428.28 lakh was spent on Village and Small Industries and Rs. 55.74 lakh on Large and Medium Industries including sericulture.

The main instrument for promoting industries in Mizoram was schemes such as industrial loan and hire purchase, grants-in-aid, power subsidy, interest subsidy etc. With these facilities, the department was able to establish 81 new SSI units during 1984 and 235 in 1985 under permanent registration and the number of SSI units under permanent registration became 857 by 1985. The department brought 391 and 641 SSI units under provisional registration during 1984 and 1985 and the number of provisionally registered SSI units reached 4421 in 1985[12].

Trade-wise Industries in Mizoram

During early Union Territory period information relating to SSI, Cottage, Village and Tiny Industries was not kept systematically. A beginning in this direction was made since 1980. However, from time to time some surveys were made by agencies and the results were published in statistical handbooks or official gazetteers of Mizoram 1989 or socio-economic review of Mizoram 1979-80. Based on all these sources, information from 1974-75 to 1989-90 is compiled and produced in Table 3.2 which reveals the following:

- During 1974-75 to 1989-90 though the budget allocation for industries in Mizoram increased 22 times from Rs. 23 lakh to Rs. 512 lakh, the number of industrial units increased 5 fold only from 460 in 1974-75 to 2,205 in 1989-90. Similarly, jobs generated grew nearly 6 times from 2,015 in 1974-75 to 11,574 in 1989-90 as against 115 times increase in investment from Rs. 90 lakh to Rs. 10,424 lakh. Per unit capital investment in industries at Rs. 0.20 lakh in 1974-75 to Rs. 4.73 lakh in 1989-90 was very low, as basically these were village and tiny units rather than SSIs. The budget outlay 3.75 per cent[13] showed that the State Government's efforts towards the promotion of industries were meagre. Perhaps the government was not exposed to industrial environment and did not give this sector due emphasis.
- Industry group-wise highest growth was recorded in chemical and chemical products, where the number of units grew 13.8 times, employment 12.3 times and investment 4 times because of inclusion of soap manufacturing units. Basic metal and allied industries (aluminium) recorded growth of 7 times in number of units, 8.6 times in jobs and 17.1 times in investment. Leaving miscellaneous group apart, next highest growth was recorded in textiles and textile goods, where the increase in number of units was 5.9 times, employment 8.5 times and investment 144.8 times. In rubber, plastics, etc. group (including tyre retreading) the number of units increased

Table 3.2: Category-wise Details of Industries in Mizoram from 1974-75 to 1989-90 (Cumulative position as on 31st March)

(*Investment : Rs. in lakh*)

Year	1975			1978			1985-86			1986-87			1987-88			1988-89			1989-90		
Name of Industry	No. of Units	No. of Employees	Investment	No. of Units	No. of Employees	Investment	No. of Units	No. of Employees	Investment	No. of Units	No. of Employees	Investment	No. of Units	No. of Employees	Investment	No. of Units	No. of Employees	Investment	No. of Units	No. of Employees	Investment
Food Product & Allied Industries	70	257	5	106	486	5	149	607	487	195	771	680	242	935	1049	284	1111	1353	252	969	1397
Wooden Products	81	282	16	93	384	16	129	564	257	195	881	498	245	1085	1117	313	1378	2118	397	1894	2231
Textile Goods	51	195	10	60	246	10	124	428	152	166	671	549	241	1043	1082	306	1352	1459	300	1652	1508
Paper Products, Publishing & Allied	26	263	15	33	378	15	45	444	340	53	502	759	61	559	1113	74	644	1150	100	698	1220
Rubber, Plastics,	6	27	1	9	56	1	9	56	1	17	106	28	21	132	42	26	165	60	35	183	123
Chemical products	4	15	1	6	23	1	6	23	1	6	23	1	6	23	1	6	23	1	55	185	5
Non-Metallic & Mineral Products	0	0	0	0	0	0	2	54	0	6	199	2	11	333	33	16	391	48	53	747	147
Basic Metal & Allied Industries	3	28	4	6	48	4	6	48	4	10	62	5	10	62	5	14	69	6	21	241	68
Metal Products & Parts	23	38	0	25	44	0	29	69	7	34	108	14	36	123	56	50	203	72	57	200	80
Leather Goods & Repairing	9	21	0	9	21	0	9	21	0	9	21	0	13	31	1	23	58	45	21	51	47
Service Based Industries	179	796	36	196	961	36	271	1556	848	415	2237	1152	568	3089	2543	661	3536	2756	841	4268	2952
Miscellaneous	8	93	1	11	105	1	38	325	326	56	420	370	86	533	436	129	760	578	73	486	652
Total	430	2015	90	554	2752	90	817	4195	2424	1162	6001	4059	1540	7948	7478	1902	9690	9647	2205	11574	10424
Investment (P.U.)			0.20			0.16			2.97			3.49			4.86			5.07			4.73
Budget Outlay on Industry			23			42			176			149			149			381			512

Source: Statistical Handbook, Mizoram, 1976 (pp. 176-183, 186-201), 1978 (pp. 125-126), 1989 (pp. 68-82).
Report on Socio-Economic Review of Mizoram, 1979-80, p. 56.
Dr. Rualkhuma Colney, Small Scale & Cottage Industries, Mizoram, L. B. Associates, Aizawl, 1997, p. 142.

5.8 times, employment 6.8 times and investment grew 99.9 times. In wood and wooden products group, there was increase of 4.9 times in number of units, 6.7 times in jobs and 143.3 times in investment. In service based industries number of units grew 4.7 times, employment 5.4 times and investment 82.5 times. Paper products, publishing and allied industries group registered a nominal increase of 3.8, 2.7, 81.1 times and food products and allied industries group 3.6, 3.8, 268.8 times respectively. The least growth was in metal products and parts and leather goods and repairing. The job oriented leather industry did not show adequate growth, perhaps because of non-availability of leather.

- It was observed that most of these units were proprietorships, as the Indian Partnership Act, 1932 is not made applicable to Mizoram. However, some units were registered as cooperative society.

Registered Small-Scale Industries in Mizoram

The year-wise and district-wise position of small-scale industries registered with the Directorate of Industries during 1972 to 1986 is given in Table 3.3. An analysis of details given in Table 3.3 revealed the following:

1. The growth of registered SSIs till 1980 was slow. In fact, in some years, there was no registration of new units. However, it picked up later and over 6 years the number increased 7 times, from 170 in 1980 to 1191 in 1986. Further, the largest number of SSIs 82.4 per cent (981 out of 1191units) were registered in Aizawl district, as against 14.3 per cent (170 units) in Lunglei district and 3.3 per cent (40 units) in Chhimtuipui district.
2. It is also observed that the budget provision for industries over the period increased nearly 10 times from Rs. 15.28 lakh in 1972 to Rs. 149 lakh in 1986, while the plan expenditure increased roughly 14 times from Rs. 437 lakh in 1972 to Rs. 6212 lakh in 1986. Thus, the relative share of industries declined from 3.50 per cent in 1972 to 2.40 per cent in 1986 which indicated that industries in the State were given low priority.
3. The slow rate of registration of SSI units, coupled with low proportion of local population engaged in household and manufacturing industries and relatively high incidence of sickness among the existing units acted as serious impediments in the progress of industrial sector. This could be regarded as an index of backwardness in industrial field.

Table 3.3: Small-Scale Industries Registered with Directorate of Industries in Mizoram from 1972 to 1986.
(As on 31st December)

	No. of SSI Units							
	Aizawl District	*Lunglei District*	*Chhimtuipui District*	*Total SSIs*	*Cumulative Total*	*Budgetary Provision for Industries (Rs. in Lakh)*	*Total Plan Expenditure (Rs. in Lakh)*	*Plan Money Spent on Promotion of Industry (per cent)*
Till 1971	8	1	Nil	9	9	N.A.	N.A.	N.A.
1972	3	Nil	Nil	3	12	15.28	437	3.50
1973	3	Nil	Nil	3	15	17.00	500	3.40
1974	Nil	Nil	Nil	Nil	15	22.52	660	3.41
1975	Nil	Nil	Nil	Nil	15	28.00	731	3.83
1976	2	Nil	Nil	2	17	41.00	864	4.74
1977	Nil	Nil	Nil	Nil	17	41.50	1081	3.84
1978	Nil	Nil	Nil	Nil	17	N.A.	1462	N.A.
1979	2	Nil	Nil	2	19	N.A.	1611	N.A.
1980	105	46	Nil	151	170	72.13	N.A.	N.A.
1981	104	24	Nil	128	298	65.67	N.A.	N.A.
1982	114	11	Nil	125	423	98.91	N.A.	N.A.
1983	117	1	Nil	118	541	78.43	N.A.	N.A.
1984	63	18	Nil	81	622	168.88	N.A.	N.A.
1985	162	44	29	235	857	176.16	4736	3.72
1986	298	25	11	334	1191	149.00	6212	2.40
Total	981	170	40	—	1191	—	—	—

Source: Directorate of Industries, Government of Mizoram, Aizawl.

Post-Statehood

The creation of statehood coincided in Mizoram with the beginning of Seventh Five Year Plan (1985-90). Systematic efforts were made during the Plan to develop large and medium industries under government ownership and to develop small scale, village and cottage industries under private entrepreneurship through promotional schemes. Special attention was paid to handloom and handicraft, and infrastructure development. A major part of the expenditure 79.36 per cent (1226.82 lakh out of 1545.98 lakh) was spent in respect of village and small industries, only 13.14 per cent (203.15 lakh out of 1545.98 lakh) was in respect of large and medium industries and the rest 7.50 per cent (116.01 lakh out of 1545.98 lakh) was for mines and minerals. During VII Plan over the years 1985-86 to 1989-90 the relative share of promotional expenditure on large and medium industries declined from 25.03 per cent in 85-86 to 6.12 per cent in 89-90. The same was reflected by corresponding increase in village and small industries (VSI) share from 74.39 per cent in 85-86 to 84.11 per cent in 89-90 and mining and geology from 0.58 per cent in 85-86 to 9.77 per cent in 89-90. This indicated relative importance of village and small industries in the economy of Mizoram.

During VII Five Year Plan, under large and medium industries sector, Agro and Allied Food Industries were given top priority due to their known advantage over other industries. A scheme for agro-industries corporation was initiated during 1989-90 with a view to forming a corporation for the development of agro-horticulture based industries in Mizoram. The Mizoram Food and Allied Industries (MFAI) was, first, created as a separate cell under the Directorate of Industry, on the recommendation of the Central Food Technological Research Institute (CFTRI), Mysore. Later, the Mizoram Food and Allied Industries Corporation Ltd. (MIFCO), was incorporated on 19th February 1989. Trial production of ginger oil and oleoresin was started and Maize Processing Unit, Khawzawl was setup. Land measuring 48 *bigha* was acquired for Fruit Juice Concentrate Plant, Chhingchhip. For village and small industries, grant-in-aid to 2,422 artisans, departmental loans to 157 entrepreneurs, interest subsidy to 6 SSIs, managerial grant to 15 industrial cooperatives, managerial subsidy and rebate on sales to 35 industrial cooperatives, EDP training to 266 entrepreneurs, soap making training in Guwahati to 5 entrepreneurs were given and 40 entrepreneurs were sent on study tour. A Rural Industrial Development Centre was setup in Aizawl for the purpose of rendering service to industrial units and for technical training to artisans and workers of local industrial units. The department of industries awarded productivity awards to 3 entrepreneurs, participated in India International Trade Fair (IITF), New Delhi and organized State Level Industrial Exhibition at Lunglei, Mizoram Industrial Convention at Aizawl, and Mizoram Industrial Fair at Aizawl. In the field of infrastructure development, the Small Industrial Estate at Kolasib was completed, industrial estate at Zuangtui was further improved and land measuring 292 acres was acquired for Industrial Growth Centre, Luangmual.

Under Handloom and Handicraft sector, promotional schemes were continued, 2 jacquard looms were procured for Research & Design Centre, 4 sheds were constructed in Handloom Complex, Thenzawl, Weavers' Service Centre buildings were constructed in 4 villages and grant-in-aid/subsidy was given to 805 weavers, and 625 craftsmen. The Mizoram Handloom and Handicrafts Development Corporation Ltd (ZOHANDCO), was incorporated on 20th December 1988, which opened sales emporia at Aizawl and Lunglei. The Zoram Electronics Development

Corporation Ltd. (ZENICS) was incorporated on 20th March 1991. A comprehensive Integrated Development Programme for Mizoram was prepared by Padmashree K.L. Nanjappa, ex-Development Commissioner (SSI). The Mizoram Preferential Stores Purchases Rules. 1986 were notified by the Government. Some portion of built-up structure at Pragati Maidan, New Delhi was acquired as permanent pavilion for Trade Fair and Mizoram Emporium. The first Industrial Policy of Mizoram, 1989 was published. First industrial directory of small industries of Mizoram was published.

Annual Plans: During two annual plans (1990-91 and 1991-92), MIFCO expanded its activities and took over all the departmental projects like Ginger Oil & Oleoresin Plant, Sairang, Fruit Juice Concentrate Plant, Chhingchhip, Fruit Preservation Factory, Vairengte, and Maize Processing Plant, Khawzawl. ZENICS started functioning. Multi Disciplinary Training-*cum*-Common Facility Centres were opened in Lunglei and Saiha. Internal roads and buildings at Industrial Growth Centre Lungmual were completed. Site for Industrial Estate at Pukpuii and Lunglei was selected. Under various promotional schemes, interest subsidy to 15 SSIs, seed margin money loans to 11 SSIs, grant-in-aid to 270 entrepreneurs were given and 60 entrepreneurs were sent on study tour, 12 entrepreneurs were trained at Entrepreneurship Development Institute (EDI), Ahmedabad and three of them had come forward with proposals to the Industrial Development Bank of India (IDBI), of which one proposal of Zonun Mat Ply Industries P. Ltd with a project cost of Rs. 162 lakh was cleared by the IDBI. Steps were taken to explore the possibilities of tea industries in Mizoram.

Under handloom sector, loom subsidy to 264 weavers, cash grant to 33 weavers were given and 3 weavers were sent for 3 years' course in handloom technology and 25 weavers were sent on study tour. Under handicrafts scheme 134 craftsmen were assisted with grant-in-aid, 20 craftsmen were sent on study tour, 162 persons were trained in knitting and tailoring and 70 in cane and bamboo. During two annual plans a sum of Rs. 1339.34 lakh were spent on industrial sector of which a major chunk was spent on VSI (82.76 per cent) and a meagre 11.15 per c only on large and medium industries, and the balance (6.09 per ce spent on mines and minerals.

Eighth Five Year Plan: During VIII Five Year Plar at Luangmual, Biate and Pawlrang were develope of tea saplings was made in 125 acres of land survey of existing tea gardens in and around

NE Bualpui, Tlungvel and Seling was conducted. Necessary machineries and equipments were procured and 315 tea grower families of Biate were not only given training but also assisted with grant-in-aid in cash and kind. Steps for establishing a tea factory in Biate were initiated. To spread electronic culture in the State, 59 local youths were given training in electronics, 6 in radio and TV technology, and 8 for computer courses at various institutes/centres. Awareness campaigns and seminars on computer and electronics and vocational training were conducted in various schools and colleges. Grant-in-aid was given to electronic entrepreneurs. Necessary machines and equipments were procured and quality control equipments were setup at Common Facility Centre.

Under handloom and handicraft sector, 680 handloom weavers were given grant-in-aid/subsidy, 170 weavers were allotted work sheds, 305 persons were trained in fly shuttle loom weaving, and 8 persons were imparted with diploma in handloom technology course. Besides, 45 weavers were sent on study tour, 796 persons were given training in knitting and tailoring and cane and bamboo, 1356 craftsmen were assisted with grant-in-aid/subsidy, 10 craftsmen were sent on study tour, and 25 primary societies were given margin money received from the Government of India. The Handloom Complex at Thenzawl was improved. A Weaving Training Centre was constructed at Lunglei. Promotional grants were given to ZOHANDCO. The department participated in India International Trade Fair (IIFT), New Delhi every year. Besides holding state level Exhibition for VSI, the department brought out quarterly publication of a bulletin "*Industry Meichher*".

Industrial Structure in Mizoram

The industrial structure in Mizoram comprises elements like state of infrastructure, industries operating, services provided, etc.

Industrial Estates

With a view to provide built up sheds along with other infrastructural facilities such as water, power, communication, etc. to small-scale industrial units, the government took up a scheme to setup some mini industrial estates at different growth centres in Mizoram. One industrial estate at Kolasib and one industrial growth centre at Lungmual (Aizawl), were setup during Fifth Five Year Plan. New estates were setup at Lunglei, and Saiha. Zuangtui industrial estate was setup to accommodate nonpolluting tiny and cottage units in Aizawl. The position regarding Zuantui and Kolasib industrial estates in 1999-2000 is shown in Table 3.4.

From Table 3.4, it is clear that the facilities created were not fully utilized by entrepreneurs, as hardly 30 per cent of the sheds were occupied in Zuantui Industrial Estate and 40 per cent in Kolasib.

To benefit from the schemes of Ministry of Commerce, Government of India, and to create infrastructural facilities of high standard for export oriented production, the Government of Mizoram has proposed for an Export Promotion Industrial Park at Pukpuii near Lengpui (National Highway–54) between Vairengte and Sairang with a provision to accommodate apart from packaging units, the units intended to export a minimum of 33 per cent of their total annual production. In view of continuously improving condition of roads, communication, power, etc., and peace in the State, it is believed that it would be a suitable place for industries requiring modern packaging facilities like fruit juice concentrate, tea, coffee, tung oil, ginger, stone polishing for export of decorative slabs, orchids, fruits, etc.

Table 3.4: Position Regarding Sheds in Zuangtui and Kolasib Industrial Estates in Mizoram (1999-2000)

Name	Facilities Offered	Number of Sheds			
		Constructed	Allocated	Occupied	Functioning
Industrial Estate, Zuangtui, Aizawl	Industrial Plots, Subsidy upto 25 per cent on development of land within the estate by entrepreneurs	20	6	6	6
Industrial Estate, Kolasib	Industrial Plots, Subsidy upto 25 per cent on development of land within the estate by entrepreneurs	5	2	2	2

Source: Directorate of Industries, Aizawl.

Registered Small-Scale Industries (SIDO)

The Directorate of Industries was setup in Mizoram in 1972. Thereafter, the Department took up registration of industries. Around 1986, the Small Industries Development Organization (SIDO) defined the terms SSI, tiny and ancillary units and laid down the norms for their registration. Presently, an enterprise having investment in plant and machinery upto Rs. 10 lakh is regarded as small scale service and business establishment, upto Rs. 25

Table 3.5: Registered Small Scale Industries (SIDO) in Mizoram from 1986-87 to 2002-03

Year	No. of Registered SSIs: Aizawl	Lunglei	Chhimtuipui	Total	Total SSIs as on 31st Dec.	No. of Persons Employed	Investment in Fixed Assets (Rs. in lakh)	Value of Annual Production (Rs. in lakh)	Production Per Unit (Rs. in lakh)	Production Per Employee (Rs. in lakh)	Production Per Rupee of Fixed Assets	Investment Per Unit (Rs. in lakh)	No. of Employees Per Unit	Budgetary Support (Rs. in lakh)	Total Plan Expenditure (Rs. in lakh)	Plan Money Spent on Promotion of Industry (%)
Till 1986-87	981	170	40	1191	1191	N.A.	N.A.	N.A.	N.A.	N.A.	N.A.	N.A.	N.A.	229.0	6212	3.69
1987-88	300	40	11	351	1542	4223	1390	1470	0.953	0.35	1.06	0.90	2.74	249.0	7262	3.43
1988-89	109	33	10	152	1694	5648	1500	1850	1.092	0.33	1.23	0.89	3.33	381.1	8411	4.53
1989-90	260	39	95	394	2088	7419	1630	2380	1.140	0.32	1.46	0.78	3.55	511.7	10096	5.07
1990-91	120	23	10	153	2241	8604	1740	3000	1.339	0.35	1.72	0.78	3.84	659.4	12500	5.28
1991-92	91	21	57	169	2410	9847	1930	3720	1.544	0.38	1.93	0.80	4.09	700.0	15229	4.60
1992-93	109	37	16	162	2572	10660	2000	5320	2.068	0.50	2.66	0.78	4.14	702.5	16517	4.25
1993-94	28	9	4	41	2613	11161	2120	5670	2.170	0.51	2.67	0.81	4.27	732.2	17482	4.19
1994-95	107	3	3	113	2726	11860	2170	8490	3.114	0.72	3.91	0.80	4.35	749.9	20215	3.71
1995-96	185	0	2	187	2913	12683	2750	9220	3.165	0.73	3.35	0.94	4.35	876.1	23341	3.75
1996-97	454	47	37	538	3451	17830	3640	10250	2.970	0.57	2.82	1.05	5.17	872.6	28678	3.04
1997-98	206	6	9	221	3672	21123	4630	11430	3.113	0.54	2.47	1.26	5.75	654.0	29525	2.22
1998-99	222	5	8	235	3907	23458	5800	12800	3.276	0.55	2.21	1.48	6.00	648.8	27235	2.38
1999-00	393	7	6	406	4313	24676	5920	14200	3.292	0.58	2.40	1.37	5.72	1221.0	37802	3.23
2000-01	117	52	8	177	4490	25974	6050	14610	3.254	0.56	2.41	1.35	5.78	1054.8	37193	2.84
2001-02	229	39	12	280	4770	26629	6110	14950	3.134	0.56	2.45	1.28	5.58	1073.8	40242	2.67
2002-03	113	71	22	206	4976	N.A.	N.A.	N.A.	N.A.	N.A.	N.A.	N.A.	N.A.	1381.4	42057	3.28
Total	4024	602	350	4976	—	—	—	—	—	—	—	—	—	—	—	—
Average	190	27	19	237	—	14786	3292	7957	2.375	0.50	2.32	1.02	4.58	746.9	22353	3.66
Growth %	—	—	—	—	8.43	13.52	12.94	18.93	10.11	4.76	5.30	4.57	-15.95	9.07	12.84	-3.35
S. D.	112.62	20.2	23.87	124	1130.2	7496.6	1809	4761	0.90	0.15	0.74	0.25	0.989	306.5	11698	0.875
C.S.D.	0.59	0.75	1.23	0.52	0.37	0.51	0.55	0.60	0.38	0.25	0.32	0.24	0.22	0.41	0.52	0.24

Legend: S.D. = Standard Deviation, C.S.D. = Coefficient of Standard Deviation.

Note: From the year 2000-01 Aizawl district was divided into five districts. However, data have been shown combined for facility of comparison.

Source: Compiled from data obtained from Directorate of Industries, Government of Mizoram, Aizawl.

lakh (old limit was Rs. 5 lakh later increased to Rs. 15 lakh) is treated as tiny unit, and upto Rs. 1 crore (earlier this limit was of 60 lakh) is recognized as SSI. For an ancillary unit, this limit is of Rs. 1 crore. Further, for the units engaged in production of 71 specified items out of 872[14] items reserved for SSIs (27 hosiery items, 14 hand tools, 13 stationery, 10 drugs and pharma and 7 sports goods), this limit is of Rs. 5 crore. According to Small Industries Development Organization (SIDO), the units though producing these reserved items but through manual process (by hand) and not through mechanized process cannot be registered as SSI. However, the various state governments continued to recognize such units as SSIs other than SIDO-SSIs. In this way, two categories of SSIs one, SIDO-SSIs and the other Non-SIDO-SSIs emerged since 1986-87. As such, the Directorate of Industries in Mizoram maintained two separate records on SSIs registration since 1989. The industrial growth in terms of number of units, number of employees, value of fixed assets, value of production, budgetary support to industrial sector, etc. is shown in Table 3.5 and also reflected through Figures 3.1, 3.2, 3.3 and 3.4.

The analysis of Table 3.5 revealed the following:

1. Of the total 4976 registered SSIs (SIDO) in the State as on 31st December 2002, 4024 units (81 per cent) were located in Aizawl district while 602 units (12 per cent) were in Lunglei and 350 units (7 per cent) in Chhimtuipui district (Figure 3.1). These industries included furniture, knitting and tailoring, bakery, automobile repair and service units, TV manufacturing-*cum*-repairing units, motor body, wood seasoning, mosaic tiles, polythene, files and bags manufacturing units, etc. Further, of the total increase of 3785 units over the period from 1986-87 (1191 units) to 2002-03 (4976 units), Aizawl district had an increase of 3043 units, Lunglei 432 units and Chhimtuipui 310 units. This clearly indicated not only disparity between districts but also heavy concentration in Aizawl district. Aizawl being the State capital provides all facilities, Lunglei, the second largest district, comes next while Chhimtuipui district is least developed, and virtually left with no development. This is supported by the fact that on the average annually 190 units were established in Aizawl district as against 27 in Lunglei and 19 in Chhimtuipui only (Figure 3.2). However, coefficient of variation at 123 per cent, 75 per cent, and 59 per cent in Chhimtuipui, Lunglei, and Aizawl districts respectively shows that average annual variation was in the reverse order.

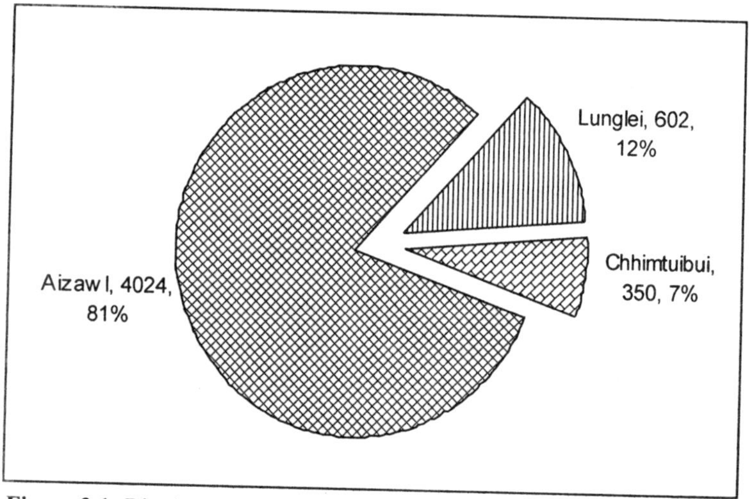

Figure 3.1: District-wise Total Registered Small Scale Industries (SIDO) in Mizoram as on 31st December 2002.

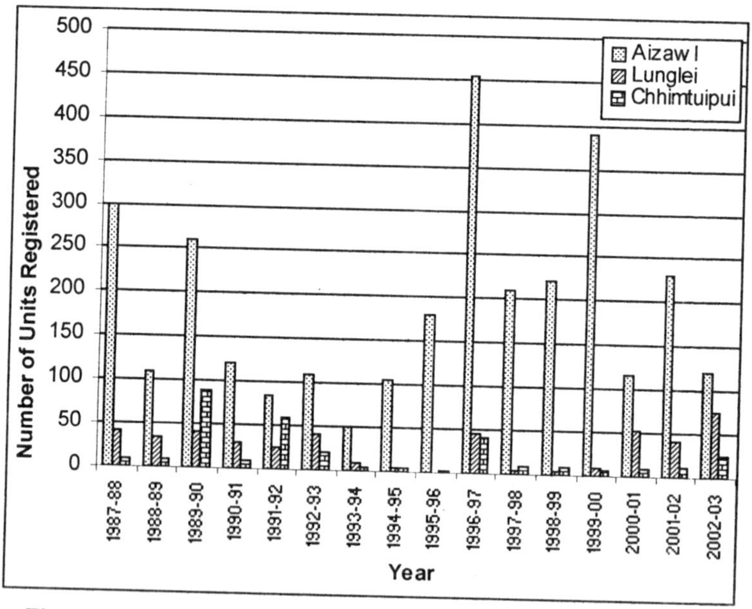

Figure 3.2: District-wise Annual Pattern of Registration of Small-Scale Industries (SIDO) in Mizoram from 1986-87 to 2002-03

2. Casual manner in industrial registration indicated lack of consistent industrial outlook at government level as well as at society level revealed that handful of persons in Aizawl district hyphen majority of funds by way of subsidies etc. in the name of fake industries as is witnessed by high sickness ratio of 43.91 per cent (Table 3.10) thereby fluid trade adoption behaviour (FTAB) is seen.
3. Employment opportunities in industrial sector of Mizoram grew on the average at 13.52 per cent p.a. (6.31 times) over 15 years from 1987-88 to 2001-02. Similarly the investment also grew on the average at 12.94 per cent p.a. (4.39 times) and the growth was 10.17 times (18.93 per cent p.a.) in the value of average annual production (Figure 3.3). Among number of persons employed, investment in fixed assets, and value of annual production, there was more variation in value of annual production 59 per cent as compared to the other two.
4. Uneducated/educated people in the State cannot be provided employment, if, in the long run the growth in registration of new industries remains at 8.43 per cent p.a. coupled with FTAB.
5. Productivity of labour first increased from 1987-88 to 1995-96 and then declined. It is a striking fact that productivity of fixed assets invested is very low (average annual turnover Rs. 2.32 against each rupee of investment in fixed assets), which first increased upto 1994-95 and declined since then. Decline in percentage plan money spent on promotion of industry in the State since 1990-91 signifies decreasing patronization of State (Figure 3.4). Though, total plan expenditure has increased at 12.84 per cent p.a. over the period, but, the proportion of it spent on promotion of industry in the State including public sector (3.66 per cent p.a.) was less and registered a negative growth of 3.35 per cent p.a. Among investment per unit and number of employees per unit, there was more variability in former (0.24) than later (0.22). This signifies that investment pattern in SSIs of Mizoram was not consistent. Similarly, among production per unit, production per employee, and production per rupee of fixed assets, variation in production per unit (0.38) was more than variation in the other two.

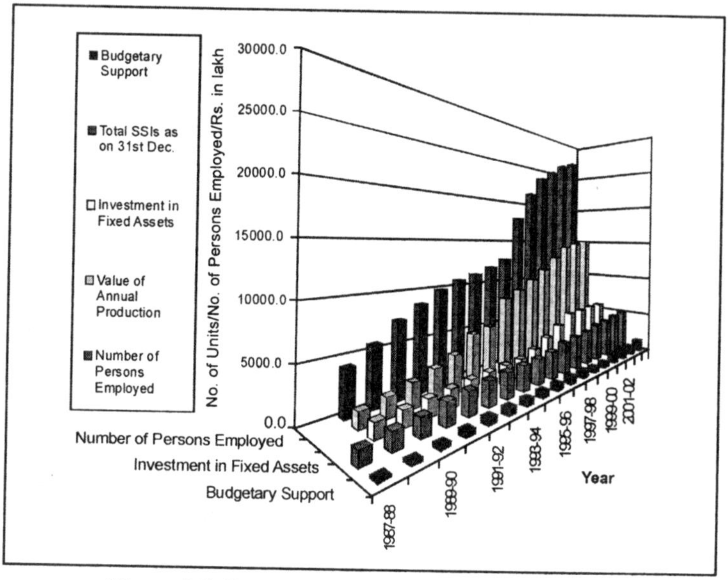

Figure 3.3: Pattern of Industrial Growth in Mizoram from 1986-87 to 2002-03

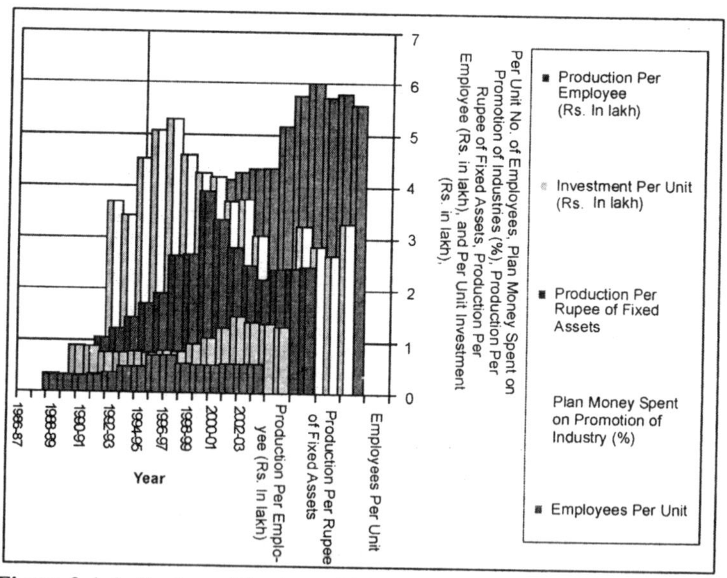

Figure 3.4: Indicators of Registered SSIs (SIDO) Performance in Mozoram from 1986-87 to 2002-03

Pearson's coefficient of correlation between certain variables of SSIs along with Student's test results were computed from base Table 3.5 and are given in Table 3.6.

Table 3.6 reveals that there is a significantly high degree positive correlation (r = 0.897) between budgetary support and total number of registered SSIs, which is significant at 1 per cent level of significance (Student's t-test). Budgetary support alone explains 80 per cent of variation in numerical growth of SSIs in the State. Similarly, coefficient of correlation, between budgetary support and investment in fixed assets (r = 0.725) was high degree positive, between budgetary support and annual value of production (r = 0.818) high degree positive are all significant at 1 per cent level of significance. There is a significant high degree positive correlation (r = 0.993) at 1 per cent level of significance between number of registered SSI units and number of persons employed. Number of SSIs alone explained 98.5 per cent variation in number of industrial jobs provided. Similarly, significant high degree positive correlation at 1 per cent level of significance is noticed between number of SSIs and investment in fixed assets (r = 0.967) and between number of SSIs and value of annual production (r = 0.978). But, there is a big question mark on their sustainability in the long-run as there has been a down fall in labour productivity (from 0.73 lakh in 1995-96 to 0.56 lakh in 2001-02), fixed assets productivity (Rs. 3.91 p.a. in 1994-95 to Rs. 2.45 p.a. in 2001-02) and budgetary support from the government (5.28 per cent in 1990-91 to 3.28 per cent in 2002-03). This is also evident from the fact that nearly 43.91 per cent of registered SSIs have turned sick. There is a need to reverse the trend immediately.

The above analyses clearly indicated that for faster industrial growth increasing budgetary support in the form of incentives and subsidy is must.

However, there was moderate correlation between budgetary support and investment per unit (r = 0.527) and was not significant at 1 per cent level of significance (Student's t-test). This showed that the budgetary support does not result in an increase in per unit investment, perhaps because of writing off of annual losses in public sector, and either withdrawal of benefits/incentives/subsidy by private entrepreneurs or keeping invested in the form of working capital rather than investing in fixed assets, technological upgradation, improved methods of production, etc. The investment per unit did not affect production per employee, may be because investment per unit does not necessarily mean investment for technological advancement, improvement in methods of production, etc.

Table 3.6: Pearson's Coefficient of Correlation between Certain Variables of SSIs in Mizoram from 1986-87 to 2002-03

Pearson's coefficient of correlation	*n*	*r*	r^2	*SE*	*t-value*	*t-value at 1per cent*	*Remarks*
Between budgetary support and total number of SSIs	17	0.897	0.804	0.048	7.8457	2.947	Significant
Between budgetary support and investment in fixed assets	15	0.725	0.525	0.123	3.7903	3.012	Significant
Between budgetary support and annual value of production	15	0.818	0.669	0.090	5.1265	3.012	Significant
Between total number of SSIs and No. of persons employed	15	0.993	0.985	0.004	29.669	3.012	Significant
Between total number of SSIs and Investment in Fixed Assets	15	0.967	0.935	0.017	13.731	3.012	Significant
Between total number of SSIs and value of annual production	15	0.978	0.957	0.011	16.962	3.012	Significant
Between budgetary support and Investment per unit	15	0.527	0.278	0.186	2.2371	3.012	Not Significant
Between investment in fixed assets and annual value of Production	15	0.951	0.904	0.020	11.085	3.012	Significant

Source: Compiled from Table 3.5

Category-wise SSIs (SIDO) of the State

The category-wise classification of registered SSIs (SIDO) as on 31st December 2001 and 2002 is given in Table 3.7 and Figure 3.5.

It may be seen from Table 3.7 and Figure 3.5 that there was no major change in category-wise number of industries from 31st December 2001 to 31st December 2002. The largest number of industries were service based industries (25.86 per cent) comprising of restaurants and hotels, education, scientific and research services, medical and health services, personal services, repair services and others, followed by apart from miscellaneous category, wood and wooden products (14.75 per cent), metal products and parts (12.44 per cent), textiles and textile goods (9.61 per cent), food products and allied industries (9.59 per cent).

Table 3.7: Category-wise Classification of SSIs (SIDO) in Mizoram
As on 31st December 2001 and 2002

Category	*2001*		*2002*	
	Number	*Percent*	*Number*	*Percent*
Food Products & Allied Industries	437	9.16	477	9.59
Wood & Wooden Industries	706	14.79	734	14.75
Textile & Textile Goods	454	9.51	478	9.61
Paper, Publishing & Allied Products	303	6.35	310	6.23
Rubber, Plastics, etc.	85	1.78	87	1.75
Chemicals & its Products	11	0.23	11	0.22
Non-Metallic & Mineral Products	25	0.52	26	0.52
Basic Metal & Allied Industries	Nil	-	Nil	-
Metal Products & Parts	594	12.45	619	12.44
Leather Goods & Repairing	19	0.40	21	0.42
Service Based Industries	1225	25.67	1287	25.86
Miscellaneous	914	19.15	926	18.61
Total	4773	100.00	4976	100.00

Source: Compiled from data obtained from Directorate of Industries Government of Mizoram, Aizawl.

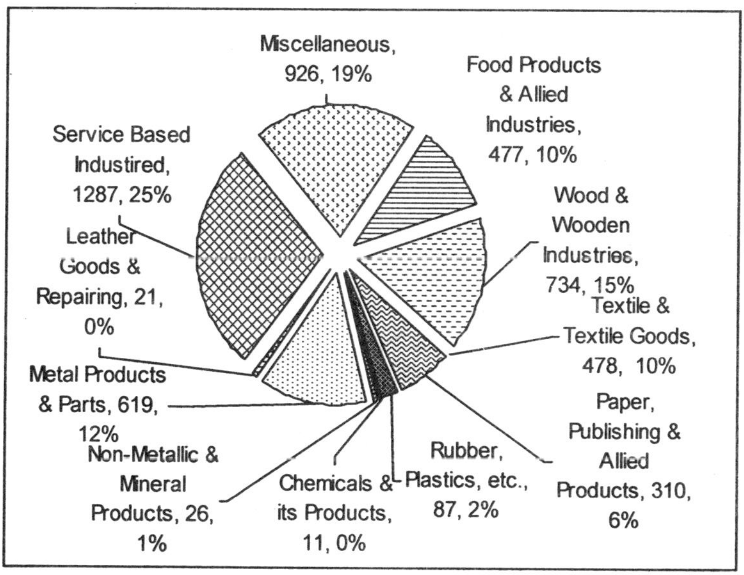

Figure 3.5: Category-wise Classification of SSIs (SIDO) in Mizoram as on 31st December 2002

Comparison of SSIs in Mizoram with NER States

The position regarding registered SSI units in all states of Northeastern region during 1996 to 2001 is given in Table 3.8 and Figure 3.6.

Table 3.8: Number of Registered SSI in Different States of NE Region From 1996 to 2001

State	*1996*	*1997*	*1998*	*1999*	*2000*	*2001*	*Growth (%)*
Arunachal	525	1200	2280	3358	4478	4520	53.95
Pradesh	(2.0)	(3.2)	(6.4)	(8.6)	(10.5)	(10.2)	(6.8)
Assam	12805	18367	20035	21514	23132	23637	11.56
	(47.7)	(49.0)	(56.5)	(55.4)	(54.1)	(53.5)	(52.7)
Manipur	4059	5034	5188	5578	5829	6000	7.30
	(15.1)	(13.4)	(14.6)	(14.4)	(13.6)	(13.6)	(14.1)
Meghalaya	1368	1977	2079	2229	2514	2621	12.24
	(5.1)	(5.3)	(5.9)	(5.7)	(5.9)	(5.9)	(5.6)
Mizoram	2478	2880	3466	3677	4028	4333	11.66
	(9.2)	(7.7)	(9.8)	(9.5)	(9.4)	(9.8)	(9.2)
Nagaland	615	731	749	779	813	982	8.01
	(2.3)	(1.9)	(2.1)	(2.0)	(1.9)	(2.2)	(2.1)
Tripura	4967	7311	1657	1697	1949	2114	-20.92
	(18.5)	(19.5)	(4.7)	(4.4)	(4.6)	(4.8)	(9.4)
Total	26817	37500	35454	38832	42743	44207	8.90
	(100)	(100)	(100)	(100)	(100)	(100)	100.00

Note: Figures in parenthesis represent percentage of total.
Source: Basic Statistics of NER, 2002, NEC Secretariat, Govt. of India, Shillong, p. 211.

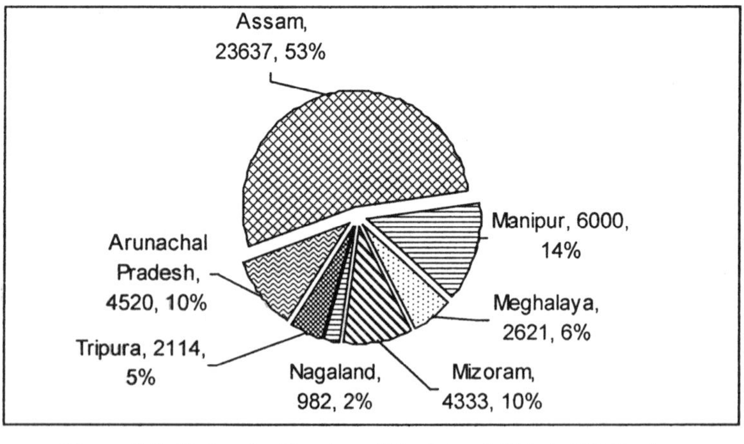

Figure 3.6: State-wise Number of Registered SSIs in NE Region during 2001

From the Table 3.8, it is clear that from 1996 to 2001, on the average 9.2 per cent of total units existed in Mizoram which was higher than Meghalaya (5.6 per cent), Nagaland (2.1 per cent), and Tripura (9.4 per cent). On the average the number of SSI units in the Northeastern region grew at 8.90 per cent p.a., In Mizoram this growth at 11.66 per cent p.a. was higher than that of Manipur (7.30 per cent p.a.), Nagaland (8.01 per cent p.a.), and Tripura, which registered a negative growth of 20.92 per cent p.a.

Some principal characteristics of SSI units of Northeastern region as on 31st March 1998 are given in Table 3.9.

Table 3.9 revealed that production per rupee of fixed investment in Mizoram at Rs. 1.06 was lowest in whole Northeastern region and even lesser than one fourth of national average of Rs. 4.65. When compared with the ratio of in-plant machinery to fixed investment, this ratio in Mizoram (33.93 per cent) was next lowest to Manipur (32.19 per cent) in whole Northeastern region. Further, it was much less than the all India average of 56.92 per cent. This showed that only one-third of total investment was made in fixed assets in Mizoram, which is less and the units seemed basically trading concerns more rather than industry in nature.

Table 3.9: Principal Characteristics of SSIs in Northeastern Region (as on 31st March 1998)

State	No. of Units	Employment (in Number)	Fixed Investment (Rs. in lakh)	In-plant Machinery (Rs. in lakh)	Production (Rs. in lakh)	Production Per Rupee of Investment (Rs.)	In-plant Machinery to Fixed Investment (%)
Arunachal Pradesh	326	2771	703	395	2624	3.3260	56.19
Assam	4430	34475	9369	5168	30235	3.2271	55.16
Manipur	2078	10216	2078	669	2988	1.4379	32.19
Meghalaya	587	3780	888	478	2700	3.0405	53.83
Mizoram	917	4223	1388	471	1470	1.0591	33.93
Nagaland	183	3059	729	489	11247	15.4280	67.08
Tripura	809	10069	1479	571	2957	1.9993	38.61
All India	582368	3665810	929603	554258	4321907	4.6492	59.62

Source : Basic Statistics of NER, 2002, NEC Secretariat, Govt. of India, Shillong, p. 211.

The position regarding sick industries of Northeastern region as on 31st March 1998 and sick industries in Mizoram as on 18th June 2001 is presented in Tables 3.10 and 3.11.

Table 3.10: State-wise Sick Industrial Units in Northeastern Region (As on 31st March 1998)

NE states	*No. of SSIs*		*Sickness (per cent)*
	Sick	*Total*	
Arunachal	36	362	9.94
Assam	1732	6162	28.10
Manipur	169	2247	7.52
Meghalaya	136	723	18.81
Mizoram	306	1223	25.02
Nagaland	83	266	31.20
Tripura	603	1412	42.70
NE region	3065	12395	24.72
All India	301390	883758	34.10

Source: Basic Statistics of North-East Region, 2002, p. 212.

From Table 3.10 sickness in SSI units of Mizoram was 25.02 per cent (306 units out of 1223 units) as on 31st March 1998, which increased to 43.91 per cent (Table 3.11) as on 18th June, 2001. It was higher than the all India average (34.10 per cent) reflecting the poor state of health of the existing industries in spite of all the incentives by the State. Further, the Table 3.10 revealed that as on 31st March 1998 the sickness in Mizoram (25.02 per cent) was higher than that of overall sickness (24.72 per cent) prevailed in whole North-East as well as Arunachal (9.94 per cent), Manipur (7.52 per cent), and Meghalaya (18.81 per cent). When compared with the ratio of increasing sickness with respective growth in number of SSIs in Northeastern region (Table 3.8), the situation seemed grimmer, may be these units were fake industries (on paper) only and flourished just to benefit from government's promotional schemes of incentives, subsidies, etc.

New District-wise SSIs

Since recently Aizawl district has been divided into five districts and Chhimtuipui into two districts, thereby, the Government organized the whole State into total eight districts. The position in respect of registered SSIs (SIDO) under new districts as on 31st March 2002 is given in Table 3.11 and Figure 3.7.

Table 3.11: District-wise Number of SSIs (SIDO) in Mizoram

District	31.12.2000	31.12.2001	31.12.2002	Sick units*
Aizawl	3706	3959	4053	1858
Champhai			7	
Kolasib			4	
Lawngtlai		89	97	
Lunglei	494	512	580	3
Mamit		6	12	
Saiha	290	202	216	111
Serchhip		3	7	
Total	4490	4770	4976	1972

* Declared on 18th June 2001.

Source: Directorate of Industries, Government of Mizoram, Aizawl.

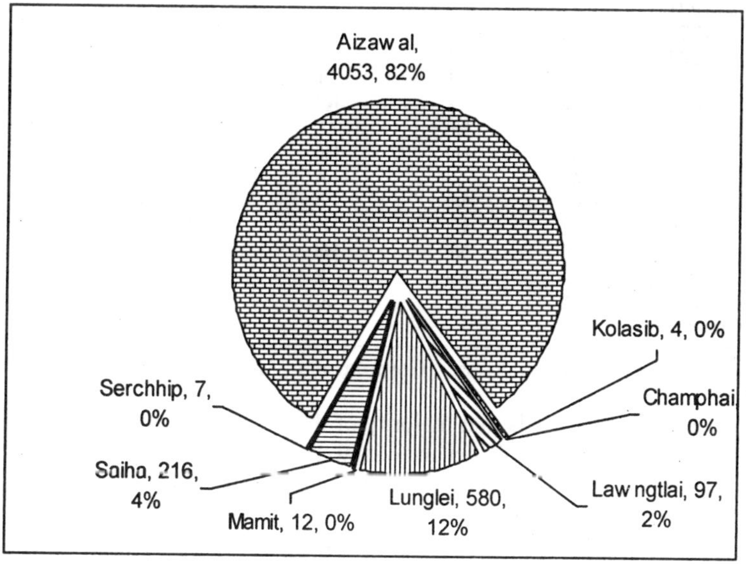

Figure 3.7: New District-wise Number of Registered SSIs (SIDO) in Mozoram as on 31st December 2002

Registered Small Scale Industries (Non-SIDO) of Mizoram

Non-SIDO industry means small scale unit producing items reserved for SSIs within maximum investment limits prescribed but processing or manufacturing manually (by hand) and not by mechanized way which could not be registered as SSI (SIDO). In Mizoram, the SSI (Non-SIDO) group mainly consisted of handloom units (making *puans*, shawls, etc.), cotton mills (making quilts, pillows and processing of raw cotton), small handicrafts and poultry, etc. These units on the average employed two to three persons but in most of the cases the owner alone managed the affairs. The position of registered SSI (Non-SIDO) in Mizoram is given in Table 3.12.

Table 3.12: Registered Small-Scale Industries (Non-SIDO) in Mizoram from 1989 to 2002

Year	*District-wise Registered SSIs*			*Total*	*Cumulative Total*
	Aizawl	*Lunglei*	*Chhimtuipui*		
Till 1989	388	13	Nil	401	401
1990	53	2	3	58	459
1991	21	4	4	29	488
1992	24	24	Nil	48	536
1993	17	1	1	19	555
1994	27	3	1	31	586
1995	42	1	Nil	43	629
1996	125	Nil	12	137	766
1997	60	Nil	Nil	60	826
1998	45	3	4	52	878
1999	47	Nil	3	50	928
2000	50	Nil	Nil	50	978
2001	6	Nil	Nil	6	984
2002	10	Nil	2	12	996
Total	915	51	30		996
Growth (%)					7.72

Source: Directorate of Industries, Government of Mizoram, Aizawl.

Table 3.12 reveals that majority of the non-SIDO units (91.87 per cent) existed in Aizawl district and rests were spread over the other districts of the State, 5.12 per cent units in Lunglei and 3.01 per cent units in Chhimtuipui district. Further, the Table 3.12 revealed that the average annual growth in number of registered SSIs (non-SIDO) over the years was 7.72 per cent. There was no consistency in the registration of SSIs from 1989 to 2002 and even in some years there was no registration in districts other than Aizawl.

Among SIDO and Non-SIDO units existed in the State, barring three or four were tiny units with investment less than Rs.10 lakh.

Village and Rural Industries under Mizoram *Khadi* & Village Industries Board (MKVIB)

Mizoram *Khadi* & Village Industries Board (MKVIB) was constituted in 1982 became functional from 14th June 1985 under the guidelines of *Khadi* and Village Industries Commission (KVIC), Government of India, Mumbai. Out of 119 industries specified by the KVIC, MKVIB presently promoting 23 trades from village industries group and 2 from *khadi* group by way of extending finance in the form of loans and grants and motivating entrepreneurs by way of giving them training. It also offers its all services to cooperatives, institutional and departmental projects besides individual projects (sole proprietorship). The total number of units registered and financed by MKVIB was 5772 upto 31st March 2001 of which 7 units were from *khadi* segment and the rests were from village industry segment. The maximum financing limit is of Rs.10 lakh for individuals and Rs.25 lakh for institutions and cooperatives.

A multi-disciplinary training centre was setup in Aizawl to train the entrepreneurs in the field of carpentry, soap making, bee keeping, cane works and oil extraction. The period of training courses varies from trade to trade. Besides, it maintains two production units viz., Community *Gur* Centre, Saitual and Khandsari Unit, Saitual and also maintains three Sales Emporiums, one each at Aizawl, Lunglei and Lawngtlai. It finances its own production units, training centre and sales emporiums. Since 1992-93, it has become a channelising agency for disbursing loans from National Scheduled Caste and Scheduled Tribe Finance and Development Corporation (NSFDC).

Village and Small Industries (VSI)

The position as regards *khadi* & village industries sponsored by MKVIB during 1985-86 to 2000-01 is given in Table 3.13.

Table 3.13 revealed that *khadi* and village industries grew from 10 units in 1985-86 to 5772 units in 2000-01 registering an average annual growth of 32.42 per cent p.a. Among these, *khadi* segment was not given due emphasis as there was negligible growth in number of cotton *khadi* units and negative growth of silk *khadi* units. The whole focus was centred round the development of village industries in Mizoram. Within village industries, greater emphasis was given to bakery and *masala* trade (1048 units) which grew at 35.48 per cent p.a. followed by carpentry and blacksmithy trade (916 units) at 28.13 per cent p.a., *gur* and *khandsari* trade (768 units) at 33.94 per cent p.a., service sector (704 units) at 23.52 per cent p.a., textile trade (653 units) at 19.18 per cent p.a., leather (255 units) at 14.32 per cent p.a., electronics (224 units), lime (213 units), cane and bamboo (188 units), pottery (160 units), fruit and vegetable preservation (122 units) and village oil (101 units). No growth was seen in match box, rubber/plastic, *polyvastra* and *gramshilpa*.

Table 3.13: Cottage, Tiny, Small and Village Industrial Units in Mizoram Assisted by Mizoram Khadi and Village Industries Board (MKVIB)
(During 1985-86 to 2000-01)

As on 31st March	*1986*	*1987*	*1988*	*1989*	*1990*	*1991*	*1992*	*1993*	*1994*	*1995*	*1996*	*1997*	*1998*	*1999*	*2000*	*2001*	*Growth*
Alluminium			8	15	24	39	42	42	52	76	76	77	77	77	77	77	16.09
Bee Keeping	1	42	77	117	141	194	203	272	356	53	53	58	58	59	60	60	6.11
Candle Making					5	17	17	17	17	30	30	46	47	47	47	47	18.68
Cane & Bamboo	1	21	43	74	114	154	164	180	196	164	164	178	178	182	188	188	21.84
Carpentry & Blacksmithy	1	91	184	270	387	503	586	678	793	728	728	867	874	891	916	916	28.13
Electronics						22	51	77	105	132	132	199	202	215	224	224	22.50
E & NCE				15	15	6	15	15	15	10	10	10	10	10	10	10	-2.63
Fibre	1	6	14	17	20	30	30	31	31	30	30	30	33	33	33	33	14.63
Fruit & Veg. Preservation	1		3	16	25	29	34	41	48	98	98	109	110	115	122	122	25.33
Gur & Khandsari		6	23	56	105	162	232	313	383	480	480	700	700	745	768	768	33.94
Gramshilpa	1	1	1	3	3	3	4	1	1	1	1	1	1	1	1	1	-3.93
Handmade Paper				1	6	13	17	25	35	54	54	96	97	116	123	123	39.88
Leather		21	44	84	122	171	191	221	221	224	224	239	239	249	255	255	14.32
Lime			8	14	29	34	44	63	88	127	127	170	174	196	213	213	27.48
Match Box				1	1	1	1	1	1	1	1	1	1	1	1	1	
NEO Soap	1	4	4	7	11	18	22	22	28	30	30	49	48	56	59	59	25.91
Pottery			5	16	26	38	48	52	52	71	71	122	131	142	160	160	24.64
Polyvastra			1	2	3	3	4	1	1	1	1	1	1	1	1	1	-6.82
P.C.P.I.(Bakery & Masala)	1	48	79	122	240	340	392	473	585	732	732	952	960	1003	1048	1048	35.48
Rubber/Plastic										1	1	1	1	1	1	1	
Service				38	92	164	229	297	410	512	512	650	660	697	704	704	23.52
Textile				54	133	207	251	308	408	499	499	639	639	648	653	653	19.18
Village Oil	1	9	19	31	46	69	79	86	89	98	98	100	101	101	101	101	22.42
Total	*9*	*249*	*513*	*953*	*1548*	*2217*	*2656*	*3216*	*3915*	*4152*	*4152*	*5295*	*5342*	*5586*	*5765*	*5765*	*32.79*
Khadi:																	
Cotton Khadi	1	1	2	4	5	5	6	6	7	4	4	5	5	5	5	5	8.42
Silk Khadi		1	2	7	8	6	7	7	7	2	2	2	2	2	2	2	-4.88
Total	1	2	4	11	13	11	13	13	14	6	6	7	7	7	7	7	5.74
Grand Total	10	251	517	964	1561	2228	2669	3229	3929	4158	4158	5302	5349	5593	5772	5772	32.42

Source: Compiled from Annual Reports from 1985-86 to 2000-01, Mizoram Khadi and Village Industries Board, Aizawl.

The proportion of defunct units was 7.86 per cent (327 out of 4158 units) as on 31.03.1996 came down to 2.89 per cent (167 out of 5772 units) as on 31.03.2001. Among defunct units majority units were from carpentry and black smithy (37 out of 916 units), service (29 out of 704 units), Bakery and *masala* (14 out of 1048 units) and *Gur* and *Khandsari* (15 out of 768 units), Textile (10 out of 653 units). The ratio of women beneficiaries was 27.29 per cent (1575 out of 5772 units) as on 31.03.2001 while it was 27.85 per cent (1477 out of 5302 units) as on 31.03.1997 has slightly declined. Of 5772 units, there were 3880 units in Aizawl (67.20 per cent), 544 in Lunglei (9.40 per cent), 438 in Champhai (7.40 per cent), 346 in Kolasib (6.00 per cent), 316 in Serchhip (5.80 per cent), 128 in Mamit (2.20 per cent), 81 in Lawngtlai (1.4 per cent) and 39 in Saiha (0.70 per cent) district.

Employment in VSI

The position as regards employment opportunities generated by the *khadi* and village industries sponsored by MKVIB is given in Table 3.14.

Table 3.14 revealed that the *khadi* and village industries as promoted by MKVIB together provided jobs (including part-time) to 15210 persons in 2000-01 from 'zero' in 1985-86. This showed an average annual growth in employment of 23.61 per cent p.a. People engaged in *khadi* segment quitted their occupation over the period. Among village industries, largest number of persons were employed in bakery and *masala* trade (2436) followed by carpentry and blacksmithy (2015), *gur* and *khandsari* (1753), textiles (1578), service segment (1520), pottery (904), lime (832), electronics (640), leather (610), handmade paper (570), candle making (429), cane and bamboo (409), soap making (378), fruit and vegetable preservation (353), aluminium (235), bee keeping (217), and village oil (195). On the average two to three part-time/full time workers are employed in these industries, but in majority cases, the industries are run and managed by the proprietor himself.

Industrial Policy

The first Industrial Policy of Mizoram was declared in 1989 with an objective of all-round development and gainful employment for local people and to create self-employment opportunities in the industry and allied sectors. The priority industries in it included agro and forest based industries, handloom and handicrafts, sericulture, electronic, village and cottage industries, consumer goods, etc.

Table 3.14: Persons Employed in Cottage, Tiny, Small & Village Industries in Mizoram Sponsored by Mizoram Khadi and Village Industries Board (During 1985-86 to 2000-01)

As on 31st March	*1986*	*1987*	*1988*	*1989*	*1990*	*1991*	*1992*	*1993*	*1994*	*1995*	*1996*	*1997*	*1998*	*1999*	*2000*	*2001*	*Growth*
Alluminium			8	14	56	115	123	180	180	219	211	224	225	231	235	235	23.51
Bee Keeping				35	206	220	256	230	216	198	183	198	199	205	214	217	5.44
Candle Making					10	42	44	55	60	42	42	102	408	426	429	429	36.87
Cane & Bamboo		20	40	100	182	220	246	260	240	288	291	350	374	390	402	409	18.06
Carpentry & Blacksmithy		135	756	282	1235	1440	1480	1650	1690	1270	1280	1574	1773	1905	1996	2015	13.50
Electronics						52	65	105	110	345	355	544	562	609	634	640	32.14
E & NCE						10		20	20	15	15	18	18	18	18	18	3.18
Fibre				8	24	60	80	90	85	57	60	68	68	74	78	78	11.00
Fruit & Veg. Preservation			5	6	122	140	135	155	166	241	288	322	329	336	353	353	30.71
Gur & Khandsari		20	57	155	170	330	340	450	460	788	876	1547	1592	1702	1748	1753	33.01
Gramshilpa										8	8	2	10	10	10	10	10.22
Handmade Paper					18	31	42	60	62	241	275	423	460	549	567	570	40.98
Leather		50	76	63	170	160	172	260	264	492	500	581	563	598	610	610	20.70
Lime			20	25	135	280	230	270	290	290	292	504	580	756	825	832	27.82
Match Box													1	1	1	1	
NEO Soap		6	8	24	53	42	55	90	86	179	181	323	323	361	376	378	34.06
Pottery			33	225	770	1050	1035	1180	530	150	165	732	792	837	897	904	11.16
Polyvastra											1	1					
P.C.P.I.(Bakery & Masala)		134	82	228	771	830	950	1155	1160	1381	1392	2169	2206	2306	2421	2436	23.99
Rubber/Plastic												1	1				
Service				38	165	330	420	530	540	782	833	1391	1418	1498	1512	1520	28.24
Textile				69	456	450	473	545	395	933	963	1479	1505	1548	1570	1578	22.05
Village Oil		10	35	55	84	165	178	180	210	135	145	162	177	195	195	195	15.21
Total (VSI)	0	375	1120	1327	4627	5967	6324	7465	6764	8054	8356	12715	13584	14555	15091	15181	24.21
Cotton Khadi		25	35	5	12	7	9	7	1	5	9	18	10	12	11	12	-2.10
Silk Khadi		25	45	15	12	10	10	10	20	17	20	20	20	21	17	17	-0.29
Total (Khadi)	0	50	80	20	24	17	19	17	21	22	29	38	30	33	28	29	-1.14
Grand Total	0	425	1200	1347	4651	5984	6343	7482	6785	8076	8385	12753	13614	14588	15119	15210	23.61

Source: Compiled from Annual Reports from 1985-86 to 2000-01, Mizoram Khadi and Village Industries Board, Aizawl.

The Policy, *inter alia,* laid stress on even development of all sectors by extending various types of support including institutional, organizational, marketing, infrastructure, and workforce apart from initiation to attract prospective entrepreneurs. This policy had forbidden non-Mizo to establish small-scale industries in the State. In medium and large-scale industries outside investment was permitted and that too through "joint and assisted sectors" only, because the policy made provision for setting up viable medium and large-scale industrial units through state owned corporations only. The incentives and subsidies included reimbursement of cost of project report, cost of land development, factory rent, manpower development, interest paid on borrowed loan, consumption of power for production, cost of drawal of power line, cost of power generating set, transportation cost of plant and machinery, price preference, exemption from sales tax, stamp duty and registration fee, equity participation by the State government in assisted sector, etc., in addition to central investment subsidy and central transport subsidy on transportation of raw materials. The policy provided that hotels, cinema halls and production of films were also entitled to these incentives, as tourism and films were also included in the list of industry.

In view of the continuing backwardness of the Northeastern region, the Government of India *vide* Notification No. EA/1/2/96—IDP dated 24th December 1997 announced the New Industrial Policy for the Northeastern region. Following this, the State also declared new "Industrial Policy of Mizoram, 2000" through which some new incentives besides maintaining the majority of the old incentives were offered to entrepreneurs in the State. However, exemptions like stamp duty and registration fee, equity participation in the assisted sector, incentives for hotels, cinema halls and films production were withdrawn. These are discussed in detail in following para under State Subsidies.

The New Industrial Policy, 2000 made a slight modification so far as investment by Non-Tribals is concerned. Keeping the interest of local entrepreneurs in mind, the policy permitted outside industrialists in joint ventures on selective basis. In case of SSIs where investment in plant and machinery exceeding Rs.50 lakh made open for outside entrepreneurs in joint ventures with local entrepreneurs. It also provided that some joint ventures by Non-Tribals from outside the State can be started with State owned public sector undertakings. The only condition to the above is non-supervisory and non-technical employments are to be kept reserved for local Mizo and in case of technical employments, preference should be given to local talents. Further, Non-Tribals holding permanent trade licence cannot recruit more than 3 non-indigenous employees for the purpose of carrying on his/her business as managers, attendants[15], etc. Furthermore, presently there is no provision for issuing "permanent trade licence" to Non-Tribals. Those Non-Tribals holding permanent trade licence issued by the erstwhile Mizo District Council also cannot have Inner-Line Pass (ILP) for more than 3 years at a time and the same is renewable by 1 year at a time. These restrictions coupled with other problems like complicated 'inner-line' regulations where there is no provision for issuing permanent inner-line pass, etc. discouraged industrialists from outside the State to invest in the State.

State Subsidies

Apart from financing of industry by the State and financial institutions, a variety of subsidies and incentives are also given. This included grants and subsidies to artisans and village level entrepreneurs, central investment subsidy, state investment subsidy, project report subsidy, power subsidy and state/central transport subsidy, etc.

Village level artisans and entrepreneurs who are not in a position to provide the security for the loans, etc. are covered under grants-in-aid/ subsidies. Interest subsidy is given to entrepreneurs borrowing funds from commercial banks. Central investment subsidy was given towards the investment in plant and machinery etc. which has now been replaced by State investment subsidy for the purpose. Power and transport subsidy are given to offset the cost disadvantage on account of high cost of power, transport, etc.

Brief description of subsidies and incentives that are presently available to entrepreneurs in the State under the Industrial Policy of Mizoram, 2000 are as follows:

1. *Project Report Subsidy*: Those newly setup or existing industrial units that have already undertaken effective steps and had paid an amount to approved consultant for making project report are given this one time subsidy within a limit of 90 per cent of cost paid subject to maximum Rs. 5,000/- per unit in case of tiny units, 75 per cent subject to maximum Rs. 25,000/- per unit in case of small-scale service establishments and 50 per cent subject to maximum Rs. 50,000/- per unit in case of large and medium units.
2. *Land Development Subsidy*: Those units established within the area of industrial estates or industrial growth centres or declared

industrial areas are given this subsidy upto 25 per cent of lease fee paid on allotment of developed/undeveloped land for a period of 5 years or 25 per cent of cost of developing an undeveloped land allotted.

3. *Factory Rent Subsidy*: Newly established or existing (in case of expansion) tiny and small scale units on having established their plant within the industrial estates or industrial growth centres or declared industrial areas are eligible to claim this subsidy equal to 50 per cent of assessed factory rent subject to maximum Rs. 30,000/- per unit per year for a period of 5 years.
4. *Manpower Development Subsidy*: This subsidy is given to newly established or existing industrial units for sending their workers with prior approval from the Directorate, outside the State for upgradation of their managerial or technical skill from duly approved, licensed, and registered industrial units/institutions. The amount of subsidy is limited to 50 per cent of actual expenditure incurred in getting them trained subject to a maximum of Rs. 3,000/- per trainee with a ceiling of Rs. 25,000/- per unit per year. The only condition which must be satisfied is that the trained employees must remain in the service of industrial unit for a minimum period of 3 years.
5. *Interest Subsidy*: To bring entrepreneurs at par with those benefited by RIP loan facility, a new scheme 'interest subsidy' was introduced for the first time in 1978-79 whereby an entrepreneur was eligible to receive a subsidy equal to an amount of interest charged in excess of 5.5 per cent per annum by nationalized bank or financial institution. Since then it continued in one form or other with minor modification here and there. According to the first industrial policy of Mizoram 1989, the interest subsidy was available to entrepreneurs at 4 per cent of the amount of term loan as well as working capital loan from bank for a period of 5 years with no maximum and minimum ceiling.

   Presently, an industrial unit may claim this recurring subsidy for a period of 5 years from the date of commissioning of the unit at a maximum rate of 4 per cent over and above 8½ per cent of interest paid by it in time on term loan or working capital loan taken from financial institutions or banks subject to maximum Rs. 3,60,000/- in case of term loan and Rs. 1,20,000/- in case of working capital loan.

6. *Power Subsidy*: This is also a recurring subsidy and is given for a period of 5 years from the date of commencement of production on power consumed by an industrial enterprise in carrying out production. The subsidy is admissible at the rate of 60 per cent of total expenditure on power consumed in case of tiny and small-scale and ancillary units, 50 per cent in case of medium scale units and 30 per cent in case of large scale units.
7. *Subsidy on Drawal of Power Line*: An industrial entrepreneur may claim this one time subsidy at a rate of 50 per cent of actual expenditure incurred on drawal of power line from main power point to factory site subject to maximum Rs. 50,000/- per unit.
8. *Subsidy on Captive Power Generating Set*: An industrial unit which has installed a new captive power generating set purchased directly from manufacturer or dealer, may claim this one time subsidy at a rate of 50 per cent of the cost of generating set and installation charges paid subject to maximum Rs. 3,00,000/- per unit. However, this subsidy is also available on purchase of second hand power generating set, but, then its value is to be worked out on the basis of its remaining life and depreciated value.
9. *State Transport Subsidy on Plant and Machinery*: This is a one time subsidy and is admissible to newly or existing industrial units at rate of 50 per cent of actual cost of transportation incurred on movement of plant and machineries from the place of purchase to factory site by rail and/or road on approved rates.
10. *State Capital Investment Subsidy*: This is also a one time subsidy and is available to newly established or existing industrial units (in case of expansion or modernization or diversification) on investment made in plant and machinery at a rate of 15 per cent of cost to artisans and tiny units, 10 per cent of cost subject to maximum Rs. 5 lakh to small-scale units and 5 per cent of cost subject to maximum Rs. 10 lakh to medium scale units. For the units setup in thrust area, this subsidy is admissible at a higher rate of 20 per cent to artisans and tiny units, 15 per cent with extended ceiling of Rs. 7 lakh to small-scale units, and 10 per cent with extended ceiling of Rs. 15 lakh to medium scale units.
11. *Subsidy on Registration with Promotion Council, etc.*: An industrial unit on obtaining a registration from recognized promotion council, commodity board, chamber of commerce,

etc. may claim reimbursement of actual registration expenses (fee) subject to maximum Rs. 20,000/- only.

12. *Subsidy on ISO Certification*: An industrial unit on obtaining a certification from International Standard Organization (ISO) or Bureau of Indian Standard (ISI) for its products may claim reimbursement of 100 per cent of expenses incurred by it on registration fee, testing fee, purchase of testing equipments, etc. subject to maximum Rs. 50,000/- only. However, this ceiling is of Rs. 1,00,000/- for units in thrust area.
13. *Additional Capital Investment Subsidy*: This is in addition to State Capital Investment Subsidy and is available to 100 per cent Export Oriented Units (EOU) at a rate of 5 per cent of investment in plant and machinery subject to maximum Rs. 5 lakh. However, for units less than 100 per cent EOU, this subsidy is available at a rate of 2 per cent with a maximum ceiling of Rs. 2 lakh.
14 *Tax Cuts*: This benefit is available to a newly setup industrial unit in the form of exemption from paying state sales tax for a period of 7 years from the date of commencement of actual commercial production. However, for units in thrust area the period of sales tax exemption is extended to 10 years.
    Besides, the units are also exempted from paying central sales tax and central excise duty under various notifications issued from time to time by Government of India in this regard.
15. *Price Preference*: Mizoram Preferential Stores Purchase Rules, 1986 were replaced by new Mizoram Preferential Stores Purchase Rules, 1994 broadening the coverage. According to these rules, while making purchase the Government departments and Government controlled organizations give preference to products manufactured by local industrial units registered with District Industries Centre (DIC) or Directorate of Industries or Mizoram *Khadi* and Village Industries Board (MKVIB). Further these units are immune from paying (depositing) earnest money and/or security deposits.
16. *Central Investment Subsidy*: To ensure balanced regional development, the Government of India had announced financial incentives for industries established in selected backward districts/areas at a rate of 10 to 15 per cent on fixed capital investment, which was in addition to the existing incentives that

were being offered by the respective State/U.T. Governments. Later, with effect from 24th December 1997, it was converted into Central Capital Investment Subsidy on Plant and Machinery at 15 per cent of cost invested in Plant and Machinery.

As the Government of India had declared whole of the Mizoram a backward area, all the industrial units setup on or after 1st October, 1970 were eligible to claim this one time subsidy. But, the scheme in Mizoram was dormant till 1977-78 as no body claimed it. Till the closure of the scheme a total number of 63 SSI units comprising 46 from Aizawl and 17 from Lunglei benefited with total disbursement of Rs. 5.50 lakh. Of the SSIs benefited, only 10 (8 from Aizawl and 2 from Lunglei) had investment above Rs. 1.0 lakh.

17. *Central Transport Subsidy*: As the State is not served by Railway the entrepreneurs have to bear additional hardship in the form of paying high transportation cost on purchase of raw materials and sale of finished goods. Keeping this in view, the Central Government decided to compensate the entrepreneurs for such an additional transport cost. This subsidy is available to an industrial enterprise in the form of reimbursement at a rate of 90 per cent of transportation charges incurred on industrial raw material from notified railway station to the location of the enterprise and similarly at the same rate on transportation cost incurred for dispatch of finished goods from place of enterprise to notified railway station.

Public Sector in Industry

Both the industrial policies of Mizoram envisaged development of large and medium scale industries under public sector only and consequent upon this, it became the duty of the State government to setup some lead industries which may encourage quick ancillarisation occupying the position of role model for private entrepreneurs. With this end, the Government of Mizoram had setup two industrial enterprises viz., MIFCO—a food processing industry and ZOHANDCO—a handloom and handicraft based industrial unit. For the purpose of knowing whether the PSUs achieved their objectives of incorporation, financial statement analysis is undertaken on the assumption that activities, working, performances, etc. of Corporations' are well reflected to a great extent in figures as are shown in their respective annual reports.

The Mizoram Handloom and Handicrafts Development Corporation Limited (ZOHANDCO)

Mizoram Handloom and Handicrafts Development Corporation Ltd. (ZOHANDCO) was incorporated on 20th December 1988 to promote, develop and protect the interests of handloom and handicrafts units, apart from extending assistance in procurement and sale of quality raw material at reasonable rates. It is a 100 per cent State Government owned company with paid up equity share capital of Rs. 604.20 lakh as on 31st March 2003. It is provided with budgetary support in the form of grant-in-aid from time to time, which was Rs. 16 lakh for 2002-03. Its main activities are to develop, aid, advise, assist, finance, protect and promote interest of handloom and handicraft units in the State, whether owned by the Government, or Statutory Body, or company, or firm or individuals and to provide them with capital, means of credit resources, technical and managerial assistance for the conduct of their process of manufacturing, management, marketing, technique of production, etc. In spite of government support, it was running into losses.

In the light of its weak financial position, the Corporation is concentrating its energy towards supply of adequate handloom raw materials[16]. To explore the talents of local weavers and artisans, training is conducted at various places with the help of resource persons from outside the State. To improve and upgrade the quality of handloom products and designs in Mizoram, a Computer Aided Textile Design Centre (CATD) with assistance from the Government of India was setup. To enhance production of bulk quantity of high quality handloom products at low cost, it has installed Semi Automatic Looms at Zuangtui Industrial Complex. Setting up of marketing complexes at strategic locations in four district headquarters is envisaged. It is planned that the stalls in these complexes be mode available weavers and crafts persons on day-to-day hire basis.

The financial statements of ZOHANDCO for the period from 1989-90 to 2001-02 were compiled for financial analysis that is given in Table 3.15, which revealed the following:

1. The profitability as reflected by the return on investment has been negative throughout the period from 11.95 per cent in 1991-92 to 48.27 per cent in 2001-02. On the average the corporation lost Rs. 29.45 annually on Rs. 100/- invested for the reason being high cost of raw materials consumed. The cost exceeded the turnover during the period from 1996-97 to

Table 3.15: Abridged Annual Accounts and Important Financial Ratios of the Mizoram Handloom and Handicrafts Development Corporation Ltd. (ZOHANDCO) from 1989-90 to 2001-02.

(Rs. in lakh)

Sl. No.	*Balance Sheet Year*	*Balances as on 31st March*													
		1990	*1991*	*1992*	*1993*	*1994*	*1995*	*1996*	*1997*	*1998*	*1999*	*2000*	*2001*	*2002*	*Growth (%)*
	Sources of Funds:														
1.	Share Capital	44.50	126.50	126.50	234.70	264.70	294.70	324.70	361.70	386.70	391.70	416.70	456.70	506.70	*16.81*
2.	Share Capital Contribution	Nil	Nil	57.70	Nil	30.00	30.00	30.00	30.00	30.00	70.00	80.00	85.00	90.00	*10.44*
3.	Reserves & Surplus	0.30	3.31	2.37	6.37	2.34	2.34	2.34	2.34	2.34	2.34	2.34	2.34	2.34	*4.23*
4.	Deferred Govt. Grants	Nil	Nil	23.02	15.34	Nil	Nil	Nil	Nil	Nil	Nil	Nil	Nil	Nil	
5.	Miscellaneous Expenses	6.97	17.76	30.39	48.95	86.16	120.68	154.40	208.25	258.93	301.55	352.93	386.06	428.52	*37.62*
6.	Retained Earnings (3+4-5)	-6.67	-14.45	-5.00	-27.24	-83.82	-118.34	-152.06	-205.91	-256.59	-299.21	-350.59	-383.72	-426.18	*-38.09*
7.	Owner's Equity (1+2+6)	37.83	112.05	179.20	207.46	210.88	206.36	202.64	185.79	160.11	162.49	146.11	157.98	170.52	*4.81*
8.	Debt	Nil	Nil	22.30	24.78	5.00	Nil	Nil	Nil	Nil	Nil	Nil	Nil	Nil	
9.	*Capital Employed (7+8)*	*37.83*	*112.05*	*201.50*	*232.24*	*215.88*	*206.36*	*202.64*	*185.79*	*160.11*	*162.49*	*146.11*	*157.98*	*170.52*	*0.00*
	Application of Funds														
10.	Fixed Assets	10.01	13.25	14.80	20.63	29.83	97.20	101.44	102.87	119.36	117.94	118.59	120.24	138.46	*26.77*
11.	Depreciation	0.94	2.64	4.36	6.53	7.68	12.76	19.26	23.44	31.38	37.02	42.84	48.20	54.45	*36.51*
12.	Net Block (10-11)	9.07	10.61	10.44	14.10	22.15	84.44	82.18	79.43	87.98	80.92	75.75	72.04	84.01	*23.76*
13.	Capital Work in Process	Nil	Nil	40.66	59.29	69.29	Nil	Nil	5.32	Nil	Nil	Nil	Nil	Nil	
14.	Total Fixed Assets (12+13)	9.07	10.61	51.10	73.39	91.44	84.44	82.18	84.75	87.98	80.92	75.75	72.04	84.01	*14.55*
15.	Investments	Nil	Nil	Nil	Nil	Nil	Nil	Nil	Nil	Nil	0.50	0.50	16.90	0.50	
16.	Cash & Bank Balances	19.95	64.16	95.62	92.38	42.16	27.87	59.10	21.79	4.12	19.82	27.56	22.76	31.97	*-8.84*
17.	Sundry Debtors	1.22	1.45	3.60	8.35	13.41	20.82	17.80	18.76	14.96	14.31	14.01	14.64	16.67	*20.82*
18.	Loans & Advances	0.91	14.23	3.09	7.91	7.36	2.02	2.56	15.63	20.40	22.99	11.41	18.40	25.73	*20.44*
19.	Other Current Assets	0.07	0.12	Nil	Nil	9.20	13.85	5.42	2.90	4.52	8.95	11.20	10.40	10.40	*45.21*
20.	Liquid Assets (16+17+18+19)	22.15	79.96	102.31	108.64	72.13	64.56	84.88	59.08	44.00	66.07	64.18	66.20	84.77	*1.48*
21.	Inventories	9.04	22.88	50.05	53.38	60.99	70.20	60.60	57.19	43.08	36.57	40.84	39.42	37.07	*4.69*
22.	Current Assets (20+21)	31.19	102.84	152.36	162.02	133.12	134.76	145.48	116.27	87.08	102.64	105.02	105.62	121.84	*2.48*
23.	Current Liabilities	2.43	1.40	1.96	3.17	8.68	12.84	25.02	15.23	14.95	21.57	35.16	36.58	35.83	*32.36*
24.	Working Capital (22-23)	28.76	101.44	150.40	158.85	124.44	121.92	120.46	101.04	72.13	81.07	69.86	69.04	86.01	*-0.94*
25.	*Funds Employed* (14+15+24)	*37.83*	*112.05*	*201.50*	*232.24*	*215.88*	*206.36*	*202.64*	*185.79*	*160.11*	*162.49*	*146.11*	*157.98*	*170.52*	*4.32*

(Contd.)

(Contd.)

Sl. No.	Income Statement / Year	1990	1991	1992	1993	1994	1995	1996	1997	1998	1999	2000	2001	2002	Growth
		for the year ended 31st March													
1.	Turnover	3.24	18.23	32.29	46.83	59.34	54.67	46.78	41.26	34.33	22.03	28.27	23.01	19.59	*4.37*
2.	Raw Materials Purchased	11.64	30.05	56.26	46.94	67.46	62.25	36.93	39.50	24.68	18.11	36.01	23.81	22.54	*-2.34*
3.	Decrease(+)/Increase(-) in Stocks	-9.04	-13.84	-27.17	-3.33	-9.41	-9.21	9.60	3.41	14.11	6.51	-4.27	1.42	2.35	*25.22*
4.	Raw Materials Consumed (2+3)	2.60	16.21	29.09	43.61	58.05	53.04	46.53	42.91	38.79	24.62	31.74	25.23	24.89	*7.63*
5.	Wages	0.56	1.09	0.58	Nil	1.99	14.29	17.40	5.40	6.02	5.85	Nil	8.10	6.87	*25.07*
6.	Gross Profit (1-4+5)	0.08	0.93	2.62	3.22	-0.70	-12.66	-17.15	-7.05	-10.48	-8.44	-3.47	-10.32	-12.17	*-9.08*
7.	Personnel Cost	3.44	6.42	9.33	15.01	12.20	3.94	5.04	21.82	24.98	24.84	64.51	35.19	35.96	*21.19*
8.	Admin., Selling & Dist. Cost	3.32	6.95	10.31	16.44	25.11	19.67	19.77	24.18	16.31	23.80	Nil	19.41	24.91	*12.42*
9.	*Operating Profit Before Depreciation (OPBD) (6-7+8)*	*-6.68*	*-12.44*	*-17.02*	*-28.23*	*-38.01*	*-36.27*	*-41.96*	*-53.05*	*-51.77*	*-57.08*	*-67.98*	*-64.92*	*-73.04*	*-34.35*
10.	Depreciation	0.91	1.70	1.72	2.16	2.49	5.07	6.51	6.45	8.03	6.99	5.82	5.36	6.24	*16.81*
11.	*Operating Profit (OF) (9-10)*	*-7.59*	*-14.14*	*-18.74*	*-30.39*	*-40.50*	*-41.34*	*-48.47*	*-59.50*	*-59.80*	*-64.07*	*-73.80*	*-70.28*	*-79.28*	*-34.96*
12.	Other Income	1.21	3.35	6.27	14.51	6.45	7.41	14.06	14.06	9.12	20.89	22.23	37.14	36.83	*24.59*
13.	*Profit Before Interest & Tax (PBIT) (11+12)*	*-6.38*	*-10.79*	*-12.47*	*-15.88*	*-34.05*	*-33.93*	*-34.41*	*-45.44*	*-50.68*	*-43.18*	*-51.57*	*-33.14*	*-42.45*	*-27.28*
14.	Interest	Nil	Nil	0.19	2.29	0.01	0.28	Nil	Nil	Nil	Nil	Nil	Nil	Nil	
15.	*Profit Before / After Tax (PBT / PAT) (13-14)*	*-6.38*	*-10.79*	*-12.66*	*-18.17*	*-34.06*	*-34.21*	*-34.41*	*-45.44*	*-50.68*	*-43.18*	*-51.57*	*-33.14*	*-42.45*	*-27.19*
16.	Accumulated Losses of P.Y.	0.30	6.68	17.47	30.10	48.65	85.87	120.39	154.12	207.96	258.64	301.26	352.64	385.78	
17.	Prior Period Expenses	Nil	Nil	-0.03	0.38	3.16	0.31	-0.68	8.40	Nil	-0.56	-0.19	Nil	Nil	
18.	*Accumulated Profits (15-16-17)*	*-6.68*	*-17.47*	*-30.10*	*-48.65*	*-85.87*	*-120.39*	*-154.12*	*-207.96*	*-258.64*	*-301.26*	*-352.64*	*-385.78*	*-428.23*	*-37.97*

(Contd.)

(Contd.)

Sl No	Important Ratios / Year	*1990*	*1991*	*1992*	*1993*	*1994*	*1995*	*1996*	*1997*	*1998*	*1999*	*2000*	*2001*	*2002*	*Mean*
1.	Return on Investment	N.A.	-18.87	-11.95	-14.01	-18.08	-19.58	-23.70	-30.64	-34.58	-39.72	-47.83	-46.22	-48.27	*-29.45*
2.	Raw Material Consumed Ratio	80.25	88.92	90.09	93.12	97.83	97.02	99.47	104.00	112.99	111.76	112.27	109.65	127.05	*101.88*
3.	Wages to Sales Ratio	17.28	5.98	1.80	0.00	3.35	26.14	37.20	13.09	17.54	26.55	0.00	35.20	35.07	*16.86*
4.	Personnel Cost to Sales Ratio	106.17	35.22	28.89	32.05	20.56	7.21	10.77	52.88	72.76	112.76	228.19	152.93	183.56	*80.31*
5.	Admn. Exp. To Sales Ratio	102.47	38.12	31.93	35.11	42.32	35.98	42.26	58.60	47.51	108.03	0.00	84.35	127.16	*57.99*
6.	Operating Profit to Sales Ratio	-234.26	-77.56	-58.04	-64.89	-68.25	-75.62	-103.61	-144.21	-174.19	-290.83	-261.05	-305.43	-404.70	*-174.05*
7.	Net Profit Ratio (PAT to Sales)	-196.91	-59.19	-39.21	-38.80	-57.40	-62.58	-73.56	-110.13	-147.63	-196.01	-182.42	-144.02	-216.69	*-117.27*
8.	Capital Turnover	N.A.	0.24	0.21	0.22	0.26	0.26	0.23	0.21	0.20	0.14	0.18	0.15	0.12	*0.20*
9.	Fixed Assets Turnover Ratio	0.36	1.72	3.09	3.32	2.68	0.65	0.57	0.52	0.39	0.27	0.37	0.32	0.23	*1.11*
10.	Debtors Turnover Ratio	N.A.	13.66	12.79	7.84	5.45	3.19	2.42	2.26	2.04	1.51	2.00	1.61	1.25	*4.67*
11.	Inventory Turnover Ratio	N.A.	1.14	0.89	0.91	1.04	0.83	0.72	0.70	0.68	0.55	0.73	0.57	0.51	*0.77*
12.	Working Capital Turnover Ratio	0.11	0.18	0.21	0.29	0.48	0.45	0.39	0.41	0.48	0.27	0.40	0.33	0.23	*0.33*
13.	Current Ratio	12.84	73.46	77.73	51.11	15.34	10.50	5.81	7.63	5.82	4.76	2.99	2.89	3.40	*21.10*
14.	Acid Test Ratio	9.12	57.11	52.20	34.27	8.31	5.03	3.39	3.88	2.94	3.06	1.83	1.81	2.37	*14.26*
15.	Super Quick Ratio	8.21	45.83	48.79	29.14	4.86	2.17	2.36	1.43	0.28	0.92	0.78	0.62	0.89	*11.25*
16.	Average Collection Period (days)	N.A.	26.73	28.54	46.57	66.92	114.27	150.67	161.71	179.26	242.48	182.82	227.23	291.68	*78.21*
17.	Inventory Holding Period (days)	N.A.	319.55	412.19	403.07	351.74	437.94	510.28	521.01	533.04	659.83	499.73	636.57	712.58	*499.79*
18.	Fixed Assets to Net Tangible Worth	23.98	9.47	25.36	31.60	42.36	40.92	40.55	45.62	54.95	49.80	51.84	45.60	49.27	*39.33*

Legend: OPBD = Operating Profit before Depreciation, OP = Operating Profit, PBIT = Profit before Interest & Tax, PBT = Profit before Tax, PAT = Profit after Tax.

Source: Compiled from Annual Accounts of Mizoram Handlooms and Handicrafts Development Corporation Ltd. from 1989-90 to 2001-02.

2001-02 and increased continuously averaging at 101.88 per cent which is a cause of concern.

2. Another factor responsible for high negative return on investment has been low capital turnover, which was on the average at around 0.20 times over the period. It is further substantiated by equally low fixed assets turnover ratio at around 1.11 times, which deteriorated continuously since 1994-95 for a simple reason of addition of new fixed assets worth Rs. 67.33 lakh which is proved unproductive and did result neither in achieving additional sales nor attaining operational efficiency, a cause of concern. Similarly, working capital turnover (0.33) was significantly low throughout the period making it clear that the Corporation's working capital was lying idle and its management was not satisfactory.
3. Among the cost components, wages though fluctuated frequently for no reason grew at 25.07 per cent p.a. from 1989-90 to 2001-02. It was even 'zero' in some years. This indicated that its products had no demand and consequently it had to halt its production activities. The cost of personnel also, though fluctuated, registered an increase of 21.19 per cent p.a. and ranged from 7.21 per cent in 1994-95 to 228.19 per cent in 1999-2000 averaging at 80.31 per cent of sales. The employees still have a mindset of government department and are not willing to accept the existence of Corporation. Similarly the Corporation's administrative expenses were more than 100 per cent of sales in 1989-90, reduced considerably in 1990-91 and stabilized since then, with fluctuations in a narrow range till 1997-98, and then increased again even beyond turnover averaging at 58 per cent of sales. This cannot be regarded as satisfactory. In fact the cost components have been the major contributors to ever increasing operating losses of the Corporation. ZOHANDCO being a public sector organization, it is not possible for the management to control the cost of personnel and administrative expenses. Hence, the only option available is to raise the operating revenue, whatever way it may be possible.
4. As regards operational efficiency as revealed by activity ratios it may be opined that the management was not conscious of the practice of operational efficiency. The inventory turnover and debtors' turnover ratios at 1.14 times and 13.66 times respectively in 1990-91 came down to 0.51 times and 1.25 times in 2001-02. This resulted into further increase in an already high

inventory-holding period from 320 days in 1990-91 to 713 days in 2001-02 and increase in average collection period from 27 days in 1990-91 to 292 days in 2001-02. All this showed that the Corporation's inventory management and receivables management were poor. Short-term solvency as depicted by current ratio, acid test ratio and super quick ratio on the average at 21.10:1, 14.26:1 and 11.25:1 respectively together indicated Corporation's inability to utilize the working capital for productive purposes. These ratios were high to very high upto 1994-95 and then declined consistently and came down to normal level thereafter. This was due to current liabilities being negligible in first half as compared to second half.

5. The growth rate in capital employed and the corresponding growth rate in turnover over the period have been more or less the same. This indicated that the Corporation's line of operations are capital intensive, though it is really not so. The organization borrowed funds for three years only and that too small amounts from 1991-92 to 1993-94. Thus, it was not trading on equity.
6. Due to poor operating results the Government of Mizoram had to compensate for the growing deficit by providing subsidies, grants, etc., which had been taken by ZOHANDCO as its other income. The Corporation, however, is not covered by Sick Industries Companies Act, 1985, owing to regular flow of additional capital contribution from Government of Mizoram[17].
7. Several points were raised by auditors in their audit reports on the accounts of ZOHANDCO during the entire period of study. Some of the points are summarized below:

   (a) *Management Related Points*: (i) Cash balance lying with sales counters at different places, which were closed down were not remitted to headquarters, and were doubtful of recovery. (ii) Periodic physical verification of cash balance and stock was not done by the management at any point of time. Quantitative and qualitative details of stocks were not maintained. (iii) Norms for damages/wastages of goods-in-transit as well as raw materials and minimum and maximum stock levels were not fixed. (iv) System of identifying and disposal of non-moving, obsolete goods etc. did not exist. Loose inventory management existed as regards to receipts and issues of materials. (v) No mechanism existed for identifying idle labour hours and idle machine hours. Thus, poor internal control system prevailed. (vi) Annual General Meeting book, Directors' Register, and other Statutory Registers except for cashbook and ledger were not maintained. (vii) Permanent secretary u/s 383A of Companies Act did not exist.

(b) *Accounting Related Points*: (i) Neither, the fixed assets register was maintained properly nor the physical verification was done. (ii) Cost records were not maintained. (iii) Preparation of periodic trial balance was not in practice. (iv) Shortages of stocks were not adjusted. (v) Grant-in-Aid received to the extent of expenses/loss recognized as profit and the balance was carried as current liability. (vi) Reconciliation of bank and Inter-office accounts were not made. (vii) Advances to managing director were not shown separately. (viii) Classifying entire sundry debtors as well as loans and advances as secured and good was wrong and did not represent true picture. (ix) Customers' records were incomplete as regards to address, etc. (x) Advances for expenses were pending for adjustment over a long time and were doubtful or recovery. No provision was made for bad and doubtful debts and for various fines and penalties against statutory defaults under different Acts and Statutes.

It may be concluded that the Government of Mizoram is putting in additional funds just to meet ZOHANDCO's annual loss, which are not being utilized for productive purposes in real sense.

The Mizoram Food and Allied Industries Corporation Ltd. (MIFCO)

The Mizoram Food and Allied Industries Corporation Limited (MIFCO) was setup on 19th December 1989 with an authorized share capital of Rs. 20 crore, with a view to harvesting the limited resources of the State and to nurture its potential by developing, promoting and improving processing and preservation of food, milk, fish, fruits, vegetables, etc.

Its objectives included[18] : (i) to promote and develop food processing industries, both in public and private sectors in Mizoram based on local agriculture and horticulture crops, (ii) to engage in the processing and preservation of products based on all food materials, be it a milk, or meat, or agro-horticulture, and pisciculture origin and to buy, stock, sell, import and export of processed food, and (iii) to promote the rapid development of aforesaid processing industries in the State, operate suitable schemes including financing of any such industry by way of underwriting the issue of shares, participating in share capital, grant of loans and offering guarantees.

The Corporation is presently running a Food Preservation Factory at Vairangte, Ginger Oil and Oleoresin Plant at Sairang, Maize-Milling Plant at Khawzawl and Food Processing Plant at Sairang. Other ongoing projects included Fruit Juice Concentrate Plant at Chhingchhip, Food Park, Chhingchhip, Pork and Poultry Processing Plants, Zemabawk, Pork Processing Plant, Poultry Processing Plant near South Hlimen, Maize Milling Plant at Paithar in Lawngtlai district, and Multipurpose Food Processing Plant at Lunglei and the Central Workshop Complex at South Hlimen. The existing production units of MIFCO are, basically, pilot projects only as they are expected to pave the way for setting up of economically viable food processing industries in the State for the benefit of prospective private entrepreneurs. In order to increase capacity utilization of the existing fruit and vegetable processing units and for employment generation for rural poor contract farming is introduced.

In doing so, the Corporation promoted its own projects, undertaken guidance and advisory assistance programmes, conducted training courses in processing and preservation of fruits and vegetables at its Food Processing and Training Centres, Sairang, Vairengte and Chhingchhip, where 25 to 30 entrepreneurs participated each programme, provided facilities to private entrepreneurs in setting up food-based industries and made available storage of all agro-horticultural products processed by them.

The total paid up capital subscribed by the State government was Rs. 14.13 crore as on 31st March 2004. Besides, the State government also gave Grants-in-Aid to the tune of Rs. 203 lakh from time to time. MIFCO's accumulated loss at Rs. 16.60 lakh in 1990-91 increased to Rs. 1265.48 lakh in 2003-04.

MIFCO had various constraints to cope up with while embarking on commercial production activities, viz. (a) old and obsolete plants and machineries of existing units, (b) absence of basic infrastructural facilities like power, water, etc, (c) insufficient quantity of raw materials, (d) low capacity of plants, (e) absence of markets. The main reasons for such a grim situation were: (i) transfer of unproductive units from the Directorate of Industries to MIFCO resulting in increasing losses, (ii) transfer of 38 people from the Directorate of Industries to MIFCO, regardless of qualification and experience, resulting into over-staffing, (iii) the State Government subscribed towards the share capital of MIFCO on installment basis year after year rather than lump sum. The authorized share capital of MIFCO Rs. 10 crore was subscribed by the State government in a span of more than 10 years, i.e. from 1989 to 2000 on quarterly installment basis. Thus, the implementation of projects was adversely affected as to time and cost overruns, and (iv) insufficient fund allocation for promotion of food processing industries in Mizoram. Since its inception the Government of Mizoram allocated barely 0.17 per cent of total State Annual Plan outlay for MIFCO despite the tremendous potentiality of agro and horticulture based industries in the State.

The annual accounts of MIFCO for the period from 1990-91 to 2003-04 were subjected to detailed analysis and are presented in Table 3.16. The analysis revealed the following:

1. The sales revenue of the Corporation throughout the period was small, when compared to investment. The investment in inventory was high when compared to sales revenue.
2. The average return on investment (ROI) at (–) 14 per cent clearly indicated grim situation of overall profitability of MIFCO.
3. The net profit after tax (PAT) on the average was drastically low at (–) 1685 per cent. The analysis of expenditure ratios shows that the excessive burden of manufacturing and other expenses (average being 1331 per cent) and depreciation (average being 388 per cent owing to improper use of fixed assets) were basically responsible for the extremely poor profit margin. Some glimpses of abnormal situation can be had from the following instances:

   (i) The manufacturing and other expenses in some cases were as high as 36 times of turnover.
   (ii) In many years the amount of raw materials consumed exceeded the amount of turnover, which in some cases had become more than 5 times of turnover.
   (iii) In some years the cost of packing materials itself had exceeded the turnover to an unbelievable extent.

4. The average capital turnover over the period at 0.02 times displayed poor activity of the Corporation. The working capital turnover and fixed assets turnover at 0.11 times and 0.03 times respectively showed a similar picture.

Table 3.16: Abridged Annual Accounts and Some Important Financial Ratios of the Mizoram Food and Allied Industries Corporation Ltd. (MIFCO) from 1990-91 to 2003-04

(Rs. in lakh)

Sl. No.	Balance Sheet Year	Balances as on 31st March														
		1991	1992	1993	1994	1995	1996	1997	1998	1999*	2000*	2001*	2002*	2003*	2004*	Growth (%)
	Sources of Funds:															
1.	Share Capital	215.25	301.76	455.76	455.76	606.66	796.41	866.41	928.01	983.51	1086.31	1170.31	1254.31	1338.31	1413.31	14.14
2.	Share Capital Contribution	Nil	Nil	Nil	118.45	72.25	Nil	30.00	Nil	Nil	Nil	Nil	Nil	Nil	Nil	
3.	Reserves & Surplus	Nil	Nil	Nil	171.82	171.82	196.10	300.25	394.62	427.12	427.12	546.73	963.54	984.79	1188.79	22.93
4.	Deferred Govt. Grants	Nil	Nil	Nil	18.06	17.90	21.22	21.08	20.90	20.90	20.90	Nil	Nil	Nil	Nil	2.65
5.	Miscellaneous Expenses	16.60	45.59	91.62	157.23	233.72	327.08	422.28	514.98	640.48	785.58	934.62	1083.60	1170.09	1265.48	34.55
6.	Retained Earnings (3+4-5)	-16.60	-45.59	-91.62	32.65	-44.00	-109.76	-100.95	-99.46	-192.46	-337.56	-387.89	-120.06	-185.30	-76.69	-18.69
7.	Owner's Equity (1+2+6)	198.65	256.17	364.14	606.86	634.91	686.65	795.46	828.55	791.05	748.75	782.42	1134.25	1153.01	1336.62	12.76
8.	Debt	Nil	15.00	Nil	Nil	Nil	Nil	Nil	Nil	Nil	Nil	Nil	Nil	Nil	Nil	
9.	Capital Employed (7+8)	198.65	271.17	364.14	606.86	634.91	686.65	795.46	828.55	791.05	748.75	782.42	1134.25	1153.01	1336.62	12.60
	Application of Funds:															
10.	Fixed Assets	72.85	127.82	221.69	251.88	280.78	280.86	308.78	309.21	715.44	719.77	724.08	661.90	658.72	658.69	16.99
11.	Depreciation	4.52	15.76	13.50	25.22	37.90	46.14	56.21	67.90	95.88	123.98	154.22	176.58	204.73	232.72	31.20
12.	Net Block (10-11)	68.33	112.06	208.19	226.66	242.88	234.72	252.57	241.31	619.56	595.79	569.86	485.32	453.99	425.97	14.25
13.	Capital Work in Process	22.96	29.63	64.50	124.72	186.82	200.07	245.85	307.49	61.83	62.24	62.72	400.94	477.53	587.97	18.07
14.	Pre-Operative Exp.	0.85	10.36	30.83	52.21	78.98	110.04	145.20	191.55	56.13	76.21	86.48	98.09	141.58	185.66	27.58
15.	Net Fixed Assets (12+13+14)	92.14	152.05	303.52	403.59	508.68	544.83	643.62	740.35	737.52	734.24	719.06	984.35	1073.10	1199.60	17.24
16.	Cash & Bank Balances	73.04	62.91	15.39	62.30	3.86	13.49	85.38	6.27	1.57	1.30	1.31	214.39	64.79	27.32	-6.44
17.	Sundry Debtors	Nil	Nil	4.38	7.29	10.33	5.66	6.25	6.24	6.19	5.88	5.86	5.54	5.54	5.54	-1.48
18.	Loans & Advances	5.50	17.56	12.58	78.37	68.76	82.70	57.39	92.31	88.55	82.27	144.04	33.84	88.22	134.00	17.66
19.	Other Current Assets	2.02	3.53	1.07	1.76	2.03	2.07	2.29	2.66	2.65	2.66	2.68	2.60	3.20	2.51	3.33
20.	Liquid Assets (16+17+18+19)	80.56	84.00	33.42	149.72	84.98	103.92	151.31	107.48	98.96	92.11	153.89	256.37	161.75	169.37	8.07
21.	Inventories	28.58	41.51	43.59	71.62	73.48	60.29	48.40	37.79	20.21	13.06	13.98	15.19	25.09	21.62	-8.87
22.	Current Assets (20+21)	109.14	125.51	77.01	221.34	158.46	164.21	199.71	145.27	119.17	105.17	167.87	271.56	186.84	190.99	3.97
23.	Current Liabilities	2.63	6.39	16.39	18.07	32.23	22.39	47.87	57.07	65.64	90.66	104.51	121.66	106.93	53.97	27.12
24.	Working Capital (22-23)	106.51	119.12	60.62	203.27	126.23	141.82	151.84	88.20	53.53	14.51	63.36	149.90	79.91	137.02	-3.33
25.	Funds Employed (15+24)	198.65	271.17	364.14	606.86	634.91	686.65	795.46	828.55	791.05	748.75	782.42	1134.25	1153.01	1336.62	12.60

(Contd.)

(*Contd.*)

Sl. No.	Income Statement Year	for the year ended 31st March														
		1991	1992	1993	1994	1995	1996	1997	1998	1999*	2000*	2001*	2002*	2003*	2004*	Growth
1.	Turnover	0.47	1.94	10.01	14.54	27.41	18.24	9.34	3.54	3.40	6.24	6.71	6.01	6.21	7.34	5.67
2.	Raw Materials Purchased	6.20	3.25	13.54	14.46	23.55	16.70	9.96	13.95	4.94	3.67	3.73	8.18	3.98	3.79	-6.55
3.	Decrease(+)/Increase(-) in Stocks	-9.20	-6.66	-11.93	-7.88	-5.59	6.14	5.09	4.53	13.40	6.62	-1.15	-1.44	-1.67	0.23	25.27
4.	Materials Consumed (2+3)	-3.00	-3.41	1.61	6.58	17.96	22.84	15.05	18.48	18.34	10.29	2.58	6.74	2.31	4.02	26.61
5.	Manufacturing & Other Exp.	16.86	25.58	55.74	60.34	59.25	53.87	67.38	52.26	75.08	110.48	120.62	120.65	72.44	80.28	10.98
6.	Packing Materials	0.89	1.73	4.97	3.08	11.89	12.89	6.20	9.06	6.29	2.00	2.85	Nil	Nil	Nil	8.14
7.	Finance Charge	Nil	Nil	Nil	Nil	Nil	Nil	Nil	Nil	Nil	Nil	Nil	8.77	0.83	0.25	
8.	*OPBD (1-[4+5+6+7])*	-14.28	-21.96	-52.31	-55.46	-61.69	-71.36	-79.29	-76.26	-96.31	-116.53	-119.34	-130.15	-69.37	-77.21	-23.24
9.	Depreciation	4.51	11.24	8.32	11.71	13.21	14.08	13.46	14.00	27.99	29.97	30.25	28.33	28.16	28.17	13.54
10.	*OP (8-9)*	-18.79	-33.20	-60.63	-67.17	-74.90	-85.44	-92.75	-90.26	-124.30	-146.50	-149.59	-158.48	-97.53	-105.38	-25.09
11.	Other Income	2.19	4.48	15.24	2.46	0.92	0.20	0.58	0.97	0.65	1.40	0.55	9.50	11.04	9.99	4.74
12.	Profit(+)/Loss(-) on Sale of F. A.	Nil	Nil	-0.52	Nil	-0.15	-4.19	-0.88	-0.84	Nil	Nil	Nil	Nil	Nil	Nil	
13.	*PBIT (10+11+12)*	-16.60	-28.72	-45.91	-64.71	-74.13	-89.43	-93.05	-90.13	-123.65	-145.10	-149.04	-148.98	-86.49	-95.39	-30.43
14.	Interest	Nil	0.27	Nil	Nil	Nil	Nil	Nil	Nil	Nil	Nil	Nil	Nil	Nil	Nil	
15.	*PAT (13-14)*	-16.60	-28.99	-45.91	-64.71	-74.13	-89.43	-93.05	-90.13	-123.65	-145.10	-149.04	-148.98	-86.49	-95.39	-30.43
16.	Accumulated Profits of P.Y.	Nil	-16.60	-45.59	-91.62	-157.23	-233.72	-327.08	-422.28	-514.98	-640.48	-785.58	-934.62	-1083.60	-1170.09	
17.	Prior Period Expenses	Nil	Nil	0.12	0.90	2.36	3.93	2.15	2.57	1.85	Nil	Nil	Nil	Nil	Nil	
18.	*Accumulated Profits (15+16-17)*	-16.60	-45.59	-91.62	-157.23	-233.72	-327.08	-422.28	-514.98	-640.48	-785.58	-934.62	-1083.60	-1170.09	-1265.48	-37.11

(*Contd.*)

(*Contd.*)

Some Important Ratios															
Year	*1991*	*1992*	*1993*	*1994*	*1995*	*1996*	*1997*	*1998*	*1999**	*2000**	*2001**	*2002**	*2003**	*2004**	*Average*
Return on Investment (ROI)	N.A.	-14	-19	-14	-12	-13	-13	-11	-15	-19	-20	-17	-9	-8	*-14*
Raw Material Consumed to Turnover	-638	-176	16	45	66	125	161	522	539	165	38	112	37	55	*76*
Mfg. Exp. To Turnover	3587	1319	557	415	216	295	721	1476	2208	1771	1798	2007	1167	1094	*1331*
Packing Cost to Turnover	189	89	50	21	43	71	66	256	185	32	42	0	0	0	*75*
Depreciation to Turnover	960	579	83	81	48	77	144	395	823	480	451	471	453	384	*388*
Operating Profit to Turnover	-3998	-1711	-606	-462	-273	-468	-993	-2550	-3656	-2348	-2229	-2637	-1571	-1436	*-1781*
Net Profit Ratio (PAT) to Turnover	-3532	-1494	-459	-445	-270	-490	-996	-2546	-3637	-2325	-2221	-2479	-1393	-1300	*-1685*
Capital Turnover Ratio	N.A.	0.01	0.03	0.03	0.04	0.03	0.01	0.00	0.00	0.01	0.01	0.01	0.01	0.01	*0.02*
Fixed Assets Turnover Ratio	0.01	0.02	0.05	0.06	0.11	0.08	0.04	0.01	0.01	0.01	0.01	0.01	0.01	0.02	*0.03*
Working Capital Turnover Ratio	0.00	0.02	0.17	0.07	0.22	0.13	0.06	0.04	0.06	0.43	0.11	0.04	0.08	0.05	*0.11*
Debtors Turnover Ratio	N.A.	Nil	4.57	2.49	3.11	2.28	1.57	0.57	0.55	1.03	1.14	1.05	1.12	1.32	*1.48*
Inventory Turnover Ratio	N.A.	0.06	0.24	0.25	0.38	0.27	0.17	0.08	0.12	0.38	0.50	0.41	0.31	0.31	*0.27*
Current Ratio	41.50	19.64	4.70	12.25	4.92	7.33	4.17	2.55	1.82	1.16	1.61	2.23	1.75	3.54	*7.80*
Liquid Ratio	30.63	13.15	2.04	8.29	2.64	4.64	3.16	1.88	1.51	1.02	1.47	2.11	1.51	3.14	*5.51*
Super Quick Ratio	27.77	9.85	0.94	3.45	0.12	0.60	1.78	0.11	0.02	0.01	0.01	1.76	0.61	0.51	*3.40*
Average Collection Period (days)	N.A.	Nil	80	146	117	160	233	644	667	353	319	346	326	275	*326*
Inventory Holding Period	N.A.	6594	1552	1446	966	1338	2124	4443	3113	973	735	886	1184	1161	*2040*
Fixed Assets to Net Tangible Worth	46.38	56.07	83.35	66.50	80.12	79.35	80.91	89.35	93.23	98.06	91.90	86.78	93.07	89.75	*81.06*

* Provisional.

Legend: OPBD = Operating Profit before Depreciation, OP = Operating Profit, PBIT = Profit before Interest & Tax, PBT = Profit before Tax, PAT = Profit after Tax.

Source: Compiled from Annual Accounts of Mizoram Food and Allied Industries Corporation Ltd. from 1990-91 to 2003-04.

5. The short term solvency position of the Corporation appears to be sound as indicated by the average current ratio, liquid ratio and super quick ratio at 7.80:1, 5.51:1, and 3.40:1 respectively. However, the dynamic situation of liquidity is indicated to be poor by the average collection period at 326 days and average inventory holding period at 2040 days. This creates doubts about the quality of trade receivables and inventory as shown in the accounts. This doubt is further substantiated as the amount of sundry debtors was constant from 1996-97 to 2003-04.
6. Loans and advances over the years have grown and accumulated to more than 24 times of the opening figure. This was perhaps because regular advances to employees remained un-recovered and/or unadjusted, advances to suppliers remained unadjusted, and advances against duty expenses etc. remained pending for adjustment for a long time.
7. The Corporation did not borrow funds except for 1991-92 when it borrowed a small amount. Thus, it did not trade on equity.
8. There was a regular stream of government grants, which had shown an average growth of 22.93 per cent over the period. Because of poor profitability, accumulated losses of the Corporation have also grown over the period at an average growth rate of 34.55 per cent. This justified the argument that the Grant-in-Aid followed losses incurred over the period and might have been given to meet the losses. Operating loss grew at an average rate of 25.09 per cent p.a. Similarly, Net loss also grew at an average rate of 30.43 per cent p.a.
9. The funds employed in the organization over the period have grown 6.73 times, registering annual growth of 12.60 per cent. However, the same could not be utilized properly for growth in turnover. In this situation, employment of more and more funds in fixed assets, capital work in process and pre-operative expenses appeared to be unjustified.
10. In nutshell, the main failure of the management can be termed as inability to generate revenue and controlling operating cost. It also failed to utilize its human resource properly so as to promote business and industry to a large extent. The concept of accountability was far away. The employees still had a mind set of government department and were not willing to accept the existence of the Corporation. The economy of scale could not be derived.

11. The Corporation was not declared sick under the Sick Industries Company Act, 1985, as the government grants besides usual share capital contribution received by the Corporation regularly, proved sufficient enough to cover the huge, accumulated loss. The Corporation has directly credited the government grants received to set off its loss to capital reserve account under Reserves and Surplus.
12. The Corporation being a public sector organization, it was not possible for the management to control the cost of personnel and administrative expenses. Hence, the only option available is to raise the sales revenue from its products whichever way is possible. No efforts were made to increase the sales revenue neither within the state nor outside the state as there was no expenditure on advertisement and publicity of its products. Brand creation was needed by way of massive advertisement and if need arises its products may be diversified, their packing may be improved, some new products with longer longevity may be introduced say, banana chips on the pattern of uncle chips, banana powder, passion fruit powder, pineapple juice powder, orange juice powder, etc. on the pattern of tomato soup powder.
13. One of the objectives of MIFCO is to give entrepreneurship training and motivation to new entrants in food-processing industry. But, if this is the financial position of the Corporation over the last fourteen years where the MIFCO was constantly carrying huge inventory against its meagre sales, cannot be taken as role model by any private entrepreneur specially when it wants to motivate them for having their own food processing industry in the State. This rather de-motivated them. So, it becomes essential that MIFCO launch marketing promotion and brand creation exercise within and outside the state to increase its turnover to a satisfactory level for which, a break-even is achieved in its operations.
14. The management contended that the implementation of projects was adversely affected due to time and cost overruns as the State Government subscribed its share capital on quarterly installment basis over 1989 to 2000 instead of lump sum. But, the point is that it could borrow from financial institutions like ZIDCO or commercial banks rather than depending wholly on the State government saying that despite of tremendous potentiality of agro-horticulture based industries in the State, the government

had barely allocated only 0.17 per cent of total State Annual Plan Outlay for MIFCO. At the same time, the State Level Bankers' Committee for Mizoram observed "at present government Corporations are not availing any bank finance. With increased scale of operations' bank credit may be required" and "while MIFCO is carrying on its thrust at agro-based industries, no finances have so far been required for their activities."[19] This clearly showed that the banks in Mizoram were ready to finance any viable project of any State Government owned Corporations, but, unfortunately, no such proposal was moved by any Government Corporation. In the light of above discussion, it may be argued that the MIFCO management could ensure timely implementation of its ongoing viable projects and could save costs overruns with the help of bank finance.

Cooperatives in Industry

Industrial activities through cooperatives in Mizoram are basically limited to the field of traditional cottage, handloom and handicrafts, sericulture, etc. There were 11 State level cooperatives as on 31st March 2002. Some of these are Mizoram State Cooperative Housing Financing Federation Ltd. (HOUSEFED) engaged in housing finance, Mizoram Apex Sericulture Cooperative Society Ltd. (MASCOS) in sericulture, Mizoram Cooperative Fish Farming Marketing and Federation Ltd. (ZOFISHFED) in fish marketing, Mizoram State Pig Producers' Federation Ltd. (PIGFED) in piggery, Mizoram Apex Handloom and Handicraft Cooperative Society Ltd. (MAHCO) in handloom and handicrafts, Mizoram State Cooperative Fruit Forestry and Vegetables Growers Federation Ltd. (MAFF), Mizoram State Women Federation (WOMENFED) in knitting and tailoring, and Mizoram Multi-Commodity Producers' Cooperative Union Ltd. (MULCO) in production of dairy products. Among these the status and operations of MULCO are discussed here.

Mizoram Multi-Commodity Producers Cooperative Union Ltd. (MULCO)

The Mizoram Multi-Commodity Producers Cooperative Union Ltd. (MULCO) is a Government of Mizoram controlled association of 25 primary societies having registered office in Aizawl and 25 branches spread all over the State. The organization is involved in the business of processing and distribution of milk and milk products. Over the years its operations expanded in length and breadth. Its product range increased from milk to milk products such as *paneer*, curd, *srikhand*, ghee, *rasagullah*, butter milk, flavoured milk, etc. Majority of its share capital was subscribed by the Government of Mizoram. Besides, it has received grants, subsidies and support from agencies like National Dairy Development Board (NDDB), Northeastern Council (NEC), Animal Husbandry and Veterinary Department (AHV), Indian Dairy Development Project (IDDP) etc. It is the second largest business organization in terms of branch network and turnover.

The financial statements of MULCO for a period from 1993-94 to 2003-04 compiled, analyzed and presented in Table 3.17.

The analysis of the statement revealed the following points:

1. A special feature worth mentioning is that it being a government controlled cooperative union; profit earning is not the motto, but, certainly not to incur loss. Further, the commodities dealt constituted essential commodities and are perishable in nature which cannot be stocked for a long time. Moreover, in view of its sizeable turnover, the gross profit margin cannot be expected to be high, but, it must be sufficient enough to cover the overheads leaving a reasonable margin to be distributed among member societies as dividend. Further more, subsidies/grants towards its revenue expenditures may not be a regular feature in future. Hence, subsidies/grants as are presently available cannot be taken into account and MULCO must sustain all its overheads on its own.
2. The Return on Investment had been negative over the entire period averaging at (-) 24.14 per cent p.a. though ranged from (–) 42.18 per cent in 1997-98 to (–) 1.80 per cent in 2003-04 because of operating loss except in the first year 1993-94. The operating loss to turnover first increased from 6.20 per cent in 1994-95 to 21.39 per cent in 1997-98 and since then reduced consistently to 0.32 per cent in 2003-04, which was definitely a good sign.
3. The average cost of raw material consumed to turnover was high at 87.31 per cent. It was even as high as 98.59 per cent in 1997-98. This indicated thin gross margin on an average at 12.69 per cent. There is a need to control it immediately, so as to leave a reasonable cover to meet the overheads.
4. Among expenses, the cost of personnel to turnover was 3 times than the cost of wages to turnover. Similarly cost of sales to turnover (3.30 per cent) though ranged between 2.89 per cent to 3.93 per cent was also high in view of large volume of sales.

Table 3.17: Abridged Annual Accounts and Some Important Financial Ratios of the Mizoram Multi-Commodity Producers' Union Ltd. (MULCO) from 1993-94 to 2003-04

(*Rs. in Lakh*)

Sl. No.	*Position Statement / Year*		*As on 30th June*					*As on 31st March*						
			1994	*1995*	*1996*	*1997*	*1998*	*1999*	*2000*	*2001*	*2002*	*2003*	*2004*	*Growth (%)*
	Sources of Funds:													
1.	Share Capital		4.29	4.28	4.29	5.19	5.22	6.22	6.22	6.22	6.22	7.37	7.43	6.15
2.	Reserves & Surplus		3.64	0.00	13.35	5.28	3.99	8.61	11.54	14.35	16.67	20.48	22.14	56.02
3.	Various Grants		4.07	30.41	98.11	73.49	46.54	57.52	110.04	66.58	43.33	33.83	96.84	14.08
4.	Misc. Exp.		Nil	0.92	Nil	Nil	Nil	Nil	Nil	Nil	Nil	Nil	Nil	
5.	Retained Earnings	(2+3-4)	7.71	29.49	111.45	78.77	50.52	66.13	121.57	80.93	60.01	54.31	118.98	14.82
6.	Owner's Equity	(1+5)	12.00	33.77	115.75	83.96	55.75	72.35	127.80	87.15	66.23	61.68	126.41	12.97
7.	Debt		0.20	0.20	Nil	Nil	Nil	4.00	Nil	Nil	Nil	Nil	Nil	
8.	*Capital Employed*	*(6+7)*	*12.20*	*33.97*	*115.75*	*83.96*	*55.75*	*76.35*	*127.80*	*87.15*	*66.23*	*61.68*	*126.41*	*12.86*
	Application of Funds:													
9.	Fixed Assets		1.52	19.32	48.83	47.99	42.16	37.82	49.73	74.09	75.11	67.36	102.04	29.39
10.	Depreciation		0.28	0.23	3.04	7.14	6.59	5.55	4.81	7.24	10.51	9.06	6.89	36.47
11.	Net Block	(9-10)	1.24	19.09	45.79	40.84	35.58	32.27	44.93	66.85	64.59	58.30	95.14	29.46
12.	Investments		0.05	0.05	0.05	0.30	0.30	0.30	0.30	0.30	0.30	0.30	0.25	20.45
13.	Cash & Bank Balance		9.17	12.17	65.17	37.67	15.40	40.67	76.67	16.31	1.70	8.99	21.64	-6.94
14.	Sundry Debtors		1.81	2.55	4.33	5.85	4.03	2.84	0.90	2.72	4.02	7.74	21.51	13.11
15.	Other Current Assets		0.08	0.08	0.08	Nil	Nil	Nil	4.99	1.02	Nil	Nil	Nil	
16.	Liquid Assets	(13+14+15)	11.05	14.79	69.58	43.53	19.43	43.51	82.56	20.05	5.72	16.72	43.15	-0.27
17.	Inventories		0.00	0.09	0.43	0.42	0.49	0.32	0.06	0.00	1.35	1.35	1.60	26.66
18.	Current Assets	(16+17)	11.05	14.88	70.01	43.94	19.92	43.83	82.62	20.05	7.07	18.07	44.75	0.68
19.	Current Liabilities		0.15	0.05	0.10	1.13	0.05	0.05	0.05	0.05	5.74	14.99	13.73	59.43
20.	Working Capital	(18-19)	10.90	14.83	69.91	42.81	19.87	43.78	82.57	20.00	1.33	3.08	31.02	-11.17
21.	*Total Funds Employed*	*(11+12+20)*	*12.20*	*33.97*	*115.75*	*83.96*	*55.75*	*76.35*	*127.80*	*87.15*	*66.23*	*61.68*	*126.41*	*12.86*

(*Contd.*)

(*Contd.*)

Sl. No.	Income Statement Year	For the year ended on 30th June					For the year ended on 31st March						
		1994	1995	1996	1997	1998	1999	2000	2001	2002	2003	2004*	Growth
1.	Turnover	68.64	95.28	155.43	181.87	137.74	209.21	257.35	343.34	372.85	483.78	532.07	21.32
2.	Raw Materials Purchased	56.06	86.15	140.41	171.27	135.86	180.89	211.07	291.30	318.02	408.86	439.33	20.46
3.	Decrease(+)/Increase(-) in Stocks	Nil	Nil	-0.32	0.01	-0.07	0.17	0.26	0.06	-1.35	0.00	-0.25	
4.	Raw Materials Consumed (2+3)	56.06	86.15	140.09	171.28	135.80	181.06	211.33	291.36	316.67	408.86	439.08	20.46
5.	Water & Energy Charges	0.09	0.50	0.47	0.87	0.79	1.69	1.97	5.12	5.67	10.01	13.04	55.56
6.	Wages	Nil	2.32	2.64	3.43	3.17	2.48	4.46	7.41	7.55	9.50	9.65	19.14
7.	Personnel Cost	2.83	2.57	6.59	10.60	8.19	11.60	17.59	18.55	19.77	19.84	20.50	23.55
8.	Administration Charges	0.39	2.34	1.97	6.30	3.85	5.09	11.53	6.55	4.56	8.67	8.26	24.56
9.	Milk Commission	2.52	3.75	5.12	5.46	4.14	7.19	9.74	9.92	12.15	15.19	15.41	19.17
10.	Packing Material Cost	Nil	Nil	Nil	6.68	Nil	3.37	10.36	16.16	16.48	4.49	16.63	12.38
11.	Distribution Expenses	0.88	3.35	7.12	7.11	4.68	7.07	8.66	8.21	6.48	5.90	4.31	10.35
12.	*OPBD[1-(4+5+6+7+8+9+10+11)]*	*5.87*	*-5.68*	*-8.57*	*-29.85*	*-22.88*	*-10.33*	*-18.26*	*-19.95*	*-16.48*	*1.31*	*5.20*	*13.41*
13.	Depreciation	0.28	0.23	3.04	7.14	6.59	5.55	4.81	7.24	10.51	9.06	6.89	36.47
14.	Operating Profit (OP) (12-13)	5.59	-5.91	-11.60	-36.99	-29.47	-15.88	-23.07	-27.18	-26.99	-7.75	-1.69	9.93
15.	Other Income	0.40	1.35	15.02	39.57	28.53	20.54	28.78	29.72	29.14	12.74	3.71	21.62
16.	Profit (+)/Loss (-) on Sale of FA	Nil	Nil	0.45	-0.61	Nil	Nil	0.21	0.28	0.15	Nil	-0.35	
17.	*PBIT (14+15+16)*	*5.99*	*-4.56*	*3.87*	*1.96*	*-0.93*	*4.66*	*5.92*	*2.82*	*2.30*	*4.98*	*1.66*	*26.06*
18.	Interest	Nil	Nil	Nil	Nil	Nil	Nil	Nil	Nil	Nil	Nil	Nil	
19.	*Profit Before Tax (PBT)(17-18)*	*5.99*	*-4.56*	*3.87*	*1.96*	*-0.93*	*4.66*	*5.92*	*2.82*	*2.30*	*4.98*	*1.66*	*26.06*
20.	Tax	Nil	Nil	Nil	Nil	Nil	Nil	Nil	Nil	Nil	Nil	Nil	
21.	Profit After Tax (PAT) (19-20)	5.99	-4.56	3.87	1.96	-0.93	4.66	5.92	2.82	2.30	4.98	1.66	26.06
22.	Accumulated Profits of P.Y.	-2.35	3.64	-0.92	2.95	4.91	3.98	8.61	5.95	8.77	11.07	4.98	
23.	Prior Period Expenses	Nil	Nil	Nil	Nil	Nil	0.03	8.58	Nil	Nil	11.07	Nil	
24.	*Accumulated Profits(21+22-23)*	*3.64*	*-0.92*	*2.95*	*4.91*	*3.98*	*8.61*	*5.95*	*8.77*	*11.07*	*4.98*	*6.64*	*34.73*

(*Contd.*)

(Contd.)

Sl. No.	Important Ratios: Year	For the year ended on 30th June 1994	1995	1996	1997	1998	For the year ended on 31st March 1999	2000	2001	2002	2003	2004*	Average
1.	Return on Investment (ROI)		-25.61	-15.50	-37.05	-42.18	-24.04	-22.60	-25.29	-35.20	-12.13	-1.80	-24.14
2.	Raw Material Consumed to Turnover	81.67	90.41	90.13	94.17	98.59	86.55	82.12	84.86	84.93	84.51	82.52	87.31
3.	Water & Energy Charges to Turnover	0.13	0.53	0.30	0.48	0.58	0.81	0.76	1.49	1.52	2.07	2.45	1.01
4.	Wages to Turnover	Nil	2.43	1.70	1.89	2.30	1.18	1.73	2.16	2.03	1.96	1.81	1.74
5.	Personnel Cost to Turnover	4 12	2.70	4.24	5.83	5.95	5.54	6.83	5.40	5.30	4.10	3.85	4.90
6.	Administration Charges to Turnover	0 57	2.45	1.27	3.46	2.80	2.43	4.48	1.91	1.22	1.79	1.55	2.18
7.	Sales Commission to Turnover	3 67	3.93	3.29	3.00	3.00	3.44	3.78	2.89	3.26	3.14	2.90	3.30
8.	Packing Cost to Turnover	Nil	Nil	Nil	3.67	Nil	1.61	4.03	4.71	4.42	0.93	3.12	2.04
9.	Distribution Cost to Turnover	1 28	3.51	4.58	3.91	3.40	3.38	3.36	2.39	1.74	1.22	0.81	2.69
10.	Operating Profit to Sales	8 14	-6.20	-7.46	-20.34	-21.39	-7.59	-8.96	-7.92	-7.24	-1.60	-0.32	-7.35
11.	Net Profit (PAT) to Turnover	8 73	-4.79	2.49	1.08	-0.68	2.23	2.30	0.82	0.62	1.03	0.31	1.29
12.	Capital Turnover Ratio		4.13	2.08	1.82	1.97	3.17	2.52	3.19	4.86	7.56	5.66	3.70
13.	Fixed Assets Turnover Ratio	55 18	4.99	3.39	4.45	3.87	6.48	5.73	5.14	5.77	8.30	5.59	9.90
14.	Debtors Turnover Ratio		43.68	45.16	35.70	27.87	60.92	137.76	189.54	110.60	82.31	36.39	76.99
15.	Inventory Turnover Ratio		2118	602	431	305	521	1354	11176	553	358	360	1778
16.	Working Capital Turnover	6.30	6.42	2.22	4.25	6.93	4.78	3.12	17.17	279.34	156.92	48.74	48.74
17.	Current Ratio	73.69	297.62	700.07	38.89	398.37	876.55	1652.40	401.03	1.23	1.21	3.26	404.03
18.	Acid Test Ratio	73.69	295.82	695.81	38.52	388.67	870.18	1651.17	401.03	1.00	1.12	3.14	401.83
19.	Super Quick Ratio	61.11	243.30	651.72	33.34	308.05	813.44	1533.38	326.16	0.30	0.60	1.58	361.18
20.	Average Collection Period (days)		8.36	8.08	10.22	13.10	5.99	2.65	1.93	3.30	4.43	10.03	6.81
21.	Inventory Holding Period (days)		0.17	0.61	0.85	1.20	0.70	0.27	0.03	0.66	1.02	1.01	0.65

Legend: OPBD = Operating Profit before Depreciation, OP = Operating Profit, PBIT = Profit before Interest & Tax, PBT = Profit before Tax, PAT = Profit after Tax.

Source: Compiled from Annual Accounts of Mizoram Multi-Commodity Producers' Cooperative Union Ltd. from 1993-94 to 2003-04.

water and energy charges seemed reasonable up to 1999-2000. Thereafter these doubled and tripled in following years. It was so because of hike in electricity rates charged by the Power and Electricity Department. As an industrial unit the expenditure on power was not controllable as it depended on the utilization of plant capacity. Due to water scarcity water transportation was done through tankers, which was a costly affair as compared to PHED supply charges. However, there existed scope to control the cost of water also. It was a happy feature that the distribution cost reduced continuously from 4.58 per cent in 1995-96 to 0.81 per cent in 2003-04.

5. The remedy to make the organization earn profit is to control some of its operating expenses such as packing cost (2.04 per cent), which explained volatile behaviour and registered an increase in size and volume. However, this cost was zero in four years out of the total period covered by study. Looking to the very nature of business, this cost cannot be taken as zero, because expenditure on primary packing is essential. It seemed that no proper accounting was done as regards packing material say stock valuation. Similarly, administration charges, sales commission, and distribution cost also need to be controlled, as these ratios on the average stood at 2.18 per cent, 3.30 per cent, and 2.69 per cent.
6. Another cost which draws attention was the cost of personnel, which seemed beyond control. Though, it is expected to pay its employees like others in government departments, the management may plan to use their services in most efficient manner ensuring increase in per employee productivity.
7. Capital turnover ratio showed a fluctuating trend. It was lowest at 1.82 times in 1996-97 and was highest at 7.56 times in 2002-03. The fixed assets turnover was high at 55.18 times in 1993-94, owing to insignificant value of fixed assets possessed by the Union. Thereafter, it settled down within the range of 3.39 times to 8.30 times. This was so because of major additions to fixed assets in phased manner from 1994-95 and onwards. Further the Union has modernized its whole production process from 2000-01 by making further additions to plant and machinery.
8. MULCO has not taken loan except in 1998-99. It was operated totally by own funds and grants from different agencies. Hence, it did not benefit from leverage.

9. MULCO had low current liabilities till 2000-01. Of course, there were sizeable current liability in the last three years from 2001-02 to 2003-04 and during these years the acid test ratio and super quick ratio were normal. However the current ratio was thin/low in these years. This showed that the organization adopted the low stocking practice, as it deals in perishable commodities. In nutshell, its short-term solvency position was quite satisfactory.
10. The average inventory holding period at less than one day was quite acceptable especially in view of the nature of its business. The average collection period at around 7 days also seemed satisfactory.
11. The officials revealed that this is the only organization managing such a large volume of business without maintaining ledger. Only cashbook and some daybooks are maintained. At the end of financial year various bills, vouchers, cash memos, etc. were sorted out head-wise to draw final accounts. As it handled such a large volume of business without ledger was quite surprising. However, accounting procedures adopted as regards distinction between capital and revenue was not clear. It was noticed that various items of capital nature were squared off through profit and loss account. Lump sum amounts of grants, subsidies from different agencies like NDDB, GOM, IDDP, NEC, etc. to the extent of expenses were treated as income. Stock recording policy of stores and spares, packing materials etc. was faulty.

State Assistance to Industries

State has an important role in the development of industries. In this respect the State provides a variety of assistance. The State assistance to industries may broadly be classified as financial assistance and non-financial assistance.

Financial Assistance to Industries

The Government of Mizoram like other state governments in the country provided financial assistance to industry in the form of grant-in-aid, Working Capital Grants as also loans from RIP Fund under the State-aid to Industrics Act and under Financial Assistance to Tea Growers besides financial subsidies to SSIs. Loans from RIP fund and State Aid to Industries Act are taken up separately in Chapter 5.

1. *Financial Assistance to Tea Growers*: Grant-in-aid/financial assistance in cash are given to adopted tea growers from Biate. However, the amount of grant/assistance varied depending on their performance.
2. *Grant-in-Aid to Artisans and Village Level Entrepreneurs*: Under the scheme, artisans engaged in different trades were given 50 per cent subsidy towards purchase of machinery tools/equipment etc. subject to maximum Rs. 1,000/-. In some cases outright cash grant was also provided. Village level artisans and entrepreneurs who could not offer sufficient securities, etc. were generally covered under the scheme. Later, the scheme was modified and a non-government registered society or institution engaged in industrial activities were made eligible to receive grant-in-aid up to Rs. 3,000/- towards working capital and Rs. 5,000/- towards purchase of tools and equipments. For an individual artisan, the grant was limited to Rs. 2,000/- towards working capital and Rs. 1,000/- towards purchase of tools and equipments.
3. *Working Capital Grant*: During U.T. period, Working Capital Grants were given to a maximum extent of Rs. 2,500/- to selected (deserving) weavers since 1973. Later, it was extended to small and village industries also. During 1973-74, 190 units from 23 different trades were given benefit under the scheme. Similarly, during 1976-78, 75 small units from 18 different trades were covered under the scheme.
4. *Subsidies to Industries by the State Government*: Details of various subsidies disbursed by different agencies to industries in Mizoram from 1991-92 to 2001-02 are given in Table 3.18.

Analysis of Table 3.18 revealed the following:

1. Though, the number of registered SSIs increased over the years, the subsidy distribution has actually decreased, rather increasing. It should have increased at least proportionately if not more.
2. The subsidies such as project report subsidy, land subsidy, power line subsidy, power generating set subsidy, state transport subsidy on plant and machinery are mainly one time in nature and are generally given at the time of establishment, while some others like interest subsidy, power subsidy, central transport subsidy

Table 3.18: Composition of Subsidies Disbursed in Mizoram From 1991-92 to 2001-02

(*Rs. in Lakh*)

Year	Project Report	Land Subsidy	Power Gen Set	Drawal of Power line	Power	Interest Subsidy	State Transport Subsidy	Equity Participation	Total	Central Transport Subsidy	Subsidy through NEDFI
1991-92	0.36	5.65	5.85	0.00	1.01	4.35	5.67	0.00	22.89	127.74	—
Per cent share	(2)	(25)	(26)		(4)	(19)	(25)		(100)		
No. of Units	3	17	3		23	16	21		83	3	
1992-93	0.21	3.80	8.48	0.00	1.02	3.05	3.86	10.00	30.42	244.69	—
Per cent share	(1)	(13)	(28)		(3)	(10)	(13)	(33)	(100)		
No. of Units	2	10	13		5	15	25	1	71	12	
1993-94	0.00	0.21	4.63	0.00	0.54	2.18	0.40	8.10	16.06	222.40	—
Per cent share		(1)	(29)		(3)	(14)	(2)	(50)	(100)		
No. of Units		2	5		12	15	7	1	42	28	
1994-95	0.27	0.50	7.12	0.50	0.03	1.32	0.05	0.00	9.78	405.33	—
Per cent share	(3)	(5)	(73)	(5)		(13)	(1)		(100)		
No. of Units	2	3	8	1	2	2	1		19	38	
1995-96	0.00	0.60	9.00	0.00	5.54	6.54	2.84	0.00	24.53	0.00	—
Per cent share		(2)	(37)		(23)	(27)	(12)		(100)		
No. of Units		1	9		35	26	13		84	63	
1996-97	0.50	0.00	6.91	0.30	3.16	13.09	0.00	0.00	23.96	103.30	0
Per cent share	(2)		(29)	(1)	(13)	(55)			(100)		
No. of Units	2		11	1	13	24			51		
1997-98	0.00	6.06	1.47	0.50	1.02	1.02	0.04	0.00	10.10	0.00	0
Per cent share		(60)	(15)	(5)	(10)	(10)			(100)		
No. of Units		1	2	1	7	7	1		19	65	
1998-99	0.00	1.04	8.03	0.00	2.26	3.76	4.23	5.00	24.32	0.00	25
Per cent share		(4)	(33)		(9)	(15)	(17)	(21)	(100)		
No. of Units		2	7		17	7	4	1	38		
1999-00	0.51	8.14	6.10	0.50	5.68	0.05	3.71	0.00	24.69	125.95	30
Per cent share	(2)	(33)	(25)	(2)	(23)		(15)		(100)		
No. of Units	2	2	2	1	26	1	9		43		
2000-01	0.00	0.00	0.00	0.00	0.00	0.00	0.00	0.00	0.00	544.57	60
2001-02	0.00	3.00	1.38	0.50	7.42	0.60	3.96	0.00	16.85	0.00	192
Per cent share		(18)	(8)	(3)	(44)	(4)	(23)		(100)		
No. of Units		1	1	1	29	2	10		44	241	
Average	(1)	(16)	(30)	(2)	(13)	(17)	(11)	(10)	(100)	161	

Note: Figures in parenthesis represent percentage share.

Source: Compiled from the data obtained from Directorate of Industries, Government of Mizoram, Aizawl.

on raw materials are given year after year as per actual expenditure under the head. It is observed that there has been variation in subsidy as well as the number of units availing the subsidy from year to year.

3. It is surprising to note that the number of units benefited as well as amount of subsidy given has fluctuated from year to year in

case of power consumption subsidy and interest subsidy. Perhaps some units lost interest and dropped out casually and again join later on or new units join as old go out on completing their tenure or there might be some other problems. Besides Government of Mizoram subsidies, the Central Government subsidy was also channelised through NEDFi. This included central transport subsidy, capital investment subsidy (central) and working capital investment subsidy. Year-wise disbursal of aggregate amount is given in Table 3.18.

4. Of the subsidies disbursed, on an average 16 per cent of funds were given in the form of land subsidy, 30 per cent as Diesel Generator Set subsidy, 10 per cent as equity participation, 17 per cent as interest subsidy. Power and state transport subsidy figured at 13 per cent and 11 per cent respectively. The 'power line subsidy' was 2 per cent and 'project report subsidy' was 1 per cent. As per Industrial Policy of Mizoram 1989, the State Government under equity participation scheme,[20] may through its Corporation, participate in 'equity contribution' by subscribing issued capital up to 10 per cent subject to maximum Rs. 10 lakh where the project cost does not exceeds Rs. 2 crores with buy-back arrangement. The purpose of the scheme was to provide share capital to promoters who find it difficult to arrange their share in capital. The scheme was discontinued in new Industrial Policy of Mizoram, 2000. It was an attractive incentive for industrial entrepreneurs. The benefit of the scheme was offered to three units one, each from brick, tyre retreading and pottery. According to the scheme the facility may be extended to corporate units only, but, no corporate unit existed neither in brick making segment nor in tyre retreading segment nor in pottery segment. This raises a doubt as to why only three units were given benefit and not the rest and why it was discontinued.

5. Central transport subsidy increased but at the same time the state transport subsidy declined. This may be due to the State machinery not promoting state transport subsidy, but central transport subsidy scheme only, just not to put strain on its own budget.

Table 3.19: Industrial Category-wise Disbursement of Subsidies in Mizoram From 1991-92 to 2001-02 (As on 31st March)

(*Rs. in Lakh*)

Industrial Category	*1992*	*1993*	*1994*	*1995*	*1996*	*1997*	*1998*	*1999*	*2000*	*2001*	*2002*	*Average*	*(%)*
Food Product &	3.65	3.80	0.33	2.60	4.99	9.35	6.85	1.82	13.98	Nil	4.72	5.21	26
Allied Industries	(12)	(8)	(3)	(3)	(9)	(8)	(4)	(2)	(7)	—	(7)	(6)	(13)
Wood & Wooden	1.98	0.49	0.20	1.49	1.53	0.12	0.02	0.33	0.81	Nil	0.65	0.76	4
Products	(18)	(7)	(7)	(5)	(19)	(4)	(2)	(4)	(9)	—	(10)	(9)	(17)
Textile & Textile	1.17	0.85	0.49	0.02	1.18	1.43	0.80	0.03	0.23	Nil	0.03	0.62	3
Goods	(10)	(5)	(6)	(1)	(12)	(8)	(5)	(1)	(4)	—	(1)	(5)	(11)
Paper Products,	0.32	1.15	0.42	0.73	1.32	0.10	0.72	0.97	0.47	Nil	0.72	0.69	3
Publishing & Allied	(4)	(9)	(5)	(2)	(8)	(1)	(1)	(3)	(3)	—	(7)	(4)	(9)
Rubber, Plastics,	12.45	3.16	8.64	0.00	3.49	1.54	0.00	1.10	0.00	Nil	0.28	3.06	15
etc.	(17)	(10)	(2)	(0)	(8)	(4)	(0)	(3)	(0)	—	(1)	(5)	(9)
Chemicals &	0.06	0.00	0.00	0.00	0.80	0.00	0.00	0.00	0.00	Nil	0.00	0.09	0
Chemical products	(2)	(0)	(0)	(0)	(2)	(0)	(0)	(0)	(0)	—	(0)	(0)	(1)
Non-Metallic &	1.47	10.09	0.02	0.00	0.73	2.25	0.00	9.19	1.00	Nil	0.00	2.47	12
Mineral Products	(5)	(2)	(1)	(0)	(2)	(5)	(0)	(5)	(2)	—	(0)	(2)	(4)
Electrical Cables	0.05	0.17	1.90	0.21	0.00	0.67	0.60	1.91	0.74	Nil	0.00	0.63	3
and Conductors	(1)	(1)	(1)	(1)	(0)	(2)	(1)	(2)	(2)	—	(0)	(1)	(2)
Metal Products	0.72	5.37	1.62	2.37	3.98	5.44	0.32	5.86	4.11	Nil	6.74	3.65	18
& Parts	(7)	(15)	(8)	(4)	(13)	(8)	(4)	(13)	(12)	—	(10)	(9)	(19)
Leather Goods	0.00	0.00	0.00	0.00	0.10	0.01	0.00	0.00	0.00	Nil	0.00	0.01	0
& Repairing	(0)	(0)	(0)	(0)	(2)	(1)	(0)	(0)	(0)	—	(0)	(0)	(1)
Service Based	0.99	5.35	1.00	2.37	6.41	2.38	0.79	3.10	3.13	Nil	3.71	2.92	14
Industries	(6)	(14)	(6)	(3)	(9)	(9)	(2)	(5)	(3)	—	(8)	(7)	(13)
Miscellaneous	0.03	0.00	1.46	0.00	0.00	0.68	0.00	0.00	0.22	Nil	0.00	0.24	1
	(1)	(0)	(3)	(0)	(0)	(1)	(0)	(0)	(1)	—	(0)	(1)	(1)
Total	22.89	30.42	16.06	9.78	24.53	23.96	10.10	24.32	24.69	Nil	16.85	20.36	100
	(83)	(71)	(42)	(19)	(84)	(51)	(19)	(38)	(43)	—	(44)	(49)	(100)

(*Contd.*)

(*Contd.*)

Industrial Category	*1992*	*1993*	*1994*	*1995*	*1996*	*1997*	*1998*	*1999*	*2000*	*2001*	*2002*	*Average*	*(%)*
Central Transport Subsidy	25.99 (3)	127.74 (12)	244.69 (28)	222.40 (33)	405.33 (63)	Nil —	103.30 (65)	Nil —	Nil —	125.95 (56)	544.57 (241)	Nil —	
Total SSIs (Nos.)	2410	2572	2613	2726	2913	3451	3672	3907	4313	4490	4770	3440	
Benefited SSI (%)	(3.44)	(2.76)	(1.61)	(0.70)	(2.88)	(1.48)	(0.52)	(0.97)	(1.00)	—	(0.92)	(1.44)	

Note :1. Figures in parenthesis represent number of units. Figures in parenthesis in Percentage column represent percentage of number of units with average total number of units

2. Food Product & Allied Industries includes Food Processing, MIFCO, Ice Plant, Rice Huller, Oil, *Masala*, Tea, Confectionary, Poultry, Spices, Chicken & Meat Processing.
3. Wood & Wooden Products includes Agro Forests & Bamboo, Cane Winding, Mat Ply, Furniture & Carpentry.
4. Textile & Textile Goods includes Handloom, Cotton Textiles, Hosiery, Tailoring, Weaving & Knitting.
5. Paper Products, Publishing & Allied includes Printing Press, Paper & Stationery
6. Rubber, Plastics, etc. includes Manufacturing of Rubber Mats, Tyre Retreading & Polythene
7. Chemicals & Chemical products includes Optical
8. Non-Metallic & Mineral Products includes Manufacturing of Cement, Cemented Flower Pots, Brick Making, Kero Gas, Stone Quarry and Pottery.
9. Electrical Cables and Conductors includes Conductors, Cables & Electricals
10. Metal Products & Parts includes Fabrication, Motor Body Building, Hardwares, Nails, Steel & Foundry
11. Leather Goods & Repairing includes Manufacturing of Shoes & their Repairing.
12. Service Based Industries includes X-Ray Clinic-*cum*-Nursing Home, Photo Services, Cable Operator, Motor Works, Auto Work Shops, Xerox Copier, Dry Cleaning, Watch Repairing, I.T./Electronics, Hotel, Engineering & Allied Services.
13. Miscellaneous includes Diesel Services, Tung Oil, & Church Services.
14. The format used for classification was drawn from the pattern used by Dr. Rualkhuma Colney in his Ph.D. thesis "Small Scale and Cottage Industries, Mizoram", published by L. B. Associates, Aizawl, 1997 p. 142.

Source: Compiled from the data obtained from Directorate of Industries, Government of Mizoram, Aizawl.

Details of subsidy distributed to different industry groups from 1991-92 to 2001-02 are given in Table 3.19.

The analysis of Table 3.19 revealed the following:

1. On an average only 1.44 per cent of total registered SSIs could be given Government support in the form of annual subsidy distribution.
2. Number of beneficiaries and their proportion has come down over the years, as the number of units doubled while the amount of subsidies though fluctuated, disbursed remained more or less same.
3. Industry-wise, 4 per cent of units benefited were from non-metallic and mineral products and were given 12 per cent of funds, 13 per cent of units from food products and allied industries got 26 per cent of funds, 9 per cent of units from rubber and plastic industry got 15 per cent of funds, 19 per cent of units from metal products and parts were given 18 per cent of funds, 13 per cent of units from service based industries were assisted with 14 per cent of funds, 9 per cent of units from paper products, publishing and allied category got 3 per cent of funds, 11 per cent of units from textile and textile goods category shared 3 per cent of total subsidy, and 17 per cent of units from wood and wooden products were distributed 4 per cent of funds.
4. Leather being a labour intensive and employment generating industry was not given adequate attention over the entire period of study.

Non-Financial Assistance to Industries

In order to promote and develop Small-Scale Industries in Mizoram, the Industries Department in collaboration with other government agencies implemented assistance programmes, which comprised of Feasibility and Consultancy Service, Industrial Estate and Area Development, Supply of raw materials (under RIP), Marketing and Turn Key Project Scheme.

1. *Feasibility and Consultancy Service*: A branch office of the Small Industries Service Institute (SISI), Government of India, Aizawl since 1973 provided services in the field of technical management, economic problems, etc. The Institute guided the new entrepreneurs in selecting items to be manufactured and in drawing up schemes. It also issued certificates in respect of technical feasibility. Besides, the SISI, Aizawl undertakes

Industrial Potential Survey, prepares State Industrial Profiles, renders Economic Information Service, provides Technical Support Service, gives Techno Economic Viability Services, makes Plan for Modernization and Technical Upgradation, helps in Locating new Markets for products, extends Consultancy Service to all entrepreneurs free of cost. Further, it undertakes project report preparation and conducts project appraisals on payment basis. In July 1996, an Industrial Potential Survey was undertaken by it. Some activities that fell within the ambit of its functional activities, but, owing to absence of tool room in Mizoram the same could not be offered to industrial entrepreneurs are (i) Common facility services to SSI units for repairs and maintenance, (ii) designing and fabrication of dies, tools, jigs and fixtures for SSI units to improve their products, (iii) use of modern instruments and tools, (iv) demonstration on the use of modern machinery and techniques, and (v) provision of technical training in different trades like fitter, machine shop and welding. Besides, The Northeastern Industrial Consultants Ltd. (NECON) extends services to entrepreneurs such as preparation of project report, project appraisal and other liaison works as well as consultancy on various matters connected with establishment of an industry. A Consultancy Bureau also works under the Directorate of Industries to render consultancy services needed by the Small Scale entrepreneurs.

2. *Industrial Estates and Area Development*: With a view to provide built sheds along with other infrastructural facilities such as water, power, communication, etc., to small-scale industrial units, the government took up scheme to setup some mini-industrial estates at different locations in Mizoram. Under the scheme, industrial estates have been setup at Zuangtui, Kolasib, Lunglei, and Champhai and an industrial growth centre at Luangmual (Aizawl). A fruit park is being developed at Chhingchhip exclusively for fruit industry. An export oriented industrial estate is being setup at Pukpuii.
3. *Rural Service Workshop*: A general engineering workshop equipped with different type of machine tools and equipments has been setup at Aizawl mainly to provide service facilities to small-scale automobile repairing workshops, which are not well equipped to perform all the works within their limited tools and equipments. A crankshaft grinding machine has been also installed within the shop.

4. *Raw Material Depot*: The Raw Material Depot functioned under RIP, Aizawl mainly designed to provide the small entrepreneurs and artisans with scarce indigenous raw materials as well as other miscellaneous type of raw materials, which were required by them, but, difficult to procure. Such raw materials were procured and stocked in the depot and sold at reasonable prices. The items that were handled by the depot are knitting wool, dyed yarn, gray yarn, paraffin wax, BP sheets, GI sheets, mutton tallow, aluminium ingots, aluminium circles, different soap making chemicals, other shoe making materials, etc.
5. *Marketing*: In order to provide like assistance marketing for products of small-scale industries in Mizoram, one marketing cell under the Directorate of Industries was constituted. This cell collects all necessary information on marketing intelligence; process and disseminates the same to the prospective entrepreneurs. Further, in order to establish proper link this cell maintains close liaisoning with various government and semi-government organisations and small-scale industries. When ZIDCO was assigned for setting up of emporia for purchase and marketing of SSI products, this cell continued providing the governmental link and acted as promotional agency for intensive marketing activity.

   There exists a Market Promotion Council under the provisions of New Industrial Policy of Mizoram, 2000 which is meant for coordinating and interacting with marketing agencies elsewhere to promote sale of local products inside and outside the country. The council focuses on export promotion of locally exportable products like garments, processed food, handicrafts and handloom products.
6. *Turn Key Project Scheme*: A proposal was taken up by the Department of Industries in setting up some demand based engineering industries under the turn key project. The government, in the first phase setup one Barbed Wire manufacturing unit in Mizoram. Under the scheme, the Industries Department had setup the factory on its own making all the necessary investments and made it operative. Later, it was handed over to private entrepreneur on "installment payment" basis to run the same independently. The objective was to develop industrial atmosphere in the region and to create demonstration effect among local entrepreneurs, so that they may also take up new ventures in setting up demand based industries in future.

Entrepreneurship Development in Mizoram

The status of entrepreneurship development in Mizoram is not different from other Northeastern states; rather it is yet to find a place on the industrial map of India being "a no industry area"[21] at national level. In Mizoram, there are one or two medium scale industries and the only small-scale, tiny, village and cottage, handloom and handicrafts industries dominated with very little investment. There is no large scale industry in Mizoram. Mizoram did not make headway in industrial development and there is a high dependence on government jobs (4.66 per cent).[22] Moreover, the Public Sector Enterprises in Mizoram were incurring huge loss year after year, and have failed to expand the base for ancillarisation and cannot be taken as role model for future entrepreneurs.

This may be attributed to historical reasons and to some extent to political and social factors, lack of entrepreneurship as well as future vision. Mizo are known to be sincere, courageous, industrious, intelligent, and capable of learning, but, lack specialization and are averse to physical labour. Mizo love white-collar jobs. One solution to the problem of educated unemployed may be the entrepreneurship development. It is a challenge for the policy makers. There is a need to change the mindset of new generation. Their horizons are to be opened up by bringing change in their thought. There are many agencies involved in entrepreneurship development. A brief description on the activities of these organizations is given here.

Directorate of Industries

The Directorate of Industries, Government of Mizoram conducts training programmes for promotion of industrial environment in the State. These included (i) One-year artisan course in handloom weaving at Weaving Training Centres at Aizawl, Lunglei and Saiha, (ii) Six month training in knitting and tailoring at Craft Centres at Aizawl, Lunglei, Saiha, Champhai and in Cane and Bamboo craft at Hnathial, Haulawng and Diltlang, (iii) One-year Certificate Course in Blacksmithy, Wireman, Carpentry, Tinsmithy, Auto-Mechanic, Turner, Welding and Foundry, and (iv) One-year PC Hardware Maintenance Course, one-year Diploma in Computer Science at Golden Republic IT Centre, Aizawl and DOEACC "O" level course, DOEACC "A" level Course and Repair and Maintenance of Consumer Electronics Course at Academy of Computer and Electronics Centre at Lunglei.

Apart from the above, Awareness Campaigns, Entrepreneurship Development Programmes (EDPs) and Management Development Programmes (MDPs) are conducted from time to time in collaboration with agencies like Northeastern Industrial Consultants Ltd. (NECON),

Small Industries Service Institute (SISI), Northeastern Development Finance Corporation Ltd. (NEDFi), Indian Institute of Entrepreneurship (IIE), etc. and some entrepreneurs were also sponsored for in-plant training outside the State.

Small Industry Service Institute

The Aizawl branch of Small Industries Service Institute (SISI) was opened in 1973 at the initiative of Small Industries Development Organization (SIDO), which is an apex body. The SISI is an agency at field level offering assistance and guidance on any problem connected with setting up and running of a small-scale industry. The Aizawl branch of SISI works in close cooperation with State Government, Zoram Industrial Development Corporation Ltd. (ZIDCO), District Industries Centre (DIC) and other agencies concerned with promotion, development and modernization of small-scale industries in Mizoram. It conducts various training programmes like (i) Entrepreneurship Development Programme (EDP) in food processing technology, refrigeration and air conditioning etc., (ii) Managerial Development Programme (MDP), (iii) Export Packaging Training Programme (EPTP), and (iv) Skill Development Programme (SDP).

Northeastern Industrial Consultants Ltd. (NECON)

The North-Eastern Industrial Consultants Ltd. (NECON) have been assigned with the responsibility of ensuring entrepreneurship development in the entire northeastern region *inter alia* other activities. With a view to provide industrial consultancy, assistance and professional services to tiny, rural, cottage, small and medium scale enterprises a branch of NECON was established on 21st November 1989 at Aizawl[23] which had organized a series of programmes for different target groups, e.g. educated unemployed youths, engineering graduates, diploma holders, science graduates, women, ex-servicemen and Prime Minister Rojgar Yojana (PMRY) beneficiaries and so on. It also helps voluntary organizations in socio-economic development activities. It has established a centre for "Science and Technology Entrepreneurship Development" (STED) at Aizawl on 8th May 2000, which became functional on 21st September 2000.

Mizoram Khadi & Village Industries Board (MKVIB)

The Mizoram Khadi and Village Industries Board maintains a Multi-Disciplinary Training Centre (MDTC), Zemabawk (Aizawl) since 1990-91 for imparting training in different trades reserved for *khadi* and village industries such as cane and bamboo crafts, carpentry, village oil, NEO soap, cane furniture, cane cap, fibre, etc. However, it had sponsored training outside the State also before MDTC came in existence.

Table 3.20 presents the year-wise training programmes conducted by different agencies.

Table 3.20: Training Programmes Conducted for Entrepreneurship Development in Mizoram (From 1971-72 to 2003-04)

Year	*Directorate of Industries*						*SISI*		*NECON*					*MKVIB*
	Weaving Crafts		*Knitting & Tailoring Crafts*		*Cane & Bamboo Crafts*									
	No. of Prog.	*No. of Participants*	*No. of Prog.*	*No. of Participants*	*No. of Prog.*	*No. of Participants*	*No. of Prog.*	*No. of Participants*	*No. of Prog.*	*No. of Participants*	*Units Established*	*No. of Jobs Generated*	*Investment (Rs. in lakh)*	
1971-72	Nil	Nil	3	16	—	—	—	—	—	—	—	—	—	—
1972-73	1	7	3	36	—	—	—	—	—	—	—	—	—	—
1973-74	Nil	Nil	3	43	—	—	N.A.	N.A.	—	—	—	—	—	—
1974-75	1	2	2	35	—	—	N.A.	N.A.	—	—	—	—	—	—
1975-76	Nil	Nil	2	30	—	—	N.A.	N.A.	—	—	—	—	—	—
1976-77	1	7	2	40	—	—	N.A.	N.A.	—	—	—	—	—	—
1977-78	1	8	2	41	—	—	N.A.	N.A.	—	—	—	—	—	—
1978-79	Nil	Nil	2	39	—	—	N.A.	N.A.	—	—	—	—	—	—
1979-80	2	23	2	42	—	—	N.A.	N.A.	—	—	—	—	—	—
1980-81	2	23	2	42	—	—	N.A.	N.A.	—	—	—	—	—	—
1981-82	4	55	2	41	—	—	N.A.	N.A.	—	—	—	—	—	—
1982-83	4	41	2	41	—	—	N.A.	N.A.	—	—	—	—	—	—
1983-84	1	4	4	90	—	—	N.A.	N.A.	—	—	—	—	—	—
1984-85	1	8	4	101	—	—	N.A.	N.A.	—	—	—	—	—	—
1985-86	1	13	4	97	—	—	N.A.	N.A.	—	—	—	—	—	—
1986-87	2	32	4	76	—	—	4	127	—	—	—	—	—	82
1987-88	2	28	6	111	—	—	9	75	—	—	—	—	—	85
1988-89	3	69	6	111	—	—	2	30	—	—	—	—	—	Nil
1989-90	3	47	6	103	1	15	2	36	—	—	—	—	—	19
1990-91	3	37	6	106	6	70	1	73	—	—	—	—	—	Nil
1991-92	3	28	6	106	5	60	N.A.	N.A.	8	200	—	—	—	21
1992-93	3	45	6	115	2	20	N.A.	N.A.	4	115	—	—	—	51
1993-94	3	41	6	115	4	51	N.A.	N.A.	3	85	—	—	—	20
1994-95	3	43	6	114	6	63	N.A.	N.A.	N.A.	N.A.	—	—	—	8
1995-96	3	37	6	109	4	39	N.A.	N.A.	N.A.	N.A.	—	—	—	Nil
1996-97	3	53	6	105	5	53	4	N.A.	N.A.	N.A.	—	—	—	Nil
1997-98	3	43	6	140	4	31	4	118	N.A.	N.A.	—	—	—	84
1998-99	3	27	6	138	1	10	1	N.A.	N.A.	N.A.	—	—	—	27
1999-00	3	29	6	152	3	35	2	70	1	25	—	—	—	34
2000-01	3	30	6	145	4	32	2	51	10	187	—	—	—	246
2001-02	N.A.	N.A.	6	144	N.A.	N.A.	1	21	6	132	48	78	76.95	N.A.
2002-03	N.A.	N.A.	N.A.	N.A.	N.A.	N.A.	3	122	10	245	96	265	129.28	N.A.
2003-04	N.A.	N.A.	N.A.	N.A.	N.A.	N.A.	2	18	7	807	89	294	110.80	N.A.

Source: Compiled from Data obtained from respective organizations.

Table 3.20 revealed the following:

- The Directorate of Industries offers training in traditional crafts through its nine craft centres established for the purpose in trades like Blacksmithy, Wireman, Carpentry, Tinsmithy, Auto-Mechanic, Turner, Welding, Foundry, PC Hardware Maintenance, Diploma in Computer Science, Repair and Maintenance of Consumer Electronics, etc. However, it is observed that these centres lack in modern industrial outlook.
- Till 1978-79, the craft centre in Lunglei somehow conducted annually one 6 month training programme in weaving and remained idle for rest of the time. Further, the period from 1971-72 to 1978-79 witnessed wide fluctuations in participation from public. Lunglei, being centre of revolutionary political movement at that time, remained disturbed and because of this, even in some years, there was no participation. Since 1983-84, the training programme in weaving was made for one year duration, each of the three centres, from 1988-89, had conducted annually one such programme. It seemed that the three weaving craft centres in Mizoram became fully operational from 1988-89. Inter-centre public participation varied and over the years from 1988-89 to 2000-01, it declined. This confirmed that people did not show interest as their problems remained unattended, which needs to be investigated. The participation from remote places like Saiha was poor. This might be because of problems such as inadequate marketing facility, inadequate finance, improper roads and communication, lack of vision, etc.
- Till 1973-74, the training programme in knitting and tailoring was of 4 month duration and thereafter, it was made of 6 month duration and from 1987-88, all the three centres regularly conducted annually 2 such programmes. Over the years, though the number of participants registered a marginal increase, there was consistency in public participation in all the three centres, which was quite encouraging. The target beneficiaries were Mizo girls who were comparatively free. The Champhai centre showed activity since 1983-84 and Lunglei centre since 1987-88. But, the capacity per programme seemed less and the number of programmes annually carried out per centre was less.

Industrial Profile of Mizoram

Handlooms, Handicraft, Sericulture are important industries of Mizoram. Besides, there are a variety of cottage and small scale industries producing items of household consumption. A brief description of these industries is given here.

1. *Handloom Weaving*: Handloom Weaving is considered one of the oldest traditional craft practiced by Mizo-Community. Mizo woman, in almost every house practices this art of weaving cloth with the help of lionlooms. With high degree of traditional skills, they turn out beautiful eye catching pieces of colourful designs, like bags, shawls and Mizo *puan* (a piece of cloth worn in the style of *Lungi* by Mizo Women). This conventional, but, outmoded method of producing cloth by Loinloom takes several hours to weave a piece of cloth which in turn results in higher cost of production. Though, not less than 50,000 weavers are engaged in the trade, the quantum of surplus production is negligible to make any appreciable impact on the consumers market inside and outside the State. On the average, handloom units attain an annual turnover of Rs. 4.92 lakh per unit and makes an annual Gross Value Addition of 43.72 per cent of their turnover.
2. *Handicrafts*: Cane and bamboo products are the only traditional handicrafts of Mizoram. Mizoram has abundant bamboo resources of twenty species which is spread over nearly 57 per cent of the geographical area. It fetches the government revenue of Rs. 80 lakh p.a. besides, annual royalty of Rs. 66 lakh. The annual availability from the total growing stock is estimated at 5.828 million MT, but, presently a small portion of it could only be utilized as the State's total bamboo consumption stands at 28315 MT only. Bamboos, though, form 30 per cent of forest department's total revenue, they are not cared properly. The culms grow upto 8 to 10 metre and are widely used for construction of *Kaccha* houses, furniture, fencing, weaving, pulping, woven products, etc., but, there is no information on the economics of trading in such items. A bamboo policy for Mizoram was framed for optimum utilization of vast untapped bamboo resource for improving rural economy and industrial development. The aims and objectives of the bamboo policy of Mizoram included (i) protection and preservation of mountain ecology by protecting bamboo forests, (ii) protection of rich

bio-diversity associated with bamboo forests and re-growth areas and their future development, (iii) sustainable development and utilization of bamboo resources through scientific management, (iv) promotion of private bamboo plantations, (v) promotion of bamboo based industries at cottage level, (vi) revitalization and promotion of local traditional bamboo crafts and art with improved technology, (vii) promotion of bamboo sector development as an essential component of rural development strategy, (viii) promotion of bamboo as an essential wood substitute by increasing bamboo production, (ix) creation of awareness and understanding of bamboo as green gold among the general public, (x) effective exploitation of the economic potential of bamboo before the impending famine ('mautam'). With this end, ply board factories have been established with investment of Rs. 162 lakh in Lengpui village and Zuangtui (Aizawl). Hnamchhantu, a NGO is actively engaged in investigating the potential for specific bamboo products. ZOHANDCO is entrusted with the responsibility to promoting handicrafts along with handlooms of the state.

Presently, among the cane and bamboo products, Mizo Hat is the exclusive item, but, if the art of bamboo crafts is properly promoted, there can be many products of it viz., baskets, stools, cups, hangers, broom sticks, handles for wall, ceiling cleaners, umbrella handles, water piping, pillows, mats, cigar pipes, fire lightening instrument, etc. Local Artisans with their traditional skill turn out beautiful Hats made of cane/bamboo and some kind of wild leaves. Though, the product has good export potential, the market has not been exploited owing to the limited quantum of production.

3. *Sericulture*: Sericulture was considered as one of the most important avenues for providing employment to rural people as the topographic features and climatic conditions of Mizoram are highly favourable for Sericulture practicing, but, negligible progress was made during the period when it was a district of Assam. After the establishment of the Rural Industries Project, 3 mulberry farms were setup at Kolasib, Mualvum and Nausel which were almost destroyed during the disturbance of 1966 and later abandoned. In the Fifth Plan, 22 sericulture farms were established in association with Northeastern Council for training to private rearers in Ceri, Muga, Mulberry, and Oak Tasar Silk

in. various suitable areas inside the Union Territory. Of these, 18 were in Aizawl district, 3 in Lunglei district and 1 in Chhimtuipui. Due emphasis was given to popularize Oak Tasar, Ceri, Muga, and Mulberry among private sericulturists. Though, the large number of seed farms and extension centres were established, the sericulture activity suffered for want of trained personnel in the field.

4. *Bakery*: Bakery is a processed food-based industry having good demand. Adoption of western life style and rapid increase in population made it an essential item of food. There are many bakery units scattered all over the State. However, their main concentration is in Aizawl. There were 1048 units registered with MKVIB as on 31st March 2001 and 434 SSIs registered with Directorate of Industries as on 31st December 2002. Apart from organized many more existed as unorganized. Among bakery units some bakeries like Zote Bakery and Mummy's Bakery each have an annual turnover of more than Rs. 3.3 crore. On the average, bakery and flour mills attain annual turnover of Rs. 1.8 crore per unit and makes an annual Gross Value Addition of 24.06 per cent of their turnover.
5. *Noodle Manufacturing*: Mizo like people from East Asia and North-East Asia like *chowmin* as a food item. It forms an essential part of their morning breakfast as well as noon time snacks. This is easily available in all restaurants and tea stalls of all towns and cities as it is a product of household industry. Its main raw material is wheat flour. It can be started as a cottage industry even with a small investment. The demand for this food item is gradually increasing and is perceived with bright scope.
6. *Wheat Flour and Wheat Products*: The dietary habits of Mizo are changing and many of them have started using wheat flour and wheat products including bakery products. Wheat flour also constitutes an ingredient for bakery units. To take advantage of the situation, two medium sized small-scale flour mills have been setup in Zuantui Industrial Estate and one in Vairengte. Among these units, Sunrise Roller Flour Mills and HP Modern Roller Flour Mills each having annual turnover of more than Rs. 3.25 crore. The industry has good prospects as the demand is expected to grow further in times to come.
7. *Carpentry and Furniture Workshop*: Carpentry and wood products have been the traditional crafts of Mizoram. Mizo have

shown high level, of skill in wood crafts. Carpentry is a competitive trade here in Mizoram because, the local demand for furniture, cabinet, etc. is not enough to keep all the carpenters fully engaged throughout the year. Non-availability of properly seasoned wood is making fine quality furniture manufacturing impossible and resulted in lack of demand from outside Mizoram. Restriction by the Supreme Court order dated 15th January 1998 has further dampened the industry. The Supreme Court order provided that there shall be no fresh felling of trees in the forest except in accordance with the Working Plan of the State Government. It is important to mention that till now, Mizoram is not having any such Working Plan.[24] However, timber working scheme existed which provided for departmental extraction of timber from areas outside reserved forests. There were 916 units registered with MKVIB as on 31st March 2001 and 734 SSI units registered with Directorate of Industries as on 31st December 2002. The number of unregistered units was more than the registered units. On the average, furniture units attain an annual turnover of Rs. 4.16 lakh per unit and make an annual Gross Value Addition of 38.34 per cent of their turnover.

8. *Blacksmithy*: Blacksmithy is a traditional old cottage industry of Mizoram. It existed in rural village economy of Lushais even before British annexed Mizoram in 1872. Blacksmith (*Thirdeng*) was considered a respected member of traditional Mizo society as he supplied tools and implements for agriculture, guns, knives and *daos*. For his services, he was remunerated in the form of a basket full of rice from each house in the village and also received a small share in every animal shot dead or trapped by any of the villager. Besides, he was exempted from coolly labour.[25] Village artisans are generally engaged in this trade. Small loans, grants, etc., in the form of cash and kind for tools and implement are given by the government to the artisans engaged in this trade. Due to competition from machine made parts and being traditional industry in nature, it is expected to get local demand only. Majority of the units were either unregistered or registered with MKVIB only. However, many more unregistered units exist.

9. *Tinsmithy*: Tinsmithy is the most commonly practiced cottage industry of the State. Besides good amount of rainfall, the drinking water supply from Public Health Engineering Department (PHED) is not regular, as there is no big reservoir

and water flows down immediately after rain. Because of this, everyone needs to harvest rain water for which big barrels generally made of tin sheets are needed. This need being basic in nature, the tinsmithy has a bright scope for further growth all over the State equally among rural and urban areas. There were 619 units registered with the Directorate of Industries as on 31st December 2002.

10. *Steel Fabrication*: Steel Fabrication industry is of recent origin in Mizoram. Its growth is mostly linked with growth in construction, more especially building construction industry and its growth is noticed during last two to three decades only owing to government patronage. Steel fabrication industry grew faster than any other industry as it is basically a service industry which does not produce standard products rather the artisans just give their services for consideration in the form of labour. This does not require large investment and an artisan with ITI qualification in welding course having some tools and implements can start it easily. On the average, steel fabrication units attain an annual turnover of Rs. 11.60 lakh per unit and make an annual Gross Value Addition of 30.83 per cent of their turnover. This industry is perceived with good prospects of further growth.
11. *Engineering Workshop*: Majority of the units among the engineering workshops in Mizoram are automobile workshops. Due to the rapid progress of road transportation in Mizoram, the scope for further development of this trade is bright. The main drawback for development of this industry was the absence of a good machine shop to provide facilities like crank shaft grinding and cylinder boring for automobile engines. One crankshaft grinding machine was installed in the Rural Service Workshop maintained under Rural Industries Project, Aizawl to overcome the difficulty. However, except for minor repairs and maintenance of automobiles, scope for major repairs and assembly of automobiles appears limited. There were altogether 631 SSIs registered with the Directorate of Industries as on 31st December 2002. Many more unregistered units also existed. On the average, automobile workshops attain annual turnover of Rs. 6.68 lakh per unit and make an annual Gross Value Addition of 37.24 per cent of their turnover.
12. *Tyre Retreading*: Like automobile workshops, tyre retreading is also one of the successful industries in Mizoram. In view of

large number of automobiles in towns and cities, the industry has a good prospects of growth subject to availability of power. On the average, tyre retreading units attain an annual turnover of Rs. 3.78 lakh per unit and make an annual Gross Value Addition of 27.49 per cent of their turnover.

13. *Paper, Publishing and Allied Products*: Majority of the units in this group are of printing press. Printing industry is among the oldest organized industry in Mizoram. The Church owned first formal unit "Synod Press" was setup in 1910-11 whose presently annual average turnover is of Rs. 22.75 lakh. The printing press in Mizoram is mainly meeting the local demand of printing jobs from different government departments and to some extent private also. Local newspapers are having their own printing press. In view of the socio-cultural background and advertising practices of business and industry in the State, it appears that the scope for further promotion of printing press other than the news paper industry is limited. However, it may grow fast, if, demand from private sector grows. There were 123 units registered with MKVIB as on 31st March 2001 and 310 SSIs registered with the Directorate of Industries as on 31st December 2002. On the average, printing press attain an annual turnover of Rs. 34.78 lakh per unit and make an annual Gross Value Addition of 40.69 per cent of their turnover.

14. *Dyeing Unit*: Dyeing and printing of textiles has been a traditional cottage industry of Mizoram. These units were using manual methods of dyeing which were time consuming and also produced poor quality at very high cost and could not meet the demand for good quality yarn to lionloom weavers of *puan* (a Mizo *lungi* wore by women as skirt) etc. To cope up with the existing problem and to supply dyed yarn at a cheaper rate to weavers the industries department had setup a semi-mechanized yarn dyeing centre at Aizawl in June 1978. The growth of the industry is linked with the growth of textile and textile products and as such is expected to have local demand only. It may have some export potential, but, their commercial viability will always be in question.

15. *Candle Making*: Owing to frequent disruption of power supply, there existed a constant demand of candles. But, paraffin wax, the basic raw material was under control and all the units were allotted with it depending on the availability of government

quota. The Raw Materials-*cum*-Sales Depot under the Rural Industries Project supplied the basic raw material needed. There were 47 units registered with MKVIB as on 31st March 2001 and 11 SSIs registered with the Directorate of Industries as on 31st December 2002.

16. *Soap Making*: Soap making is a village and cottage industry of Mizoram. Though, there is a good demand for washing soap in the market, the units are facing shortage of working capital. There were 59 units registered with MKVIB as on 31st March 2001.
17. *Vaihlozial*: Vaihlozial is a local tobacco relished by the Mizo. It is a type, which has got some similarity with *Bidi* and can be placed between *Bidi* and Cigarettes. The locally grown tobacco leaves known as 'Vaihlo' are used as basic raw material along with a thin piece of paper and cotton thread to manufacture Vaihlozial. This trade of manufacturing Vaihlozial is a household, which is practiced all over the state. Mostly, Mizo women are engaged in this trade. They utilize their leisure in making Vaihlozial, which is a means of some extra earnings. There were 43 units registered with the Directorate of Industries as on 31st December 2002.
18. *Fruit Preservation*: The climate and topography of Mizoram offer good prospects for growing a variety of fruits. However, efforts in this direction started late. The main products are pineapple juice, squash, canned pineapple, orange juice, passion fruit juice, etc. With MIFCO having plants at Sairang, Vairengte and Chhingchhip, the industry is developing as an organized industry in the State. A food park is being setup at Chhingchhip to accommodate private sector units for processing and preservation of fruits and fruit products. Of the total 11 state level cooperatives as on 31st March 2002, one, Mizoram State Cooperative Fruit Forestry and Vegetables Growers Federation Ltd. (MAFF) with total investment of Rs. 28.07 lakh having one branch and 39 member cooperative societies engaged in it. There were 122 units registered with MKVIB as on 31st March 2001.

Special Features of Industries in Mizoram

To know the important characteristic features of industry in Mizoram a sample of 130 industrial units was taken. These units were located in five districts out of eight districts of the State viz., Aizawl, Champhai, Kolasib, Mamit, and Serchhip. However, looking to industrial concentration the same may be taken as representative of the entire State. The findings pertaining to these 130 randomly selected industrial units have been discussed as under:

1. *Location-wise Classification*: Classification of enterprises as presented in Table 3.21 reveals that out of total 130 unit, 85 were from Aizawl, 11 from Champhai, 17 from Kolasib, 11 from Mamit and 12 from Serchhip districts.
2. *Industry-wise Classification*: Of total 130 units, 19 were Automobile Workshops, 16 Bakery & Flour Mills, 6 Electricals and Electronics, 16 Fabrication, 24 Furniture, 8 Handloom, 3 Motor Body, 8 Printing Press, 23 Tailoring and Textile Trading and 7 Tyre Works.
3. *Organization of Enterprises*: All the units were proprietorship firms, as there are no partnership firms and company form of enterprises in general, except state government owned Public Sector Undertakings. The Indian Partnership Act, 1932 is yet to be extended to Mizoram. In reality, there may be some partnership firms, but, they are registered either as cooperative societies or individual proprietorship. These cooperative societies are far away from the spirit of cooperation and are true business houses.

Table 3.21: Location-wise, Industry-wise and Sex-wise Classification of Sample Enterprises in Mizoram

	District																	
	Aizawl			*Champhai*			*Kolasib*			*Mamit*			*Serchhip*			*Total*		
Industrial Category	*M*	*F*	*T*	*M*	*F*	*T*	*M*	*F*	*T*	*M*	*F*	*T*	*M*	*F*	*T*	*M*	*F*	*T*
Automobile Workshop	8	1	9	2	0	2	4	0	4	2	0	2	2	0	2	18	1	19
Bakery & Flour Mills	8	4	12	1	0	1	—	—	—	1	0	1	2	0	2	12	4	16
Electrical & Electronics	4	0	4	—	—	—	2	0	2	—	—	—	—	—	—	6	0	6
Fabrication	8	0	8	2	0	2	2	0	2	2	0	2	2	0	2	16	0	16
Furniture	15	0	15	2	0	2	2	0	2	3	0	3	2	0	2	24	0	24
Handloom	3	5	8	—	—	—	—	—	—	—	—	—	—	—	—	3	5	8
Motor Body	1	1	2	—	—	—	—	—	—	—	—	—	1	0	1	2	1	3
Printing Press	5	0	5	1	0	1	1	0	1	—	—	—	1	0	1	8	0	8
Tailoring & Textile Trading	5	12	17	1	0	1	1	2	3	1	0	1	0	1	1	8	15	23
Tyre Works	4	1	5	1	0	1	1	0	1	—	—	—	—	—	—	6	1	7
Total	61	24	85	10	0	10	13	2	15	9	0	9	10	1	11	103	27	130

Legend: M=Male, F=Female, T=Total

4. *Age and Background of Entrepreneurs*: The sample survey revealed that nearly 70 per cent (90 out of 130) of entrepreneurs

were of less than 20 years' held in their respective trade. None of the entrepreneurs' grandfather/mother and great grandfather/ mother had ever engaged in industry. In 23 per cent (30 out of 130) cases, the father/mother of the entrepreneur had chosen industry as their entrepreneurial career. In 38 per cent (50 out of 130) cases, entrepreneurs opted for industrial activity as a means of their career for the first time in their family history. Only 7 per cent (10 out of 130) entrepreneurs accepted of their family support behind their choosing to a particular industrial activity. Other 84 per cent (110 out of 130) entrepreneurs reported that nothing motivated them to engage in a particular industry, except their own ambitions. Again, 60 per cent entrepreneurs were such who could not be given any exposure through governments' motivational programmes like EDPs, MDPs and SDPs. All these makes it clear that majority of entrepreneurs in industry are of first generation entrepreneurs having no family background (support). Further, governments' motivational programmes have brought a little impact only in this regard. It may be argued that the roots of modern industry in Mizoram are two decades old only and yet to sprawl deeper.

5. *Education and Training of Entrepreneurs*: Education is an important strength of people in Mizoram and it was observed that only 47 per cent (60 out of 130) of the entrepreneurs were below plus two level of education and the rest had higher education exposure. Nearly 40 per cent of the entrepreneurs had some exposure to training or exposure about the working of industry through various promotional programmes like EDPs, MDPs, SDPs, etc. This showed that young persons with experience and exposure are not joining industry as freely as any other profession.
6. *Sex of Entrepreneurs*: Of the 130 enterprises' 27 were owned, run, and managed by females. Of the 27 females, 24 were from Aizawl district, 2 from Kolasib district, and 1 from Serchhip district. Majority of the females in Mizoram were engaged in occupations like tailoring and textile (15 out of 27), handloom (5 out of 27), Bakery (4 out of 37). Basically these trades are traditional in-house trades and are best suited for female participation. Their non-traditional participation was also seen in Mizoram such as automobile workshops, motor body workshops and tyre works. But, their participation was low

and may be by chance and not by choice. Those who were engaged in non traditional trades were managing with hired workers only.

7. *Management of Enterprises*: In all the cases the firm's affairs were either managed by entrepreneur himself or by his family members. Professional managers were not engaged. Nearly 53 per cent (70 out of 130) entrepreneurs reported that they did not like to recruit professionally qualified people. This indicated that professional outlook was lacking in entrepreneurs in Mizoram.

   About 68 per cent (80 out of 130) entrepreneurs maintained books of accounts relating their firm. However, 15 per cent (20 out of 130) get it done by an outside accountant only 7 per cent (10 out of 130) entrepreneurs keep their accounts under double entry system and the rests under single entry system as per their need, convenience, ability and knowledge. It may be understood that accounting records are not kept systematically, as there is no incentive force to do so as the tax authorities do not insist upon it. Moreover, tribal people in Mizoram are not liable to pay income tax and they need not to determine annual profit accurately. Perhaps, this may be the reason why entrepreneurs in general do not hire the services of an 'accountant'. Another reason might be that due to small scale of operation they find it difficult to afford the services of hired accountants.

Table 3.22: Per Employee Annual Wages Prevailing in Industries of Mizoram For the year 2002-03

(Figures in Rupees)

District	*Aizawl*	*Champhai*	*Kolasib*	*Mamit*	*Serchhip*	*Mean*
Automobile Workshops	26632	51710	21750	34800	44400	28991
Bakery & Flour Mills	18348	42013	N.A.	23600	N.A.	18776
Electrical & Electronics	29333	N.A.	N.A.	N.A.	N.A.	29333
Fabrication	33518	48105	14000	38000	31125	33381
Furniture	31593	66190	32160	48625	41800	37043
Handloom	29447	N.A.	N.A.	N.A.	N.A.	29447
Motor Body	26441	N.A.	N.A.	N.A.	48750	28789
Printing Press	60470	4350	N.A.	N.A.	52750	56224
Tailoring & Textile	30114	42000	28286	N.A.	42000	30622
Trading						
Tyre Works	34335	43500	21600	N.A.	N.A.	33625
Mean	25633	35160	23929	20310	39200	26405

8. *Average Annual Wages*: Table 3.22 shows per employee average annual wages. Though, it varied between Rs. 20,310/- the lowest in Mamit district and Rs. 39,200/- the highest in Serchhip district, it works out to be at Rs. 26,405/- per each worker. The wage rate of Aizawl district was little below the average. Category-wise, it ranged between Rs. 18,776/- in bakery and flour mills and Rs. 56,224/- in printing press category. Except for bakery, the annual wage per employee was higher than the weighted average in all other trades.
9. *Material Cost Component in Total Cost*: Table 3.23 shows the material cost component in total cost, which revealed that on the average it comprised 68 per cent in Mizoram. Which seemed high and is reflexive of the industries in Mizoram a material intensive. Among districts, it varied between 55 per cent in Kolasib to 68 per cent in Aizawl. Similarly, among different industries, it ranged between 37 per cent in handloom to 77 per cent in fabrication, which is an indicative of handloom industry a labour intensive one and fabrication and bakery trades are highly competitive. However, the material cost component in fabrication industry in Aizawl district (80 per cent), in Kolasib district (81 per cent), in bakery trade in Mamit (83 per cent), Serchhip (86 per cent), in printing press trade in Kolasib (85 per cent), in tailoring and textile trade in Mamit district (88 per cent) were higher than the weighted average.

Table 3.23: Material Cost Component in Total Cost in Industries of Mizoram For the year 2002-03

(*Figures in percentage*)

District	*Aizawl*	*Champhai*	*Kolasib*	*Mamit*	*Serchhip*	*Total*
Automobile Workshops	71	70	51	68	59	68
Bakery & Flour Mills	70	56	N.A.	83	86	70
Electrical & Electronics	47	N.A.	38	N.A.	N.A.	47
Fabrication	80	63	81	63	67	77
Furniture	60	51	43	42	63	56
Handloom	37	N.A.	N.A.	N.A.	N.A.	37
Motor Body	65	N.A.	N.A.	N.A.	51	63
Printing Press	63	76	85	N.A.	63	63
Tailoring & Textile Trading	51	69	30	88	10	49
Tyre Works	44	35	61	N.A.	N.A.	45
Total	68	60	55	61	62	68

10. *Purchase of Inputs*: It was reported that 40 out of 130 industries (31 per cent) were totally depending upon supply from outside the State, while other 60 out of 130 (46 per cent) procured goods both from within and out side the State.
    About 15 per cent (20 out of 130) of the entrepreneurs recognized the role of middleman in purchases. However, the entrepreneurs denied any role of middleman in selling their products. This is how brokers, commission agents, *dalals* and *arhatiya* do not exist in Mizoram.
    Around three-fourth (100 out of 130) entrepreneurs confirmed the practices of credit facility from suppliers and producers for 40 days to 4 months depending upon the custom of trade. Further, they confirmed that they give credit to retailers, for 1 month to 5 months.
11. *Marketing of Product*: Approximately 61 per cent (80 out of 130) units were producing and selling in Aizawl district only. This signifies that the products of industries are for local consumption and their area of operation is limited.
12. *State Assistance Programme*: State incentive programmes play an important role in promotion of industries. However, as per the survey, only 23 per cent (30 out of 130) units benefited from project report subsidy and captive power consumption subsidy, 7 per cent (10 out of 130) units received subsidy on transportation of plant and machinery. Similarly, 15 per cent (20 out of 130) received assistance under central transport subsidy. Among the sample units none received neither land subsidy or D.G. Set subsidy nor interest subsidy nor grant-in-aid nor working capital grant. Over all, only 23 per cent (30 out of 130) entrepreneurs confirmed that the benefits of incentives and promotional programmes of industrial policy reach grassroots level. Surprisingly, 46 per cent (60 out of 130) entrepreneurs expressed "no idea" on the question of reaching benefits of policy measures to grassroots level. All the entrepreneurs denied the existence of marketing support from government.
13. *Gross Value Added*: Table 3.24 reveals the gross value added by industries in Mizoram.

Table 3.24 reveales that on the average the gross value addition by industry in Mizoram was 30 per cent. It may be considered satisfactory.

However, it varied among districts between 28.35 per cent in Aizawl to 51.91 per cent in Kolasib. Similarly, among different industries, it ranged from 24.06 per cent in bakery and flour mills to 61 per cent in electricals and electronics. This indicated that bakery and flour mills are most competitive and electricals and electronics industry is most promising. However, it was highest in tailoring in Mamit district (86.44 per cent), bakery in Serchhip (74.15 per cent) and printing in Champhai (73.65 per cent) and Kolasib district (72.81 per cent). This indication may attract new entrepreneurs in future to these industries.

Table 3.24: Gross Value Added by Industries in Mizoram
For the year 2002-03

(*Figures in percentage*)

District	*Aizawl*	*Champhai*	*Kolasib*	*Mamit*	*Serchhip*	*Mean*
Automobile Workshops	37.81	21.62	44.23	42.09	36.03	37.24
Bakery & Flour Mills	23.94	22.36		28.44	74.15	24.06
Electrical & Electronics	56.55		83.74			61.11
Fabrication	29.47	25.47	47.72	41.45	32.06	30.83
Furniture	36.42	36.91	51.59	41.23	43.57	38.34
Handloom	43.72					43.72
Miscellaneous	46.64	11.55	51.44	57.22	71.00	44.93
Motor Body	31.46				35.39	32.01
Printing Press	38.33	73.65	72.81		20.58	39.05
Tailoring & Textile Trading	36.84	24.37	61.46	86.44	38.85	40.69
Tyre Works	23.90	58.30	44.98			27.49
Mean	28.35	31.98	51.91	43.96	34.64	29.72

NOTES

1. IBM World Book, 1997.
2. Anuradha, A. and Rao, A.V.V.S.K., An Analysis of Inter-State Industrial Disparities in India, *Indian Journal of Regional Science*, Vol. XXVII, No. 1 & 2, 1995, p. 33.
3. Yogi A. K., *Development of the Northeast Region: Problems and Prospects*, Spectrum Publications, Guwahati, 1991, p. 175.
4. Department of Art & Culture, *District Gazetteers, Mizoram*, Government of Mizoram, 1989, p. 127.
5. *Ibid.*
6. *Ibid*, p. 136.
7. Roy Burman, B.R., *Demographic and Socio-Economic Profiles of the Hill Areas of Northeast India*, Department of Publications, Delhi, 1970, p. 279.
8. Small Scale Industries Development Organization, *Report on Development of Industries in Mizo Hills*, Ministry of Industrial Development and Internal Trade, New Delhi, 1971, pp. 23-29.

9. Directorate of Industries, *Mizoram Progress of Industrial Development*, Souvenir Sl. No. 1, Government of Mizoram, Aizawl, p. 55.
10. Administration Report, Government of Mizoram, 1984, p. 53.
11. *Ibid.*
12. *Ibid*, pp. 52 and 62.
13. Various Plan Documents (U.T. Period) of Government of Mizoram, Aizawl.
14. As on 31st March 1984.
15. The Mizoram Gazette (Extraordinary): Guidelines for the Enforcement of the Inner Line Regulation in Mizoram, Vol. XXXIII, issue no. 205 Dated 24th June 2004, p. 4.
16. State Presentation to the Twelfth Finance Commission, Government of Mizoram, 1st June 2004, p. 30.
17. Auditors' Report on Annual Accounts of ZOHANDCO, 2001-02, p. 5.
18. Memorandum to the Twelfth Finance Commission, Government of Mizoram, February 2004, p. 31.
19. Report on the Sub-Committee of State Level Bankers' Committee for Mizoram on Credit-Deposit ratio dated 15th November 1996, State Bank of India, Regional Office Aizawl, pp. 4-5.
20. The Industrial Policy of Mizoram, 1989, p. 27.
21. NEC Secretariat, Basic statistics of NE Region, Shillong, 1980, p. 143. Quoted in Lianzela, (Dr.), *Economic Development of Mizoram,* Spectrum Publications, Delhi, 1994, p. 142. Also quoted in Datta, P.S., *India's North-East: A Study in Transition*, Har Anand Publications, New Delhi, 1992, p. 108.
22. Directorate of Economics & Statistics, *Statistical Handbook of Mizoram*, Government of Mizoram, 2002, p.40.
23. Singha, R.K.P.G. & Gupta, A.D., Industrial Development in Mizoram-Towards Sustainable Development, In edited volume *Modernization of the Mizo Society,* Prasad, R.N. & Agarwal, A.K., Mittal Publications, New Delhi, 2003, p. 92.
24. Department of Environment & Forests, *Mizoram Forest, 2003*, Government of Mizoram, Aizawl, p. 35.
25. Dutta, P.S., *India's North-East: A Study in Transition*, Har Anand Publications, New Delhi, 1992, p. 103.

4

FINANCING OF BUSINESS AND INDUSTRY IN MIZORAM

Introduction

The term finance refers to funds or conduct of monetary affairs of an entity. It implies to a system by which money-matters of a nation, state, a firm, or a corporation are managed. It also refers to money or credit for and to conduct or engage in financial operations[1]. In general sense 'finance' is money resources or revenues. It connotes the resources of an individual or a group of persons computed in terms of money. In wider sense, the term 'finance' also includes credit.

Traditionally, finance was concerned with raising funds necessary to meet the operating requirements of a business, choosing optimum source. But, according to modern concept, finance is an integral part of management rather than specially concerned with raising funds for operations. It is concerned with all financial activities including planning, raising, allocating, and controlling and not with just any one of them.

Finance includes both public and private finance. It is concerned with procuring money for private organizations and management of money by individuals, associations of people and corporations. With the development of nation-state, public finance i.e., the management of revenues, expenditures, and debts of State has assumed great political as well as economic importance. Though, the most important source of government revenue is tax, sale of public properties and franchises, sale of interest-bearing bonds also contribute.

Finance and Business

Finance is not only needed for a business but is an integral part of corporate management and affects almost every aspects of corporate life as every problem and every decision entails financial implications. Business finance can broadly be defined as the activity concerned with planning, raising, controlling and administering funds used in business. It is related with principles, practices, procedures and problems concerning the financial management of business, industry, trade, commerce, service and mining. The field of corporate finance comprises of the study of financial operations of a company from its inception to its growth and expansion including its winding up also. This includes designing pattern of capitalization that may be helpful in maximizing owners' equity and the market value of shares.

Sources of Finance for Business and Industry

Sources of finance for business and industry may broadly be divided into two groups, viz., internal sources and external sources. Internal sources include retained earnings, internal cash flows from operations, etc. and external sources include equity—proprietors' capital (for non-corporates), shares (equity and preference including right shares, and bonus shares), debt (from institutions), public deposits, debentures, loans (from non-banking financial institutions), bank advance, money market instruments, lease finance, etc.

The study of economic history of countries reveals that economic development and growth of financial infrastructure have gone hand in hand. There is a close interaction between the two. Without the growth of financial infrastructure, there cannot be any development and the former in turn changes the shape and size of financial institutions. Banks constitute an important segment of financial structure of a country. In recent years, commercial banks have faced increasing competition in their traditional service market:

Financing of Business and Industry in Mizoram

Mizoram is among new States of Indian Union and it has witnessed the growth of business and industry over the last 100 years or so. This growth had the support of finance since the out set, though, initially it was drawn from individuals, but, later on certain institutions developed to take care of the need of finance for business and industry. The history of this interesting development is described here.

Pre-British Era (Before 1871)

As there existed no organized economic activity during pre-British period in Mizoram, use of finance was non-existent. People lived in the lap of 'mother nature' and consumed whatever was available from that source. Even at a later stage the transactions were settled through barter of commodities. Gradually, people organized themselves under the Chiefs and started living in settled habitats. Exchange of surplus commodities they raised or collected for certain items of necessity with outside traders was also done through Chiefs. At a later stage, some Bengali traders entered the territory, established market centers and started organized exchange of commodities under the patronage of some Chiefs. However, finance in the modern sense did not form part of these dealings.

British Era (1872-1947)

When the British established their post in Mizoram after 1872, there was no organized finance activity. There were no village money lenders among Mizo, still borrowing of items from person to person was in vogue and interest was also charged. The rate of interest varied from place to place and person to person in between 10 to 15 per cent per annum. In Demagiri of Lunglei district, it is understood that there were *Mahajans* who lend money to poor Chakmas at the time of cultivation and realized the same at the time of harvest, mostly in kind. By this process of realization, the *Mahajans* secured double benefit; firstly, they got back their money and realized interest at a high rate in the form of paddy, oil seeds, cotton etc., and secondly, they made a lucrative business having obtained paddy at a low rate. The cultivators usually had no alternative except to sell their produce to *Mahajans*, as the facility for transportation of goods to organized markets did not exist. The rate of interest among Chakmas of Demagiri area increased sometimes over 50 per cent per annum.

Post Independence

After partition of India, the East Pakistan authorities did not allow Mizo to trade freely with Chittagong and Sylhet, which depressed the inter-dependent Mizo economy that resulted in serious depression in trade and commerce in *Lushai* Hills district (Mizoram). This adversely affected its economy, more especially in south-west part of the district. After independence, the regulation and control of business related activities passed on to the *Lushai* Hills District Council's administration, which under the special powers of Paragraph 10 of Schedule VI of the Indian Constitution enacted the *Lushai* Hills District (Trading by Non-Tribals) Regulations 1953 and Rules 1954 with a view to regulate and control money lending, apart from trading to save simple Mizo from exploitation by money lenders[2]. The Regulations, without creating alternative source of credit discouraged money lenders. Whatever money-lending business that existed came to a halt.

Under the *Lushai* Hills District (Trading by Non-Tribals) Regulation 1953, the non-tribals were prohibited from granting any advance whether of money or kind at interest except under a licence issued by the District Council. They were further prohibited from charging interest exceeding 6½ per cent p.a. in case of secured loan and 12½ per cent in case of unsecured loan. Further, the interest could accrue to the tune of principal amount of loan only. Consequently, the aggregate of principal and interest could not be more than double the principal. The officers of the District Council could inspect the accounts of licensed money lenders. The *Kabuliwalas* who thrived in the plains and other districts of Assam were rarely found in Mizoram.

However, the cooperative credit societies formed an integral part of the credit structure in Mizoram. Actually the cooperative movement started in Mizoram in 1947 and the first cooperative society was established in 1949. Since then it made a steady progress and the number of societies increased to 54 in 1964 and 80 in 1966. During insurgency, all these societies became defunct, as their operations were disturbed, properties damaged, and members scattered to different group centres. The only bank branch of the Assam Cooperative Apex Bank was closed down. The mobile branch of State Bank of India (SBI) handled government business only. It had not been possible for it to assist industry, agriculture, artisans or workers.

There was no indigenous system of banking in Mizoram. The volume of circulation of money in the rural sector was small, particularly in the interior areas. The peculiar system of agriculture upon which bulk of population depends provided little scope for investment in land. Manual labour is required to till the soil as the hillsides are not amenable to mechanized cultivation. Improved seeds and manure were hardly purchased from market. The funds for construction of houses and other purposes were usually derived from the sale proceeds of crops grown in *jhum* and/or pigs, which are reared by almost every family. Moreover, the need for credit was not felt acutely in rural areas as in urban or semi-urban areas. However, among the Chakmas, the indebtedness prevailed subject to availability of credit. The economic condition of Chakmas was worse than Mizo. The *Riang* families also possessed very few tangible assets. They looked outside for assistance either in the form of relief or loan to ameliorate their condition. Periodic natural calamities added to their indebtedness.

The State government distributed interest free loans to the tune of Rs.59.89 lakh among the villagers in distress in the form of rice and other foodstuff, When 'famine' (*Mautam*) of 1960 affected the entire territory. After the outbreak of disturbance in 1966, there was widespread crop failure in two successive years 1966-67 and 1967-68 that caused acute food scarcity in all parts of the territory. The State government embarked upon several plans to enhance the purchasing power of people, who were shifted to Group Centres and also gave ration worth more than Rs.71 lakh on credit to people until the end of 1969.

Union Territory Period (1972-86)

Modern banking activity ushered in Mizoram with the establishment of first branch of State Bank of India (SBI) at Aizawl on 29th December 1971. Ever since the business started growing in terms of both deposits and advances, which induced branch expansion.

Until mid-1976, there were only two branches of SBI in Mizoram, one at Aizawl and the other at Lunglei. The biggest trading complex - Bara Bazaar in Aizawl had no branch of any Commercial Bank. Mizoram remained most poorly served area in the whole Northeastern region. Upto 1976, while one bank branch in Meghalaya and Nagaland served 36,000 people, in Mizoram one bank branch served 1,66,000 people. Out of total 20,968 bank offices in the country as on 31st March 1976, Mizoram had only two. Later in 1976, SBI established 4 branches in Mizoram, one each at Aizawl, Kolasib, Champhai and Serchhip. Thereafter, the United Commercial Bank (UCO) established a branch at Aizawl on 16th September 1976, and Vijaya Bank (VB) at Aizawl on 23rd September 1977. Mizoram Cooperative Apex Bank (MCAB) formed on 5th December 1978 became operational on 31st July 1982; Mizoram Rural Bank (MRB) was established on 23rd September 1983[3]. With widening of branch network not only neglected sections of people but the primary sector and secondary sector received increased financial assistance from banks.

Post Statehood

In 1987, when Mizoram was accorded statehood, there existed 51 bank branches in the State, 13 of SBI, 1 each of UCO, and Vijaya Bank, 2 of MCAB and 34 of MRB. An important aspect of the branch expansion was spread of banking in unbanked areas, particularly in rural areas. Of the 51 bank offices by June 1986, 37 were in rural areas and 14 in semi-urban /urban areas. The emphasis was on geographic expansion of banking facilities to rural areas, which was amply demonstrated by the progressive increase in rural coverage as distinguished from semi-urban or urban areas. By June 1987, the population served per bank office in Mizoram was 10,000 people, as against the regional average of 21,000 and national average of 13,000. Evidently population in the State was better served with wider banking facilities compared to the Northeastern region and the country as a whole. However, inter-district disparity in bank offices existed. On 31st March 2002, there were maximum number of bank offices in Aizawl district (30) followed by Lunglei (13), Champhai (11), Kolasib (10), Mamit and Serchhip (9 each), Saiha (5) and Lawngtlai (3). The distribution of branch network broadly covered almost all the blocks in the State except Bunghmun and Chawngte RD block. SBI had spread its network in all the district headquarters and established some branches even in remotest corners of Mizoram, covering places like Saiha, Demagiri, Zawlnuam, and Thingsai. MRB with 54 branches located in almost every nook and corner of Mizoram, along with SBI served the rural population of the State. MCAB had 10 branches established in all district headquarters except Mamit. However, UCO Bank and Vijaya Bank with only 1 branch each at Aizawl concentrated mainly on urban population.

The district-wise distribution of bank branches in Mizoram in 2003 is shown in Table 4.1.

Table 4.1: District-wise Distribution of Bank Branches in Mizoram in 2003

District	*SBI*	*MRB*	*UCO*	*VB*	*MCAB*	*MUCO*	*Total*
Aizawl	7	17	1	1	4	1	31
Champhai	1	9	Nil	Nil	1	Nil	11
Kolasib	3	6	Nil	Nil	1	Nil	10
Mamit	3	6	Nil	Nil	Nil	Nil	9
Lawngtlai	1	1	Nil	Nil	1	Nil	3
Lunglei	6	6	Nil	Nil	1	Nil	13
Saiha	1	3	Nil	Nil	1	Nil	5
Serchhip	2	6	Nil	Nil	1	Nil	9
Total	24	54	1	1	10	1	91

Legend: SBI = State Bank of India, MRB = Mizoram Rural Bank, UCO = United Commercial Bank, VB = Vijaya Bank, MCAB = Mizoram Cooperative Apex Bank, and MUCO = Mizoram Urban Cooperative Bank.

Source: Status Paper on Banking Scenario in Mizoram, SBI, Regional Office, Aizawl.

In 2003, there were 91 bank branches, most of which were rural branches catering to the population of 8,91,058 i.e., one bank branch served 9800 persons. State Bank of India with total 24 branches (5 in semi-urban areas viz. Aizawl, Bawngkawn, Dawrpui, Mission Veng and Lunglei and 19 in rural areas) spread over 8 districts and 22 blocks in the State, opened its regional office at Aizawl on 23rd August 1990. There had been an increase in the number of bank offices in Mizoram and the North-East as well, which placed Mizoram at first in terms of population served per bank office as compared to other States of the region.

Apart from the commercial banks in providing long-term funds to business and industry, some development banks also came up in the State. Among these, Zoram Industrial Development Corporation Ltd. (ZIDCO), a state level financial institution was set up at Aizawl on 19th February 1978. The Industrial Development Bank of India (IDBI) established its office at Aizawl on 8th October 1986 and started its operations in the State. Later, this activity was transferred to Small Industries Development Bank of India (SIDBI) from 2nd April 1990, which acts as an agency of IDBI. SIDBI is not involved in direct financing in Mizoram. It refinances projects through prime lending institutions like ZIDCO, MRB, etc. Northeastern Development Finance Corporation Ltd. (NEDFi) extended its operations to Mizoram by setting up office at Aizawl from November 2000. Thus, over the period a structure of commercial banking and development banking grew in the State. The contribution of these institutions in terms of financing of business and industry in Mizoram is examined here.

Financing by State Government

During UT period, since the financial infrastructure and institutions could not be developed in Mizoram, the State like other state governments in the country had to shoulder the responsibility of providing financial assistance to small industries. The Government of Mizoram through its Directorate of Industries provided finance to small-scale industries in the state under various plan schemes like loan from RIP Fund and under the State-aid to Industries Act.

Under the "State Aid to Industries Act", the maximum amount of loan to be given to an individual enterprise was Rs. 20,000/-. Small loans upto Rs. 2,500/- were provided to entrepreneurs against one surety and upto Rs. 5,000/- against two sureties. Loans above Rs. 5,000/- and upto

Rs. 20,000/- were given only against mortgage of fixed property and hypothecation of machinery. Loans at an interest of 5.5 per cent p.a. were generally given in cash, but in kind also when machinery was purchased on hire purchase. The Directorate of Industries and District Industries Centres disbursed the loans up to Rs. 2500/-. Different types of industrial units financed under the State Aid to Industries Act were printing press, carpentry works, aluminium metal works, cane and bamboo works, tailoring industries, motor workshops, tyre retreading, saw mill, soap making, fruit preservation, knitting industries, watch repairing, shoe making, handloom industry, blacksmithy, etc. Later, the scheme was discontinued from 1985-86. Under the loan from RIP scheme, greater stress seemed to have been given to wood and wooden products, food products and allied industries, service based industries, metal products and parts, and textile and textile goods. With the conversion of RIP into DIC, the scheme of RIP loan fund was discontinued.

The financial assistance was given from year to year within the availability of funds under Plan. Obviously, there were year to year fluctuations. How far this was adequate and served the cause of industrialization cannot be clearly stated. As a pioneering effort in a zero industry region, it must have been a bold initiative.

Financing by Development Banks

Considering the significance of development banking besides commercial banks and other banks, apex financial institutions like SIDBI, IDBI, NABARD, NEDFi have set up their offices in the State. The Zoram Industrial Development Corporation (ZIDCO) was set up on 19th February 1978. All these institutions are active in the State. The contribution made by each of these institutions in terms of financing of business and industry in Mizoram is discussed here.

Industrial Development Bank of India (IDBI)

Industrial Development Bank of India (IDBI) maintains its office in Mizoram at Aizawl since 8th October 1986 under the policy of having offices in all state capitals. IDBI is expected to extend refinancing facility to financial institutions. In Mizoram, it did so by giving loans to ZIDCO in addition to share capital contribution of Rs.428 lakh. Normally, it does not finance directly but in case of Zonun Mat Ply (P.) Ltd., a project of Rs.162 lakh was financed by it directly. Since inception of SIDBI on

2nd April 1990, it has stopped re-financing from 1991-92 and now the Aizawl office keeps busy in mobilizing household savings. The position of refinance disbursed by IDBI in Mizoram from 1982-83 to 2000-01 is given in Table 4.2.

Table 4.2: Loans under Refinance by Industrial Development Bank of India in Mizoram (from 1982-83 to 2000-01)

(*Rs. in lakh*)

Year	*Amount of Refinance*	*Cumulative Refinance*
1982-83	69.01	69.01
1983-84	35.89	104.90
1984-85	87.67	192.57
1985-86	115.08	307.65
1986-87	378.38	686.03
1987-88	258.99	945.02
1988-89	514.66	1459.68
1989-90	273.51	1733.19
1990-91	326.83	2060.02
1991-92	139.38	2199.40
2000-01	(SIDBI) 5.22	2204.62

Source: Annual Report, 2000-01, ZIDCO, Aizawl.

The Table 4.2 revealed that IDBI refinanced to ZIDCO in an increasing manner till 1988-89 and then showed less interest and ultimately stopped refinancing from the middle of 1991-92 on the ground of poor repayment of over dues by ZIDCO.[4] However, the same was resumed by SIDBI again since 2000-01 after negotiations at tri-party meeting between officials of ZIDCO, IDBI, and SIDBI held at Guwahati on 23rd November 2000.

Small Industries Development Bank of India (SIDBI)

Small Industries Development Bank of India (SIDBI) was incorporated as a wholly owned subsidiary of IDBI and became operational on 2nd April 1990. *Inter alia* other things, it has been assigned the task of term financing to SSI sector. It operates many schemes such as composite loan scheme (CLS), mahila udyam nidhi (MUN), project finance scheme (PFS), venture capital scheme (VCS), small road transport operators' scheme (SRTO), scheme for professionals, seed capital scheme, national equity fund, single window scheme (SWS), scheme for export bills financing, ISO 9000 scheme, direct discounting scheme (DDS), bills rediscounting scheme (BRS), working capital term loan scheme (WCTL), scheme for ancillary etc. Some of these schemes are for direct financing and others are for refinancing through prime lending institutions (PLI). The contribution made by SIDBI in advancing loans in Northeastern states over the period from 1990-91 to 2001-02 is presented in Table 4.3.

Table 4.3: Loans Disbursed by SIDBI to Northeastern States from 1996-97 to 2001-02 (As on 31st March)

(Rs. in lakh)

NER States	*1996-97*	*1997-98*	*1998-99*	*1999-00*	*2000-01*	*2001-02*	*Growth (%)*
Arunachal Pradesh	462	629	776	924	1091	1304	22.19
Assam	7095	8101	9066	10373	12389	14325	15.10
Manipur	1268	1510	1578	1996	2723	2875	19.03
Meghalaya	1680	2336	2630	3032	3575	4047	18.07
Mizoram	675	745	843	943	1094	1175	12.22
Nagaland	716	868	1010	1158	1440	1687	18.50
Tripura	1485	1868	2248	2758	3408	3535	19.87
Total	13381	16057	18151	21184	25720	28948	16.77

Source: SIDBI, Aizawl.

It may be observed from Table 4.3 that out of the total loans disbursed for Rs. 28948 lakh, the highest share was given to Assam which received nearly 49.49 per cent to total loans (Rs.14325 lakh). But, the annual growth in advances of SIDBI was highest in case of Arunachal Pradesh (22.19 per cent p.a.). Mizoram received only 4 per cent (lowest proportion) of total finance (Rs.1175 lakh) among all Northeastern states. The growth over the years from 1996-97 to 2001-02 was at 12.22 per cent p.a. only, which was below the overall growth at 16.77 per cent p.a. as well as lowest among the Northeastern region. It may be understood that from 1996-97 to 2001-02, SIDBI in spite of volume difference gave increasing emphasis on loan proposals of other NER States except Mizoram and Assam.

The position regarding loans disbursed in Northeastern states under refinance schemes is presented in Table 4.4.

It may be seen from Table 4.4 that among Northeastern states from 1996-97 to 2001-02, the share of Mizoram in total refinance was mere

4.46 per cent (Rs.1102 lakh out of Rs.24682 lakh), which was lowest. It may also be seen that out of total disbursal of Rs.1175 lakh in Mizoram by SIDBI, Rs.1102 lakh was by way of refinance, which indicates that the other schemes of SIDBI especially the direct finance were not operational in Mizoram, may be because, the entrepreneurs in Mizoram might not be aware of these schemes.

Table 4.4: Refinance Disbursed by SIDBI to Northeastern States from 1996-97 to 2001-02 (As on 31st March)

(Rs. in lakh)

NER States	*1996-97*	*1997-98*	*1998-99*	*1999-00*	*2000-01*	*2001-02*	*Growth (%)*
Arunachal Pradesh	480	588	737	885	1052	1265	21.35
Assam	5965	6611	7187	8484	9361	10657	12.46
Manipur	1268	1510	1578	1996	2604	2756	17.86
Meghalaya	1680	2336	2612	2986	3524	3905	17.30
Mizoram	706	740	838	938	1054	1102	10.20
Nagaland	756	847	989	1137	1328	1574	15.87
Tripura	1472	1852	2227	2737	3320	3423	19.30
Total	12327	14484	16168	19163	22243	24682	15.12

Source: SIDBI, Aizawl.

North Eastern Development Finance Corporation Ltd. (NEDFi)

Northeastern Development Finance Corporation Ltd. (NEDFi) provides financial assistance to entrepreneurs in the form of rupees term loan (RTL), north-east equity fund (NEEF), working capital term loan (WCTL), micro finance (MIF), equipment finance (EQF), bridge loan (BL), equipment leasing (EQL), scheme for north-east handloom and handicrafts (SNEHH), jute enterprise development scheme (JEDS) and women enterprise development scheme (WEDS). Normally, NEDFi finances projects of Rs.25 lakh and above. It started giving loans in Mizoram from 1997-98. The position regarding loans disbursed by NEDFi from 1997-98 to 2002-03 is given in Table 4.5.

It may be observed from Table 4.5 that there were significant ups and downs in loans disbursed by NEDFi from year to year. NEDFi Advances increased sharply upto 1999-2000 and thereafter grew at slow pace. However, overall growth in NEDFi advances in Mizoram was 82.77 per cent p.a.

Table 4.5: Financing by Northeastern Development Finance Corporation in Mizoram from 1997-98 to 2002-03 (As on 31st March)

(Rs. in lakh)

Year	Annual Loan Disbursement	Cumulative Total
1997-98	25.00	25.00
1998-99	63.10	88.10
1999-00	190.70	278.80
2000-01	148.90	427.70
2001-02	45.05	472.75
2002-03	97.85	570.60
Growth (%)		82.77

Source: NEDFi, Aizawl.

Zoram Industrial Development Corporation Ltd. (ZIDCO)

Zoram Industrial Development Corporation Ltd. (ZIDCO) was set up on 19th February 1978 under co-sponsorship of Government of Mizoram and IDBI with an objective of industrial development of economically backward State of Mizoram. It is the only non-banking financial institution in Mizoram involved in direct financing through long-term loans. It has registered office at Aizawl and one branch office at Lunglei. As per the agreement between Government of Mizoram and IDBI, both were to make matching contribution towards the share capital of ZIDCO, and it was so till 1990-91. However, as a result of economic liberalization, the Government of India stopped subscribing additional share capital to IDBI and consequent upon this from 1991-92, IDBI declined to subscribe any more towards share capital of ZIDCO under matching pool. It received refinance from IDBI upto 1991-92 and from SIDBI from 2000-01 onwards under agreement. For the intermittent period, ZIDCO was deprived of refinancing facility as neither IDBI nor SIDBI extended support owing to default in payment of over dues. ZIDCO is a channelising agency for various loans under National Minorities Development and Finance Corporation Ltd. (NMDFC). It had drawn funds from this source Rs.1226.58 lakh inclusive of Rs.300.00 lakh meant for small and marginal ginger growers. Besides NMDFC schemes, ZIDCO sanctioned and disbursed loans to various entrepreneurs of the State. Total advances made by it may be divided into two categories, *viz.*, small-scale industries (SSIs) and small business finance (SBF). The advances made by ZIDCO from 1986-87 to 2001-02 are produced in Table 4.6, which revealed the following:

1. Over the years from 1986-87 to 2001-02, SSI advances constituted 72.9 per cent of total advances as against 27.1 per cent to SBF category. Though, the main emphasis was on industry, its relative share in total advances has declined over the years from 81.2 per cent in 1986-87 to 63.1 per cent in 2001-02, which is contrary to its very objective of incorporation and at the same time, small road transport operators' advances (SRTO-SBF) were given due preference such as 18.8 per cent in 1986-87 increased to 36.9 per cent in 2001-02.

Table 4.6: Financing of Business and Industry by ZIDCO in Mizoram from 1986-87 to 2001-02 (As on 31st March)

(*Rs. in lakh*)

Year	*No. of New Loans*		*SSI*		*SBF*		*Total*
	All	*SRTO*					
1886-87	258	3	777.83	(81.2)	179.67	(18.8)	957.50
1987-88	201	48	1111.37	(80.6)	268.04	(19.4)	1379.41
1988-89	513	202	1446.52	(72.6)	544.86	(27.4)	1991.38
1989-90	101	42	1702.20	(72.2)	656.31	(27.8)	2358.51
1990-91	103	16	1973.98	(74.2)	687.17	(25.8)	2661.15
1991-92	70	5	2216.84	(76.3)	686.78	(23.7)	2903.62
1992-93	87	9	2203.41	(77.7)	632.09	(22.3)	2835.50
1993-94	106	35	2302.06	(76.8)	697.03	(23.2)	2999.09
1994-95	114	46	2324.76	(74.5)	797.76	(25.6)	3122.52
1995-96	130	67	2568.20	(73.9)	906.79	(26.1)	3474.99
1996-97	102	54	2566.06	(71.0)	1048.74	(29.0)	3614.80
1997-98	101	60	2662.46	(70.4)	1117.13	(29.6)	3779.59
1998-99	181	53	2844.36	(69.3)	1259.61	(30.7)	4103.97
1999-00	530	27	3009.59	(66.9)	1487.72	(33.1)	4497.31
2000-01	242	24	3097.60	(65.9)	1602.98	(34.1)	4700.58
2001-02	441	63	3131.46	(63.1)	1830.12	(36.9)	4961.58
Growth (%)			7.66	(72.9)	12.77	(27.1)	9.03

Note: 1. Figures in parenthesis represent percentage of total.
2. Figures in parenthesis in growth row show average relative share.

Legend: SSI = Small-Scale Industries, SBF = Small Business Finance.

Source: ZIDCO, Aizawl.

2. Overall growth in total advances over the period was 5 times and it registered an annual growth of 9.03 per cent p.a. In SSI segment, it was 4 times only and marked an annual average growth of 7.66 per cent. Perhaps either the management did not receive proposals from new industrial units or the management discouraged SSI advances may be for various reasons. On the other hand SBF

> advances grew by more than 10 times and registered an annual average growth of 12.77 per cent. Its major component was Small Road Transport Operators' loan (SRTO) through which mostly city buses were financed. This shows that the growth of industry in the State was slower than business.

Industrial category-wise advances of ZIDCO from 1987-88 to 1992-93 are presented in Table 4.7.

It may be observed from Table 4.7 that average per unit finance by ZIDCO registered a marginal increase from Rs.1.68 lakh on 21st July 1987 to Rs.1.74 lakh on 31st March 1993. This showed that per unit quantum of finance was small.

Table 4.7: Industry Group-wise Loans Disbursed by ZIDCO in Mizoram During 1987 to 1993

(Rs. in lakh)

Name of Trade	*21.7.1987*		*31.7.1991*		*31.3.1993*	
	Units	*Amount*	*Units*	*Amount*	*Units*	*Amount*
Electrical Cables & Conductors			30	17.14	30	25.84
Chemicals & Chemical Products	5	1.50	8	1.87	8	4.21
Food Product & Allied Industries	121	85.67	188	192.45	206	348.47
Leather Goods & Repairing	7	7.37	12	10.42	11	13.92
Metal Products & Parts	32	43.00	45	64.13	50	108.03
Non-Metallic & Mineral Products	49	127.33	69	182.68	74	198.70
Paper Products, Publishing & Allied Industries	38	84.65	54	116.54	57	131.01
Rubber, Plastics, etc.	13	76.72	23	91.61	25	134.60
Service Based Industries	159	577.49	529	1117.69	560	1388.99
Textile & Textile Goods	205	148.64	322	199.56	360	300.40
Wood & Wooden Products	118	104.82	179	163.12	189	181.50
Total	747	1257.19	1459	2157.21	1570	2835.07

Note: (i) Electrical Cables and Conductors include Conductors, Cables, Electricals, Aluminium Casting and Aluminium Conductors.

(ii) Chemicals & Chemical products include Optical, Candle, and Soap Making.

(iii) Food Product & Allied Industries includes Food Processing, Bee-keeping, Ice Plant, Rice Huller, Oil, Masala, Tea, Poultry, Spices, Chicken & Meat Processing, Flour Mills, Cold Drinks, Chow making, and Confectionary.

(iv) Leather Goods & Repairing includes Manufacturing of Shoes & their Repairing, Leather Tanning.

(v) Metal Products & Parts includes Fabrication, Motor Body Building,

Hardware, Nails, Steel, Foundry, Tinsmithy, Blacksmithy, Goldsmithy, Paper Pin and Barbed Wire.

(vi) Non-Metallic & Mineral Products includes Manufacturing of Cement, Cemented Flower Pots, Brick Making, Kero Gas, Stone Quarry and Pottery.

(vii) Paper Products, Publishing & Allied includes Printing Press, Paper & Stationery, Paper Bag, and Exercise Books.

(viii) Rubber, Plastics, etc. includes Manufacturing of Rubber Mats, Tyre Retreading, Slipper Manufacturing, Hume Pipe and Polythene.

(ix) Service Based Industries includes Health Clinic and Laboratory, Photo Services, Cable Operator, Motor Works, Auto Work Shops, Xerox Copier, Dry Cleaning, Watch Repairing, IT/Electronics, Hotel, Engineering & Allied Services, Dyeing and Laundry, Bike Works, Bicycle Repairing, and Speed Boat Service,

(x) Textile & Textile Goods includes Handloom, Cotton Textiles, Hosiery, Tailoring, Weaving and Knitting, Silk Kurta, and Cotton Mills.

(xi) Wood & Wooden Products includes Agro Forests & Bamboo, Cane Winding, Mat Ply, Furniture and Carpentry, Timber Seasoning, and Saw Mills.

Source: Statistical Handbook of Mizoram, 1987, pp. 114-19.
ZIDCO, Aizawl (for 1991 and 1993).

Further, the Corporation gave major emphasis on promotion of service based industries, which included small road transport operators' loans whereby larger funds (47 per cent) were invested. Out of 1570 units financed with total assistance of Rs. 2835.67 lakh as on 31st March 1993, 560 units from to service based industry, which were given Rs.1388.99 lakh. If SRTO loans are separated then the picture that emerge produces poor financing pattern for rest of the industries because 1010 units from industries other than service based industries were given loan of Rs.1446.68 lakh averaging at Rs.1.43 lakh per unit. Besides SRTO loans, major focus was on food products and allied industries where 206 units were financed with Rs.348.47 lakh, followed by textile and textile goods where 360 units were financed with Rs.300.4 lakh, and wood and wooden products where 189 units were financed with Rs.181.5 lakh.

ZIDCO had initiated a "*One Time Settlement Scheme*" *(OTS)* under Restructuring Programme[5] for speedy recovery of overdue loans. This initiative received some response. The position regarding recovery of principal amount of loans advanced by ZIDCO from 1980-81 to 2001-02 is given in Table 4.8.

Table 4.8: Recovery of Principal Amount of Loans Advanced by ZIDCO From 1980-81 to 2001-02 (As on 31st March)

(*Rs. in lakh*)

Year	Amount Disbursed (Rs.)	Recovery of Principal (Rs.)	Net Due Cumulative (Rs.)	Percentage Recovery
1980-81	0.51	0.00	0.51	—
1981-82	19.73	0.00	20.24	—
1982-83	56.85	0.00	77.09	—
1983-84	41.01	0.19	117.92	0.24
1984-85	118.24	10.72	225.45	9.09
1985-86	260.89	12.03	474.30	5.34
1986-87	350.75	19.89	805.17	4.19
1987-88	505.17	72.52	1237.82	9.01
1988-89	515.27	82.51	1670.59	6.67
1989-90	311.18	100.92	1880.84	6.04
1990-91	303.22	110.67	2073.40	5.88
1991-92	152.96	100.81	2125.55	4.86
1992-93	89.66	102.98	2112.23	4.84
1993-94	143.77	181.38	2074.62	8.59
1994-95	147.86	157.47	2065.01	7.59
1995-96	134.63	112.35	2087.29	5.44
1996-97	129.92	153.25	2063.96	7.34
1997-98	112.72	101.09	2075.58	4.90
1998-99	152.91	78.04	2150.46	3.76
1999-00	217.83	91.92	2276.37	4.27
2000-01	137.36	150.68	2263.04	6.62
2001-02	274.27	172.33	2364.98	7.62
Average				5.91

Note: Recovery percentage has been calculated on immediately previous year's cumulative outstanding of principal amount. Interest figures have not been included here and consequently the recovery figures also do not include the amount realized towards the interest due.

Source: Compiled from various annual reports of ZIDCO, Aizawl.

The Table 4.8 revealed the following:

1. On the average ZIDCO was able to recover 5.91 per cent of principal advances made till immediately preceding year. Obviously, it cannot be considered satisfactory and was responsible for low capital turnover. In view of the poor recovery, new advances could not be made. Most of the existing advances are dormant. As a result, the contribution made by the Government of Mizoram towards the additional share capital of ZIDCO year after year could be utilized for industrial development of the State. Since poor recovery

discouraged the management from making advances, the additional share capital subscribed remained accumulated as cash and bank balance with the Corporation.

2. The management, in recent past, concentrated on recovery as is revealed from Directors' Report[6]. But, in the absence of repayment culture among the entrepreneurs, the results were far from satisfaction. The management has reported several reasons for poor recovery of overdues, such as projects not implemented and loanees not in position to repay their loans, projects implemented but could not run properly due to lack of skill in their management; lack of market for finished goods, insufficient power supply, and loanees not willing to repay the loans[7].

Mizoram Khadi and Village Industries Board (MKVIB)

Steps were initiated to form the Mizoram *Khadi* and Village Industries Board (MKVIB) in 1982-83 and it came in existence on 14th June 1985 under the MKVIB Act 1982 and became fully functional from 1986-87. It functions under the policy directives of KVIC, Mumbai and looks after village industries. Out of total 119 industries as notified by KVIC, it sponsors in Mizoram only 23 village industries and 2 from *khadi*. Till 2000-01, the board had financed 5772 units with maximum finance of Rs.10 lakh per unit. It receives funds from 4 different sources viz., KVIC, consortium bank credit (CBC), National Scheduled Caste and Scheduled Tribe Finance and Development Corporation (NSFDC) and the State Government in the form of grants and loans. The State Government gave grants towards meeting the establishment cost. Funds from other three sources were utilized in assisting the entrepreneurs in Mizoram. Grants received were distributed as non-refundable grants to entrepreneurs. Loans received were disbursed among entrepreneurs as loan assistance recoverable periodically. For the purpose of disbursing loans, it has established certain funds like establishment fund, project fund, consortium fund, NSFDC fund, reserve fund and SEP fund since 1995-96.

Information regarding the grants-in-aid and loans disbursed by MKVIB to its own units and other eligible industries in Mizoram is given in Table 4.9.

It may be observed from Table 4.9 that out of the total financial assistance made on the average, 3.88 per cent was given to its own units,

93.42 per cent was given to village and small industries as specified by KVIC and the balance 2.97 per cent was given to village industries but as specified by NSFDC and SEMFEX schemes.

Table 4.9: Financing by Mizoram Khadi & Village Industries Board in Mizoram during 1985-86 to 2000-01 (As on 31st March)

(*Rs. in lakh*)

	Loans (Rs.)							Grants (Rs.)	
Year	Own Units		VSI		Other VSI		Total	SEMFEX	KVIC
	Amount	(%)	Amount	(%)	Amount	(%)	Amount	Amt.	Amt.
1985-86	Nil	Nil	6.18	Nil	Nil	Nil	6.18	Nil	6.09
1986-87	Nil	Nil	26.62	Nil	Nil	Nil	26.62	Nil	14.70
1987-88	Nil	Nil	20.43	Nil	Nil	Nil	20.43	Nil	8.15
1988-89	Nil	Nil	143.85	Nil	Nil	Nil	143.85	Nil	18.43
1989-90	Nil	Nil	152.94	Nil	Nil	Nil	152.94	Nil	48.48
1990-91	6.31	(2.69)	228.31	(97.31)	Nil	Nil	234.62	Nil	40.27
1991-92	6.64	(2.63)	234.62	(92.90)	11.30	(4.47)	252.56	Nil	Nil
1992-93	22.50	(5.43)	382.05	(92.23)	9.70	(2.34)	414.25	Nil	Nil
1993-94	22.50	(4.35)	491.91	(95.20)	2.30	(0.45)	516.71	0.53	14.18
1994-95	22.28	(3.25)	660.32	(96.36)	2.63	(0.38)	685.23	0.56	Nil
1995-96	31.77	(4.18)	698.48	(91.88)	30.00	(3.95)	760.25	Nil	Nil
1996-97	85.33	(4.04)	1990.18	(94.31)	34.66	(1.64)	2110.17	1.47	Nil
1997-98	94.48	(4.10)	2165.51	(94.08)	41.90	(1.82)	2301.89	Nil	Nil
1998-99	117.62	(4.11)	2639.38	(92.16)	106.84	(3.73)	2863.84	Nil	Nil
1999-00	126.01	(3.86)	3070.06	(94.09)	66.69	(2.04)	3262.76	Nil	Nil
2000-01	151.89	(4.02)	3292.95	(87.08)	336.60	(8.90)	3781.44	Nil	Nil
Average	62.48	(3.88)	1012.74	(93.42)	64.26	(2.97)	1095.86		
Growth (%)	39.80		46.72		54.41		47.77		

Note: Figures in parenthesis represent percentage of total. These have been worked out from 1990-91.

Source: Annual Reports, Mizoram Khadi & Village Industries Board, Aizawl.

Of the funds advanced to its own units, nearly 60 per cent funds were advanced in *Khandsari* unit, Saitual and 28 per cent funds were made available to MDTC, Zemabawk. Loans to its own units increased from Rs.6.31 lakh in 1990-91 to Rs.151.89 lakh in 2000-01 at 39.80 per cent p.a.

Likewise, in case of village industries as specified by KVIC, the outstanding loans increased from Rs.6.18 lakh in 1985-86 to Rs.3292.95 lakh in 2000-01 registered an annual average increase of 46.72 per cent which was more or less at par with increase in overall advances at 47.77 per cent p.a.

Out of the total funds advanced as on 31st March 2001, maximum were outstanding against service units (448.10 lakh), followed by bakery and *masala* units (Rs. 368.14 lakh), carpentry and blacksmithy (Rs.366.85 lakh), lime units (Rs.310.23 lakh), pottery (Rs.266.61 lakh), electronics (Rs.219.85 lakh), textile units (Rs.175.94 lakh), *gur* and *khandsari* units (Rs.121.48 lakh), etc[8]. No new loans were disbursed to village industries under KVIC during 1991-92, 1992-93, and 2000-01.

Similarly, the growth in advances to village industries as specified under NSFDC and SEMFEX schemes was at 54.41 per cent p.a., sharper than any other. However, the figures for both the grants of SEMFEX and KVIC fluctuated from year to year perhaps due to change in focus or change in number of eligible units over the period as also availability of budget. No unit as specified by KVIC was given any grant since 1994-95.

Majority of the benefits of MKVIB assistance went in Aizawl district only as more than 2/3rd of beneficiary units existed there. The 1/3rd assistance were shared between other seven districts. Among them the least recipient were Saiha, Lawngtlai and Mamit districts. All the trades were not given equal weightage, neither in case of KVIC schemes nor in case of NSFDC etc. SEMFEX loans increased over the years, but, decreased in number showed that MKVIB preferred financing big projects only.

Financing by Commercial Banks

There are three commercial banks viz., State Bank of India (SBI), Vijaya Bank (VB), and United Commercial Bank (UCO) and three other banks namely, Mizoram Rural Bank (MRB), Mizoram Cooperative Apex Bank (MCAB), and Mizoram Urban Cooperative Bank (MUCO) that undertake financing of business and industry in Mizoram. The financing of commercial banks can be classified into 4 categories *viz.,* small scale industry advances (SSIs), small business finance advances (SBF), agricultural advances (AGL), and Personal advances. Financing to business and industry in Mizoram by each bank is discussed hereunder.

State Bank of India

The State Bank of India having second largest branch net work in Mizoram not only handled government business, but, also sowed the seeds of credit expansion for the first time. The data regarding advances by SBI to SSI and SBF from 1990-91 to 2001-02 are compiled and presented in Table 4.10. No comments can be given on the performance for the period from 1971 to 1989 as the data were not available.

Table 4.10: Segment-wise Advances of State Bank of India in Mizoram From 1990-91 to 2001-02 (As on 31st March)

(*Rs. in lakh*)

Year	*C & I*	*SSI*	*SBF*	*AGL*	*Personal*	*Total*
1990-91	263.32	315.88	538.24	163.64	252.18	1533.26
Share (%)	(17)	(21)	(35)	(11)	(16)	(100)
1991-92	242.73	291.74	510.50	189.87	255.01	1489.85
Share (%)	(16)	(20)	(34)	(13)	(17)	(100)
1992-93	231.36	365.64	356.92	264.06	265.18	1483.16
Share (%)	(16)	(25)	(24)	(18)	(18)	(100)
1993-94	228.71	407.97	400.51	297.69	290.44	1625.32
Share (%)	(14)	(25)	(25)	(18)	(18)	(100)
1994-95	220.39	371.40	345.24	309.43	316.14	1562.60
Share (%)	(14)	(24)	(22)	(20)	(20)	(100)
1995-96	279.11	485.84	520.62	355.01	404.89	2045.47
Share (%)	(14)	(24)	(25)	(17)	(20)	(100)
1996-97	295.40	521.59	640.56	368.00	485.51	2311.06
Share (%)	(13)	(23)	(28)	(16)	(21)	(100)
1997-98	307.45	584.48	897.70	378.12	772.51	2940.26
Share (%)	(10)	(20)	(31)	(13)	(26)	(100)
1998-99	394.03	720.32	1338.96	410.53	1361.37	4225.21
Share (%)	(9)	(17)	(32)	(10)	(32)	(100)
1999-00	304.51	781.15	1721.35	469.58	2038.05	5314.64
Share (%)	(6)	(15)	(32)	(9)	(38)	(100)
2000-01	346.84	837.01	1647.91	468.62	3047.20	6347.58
Share (%)	(5)	(13)	(26)	(7)	(48)	(100)
2001-02	471.21	781.30	1729.90	500.61	4788.61	8271.63
Share (%)	(6)	(9)	(21)	(6)	(58)	(100)
Average	*(12)*	*(20)*	*(28)*	*(13)*	*(28)*	*(100)*
Growth (%)	*5.50*	*10.69*	*16.43*	*9.79*	*32.08*	*17.99*
C. V.	*24*	*35*	*61*	*30*	*115*	*67*

Note: Figures in parenthesis represent percentage of total.

Legend: C & I = Commercial and Institutional Advances, SSI = Small Scale Industry Advances, SBF = Small Business Finance Advances, AGL = Agricultural Advances, C.V. = Coefficient of Variation.

Source: Regional Office, State Bank of India, Aizawl.

Table 4.10 revealed the following:

1. On the average, except for AGL and C and I advances the bank had given more or less equal weightage to all other categories of advances. AGL and C and I category though received equal share but less weightage than others. Except for the personal category advances, the relative share of all other advances registered a gradual decline over the period from 1990-91 to 2001-02.

2. Though, all the advances increased in absolute over the period, the relative share of SSI advances declined from 25 per cent in 1993-94 to 9 per cent in 2001-02, AGL advances from 20 per cent in 1994-95 to 6 per cent in 2001-02. On the average, both the SBF and Personal category advances dominated the portfolio each acquiring 28 per cent share in total advances, but, relatively recorded opposite trend as the former declined from 35 per cent in 1990-91 to 21 per cent in 2001-02, while the later, at the same time, jumped from 16 per cent to 58 per cent.
3. From 1990-91 to 2001-02 the total advances grew at 17.99 per cent p.a. (5.39 times). Among these, Personal advances marked highest growth at 32.08 per cent p.a. (18.99 times) followed by SBF advances at 16.43 per cent p.a. (3.21 times) and SSI advances at 10.69 per cent p.a. (2.47 times). The growth in all the advances except for Personal category was lower than that of over all (17.99 per cent p.a.). The lowest growth was in C & I (5.50%) and AGL (9.79%) advances.
4. From year to year, there was 67 per cent variation in total advances of the bank. Among different categories, the Personal advances contained highest variation (115 per cent). Variation in all other categories was low than that of variation in total advances. The least variation was in C & I at 24 per cent and AGL at 30 per cent.

The position regarding district-wise advances by SBI in Mizoram from 1990-91 to 2001-02 is given in Table 4.11.

Table 4.11 revealed the following:

1. The SBI distributed most of loanable funds in Aizawl district (59%). Of the remaining 41 per cent of funds, Lunglei district got 15 per cent; Serchhip district received 9 per cent, followed by Kolasib district which received 6 per cent. The balance 12 per cent of the funds were distributed among Lawngtlai (4%), Champhai (3%) and Saiha (3%) districts. The least one per cent share was given in Mamit district, though, it is an orange garden of the State with most promising horticulture base. There is a need for change in the attitude of farmers and to create awareness among them, as they may not know how they can avail loan for raising commercial crop of oranges.
2. The overall growth in total advances of SBI in Mizoram was 17.99 per cent p.a. The growth was higher than the average in Lawngtlai

(22.54%) and Aizawl (19.63%) districts but in, Serchhip (17.55%), Lunglei (17.51%), Mamit (16.99%), Chaphai (14.74%), Saiha (13.70%) and Kolasib (9.39%) districts, it was below the average.

3. The variation in advances of Lawngtlai (85%), Saiha (74%) and Aizawl (72%) districts were more than the variation in overall advances (67%), while in case of Kolasib (41%), Serchhip (49%), Champhai (53%), Mamit (62%), and Lunglei (63%) districts, it was less than the variation in overall advances.

Table 4.11: District-wise Advances by State Bank of India in Mizoram From 1990-91 to 2001-02 (As on 31st March)

(Rs. in lakh)

District	*Aizawl*	*Cham-phai*	*Kolasib*	*Lawng-tlai*	*Lunglei*	*Mamit*	*Serchhip*	*Saiha*	*Total*
1990-91	934.90	37.25	116.58	44.72	217.45	20.30	39.68	122.38	1533.26
Share (%)	(61)	(2)	(8)	(3)	(14)	(1)	(3)	(8)	(100)
1991-92	827.26	50.83	115.71	52.63	237.83	20.93	144.12	40.54	1489.85
Share (%)	(56)	(3)	(8)	(4)	(16)	(1)	(10)	(3)	(100)
1992-93	780.11	55.50	123.92	59.05	232.25	25.61	169.15	37.57	1483.16
Share (%)	(53)	(4)	(8)	(4)	(16)	(2)	(11)	(3)	(100)
1993-94	873.65	58.71	120.89	66.79	261.70	23.36	180.99	39.23	1625.32
Share (%)	(54)	(4)	(7)	(4)	(16)	(1)	(11)	(2)	(100)
1994-95	894.06	63.84	118.41	67.15	163.73	27.08	182.70	45.63	1562.60
Share (%)	(57)	(4)	(8)	(4)	(10)	(2)	(12)	(3)	(100)
1995-96	1155.30	76.22	123.98	80.06	328.27	36.06	202.34	43.24	2045.47
Share (%)	(56)	(4)	(6)	(4)	(16)	(2)	(10)	(2)	(100)
1996-97	1379.26	66.35	118.96	103.45	337.38	32.55	224.99	48.12	2311.06
Share (%)	(60)	(3)	(5)	(4)	(15)	(1)	(10)	(2)	(100)
1997-98	1805.85	70.66	135.31	115.33	461.90	38.43	264.50	48.28	2940.26
Share (%)	(61)	(2)	(5)	(4)	(16)	(1)	(9)	(2)	(100)
1998-99	2630.71	123.90	187.23	153.33	672.73	57.06	308.03	92.22	4225.21
Share (%)	(62)	(3)	(4)	(4)	(16)	(1)	(7)	(2)	(100)
1999-00	3321.68	138.84	238.54	255.98	784.67	82.06	336.04	156.83	5314.64
Share (%)	(63)	(3)	(4)	(5)	(15)	(2)	(6)	(3)	(100)
2000-01	3963.05	166.23	278.57	312.02	905.45	86.99	427.53	207.74	6347.58
Share (%)	(62)	(3)	(4)	(5)	(14)	(1)	(7)	(3)	(100)
2001-02	5363.35	197.24	306.12	467.45	1091.33	108.99	496.23	240.92	8271.63
Share (%)	(65)	(2)	(4)	(6)	(13)	(1)	(6)	(3)	(100)
Average	(59)	(3)	(6)	(4)	(15)	(1)	(9)	(3)	(100)
Growth (%)	19.63	14.74	9.39	22.54	17.51	16.99	17.55	13.70	17.99
C. V.	72	53	41	85	63	62	49	74	67

Note: Figures in parenthesis represent percentage of total.

Legend: C.V. = Coefficient of Variation.

Source: Regional Office, State Bank of India, Aizawl.

The position regarding district-wise SSI advances by SBI in Mizoram from 1990-91 to 2001-02 is given in Table 4.12.

Table 4.12: District-wise Small Scale Industry Advances by State Bank of India in Mizoram From 1990-91 to 2001-02 (As on 31st March)

(*Rs. in lakh*)

Year	*Aizawl*	*Cham-phai*	*Kolasib*	*Lawng-tlai*	*Lunglei*	*Mamit*	*Serchhip*	*Saiha*	*Total*
1990-91	150.43	3.70	7.79	7.03	82.35	0.32	6.94	57.32	315.88
Share (%)	(48)	(1)	(2)	(2)	(26)	(0)	(2)	(18)	(100)
1991-92	144.07	6.16	10.33	8.84	90.71	0.22	25.12	6.29	291.74
Share (%)	(49)	(2)	(4)	(3)	(31)	(0)	(9)	(2)	(100)
1992-93	143.01	2.92	12.19	10.23	98.30	0.15	91.41	7.43	365.64
Share (%)	(39)	(1)	(3)	(3)	(27)	(0)	(25)	(2)	(100)
1993-94	144.45	7.94	13.14	15.74	112.02	0.53	106.10	8.05	407.97
Share (%)	(35)	(2)	(3)	(4)	(27)	(0)	(26)	(2)	(100)
1994-95	161.41	8.14	11.32	17.39	53.41	1.31	107.33	11.09	371.40
Share (%)	(43)	(2)	(3)	(5)	(14)	(0)	(29)	(3)	(100)
1995-96	187.73	11.26	9.11	19.13	128.76	1.36	115.13	13.36	485.84
Share (%)	(39)	(2)	(2)	(4)	(27)	(0)	(24)	(3)	(100)
1996-97	208.41	11.10	13.81	23.74	130.01	1.70	120.26	12.56	521.59
Share (%)	(40)	(2)	(3)	(5)	(25)	(0)	(23)	(2)	(100)
1997-98	237.70	9.03	17.16	27.31	156.85	2.39	122.53	11.51	584.48
Share (%)	(41)	(2)	(3)	(5)	(27)	(0)	(21)	(2)	(100)
1998-99	309.64	11.60	20.54	39.78	189.44	2.98	133.31	13.03	720.32
Share (%)	(43)	(2)	(3)	(6)	(26)	(0)	(19)	(2)	(100)
1999-00	320.39	16.72	25.70	51.89	209.05	4.85	132.38	20.17	781.15
Share (%)	(41)	(2)	(3)	(7)	(27)	(1)	(17)	(3)	(100)
2000-01	336.44	18.26	29.95	88.17	191.05	8.05	142.79	22.30	837.01
Share (%)	(40)	(2)	(4)	(11)	(23)	(1)	(17)	(3)	(100)
2001-02	272.24	17.48	19.81	97.76	205.58	7.45	139.46	21.52	781.30
Share (%)	(35)	(2)	(3)	(13)	(26)	(1)	(18)	(3)	(100)
Average	*(41)*	*(2)*	*(3)*	*(5)*	*(26)*	*(0)*	*(19)*	*(4)*	*(100)*
Growth (%)	*9.09*	*15.52*	*10.66*	*26.50*	*10.25*	*42.86*	*20.28*	*3.58*	*10.69*
C. V.	*33*	*47*	*41*	*86*	*37*	*101*	*40*	*77*	*35*

Note: Figures in parenthesis represent percentage of total.

Legend: C.V. = Coefficient of Variation.

Source: Regional Office, State Bank of India, Aizawl.

Table 4.12 revealed the following:

1. Three major districts namely Aizawl, Lunglei and Serchhip got nearly 86 per cent of the SSI advances and remaining 5 districts shared the balance 14 per cent funds, while in Mamit district it was almost 'Nil' and in Champhai (2 %), Kolasib (3 %), Saiha (4 %) and Lawngtlai (5 %), districts also near to negligible. In Lunglei district there was no change in relative share in SSI advances over the period, in Serchhip and Lawngtlai districts the relative share increased from 2 per cent each in 1990-91 to 18 per cent and 13 per cent respectively in 2001-02. On the contrary the relative share of Aizawl and Saiha district came down from 48 per cent and 18 per cent respectively in 1990-91

to 35 per cent and 3 per cent respectively in 2001-02. Change in relative share of other districts was negligible.

2. The growth in SSI advances of Mamit (42.86% p.a.), Lawngtlai (26.50% p.a.), Serchhip (20.28% p.a.), and Champhai (15.52% p.a.) districts were more than the overall growth in SSI advances at 10.69 per cent p.a. There was highest increase in Mamit district and moderate increase in Lawngtlai, Serchhip and Champhai districts. Growth in case of Kolasib and Lunglei districts was at par with overall growth in SSI advances. The least increase was noticed in Saiha district (3.58% p.a.). In case of Aizawl district SSI advances grew at the rate (9.09% p.a.) little lesser than that of the overall growth in SSIs advances.
3. Among district-wise SSI advances there was larger variation in Mamit (101%), Lawngtlai (86%) and Saiha (77%) districts as compared to variation in overall SSI advances (35%). Variation in other districts was less than the variation in overall SSI advances.

The position regarding district-wise SBF advances by SBI in Mizoram from 1990-91 to 2001-02 is given in Table 4.13.

Table 4.13 revealed the following:

1. The relative share of Aizawl district had declined from 59 per cent in 1990-91 to 51 per cent in 2001-02, but, on an average it remained at 56 per cent. Next largest share 15 per cent went to Lunglei district and the relative share increased from 14 per cent in 1990-91 to 22 per cent in 2001-02. Kolasib and Serchhip districts got more or less equal funds (8%), but, in case of Kolasib the relative share declined from 9 per cent in 1990-91 to 5 per cent in 2001-02 and that of Serchhip district increased from 4 per cent in 1990-91 to 9 per cent in 2001-02. The share of Lawngtlai district in SBF advances consistently remained at 5 per cent. The balance 9 per cent funds were shared by remaining three districts Saiha (4%), Champhai (3%) and Mamit (2%).
2. The growth of SBF financing in Mamit (29.12% p.a.), Champhai (26.53% p.a.), Lunglei (22.48% p.a.) districts was higher than the overall growth in SBF advances (16.43% p.a.). Growth in Serchhip (17.81% p.a.), Lawngtlai (16.74% p.a.) and Aizawl (15.56% p.a.) districts was near the over all growth in SBF advances (16.43% p.a.). However, Saiha district did register

growth at 13.27 per cent p.a. that was less than the average and the least growth in SBF advances was in Kolasib district at 7.55 per cent p.a.

Table 4.13: District-wise Small Business Finance by State Bank of India in Mizoram From 1990-91 to 2001-02 (As on 31st March)

(*Rs. in lakh*)

Year	*Aizawl*	*Cham-phai*	*Kolasib*	*Lawng-tlai*	*Lunglei*	*Mamit*	*Serchhip*	*Saiha*	*Total*
1990-91	320.11	7.41	47.55	27.26	77.37	3.97	21.66	32.91	538.24
Share (%)	(59)	(1)	(9)	(5)	(14)	(1)	(4)	(6)	(100)
1991-92	256.75	12.04	43.33	24.25	63.17	3.41	86.85	20.70	510.50
Share (%)	(50)	(2)	(8)	(5)	(12)	(1)	(17)	(4)	(100)
1992-93	201.55	3.84	35.67	20.01	47.15	3.57	27.58	17.55	356.92
Share (%)	(56)	(1)	(10)	(6)	(13)	(1)	(8)	(5)	(100)
1993-94	234.89	8.35	31.24	19.06	61.88	2.75	24.91	17.43	400.51
Share (%)	(59)	(2)	(8)	(5)	(15)	(1)	(6)	(4)	(100)
1994-95	216.48	17.57	30.21	18.11	19.60	3.57	27.70	12.00	345.24
Share (%)	(63)	(5)	(9)	(5)	(6)	(1)	(80)	(3)	(100)
1995-96	294.73	26.69	44.78	27.48	71.92	7.93	34.58	12.51	520.62
Share (%)	(57)	(5)	(9)	(5)	(14)	(2)	(7)	(2)	(100)
1996-97	360.20	25.59	39.34	41.96	89.98	10.37	56.28	16.84	640.56
Share (%)	(56)	(4)	(6)	(7)	(14)	(2)	(9)	(3)	(100)
1997-98	520.61	30.61	42.88	54.98	133.98	13.90	83.33	17.41	897.70
Share (%)	(58)	(3)	(5)	(6)	(15)	(2)	(9)	(2)	(100)
1998-99	735.74	49.08	79.15	82.43	217.19	24.53	108.40	42.44	1338.96
Share (%)	(55)	(4)	(6)	(6)	(16)	(2)	(8)	(3)	(100)
1999-00	978.77	51.72	79.22	90.92	301.93	39.28	118.49	61.02	1721.35
Share (%)	(57)	(3)	(5)	(5)	(18)	(2)	(7)	(4)	(100)
2000-01	844.26	54.11	68.89	86.74	349.23	34.31	139.95	70.42	1647.91
Share (%)	(51)	(3)	(4)	(5)	(21)	(2)	(8)	(4)	(100)
2001-02	873.97	72.50	78.41	74.88	374.04	24.98	149.25	81.87	1729.90
Share (%)	(51)	(4)	(5)	(4)	(22)	(1)	(9)	(5)	(100)
Average	*(56)*	*(3)*	*(7)*	*(5)*	*(15)*	*(2)*	*(8)*	*(4)*	*(100)*
Growth (%)	*15.56*	*26.53*	*7.55*	*16.74*	*22.48*	*29.12*	*17.81*	*13.27*	*16.43*
C. V.	*57*	*71*	*35*	*59*	*80*	*87*	*62*	*70*	*61*

Note: Figures in parenthesis represent percentage of total.

Legend: C.V. = Coefficient of Variation.

Source: Regional Office, State Bank of India, Aizawl.

3. Among district-wise SBF advances, there was larger variation in Mamit (87%), Lunglei (80%), Champhai (71%), and Saiha (70%) districts as compared to overall variation in SBF advances (61%), while variation in other districts was less than the overall variation in SBF advances. Further, variation in SBF advances was more or less in tune with variation in total SBI advances, but at the same time SSI advances were more consistent.

4. Thus, though the total advances of Aizawl district grew at an average rate of 19.63 per cent p.a., SSI and SBF advances did not grew at the same pace. It seemed SBI had given more emphasis on consumer advances from personal category in Aizawl district. Similarly, in case of Mamit, Champhai and Serchhip districts SSI and SBF advances were given greater priority over others. In case of Lunglei district, SBF advances were preferred over SSI advances, but in case of Kolasib district SSI advances were preferred against SBF advances.

Mizoram Rural Bank

Mizoram Rural Bank (MRB) has the widest network of 54 branches in Mizoram spread all over the eight districts of the State with head office in Aizawl. Its branches are located in every nook and corner of the State serving deep into Mizoram even in an un-banked area. Its role in the development of Mizoram's business, trade and commerce may be understood from the analysis of data relating to its advances for the period from 1990-91 to 2001-02 is compiled and presented in Tables 4.14, 4.15, 4.16, and 4.17

Table 4.14 on segmentwise Advances of MRB revealed the following:

1. On the average, SBF advances dominated consistently at 54 per cent which ranged between 49 per cent and 61 per cent. AGL advances at 26 per cent ranged between 15 per cent and 34 per cent. Relative share of Personal advances recorded stagnation in first half period, thereafter, jumped sharply and became more or less constant. While SSI advances at 11 per cent declined from 15 per cent in 1990-91 to 7 per cent in 2001-02.
2. Overall growth in total advances was 15.91 per cent p.a. The highest growth was in personal segment at 51.25 per cent p.a. The annual growth in SBF, AGL, and SSI advances was at 16.51 per cent, 9.00 per cent, and 6.90 per cent respectively. This showed that MRB neither focused on SSI advances nor on SBF advances, rather it focused on personal advances that contributed to the growth of business and industry indirectly by boosting demand for industrial products of other state.
3. The variation in SSI advances and AGL advances over the years was similar, but lesser than the variation in total advances. However, the variation in SBF advances was more than the variation in total advances; highest variation was in Personal advances.

Table 4.14: Segment-wise Advances of Mizoram Rural Bank in Mizoram From 1990-91 to 2001-02 (As on 31st March)

(*Rs. in lakh*)

Year	*SSI*	*SBF*	*AGL*	*Personal*	*Total*
1990-91	66.37	255.17	109.37	8.58	439.49
Share (%)	(15)	(58)	(25)	(2)	(100)
1991-92	70.41	256.16	133.98	7.18	467.73
Share (%)	(15)	(55)	(29)	(2)	(100)
1992-93	83.26	279.93	171.22	11.95	546.36
Share (%)	(15)	(51)	(31)	(2)	(100)
1993-94	85.28	321.94	218.64	15.03	640.89
Share (%)	(13)	(50)	(34)	(2)	(100)
1994-95	71.25	365.33	229.47	36.01	702.06
Share (%)	(10)	(52)	(33)	(5)	(100)
1995-96	89.65	386.91	265.80	42.21	784.57
Share (%)	(11)	(49)	(34)	(5)	(100)
1996-97	66.62	463.72	237.23	104.03	871.60
Share (%)	(8)	(53)	(27)	(12)	(100)
1997-98	93.68	494.77	235.05	181.73	1005.23
Share (%)	(9)	(49)	(23)	(18)	(100)
1998-99	96.02	557.72	241.98	207.95	1103.67
Share (%)	(9)	(51)	(22)	(19)	(100)
1999-00	118.50	724.57	269.73	277.13	1389.93
Share (%)	(9)	(52)	(19)	(20)	(100)
2000-01	129.94	1195.14	298.99	320.01	1944.08
Share (%)	(7)	(61)	(15)	(16)	(100)
2001-02	164.51	1480.48	382.38	438.40	2465.77
Share (%)	(7)	(60)	(16)	(18)	(100)
Average	(11)	(54)	(26)	(10)	(100)
Growth (%)	6.90	16.51	9.00	51.25	15.91
C. V.	30	66	30	102	58

Note: Figures in parenthesis represent percentage of total.

Legend: SSI = Small Scale Industry Advances, SBF = Small Business Finance Advances, AGL = Agricultural Advances, CV = Coefficient of Variation.

Source: Head Office, Mizoram Rural Bank, Aizawl.

The details of district-wise advances of MRB in Mizoram from 1990-91 to 2001-02 are given Table 4.15, which revealed the following:

1. Being a rural bank, MRB should have given greater emphasis to advances in rural/remote areas. But, district-wise analysis of advances showed a reverse picture and confirmed that the bank mainly concentrated in advancing loans in Aizawl district (52 per cent) and very little credit was made available to Siaha

(2%) and Lawngtlai (0%) districts. Champhai, Lunglei, Kolasib, and Serchhip districts were given more or less equal weightage in the range of 8 per cent to 11 per cent of total advances in each district over the period from 1990-91 to 2001-02. The relative share of Kolasib and Serchhip districts reduced slightly in second half. The relative share of Mamit district (6%) declined to half of what was at the beginning.

Table 4.15: District-wise Advances of Mizoram Rural Bank in Mizoram From 1990-91 to 2001-02 (As on 31st March)

(Rs. in lakh)

District	*Aizawl*	*Cham-phai*	*Mamit*	*Kolasib*	*Serchhip*	*Lunglei*	*Saiha*	*Lawng-tlai*	*Total*
1990-91	215.02	46.59	35.72	47.83	45.37	35.22	13.41	0.33	439.49
Share (%)	(49)	(11)	(8)	(11)	(10)	(8)	(3)	(0)	(100)
1991-92	217.96	55.10	39.94	51.98	47.01	37.89	16.54	1.31	467.73
Share (%)	(47)	(12)	(9)	(11)	(10)	(8)	(4)	(0)	(100)
1992-93	258.30	66.58	45.15	59.13	56.57	41.80	16.86	1.97	546.36
Share (%)	(47)	(12)	(8)	(11)	(10)	(8)	(3)	(0)	(100)
1993-94	301.48	87.15	52.03	64.36	61.36	47.84	22.63	4.04	640.89
Share (%)	(47)	(14)	(8)	(10)	(10)	(7)	(4)	(1)	(100)
1994-95	340.82	80.15	58.56	75.81	63.36	59.22	20.41	3.73	702.06
Share (%)	(49)	(11)	(8)	(11)	(9)	(8)	(3)	(1)	(100)
1995-96	373.54	89.79	65.36	80.62	63.15	84.99	22.80	4.32	784.57
Share (%)	(48)	(11)	(8)	(10)	(8)	(11)	(3)	(1)	(100)
1996-97	474.50	102.52	41.96	71.43	67.25	98.44	13.28	2.22	871.60
Share (%)	(54)	(12)	(5)	(8)	(8)	(11)	(2)	(0)	(100)
1997-98	580.73	106.31	39.83	74.71	68.25	120.46	12.55	2.39	1005.23
Share (%)	(58)	(11)	(4)	(7)	(7)	(12)	(1)	(0)	(100)
1998-99	586.57	105.65	40.91	110.74	77.50	168.44	11.53	2.33	1103.67
Share (%)	(53)	(10)	(4)	(10)	(7)	(15)	(1)	(0)	(100)
1999-00	780.12	111.98	53.32	129.46	109.64	186.50	16.59	2.32	1389.93
Share (%)	(56)	(8)	(4)	(9)	(8)	(13)	(1)	(0)	(100)
2000-01	1057.02	170.90	91.79	173.26	164.99	248.57	27.22	10.33	1944.08
Share (%)	(54)	(9)	(5)	(9)	(8)	(13)	(1)	(1)	(100)
2001-02	1398.20	213.09	111.39	201.51	185.33	300.76	43.35	12.14	2465.77
Share (%)	(57)	(9)	(5)	(8)	(8)	(12)	(2)	(0)	(100)
Average	(52)	(11)	(6)	(10)	(9)	(11)	(2)	(0)	(100)
Growth (%)	18.15	12.03	6.63	12.90	12.18	23.15	4.25	21.05	15.91
C. V.	64	44	39	50	52	71	43	87	58

Note: Figures in parenthesis represent percentage of total.

Legend: C.V. = Coefficient of Variation.

Source: Head Office, Mizoram Rural Bank, Aizawl.

2. The growth in advances of Lunglei district was highest at 23.15 per cent p.a. Next highest growth was in Lawngtlai district at 21.05 per cent p.a. (though, the overall share was very less). Growth in Aizawl district at 18.15 per cent p.a. was more than the over all growth in total advances. The least growth was in Saiha district at 4.25 per cent p.a. In Mamit district the growth was at 6.63 per cent p.a. Kolasib, Serchhip and Champhai districts registered growth, of course below the average, at around 12.00 per cent p.a.
3. Variation in advances of Lawngtlai (87%), Lunglei (71%) and Aizawl (64%) districts was greater than overall variation in total advances (58%), while in case of advances of other districts there existed consistency as the variation was less than that of overall variation.

The details of district-wise SSI advances of MRB in Mizoram from 1990-91 to 2001-02 are given in Table 4.16, which revealed the following:

1. District-wise SSI financing pattern of MRB in Mizoram revealed that Aizawl district dominated the rest of the State as it attracted on the average nearly 48 per cent of SSI advances. Rests of the loans were disbursed in the range of 9 per cent to 11 per cent, averaging at 10 per cent each among Kolasib, Mamit, Serchhip, Lunglei and Champhai districts. Saiha (2%) and Lawngtlai (0%) districts were given least almost 'Nil'. It may be concluded that no disbursement was made in old Chhimtuipui district.
2. The highest growth was in Lunglei district at 11.02 per cent p.a. In Serchhip, Aizawl and Champhai districts, it was above the overall growth of SSI advances, but, at 8.33 per cent, 8.26 per cent and 7.86 per cent p.a. respectively. In Saiha and Lawngtlai districts negative growth was noticed at 6.92 per cent and 0.84 per cent p.a. respectively. In case of Kolasib and Mamit districts, a nominal increase was recorded at 1.65 per cent and 0.72 per cent p.a. respectively.
3. Variation in SSI advances 30 per cent was less than the variation in total advances 58 per cent (Table 4.15). Further, among inter-district SSI advances, the variation in Mamit and Kolasib districts was lowest, while in Aizawl, Champhai, Saiha and Lawngtlai districts, it was almost at par, and in Serchhip and Lunglei districts, it was greater than the variation in overall SSI advances.

Table 4.16: District-wise Small Scale Industry Advances by Mizoram Rural Bank in Mizoram, from 1990-91 to 2001-02 (As on 31st March)

(*Rs. in lakh*)

District	*Aizawl*	*Cham-phai*	*Mamit*	*Kolasib*	*Serchhip*	*Lunglei*	*Saiha*	*Lawng-tlai*	*Total*
1990-91	29.53	6.10	6.68	8.31	7.49	6.15	2.11	0.00	66.37
Share (%)	(44)	(9)	(10)	(13)	(11)	(9)	(3)	(0)	(100)
1991-92	30.29	7.13	8.27	7.31	8.17	6.74	2.46	0.04	70.41
Share (%)	(43)	(10)	(12)	(10)	(12)	(10)	(3)	(0)	(100)
1992-93	38.31	7.53	9.50	9.85	8.55	6.91	2.54	0.07	83.26
Share (%)	(46)	(9)	(11)	(12)	(10)	(8)	(3)	(0)	(100)
1993-94	37.80	8.17	10.33	11.75	7.69	6.44	3.05	0.05	85.28
Share (%)	(44)	(10)	(12)	(14)	(9)	(8)	(4)	(0)	(100)
1994-95	27.86	5.16	10.25	11.49	6.75	7.25	2.44	0.05	71.25
Share (%)	(39)	(7)	(14)	(16)	(9)	(10)	(3)	(0)	(100)
1995-96	47.08	5.18	10.20	10.07	5.78	9.08	2.16	0.10	89.65
Share (%)	(53)	(6)	(11)	(11)	(6)	(10)	(2)	(0)	(100)
1996-97	39.22	5.89	6.05	6.33	3.66	4.44	0.99	0.04	66.62
Share (%)	(59)	(9)	(9)	(10)	(5)	(7)	(1)	(0)	(100)
1997-98	47.41	8.34	5.45	13.50	6.71	11.22	1.00	0.05	93.68
Share (%)	(51)	(9)	(6)	(14)	(7)	(12)	(1)	(0)	(100)
1998-99	46.61	11.30	5.43	11.52	8.71	10.91	1.49	0.05	96.02
Share (%)	(49)	(12)	(6)	(12)	(9)	(11)	(2)	(0)	(100)
1999-00	52.44	11.91	8.19	11.79	14.30	18.62	1.20	0.05	118.50
Share (%)	(44)	(10)	(7)	(10)	(12)	(16)	(1)	(0)	(100)
2000-01	59.96	12.63	10.65	10.00	17.20	18.21	1.24	0.05	129.94
Share (%)	(46)	(10)	(8)	(8)	(13)	(14)	(1)	(0)	(100)
2001-02	86.99	15.26	12.01	8.85	23.21	16.39	1.75	0.05	164.51
Share (%)	(53)	(9)	(7)	(5)	(14)	(10)	(1)	(0)	(100)
Average	(48)	(9)	(10)	(11)	(10)	(10)	(2)	(0)	(100)
Growth (%)	8.26	7.86	0.72	1.65	8.33	11.02	-6.92	-0.84	6.90
C. V.	35	36	25	20	54	47	35	30	30

Note: Figures in parenthesis represent percentage of total.

Legend: C.V. = Coefficient of Variation.

Source: Head Office, Mizoram Rural Bank, Aizawl.

The details of district-wise SBF advances of MRB in Mizoram from 1990-91 to 2001-02 are given in Table 4.17.

The Table 4.17 revealed the following:

1. District-wise SBF financing pattern of MRB revealed that Aizawl district dominated on the portfolio at 58 per cent of total SBF loans disbursed. Lunglei district shared 11 per cent. Serchhip, Champhai, and Kolasib districts shared more or less equal at 8 to 9 per cent. Mamit district got only 4 per cent of funds. Saiha (2%) and Lawngtlai (0%) districts were more or less ignored.

Table 4.17: District-wise Small Business Finance by Mizoram Rural Bank in Mizoram From 1990-91 to 2001-02 (As on 31st March)

(*Rs. in lakh*)

District	*Aizawl*	*Cham-phai*	*Mamit*	*Kolasib*	*Serch-hip*	*Lunglei*	*Saiha*	*Lawn-gtlai*	*Total*
1990-91	146.83	25.92	12.11	22.22	24.52	17.92	5.65	0.00	255.17
Share (%)	(58)	(10)	(5)	(9)	(10)	(7)	(2)	(0)	(100)
1991-92	147.56	25.54	11.67	23.72	23.39	16.85	7.08	0.35	256.16
Share (%)	(58)	(10)	(5)	(9)	(9)	(7)	(3)	(0)	(100)
1992-93	166.75	25.52	12.28	24.38	28.76	16.24	5.58	0.42	279.93
Share (%)	(60)	(9)	(4)	(9)	(10)	(6)	(2)	(0)	(100)
1993-94	189.47	30.55	14.58	23.83	31.18	21.34	8.69	2.30	321.94
Share (%)	(59)	(9)	(5)	(7)	(10)	(7)	(3)	(1)	(100)
1994-95	218.76	22.79	17.95	30.39	33.64	33.24	7.08	1.48	365.33
Share (%)	(60)	(6)	(5)	(8)	(9)	(9)	(2)	(0)	(100)
1995-96	231.79	20.01	20.62	32.97	34.00	37.49	8.53	1.50	386.91
Share (%)	(60)	(5)	(5)	(9)	(9)	(10)	(2)	(0)	(100)
1996-97	281.50	45.71	12.15	29.06	32.39	55.86	6.33	0.72	463.72
Share (%)	(61)	(10)	(3)	(6)	(7)	(12)	(1)	(0)	(100)
1997-98	307.76	49.58	14.51	21.07	34.01	60.88	6.15	0.81	494.77
Share (%)	(62)	(10)	(3)	(4)	(7)	(12)	(1)	(0)	(100)
1998-99	292.52	45.10	15.87	51.58	42.88	104.32	4.65	0.80	557.72
Share (%)	(52)	(8)	(3)	(9)	(8)	(19)	(1)	(0)	(100)
1999-00	629.16	98.48	56.93	113.82	113.55	166.52	13.49	3.19	1195.14
Share (%)	(53)	(8)	(5)	(10)	(10)	(14)	(1)	(0)	(100)
2000-01	405.78	43.23	23.75	65.62	62.29	114.79	8.34	0.77	724.57
Share (%)	(56)	(6)	(3)	(9)	(9)	(16)	(1)	(0)	(100)
2001-02	798.40	126.62	61.54	136.24	121.29	212.80	17.57	6.02	1480.48
Share (%)	(54)	(9)	(4)	(9)	(8)	(14)	(1)	(0)	(100)
Average	(58)	(8)	(4)	(8)	(9)	(11)	(2)	(0)	(100)
Growth (%)	15.18	13.71	12.73	16.03	14.05	28.15	5.86	15.43	16.10
C. V.	61	68	73	77	67	87	43	96	66

Note: Figures in parenthesis represent percentage of total.

Legend: C.V. = Coefficient of Variation.

Source: Head Office, Mizoram Rural Bank, Aizawl.

2. Further, it may be understood that the highest growth was registered in Lunglei district at 28.15 per cent p.a. In all other districts the growth of SBF advances was less than that of overall growth at 16.10 per cent p.a. The least growth was in Saiha district at 5.86 per cent p.a. Though, the growth in per cent was higher in Lawngtlai district but it did not get a sizeable share.
3. Among inter-district SBF advances, the degree of fluctuation from year to year was greater in Lawngtlai (96 %), Lunglei (87 %), Kolasib (77 %), and Mamit (73 %) districts as

compared to variation in overall SBF advances (66%) and as also other districts. The least variation was in Saiha district at 43 per cent.

4. It may be concluded that the bank provided banking facility extensively in rural areas, but, paid attention to SBF advances only. It played little role in industrial development of the State. Its emphasis on credit expansion was centered only to urban areas, which was contrary to the objective of rural bank.

On the whole, it may be concluded that there existed disparity between Aizawl district and rest of the State giving an indication of unbalanced development in the State, which needs to be set right. If not checked, it may cause increased migration from remote and rural areas to urban areas and increasing concentration in urban centers may lead to further complications of increased urbanization.

Vijaya Bank

Though the Vijaya Bank has completed Silver Jubilee of its existence in Mizoram, its business grew in volume, but, it did not spread in size (number of branches) and kept confined to Aizawl. It does not cover the whole State in the ambit of its operations. The data on advances of Vijaya Bank from 1989-90 to 2001-02 are compiled and presented in Table 4.18.

Table 4.18 revealed the following:

1. The SSI advances increased in absolute amout but the relative share on the average at 9 per cent declined continuously and registered a negligible growth of 0.51 per cent p.a. over the period. Of the total advances, on the average SBF loans and Personal advances constituted 58 per cent and 25 per cent respectively.
2. It concentrated on SBF advances throughout the period, except for 1991-92 to 1992-93, when personal advances were given higher priority and during these two years such advances constituted 50 per cent of total advances. In the first two years of study period, SSI, AGL, and Personal advances were given almost same weightage. Since 1997-98, it started ignoring the SSI sector.

Table 4.18: Segment-wise Advances of Vijaya Bank in Mizoram from 1990-91 to 2001-02 (As on 31st March)

(*Rs. in lakh*)

Year	*SSI*	*SBF*	*AGL*	*Personal*	*Total*
1989-90	34.75	94.64	34.54	44.15	208.08
Share (%)	(17)	(45)	(17)	(21)	(100)
1990-91	32.67	93.65	29.39	29.64	185.35
Share (%)	(18)	(51)	(16)	(16)	(100)
1991-92	25.00	60.00	6.80	88.20	180.00
Share (%)	(14)	(33)	(4)	(49)	(100)
1992-93	25.00	60.00	5.00	110.00	200.00
Share (%)	(13)	(30)	(3)	(55)	(100)
1993-94	N.A.	N.A.	N.A.	N.A.	N.A.
Share (%)	N.A.	N.A.	N.A.	N.A.	N.A.
1994-95	26.45	166.04	2.65	49.14	244.28
Share (%)	(11)	(68)	(1)	(20)	(100)
1995-96	31.95	269.98	5.47	76.39	383.79
Share (%)	(8)	(70)	(1)	(20)	(100)
1996-97	30.94	269.44	12.76	72.16	385.30
Share (%)	(8)	(70)	(3)	(19)	(100)
1997-98	28.86	425.63	14.83	71.65	540.97
Share (%)	(5)	(79)	(3)	(13)	(100)
1998-99	26.89	351.01	79.91	94.55	552.36
Share (%)	(5)	(64)	(14)	(17)	(100)
1999-00	21.85	368.14	106.35	162.73	659.07
Share (%)	(3)	(56)	(16)	(25)	(100)
2000-01	32.25	430.71	78.78	140.31	682.05
Share (%)	(5)	(63)	(12)	(21)	(100)
2001-02	32.86	715.95	60.07	210.97	1019.85
Share (%)	(3)	(70)	(6)	(21)	(100)
Average	(9)	(58)	(8)	(25)	(100)
Growth (%)	0.51	23.68	20.12	26.74	11.61
C. V.	13	65	98	50	55

Note: Figure in parenthesis represent percentage of total.

Legend: SSI = Small Scale Industry Advances, SBF = Small Business Finance Advances, AGL = Agricultural Advances, C.V. = Coefficient of Variation.

Source: Vijaya Bank, Aizawl.

3. Total advances of the bank increased 5 times and registered an average annual growth of 11.61 per cent, wheareas the increase

in SSI advances was '*Nil*'. The trend showed that these advances declined over the entire period. No attention was paid to Industrial advances. At the same time the trend in SBF advances showed an upward movement recording an average annual growth of 23.68 per cent p.a. The AGL advances decreased in first half, then increased in second half and ultimately recorded a jump of almost 100 per cent. Personal advances continued to grow at second place.

4. Variation in year to year advances of AGL (98%) and SBF (65%) was larger than that that of overall variation (55%). However, there was higher degree of consistency in SSI advances as variation was least (13%). Further, variation in personal advances was almost at same pace as was in total advances.

It may be concluded that only trade and services (commercial) loans were preferred by the bank over the period of study. It did not realize its responsibility towards industrial development in Mizoram. Of course, it contributed towards development of business in Mizoram.

United Commercial Bank

United Commercial Bank (UCO) branch was set up in Aizawl on 16th September 1976. It kept confined to Aizawl city only and did not cover the whole Mizoram in its operations. The details of advances from 1981-82 to 2001-02 by the bank are presented in Table 4.19. The data from 1989-90 and onwards were analyzed to maintain comparability between UCO Bank and Vijaya Bank as both banks have one branch each at Aizawl and became operational together from 1977.

The Table 4.19 revealed the following:

1. The advances made by UCO Bank during pre-statehood period from 1981-82 to 1988-89 revealed that though the relative share of SBF advances declined over the years, the average dominated the portfolio at 60 per cent in total advances. However, SSI advances on the average (8 per cent) was lowest increased continuously from near 'zero' per cent in 1981-82 to 25 per cent in 1988-89. Personal and AGL loans constituted 18 per cent, and 14 per cent respectively. The bank appeared mainly interested in Small Business Finance and it gave least weightage to Small Scale Industry loans. AGL advances were not large,

Table 4.19: Segment-wise Advances of United Commercial Bank in Mizoram From 1981-82 to 1989-90 (As on 31st March)

(Rs. in lakh)

Year	SSI	SBF	AGL	Personal	Total
1981-82	0.04	27.84	1.22	3.70	32.80
Share (%)	(0)	(85)	(4)	(11)	(100)
1982-83	0.44	28.75	2.90	4.77	36.86
Share (%)	(1)	(78)	(8)	(13)	(100)
1983-84	1.60	28.71	2.43	7.93	40.67
Share (%)	(4)	(71)	(6)	(19)	(100)
1984-85	3.04	27.45	4.50	7.54	42.53
Share (%)	(7)	(65)	(11)	(18)	(100)
1985-86	4.43	22.94	4.56	8.10	40.03
Share (%)	(11)	(57)	(11)	(20)	(100)
1986-87	4.25	19.55	14.19	11.23	49.22
Share (%)	(9)	(40)	(29)	(23)	(100)
1987-88	6.43	27.44	16.44	17.22	67.53
Share (%)	(10)	(41)	(24)	(25)	(100)
1988-89	26.70	46.03	18.62	15.20	106.55
Share (%)	(25)	(43)	(17)	(14)	(100)
Average upto 1988-89	***(8)***	***(60)***	***(14)***	***(18)***	***(100)***
1989-90	38.82	60.24	27.62	17.61	144.29
Share (%)	(27)	(42)	(19)	(12)	(100)
1990-91	47.88	84.72	16.41	21.06	170.07
Share (%)	(28)	(50)	(10)	(12)	(100)
1991-92	58.10	78.96	16.19	18.62	171.87
Share (%)	(34)	(46)	(9)	(11)	(100)
1992-93	63.72	86.79	18.03	21.31	189.85
Share (%)	(34)	(46)	(9)	(11)	(100)
1993-94	60.51	81.73	13.13	22.40	177.77
Share (%)	(34)	(46)	(7)	(13)	(100)
1994-95	62.50	70.77	18.05	26.71	178.03
Share (%)	(35)	(40)	(10)	(15)	(100)
1995-96	59.93	89.53	18.35	34.80	202.61
Share (%)	(30)	(44)	(9)	(17)	(100)
1996-97	30.49	140.14	22.43	62.46	255.52
Share (%)	(12)	(55)	(9)	(24)	(100)
1997-98	17.94	123.43	19.99	53.21	214.57
Share (%)	(8)	(58)	(9)	(25)	(100)
1998-99	13.36	89.32	15.70	33.84	152.22
Share (%)	(9)	(59)	(10)	(22)	(100)
1999-00	11.21	85.60	8.35	36.98	142.14
Share (%)	(8)	(60)	(6)	(26)	(100)
2000-01	18.30	93.13	7.61	47.35	166.39
Share (%)	(11)	(56)	(5)	(28)	(100)
2001-02	14.15	76.81	6.64	64.86	162.46
Share (%)	(9)	(47)	(4)	(40)	(100)
Average from 1989-90	(21)	(50)	(9)	(20)	(100)
Growth (%) from 1989-90	-12.97	2.14	-7.61	10.75	-0.05
C. V. (from 1989-90)	54	23	36	45	17

Note: Average, Growth and C.V. have been calculated from 1989-90.

Legend: SSI = Small Scale Industry, SBF = Small Business Finance, AGL = Agricultural Advances, C.V. = Coefficient of Variation.

Source: United Commercial Bank, Aizawl.

but, picked up sharply in second half. Personal advances increased consistently till 1987-88.

2. During pre-statehood period from 1981-82 to 1988-89 there was very little growth in financing by the bank. Even in later years also it did not make much headway as the bank confined its activities in and around Aizawl town only.
3. During post-statehood period from 1989-90 and onwards, the average composition of SBF, SSI, Personal and AGL advances was 50 per cent, 21 per cent, 20 per cent, and 9 per cent respectively.
4. There was a shift in focus of the bank and it gave progressive attention to SSI advances especially up to 1995-96, but, then its relative share in total advances declined sharply. However, SBF and Personal segment continued to receive same emphasis. On the other hand AGL advances seemed to be discouraged.
5. The total advances increased up to 1996-97 and thereafter declined owing to write off of bad debts (protested bill accounts) and as a result recorded a negative growth of 0.05 per cent p.a. The highest fall was in SSI advances at 12.97 per cent p.a. Next was in AGL advances at 7.61 per cent p.a., whereas SBF advances recorded a marginal growth of 2.14 per cent p.a. This indicated that the bad debts written off were more from SSI and AGL sector and least from SBF category. This also signified that the branch management took least interest in SSI advances and mainly focused on SBF advances.
6. When compared to Vijaya Bank, the bank had much less business in Mizoram after suffering loss due to huge bad debts written off and showed least interest in SSI advances and its role was declined as is evident from the fact that during 1989-90 to 2001-02, UCO Bank registered decline in its advances at 0.05 per cent p.a., whereas Vijaya Bank's advances grew at 11.61 per cent p.a. Further, UCO Bank's SSI advances declined sharply at 12.97 per cent p.a. as against 0.51 per cent p.a. growth in Vijaya Bank's SSI advances. Similarly, UCO Bank's SBF advances grew only at 2.14 per cent p.a. as against 23.68 per cent growth in Vijaya Bank's SBF advances. Again, AGL advances of UCO Bank declined at 7.61 per cent p.a. as against increase in Vijaya Bank at 20.12 per cent p.a. Though personal advances of UCO increased at 10.75 per cent p.a. while the increase in Vijaya Bank was high at 26.74 per cent p.a.

Cooperatives in Financing

The cooperative credit societies formed an important part of the credit structure in Mizoram. The idea of co-operation was present even among the early inhabitants of this region. People used to cut jungles for *jhum*, sow seeds, and weed *jhums* together. They maintained a well-knit corporate life and used to help one another in times of need. In fact, the very nature of day-to-day life accustomed Mizo to live and work in cooperation and embrace unity. Of course, the type of cooperation practiced was not planned and systematic. It was only in 1949 that planned cooperative movement reached Mizoram with the establishment of office of the Senior Inspector of Cooperative Societies at Aizawl. The first cooperative society was established in 1949 and since then a number of societies gradually grew.

During Five Year Plans, the Cooperative movement underwent several changes. In the First Five Year Plan, the cooperatives aimed at rehabilitation of the shattered economy. In the Second Five Year Plan emphasis was given to systematic development of cooperative movement and on its viability with greater government participation in its every aspect. The cooperatives were structured on the lines of recommendations of the Rural Credit Survey Committee of the Reserve Bank of India. Accordingly, the State Cooperative Department was reoriented and the office of the Assistant Registrar, Cooperative Societies was established at Aizawl in 1956. In pursuance of the National Development Council's policy decision a Cooperative Office was also opened at Lunglei in 1958. The emphasis of the Cooperative movement was shifted from viability to close contact, removing social cohesion and spread of national obligation among members.

During the Third Five Year Plan, intensive efforts were made to amalgamate the weak and uneconomic societies with the strong and viable ones and stress was placed on production oriented rural credit. However, in spite of difficulties of communication, transport, and disturbance of 1966, Cooperative movement made head way in Mizoram, particularly in the field of agricultural credit. The number of agricultural credit societies from 72 in 1970 increased to 152 in 1975. Until the Union Territory status in January 1972, the Assistant Registrar of Cooperative Societies at Aizawl was the district head of the Cooperative Societies Department in Mizoram and was assisted by Senior and Junior Cooperative Auditors. There was also one Liquidation Officer for the liquidation of moribund societies.

During the Fifth Five Year Plan, primary emphasis was laid on adequate provision of Cooperative credit for the rural population and fair distribution of essential commodities at cheaper rates both for rural and urban population. Provision of rural credits on easy terms was an important element of the Cooperative movement. Mizoram Cooperative Apex Bank Ltd. was registered under the Cooperative Societies Act on 5th December 1978 for which Rs.13 lakh were provided towards the share capital contribution, loan subsidy for purchase of furniture and fixtures, administrative charges, etc. In all, 155 service cooperative societies were organized and a provision of Rs.19.60 lakh was made for improvement of their business, strengthening of their share capital and for construction of godowns on loan. The Study Group on Agricultural Refinance and Development Cooperation had recommended organization of Large sized Agricultural Multipurpose Cooperative Societies (LAMPs) in the hill areas.

During VI Five Year Plan, four (4) LAMPS were organized in 1980-81 to serve the entire State for which Rs.10.50 lakh was provided as share capital contribution, managerial subsidy, transport subsidy, building subsidy and loan. The Marketing Cooperative Society Ltd. was setup at Aizawl to undertake procurement and marketing of agricultural produce mainly cash crops grown in Mizoram for which Rs.10.50 lakh was provided to foster and strengthen the business capacity of the society. Financial assistance and loan of Rs.13.85 lakh was provided under "Consumer Cooperatives" to foster the existing state level consumer cooperative societies, *viz.*, the Mizoram Wholesale Cooperative Stores Ltd. and the Mizoram Cooperative Super Market Ltd. The Mizoram Cooperative Union Ltd. was also given Rs.2 lakh for taking up the programme of cooperative education and training in an organized manner.

There were 7 State Level Cooperative Societies *viz.*, Mizoram Apex Marketing Cooperative Society Ltd., Mizoram Wholesale Cooperative Stores Ltd., Mizoram Cooperative Super Market Ltd., Mizoram State Cooperative Union Ltd., Mizoram Apex Weavers Service & Marketing Cooperative Society Ltd., Mizoram Cooperative Apex Bank Ltd., and Mizoram Cadre Management Cooperative Society Ltd. at Aizawl as on 1st October 1979. Among these, Mizoram Cooperative Apex Bank Ltd. and Mizoram Urban Cooperative Bank are financial institutions. The financing function of these banks is described here.

The Mizoram Cooperative Apex Bank (MCAB)

The Mizoram Cooperative Apex Bank (MCAB) was set up on 5th December 1978 for providing rural credit. However, the Reserve Bank of India approved its byelaws on later date and it became functional from

31st July 1982. During 1979-80, financial assistance was provided to it at Rs. 5.00 lakh as share capital contribution, Rs.0.50 lakh as loan for building, Rs. 0.50 lakh as subsidy for building, and Rs.1.00 lakh as grant for administrative charges totalling Rs.7.00 lakh. It has 10 branches spread over the 7 districts of Mizoram. However, it does not serve Mamit district yet. Data relating to advances of MCAB from 1982-83 to 2001-02 has been compiled and presented in Table 4.20.

For want of inter-bank comparison, the advances made by MCAB are analysed in two parts, *viz.*, advances made during pre-statehood period broadly covering upto 1989-90 and during post-statehood period from 1990-91 to 2001-02. The analysis of Table 4.20 revealed the following:

1. No advance was given to SSI sector during pre-statehood period. The whole focus of the bank was centred on SBF advances, which on the average comprised of 84 per cent of total advances followed by personal advances 12 per cent and AGL advances 4 per cent. During post statehood period also, the bank did not encourage SSI advances till 1997-98 and thereafter it started giving SSI loans, which were nearly 4 per cent of total advances. The SBF advances continued to dominate on the average at 76 per cent of total advances. AGL advances were also not given enough attention till 1997-98 and as a result, on the average, only 8 per cent of total advances could be given to this segment. Personal category advances, however, remained more or less stagnant till 1996-97 and thereafter increased every year and its composition, on the average was 15 per cent of total advances. From the above analysis, it is clear that till 1996-97, the bank preferred SBF advances only. In 1998-99, for the first time, it started giving loans to other categories of advances *viz.*, SSI, AGL, and Personal loans, resulting into an overall decrease in the share of SBF advances in the portfolio.
2. As regards growth in advances of the bank, though the total advances grew at 5.52 per cent p.a., the highest growth was recorded in AGL advances (41.62% p.a.) and Personal loan segment at 23.57 per cent p.a. At the same time, the SBF advances though increased in absolute figure till 1997-98 and thereafter declined both in terms of absolute and relative terms and had a negative growth of 2.17 per cent annually.

Table 4.20: Segment-wise Advances of Mizoram Cooperative Apex Bank in Mizoram from 1982-83 to 2001-02 (As on 31st March)

(Rs. in lakh)

Year	*SSI*	*SBF*	*AGL*	*Personal*	*Total*
1982-83	0.00	2.69	1.31	5.36	9.36
Share (%)	(0)	(29)	(14)	(57)	(100)
1983-84	0.00	20.02	0.00	0.00	20.02
Share (%)	(0)	(100)	(0)	(0)	(100)
1984-85	0.00	80.48	8.76	8.54	97.78
Share (%)	(0)	(82)	(9)	(9)	(100)
1985-86	0.00	220.31	7.16	15.72	243.19
Share (%)	(0)	(91)	(3)	(6)	(100)
1986-87	0.69	370.62	9.80	29.22	410.33
Share (%)	(0)	(90)	(2)	(7)	(100)
1987-88	3.23	651.70	8.87	43.27	707.07
Share (%)	(0)	(92)	(1)	(6)	(100)
1988-89	0.00	975.34	11.26	69.30	1055.90
Share (%)	(0)	(92)	(1)	(7)	(100)
1989-90	0.00	1242.46	13.84	89.60	1345.90
Share (%)	(0)	(92)	(1)	(7)	(100)
Average	***(0)***	***(84)***	***(4)***	***(12)***	***(100)***
1990-91	0.00	1348.25	16.20	113.08	1477.53
Share (%)	(0)	(91)	(1)	(8)	(100)
1991-92	0.00	1448.92	38.68	115.62	1603.22
Share (%)	(0)	(90)	(2)	(7)	(100)
1992-93	0.00	1641.82	17.67	137.67	1797.16
Share (%)	(0)	(91)	(1)	(8)	(100)
1993-94	4.99	1765.51	22.54	150.65	1943.69
Share (%)	(0)	(91)	(1)	(8)	(100)
1994-95	25.91	1887.91	34.17	141.64	2089.63
Share (%)	(1)	(90)	(2)	(7)	(100)
1995-96	0.00	2063.80	31.01	144.09	2238.90
Share (%)	(0)	(92)	(1)	(6)	(100)
1996-97	0.00	2190.27	47.22	222.27	2459.76
Share (%)	(0)	(89)	(2)	(9)	(100)
1997-98	0.00	2371.05	73.38	325.13	2769.56
Share (%)	(0)	(86)	(3)	(12)	(100)
1998-99	63.71	998.07	399.06	373.62	1834.46
Share (%)	(3)	(54)	(22)	(20)	(100)
1999-00	63.34	1149.74	463.07	421.36	2097.51
Share (%)	(3)	(55)	(22)	(20)	(100)
2000-01	107.22	1269.73	580.56	732.08	2689.59
Share (%)	(4)	(47)	(22)	(27)	(100)
2001-02	130.22	1290.04	397.10	1523.67	3341.03
Share (%)	(4)	(39)	(12)	(46)	(100)
Average	**(1)**	**(76)**	**(8)**	**(15)**	**(100)**
Growth (%)	30.62	-2.17	41.62	23.57	5.52
C. V.	136	26	116	106	24

Note: 1. Figures in Parenthesis represent share in total advances.

2. Average, Growth and C.V. have been from 1990-91.

Legend: SSI = Small Scale Industries; SBF = Small Business Finance; AGL = Agricultural Advances, C.V. = Coefficient of Variation.

Source: Compiled from Balance Sheets of Mizoram Apex Cooperative Bank.

3. From year to year though there was more or less consistency among SBF advances and total advances, there were larger variations in SSI, AGL, and personal advances.

The data relating to district-wise advances of MCAB from 1991-92 to 2001-02 are analyzed and presented in Table 4.21.

Table 4.21: District-wise Advances of Mizoram Cooperative Apex Bank in Mizoram from 1991-92 to 2001-02 (As on 31st March)

(*Rs. in lakh*)

Year	*Aizawl*	*Champhai*	*Kolasib*	*Lawngtlai*	*Lunglei*	*Saiha*	*Serchhip*	*Total*
1991-92	1282.83	76.25	19.62	0.94	132.02	73.64	18.86	1604.16
Share (%)	(80)	(5)	(1)	(0)	(8)	(5)	(1)	(100)
1992-93	1371.84	88.10	23.08	3.14	181.10	90.24	96.37	1853.87
Share (%)	(74)	(5)	(1)	(0)	(10)	(5)	(5)	(100)
1993-94	1469.97	91.59	25.66	11.86	203.62	99.22	41.80	1943.72
Share (%)	(76)	(5)	(1)	(1)	(10)	(5)	(2)	(100)
1994-95	1570.32	92.41	26.45	18.67	226.21	112.69	42.90	2089.65
Share (%)	(75)	(4)	(1)	(1)	(11)	(5)	(2)	(100)
1995-96	1613.54	99.09	21.83	19.20	254.32	115.48	44.55	2168.01
Share (%)	(74)	(5)	(1)	(1)	(12)	(5)	(2)	(100)
1996-97	1861.89	124.17	24.90	40.64	267.49	129.28	42.48	2490.85
Share (%)	(75)	(5)	(1)	(2)	(11)	(5)	(2)	(100)
1997-98	2022.24	167.76	38.74	41.01	285.64	135.34	42.34	2733.07
Share (%)	(74)	(6)	(1)	(2)	(10)	(5)	(2)	(100)
1998-99	1218.25	152.24	40.01	41.66	145.89	106.10	44.10	1748.25
Share (%)	(70)	(9)	(2)	(2)	(8)	(6)	(3)	(100)
1999-00	1490.52	166.25	44.70	42.46	154.15	137.13	62.33	2097.54
Share (%)	(71)	(8)	(2)	(2)	(7)	(7)	(3)	(100)
2000-01	1983.66	162.51	65.46	62.88	194.22	139.39	81.46	2689.58
Share (%)	(74)	(6)	(2)	(2)	(7)	(5)	(3)	(100)
2001-2002	2249.03	139.98	86.00	90.99	243.12	183.25	66.05	3058.42
Share (%)	(74)	(5)	(3)	(3)	(8)	(6)	(2)	(100)
Average	(74)	(6)	(2)	(1)	(9)	(5)	(2)	(100)
Growth (%)	3.74	8.33	14.22	45.22	1.59	6.87	6.37	4.48
C. V.	19	27	53	76	24	23	39	20

Note: Figures in parenthesis represent share in total advances.

Legend: SSI = Small Scale Industries; SBF = Small Business Finance; AGL = Agricultural, C. V. = Coefficient of Variation.

Source: Compiled from Balance Sheets of Mizoram Apex Cooperative Bank.

The analysis of Table 4.21 revealed the following:

1. On the average 74 per cent of total advances were consistently made in Aizawl district. This placed Aizawl district much ahead of other districts over the entire period of study. Next was Lunglei district, which was provided with on the average 9 per cent of total advances. Champhai and Saiha districts received 6 per cent

and 5 per cent of total loanable resources of the bank respectively. The least weightage was given to Kolasib, Lawngtlai and Serchhip districts, each of which shared on the average 2 per cent of total advances given by the bank. Though the total advances grew at 4.48 per cent p.a., the highest growth was in advances of Lawngtlai district at 45.22 per cent p.a. The share of Lawngtlai district in total advances was much less during earlier years and financing by bank in later years was useful in building the necessary credit base needed for operations. In Kolasib district the advances increased at 14.22 per cent p.a., Serchhip district at 6.37 per cent. Advances in Champhai district registered a moderate increase of 8.33 per cent p.a. Till 1995-96, the advances in Champhai district were almost stagnant and thereafter, showed a large increase in absolute terms. The advances grew consistently at 6.87 per cent p.a. in Saiha district. The least increase was in Lunglei district (1.59% p.a.) and Aizawl district (3.74% p.a.).

2. Nearly 3/4th of total advances were made by the bank in Aizawl district only and 1/4th to remaining districts. This showed that disparity between Aizawl and other districts may be due to concentration of population in Aizawl district. This also makes it clear that most advances were given in urban areas of the State, as the bank had all its branches located at district headquarters only and not elsewhere. This was contrary to the prime objective of the bank.
3. Except for Lawngtlai, Kolasib and Serchhip districts, the variation in advances of all other districts was of low degree and was more or less at par with variation in total advances.
4. All other banks have ignored Saiha district but MCAB has made advances consistently at 5 per cent of total advances. This is a good feature to note.

The data relating to district-wise SSI advances of MCAB from 1991-92 to 2001-02 has been analyzed and presented in Table 4.22.

The analysis of Table 4.22 revealed that the bank started giving SSI loans from 1999-00 only. The SSI advances of the bank were mainly distributed in three districts *viz.*, Aizawl (70 %), Lunglei (12 %), and Saiha (11 %) over the three years period from 1999-00 to 2001-02. However, there were wide fluctuations in advances of Saiha and Champhai districts and was either at par or below the overall average variation (48 %)

in all other districts. As regards SSI advances also, all other banks ignored Saiha district but MCAB, advanced nearly 11 per cent of total SSI advance. This is a good feature.

Table 4.22: District-wise Small-Scale Industry Advances of Mizoram Cooperative Apex Bank from 1999-2000 to 2001-02 (As on 31st March)

(*Rs. in lakh*)

Year	*Aizawl*	*Champhai*	*Kolasib*	*Lawngtlai*	*Lunglei*	*Saiha*	*Serchhip*	*Total*
1999-00	42.27	1.32	0.92	0.96	11.20	4.61	2.05	63.33
Share %	(67)	(2)	(1)	(2)	(18)	(7)	(3)	(100)
2000-01	85.11	1.24	1.02	0.86	11.15	5.58	2.26	107.22
Share %	(79)	(1)	(1)	(1)	(10)	(5)	(2)	(100)
2001-02	132.99	5.87	0.72	2.23	18.13	40.75	5.72	206.41
Share%	(64)	(3)	(0)	(1)	(9)	(20)	(3)	(100)
Average	(70)	(2)	(1)	(1)	(12)	(11)	(3)	(100)
Growth (%)	77.38	110.88	-11.53	52.41	27.23	197.31	67.04	80.53
C. V.	43	77	14	46	24	99	50	48

Note: Figures in parenthesis represent percentage of total advances.

Legend: C. V. = Coefficient of Variation.

Source: Compiled from Balance Sheets of Mizoram Apex Cooperative Bank.

The data relating to district-wise SBF advances of MCAB from 1991-92 to 2001-02 has been analyzed and presented in Table 4.23.

Table 4.23 revealed the following:

1. In SBF advances highest increase was noticed in Lawngtlai district. The SBF advances in all other districts decreased, except for Kolasib district which recorded a marginal increase of 1.28 per cent p.a. The highest decrease was in Serchhip district at 10.21 per cent p.a., followed by Lunglei (7.41% p.a.), Aizawl (3.39% p.a.), Saiha (2.59% p.a.) and Champhai (2.33% p.a.). The SBF advances continued to increase upto 1997-98 and then declined sharply and registered an average annual fall of 3.51 per cent. Overall it appears that the bank discouraged SBF advances since 1998-99, diversifying its loans and advances portfolio by including other segments in its basket. Till 1998-99, the bank management seemed conservative as far as SBF advances are concerned.
2. There has been a sharp decline of 34 per cent in total advances of all categories except SSI and in all districts except Kolasib,

Lawngtlai and Serchhip due to writing off of huge bad debts amounting to 10 crore[9] approximately in 1997-98.

Table 4.23: District-wise Small Business Finance by Mizoram Cooperative Apex Bank from 1991-92 to 2001-02 (As on 31st March)

(*Rs. in lakh*)

Year	*Aizawl*	*Champhai*	*Kolasib*	*Lawngtlai*	*Lunglei*	*Saiha*	*Serchhip*	*Total*
1991-92	1162.71	62.58	17.65	0.82	125.26	66.74	14.10	1449.86
Share (%)	(80)	(4)	(1)	(0)	(9)	(5)	(1)	(100)
1992-93	1260.54	72.93	18.47	1.77	173.35	79.81	91.58	1698.45
Share (%)	(74)	(4)	(1)	(0)	(10)	(5)	(5)	(100)
1993-94	1354.22	75.01	21.26	3.98	193.97	88.80	34.95	1772.19
Share (%)	(76)	(4)	(1)	(0)	(11)	(5)	(2)	(100)
1994-95	1459.03	76.61	21.94	12.53	215.13	97.80	36.10	1919.14
Share (%)	(76)	(4)	(1)	(1)	(11)	(5)	(2)	(100)
1995-96	1489.07	83.54	16.54	9.22	247.21	104.51	38.42	1988.51
Share (%)	(75)	(4)	(1)	(0)	(12)	(5)	(2)	(100)
1996-97	1638.00	108.66	18.09	26.86	254.01	115.24	29.44	2190.30
Share (%)	(75)	(5)	(1)	(1)	(12)	(5)	(1)	(100)
1997-98	1766.02	138.86	20.12	24.35	270.63	121.52	29.58	2371.08
Share (%)	(74)	(6)	(1)	(1)	(11)	(5)	(1)	(100)
1998-99	987.30	128.97	26.58	26.82	129.14	95.16	28.65	1422.62
Share (%)	(69)	(9)	(2)	(2)	(9)	(7)	(2)	(100)
1999-00	873.31	65.14	22.28	16.15	83.13	76.96	12.79	1149.76
Share (%)	(76)	(6)	(2)	(1)	(7)	(7)	(1)	(100)
2000-01	992.99	64.24	22.99	16.92	85.52	68.08	18.97	1269.71
Share (%)	(78)	(5)	(2)	(1)	(7)	(5)	(1)	(100)
2001-02	968.79	32.89	16.98	22.00	81.09	45.49	9.83	1177.07
Share (%)	(82)	(3)	(1)	(2)	(7)	(4)	(1)	(100)
Average	(76)	(5)	(1)	(1)	(10)	(5)	(2)	(100)
Growth (%)	-3.39	-2.33	1.28	33.97	-7.41	-2.59	-10.21	-3.51
C. V.	22	36	14	64	41	25	68	24

Note: Figures in parenthesis represent percentage of total advances.

Legend: C. V. = Coefficient of Variation.

Source: Compiled from Balance Sheets of Mizoram Apex Cooperative Bank.

The primary objective of establishing MCAB is to extend banking and financial services to the inhabitants of rural areas in Mizoram. Aizawl, being state capital, the entire district is considered better developed in terms of economic activities as compared to other districts of the State. Further, in all the districts the bank has a branch located at district headquarter. Based on this, it may be concluded that a major part of the advances was made in urban areas, which was contrary to its objectives.

The performance of MCAB in terms of credit expansion was satisfactory throughout the period of study in general and last few years in particular, but it had diverted from its objective of providing rural credit.

Mizoram Urban Cooperative Bank (MUCO)

Mizoram Urban Cooperative Bank (MUCO) is a single branch bank located in Aizawl. However, it financed all the four segments, *viz.*, SSI, SBF, AGL and personal advances. Unfortunately, the financial position of the bank was in bad shape and it functioned under the control of administrator appointed by the Reserve Bank of India. For this reason, complete information about its financing activities could not be obtained. The data relating to advances of MUCO Bank from 1993-94 to 2001-02 are given in Table 4.24.

An analysis of Table 4.24 revealed the following:

1. Over the years from 1993-94 to 2001-02 the focus of MUCO on industrial advances was almost negligible. Its major concentration was on SBF advances which also fluctuated from year to year. The share of SBF advances in total advances was nearly 62 per cent in all the years from 1993-94 to 2001-02, except the year 1994-95 and 1995-96, when it was only 54 per cent and 48 per cent respectively, as personal advances were given higher priority.
2. Its emphasis on Agricultural and Personal advances was more or less the same, especially during 1997-98 to 2001-02. During 1993-94 to 1995-96 agricultural advances were ignored.
3. The highest average annual growth at 63.42 per cent p.a. was noticed in agricultural advances as against overall growth in total advances at 20.75 per cent p.a., while SSI segment registered growth of 13.71 per cent only, which was below the average growth. The growth in SBF segment was slightly better at 23.90 per cent p.a. and least growth was recorded at 6.76 per cent in Personal advances.
4. Variation in AGL and SBF advances was higher than the other two segments and in total advances. Variation in SSI advances was equal to and in Personal advances was just half of the variation in total advances.

It may be concluded that MUCO Bank does not play any role in industrial advancement of Mizoram but it only welcomes small business finance proposals besides advancing personal and agricultural loans.

Table 4.24: Segment-wise Advances of Mizoram Urban Cooperative Bank in Mizoram from 1993-94 to 2001-02 (As on 31st March)

(*Rs. in lakh*)

Year	*SSI*	*SBF*	*AGL*	*Personal*	*Total*
1993-94	6.43	93.57	1.66	52.39	154.05
Share (%)	(4)	(61)	(1)	(34)	(100)
1994-95	10.38	130.46	16.40	82.98	240.22
Share (%)	(4)	(54)	(7)	(35)	(100)
1995-96	10.07	87.14	1.96	83.73	182.90
Share (%)	(6)	(48)	(1)	(46)	(100)
1996-97	10.07	252.77	70.46	82.22	415.52
Share (%)	(2)	(61)	(17)	(20)	(100)
1997-98	10.07	333.98	69.85	80.81	494.71
Share (%)	(2)	(68)	(14)	(16)	(100)
1998-99	9.82	379.02	72.12	74.26	535.22
Share (%)	(2)	(71)	(13)	(14)	(100)
1999-00	14.70	411.22	98.73	98.20	622.85
Share (%)	(2)	(66)	(16)	(16)	(100)
2000-01	19.56	425.93	98.34	114.26	658.09
Share (%)	(3)	(65)	(15)	(17)	(100)
2001-02	22.87	399.08	96.07	104.19	622.21
Share (%)	(4)	(64)	(15)	(17)	(100)
Average	(3)	(62)	(11)	(24)	(100)
Growth	13.71	23.90	63.42	6.76	20.75
C.V.	40	48	66	22	43

Note: Figures in Parenthesis represent share in total advances.

Legend: SSI = Small Scale Industries; SBF = Small Business Finance; AGL = Agricultural, C. V. = Coefficient of Variation.

Source: MUCO Bank, Aizawl.

On the whole, it may be concluded from the above that in respect of finance, Mizoram is much behind the national average and there is ample scope for expanding the operations in future. MCAB being a cooperative institution for rural area MRB being rural bank should take up the challenge of meeting the credit needs and return back to their original objective of financing the needs of rural areas by opening more branches particularly in rural unbanked areas.

Overall Financing Scenario

Besides commenting upon individual institution-wise advances, a comparative study has been made to know the relative role played by different financial institutions including banks in promotion of small business finance and small-scale industry in the State. Further, a comparative study has also been made to know about their relative performance as regards to loan targets achieved, recovery attained, and credit-deposit ratio.

Overall Financing of Business

Financial institutions including commercial banks are the most important source of finance for business. The financing of business by financial institutions in Mizoram from 1990-91 to 2001-02 is presented in Table 4.25 and Figure 4.1.

Table 4.25: Composition of Small Business Financing in Mizoram from 1990-91 to 2001-02

(*Rs. in lakh*)

Year	*SBI*	*MRB*	*VB*	*UCO*	*MCAB*	*MUCO*	*ZIDCO*	*Total*
1990-91	538.24	282.03	93.65	84.72	1448.92	N.A.	687.17	3134.73
Share (%)	(17)	(9)	(3)	(3)	(46)		(22)	(100)
1991-92	510.50	288.23	60.00	78.96	1641.82	N.A.	686.78	3266.29
Share (%)	(16)	(9)	(2)	(2)	(50)		(21)	(100)
1992-93	356.92	320.97	60.00	86.79	1765.51	N.A.	632.09	3222.28
Share (%)	(11)	(10)	(2)	(3)	(55)		(20)	(100)
1993-94	400.51	382.85	N.A.	81.73	1887.91	85.06	697.03	3535.09
Share (%)	(11)	(11)		(2)	(53)	(2)	(20)	(100)
1994-95	345.24	503.38	166.04	70.77	2063.80	122.82	797.76	4069.81
Share (%)	(8)	(12)	(4)	(2)	(51)	(3)	(20)	(100)
1995-96	520.62	530.41	269.98	89.53	2190.27	78.84	906.79	4586.44
Share (%)	(11)	(12)	(6)	(2)	(48)	(2)	(20)	(100)
1996-97	640.56	663.10	269.44	140.14	2371.05	243.60	1048.74	5376.63
Share (%)	(12)	(12)	(5)	(3)	(44)	(5)	(20)	(100)
1997-98	897.70	662.47	425.63	123.43	1423.54	325.31	1117.13	4975.21
Share (%)	(18)	(13)	(9)	(2)	(29)	(7)	(22)	(100)
1998-99	1338.96	765.90	351.01	89.32	998.07	370.17	1259.61	5173.04
Share (%)	(26)	(15)	(7)	(2)	(19)	(7)	(24)	(100)
1999-00	1721.35	932.75	368.14	85.60	1149.74	401.62	1487.72	6146.92
Share (%)	(28)	(15)	(6)	(1)	(19)	(7)	(24)	(100)
2000-01	1647.91	1396.93	430.71	93.13	1269.73	416.18	1602.98	6857.57
Share (%)	(24)	(20)	(6)	(1)	(19)	(6)	(23)	(100)
2001-02	1729.90	1678.81	715.95	76.81	1177.07	389.68	1830.12	7598.34
Share (%)	(23)	(22)	(9)	(1)	(15)	(5)	(24)	(100)
Average	**(17)**	**(13)**	**(5)**	**(2)**	**(37)**	**(4)**	**(22)**	**(100)**
Growth	16.43	17.37	23.68	1.04	- 4.05	25.07	10.48	8.60

Note: In case of MUCO Bank, Growth rate has been calculated from 1993-94, as the figures for earlier years were not available.

Legend: SBI = State Bank of India, MRB = Mizoram Rural Bank, VB = Vijaya Bank, UCO = United Commercial Bank, MCAB = Mizoram Cooperative Apex Bank, MUCO = Mizoram Urban Cooperative Bank, and ZIDCO = Zoram Industrial Development Corporation Ltd.

Source: Data from respective organizations.

Table 4.25 and Figure 4.1 shows that the relative share of different institutions in Rs.100/- advanced to small business in Mizoram, on the average MCAB provided Rs. 37/-, ZIDCO contributed Rs. 22/-, SBI gave Rs.17/-, MRB shared Rs. 13/-, Vijaya Bank afforded Rs. 5/-, MUCO bank gave Rs. 4/-, and the balance Rs. 2/- was shared by UCO bank. The relative share of all the banks and institutions has increased over the period from 1990-91 to 2001-02 except for MCAB and UCO Bank. In these two cases though the total advances in absolute terms increased their relative share in total declined over the period.

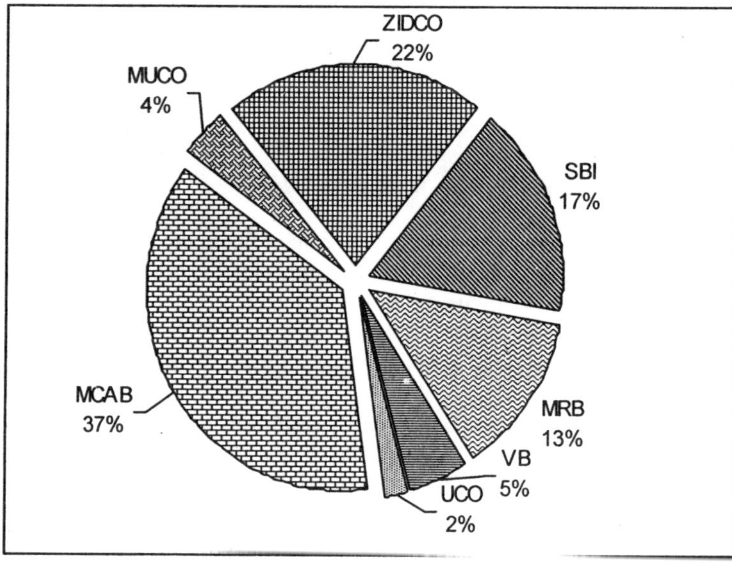

SBI = State Bank of India
MCAB = Mizoram Cooperative Apex Bank
UCO = United Commercial Bank
ZIDCO = Zoram Industrial Development Corporation
MRB = Mizoram Rural Bank
MUCO = Mizoram Urban Cooperative Bank
VB = Vijaya Bank

Figure 4.1: Average Share of Financial Institutions in Small Business Financing in Mozoram from 1990-91 to 2001-02

Further, on the average, total Small Business Finance (SBF) advances in Mizoram increased 2.42 times marking an average annual growth of 8.60 per cent from 1990-91 to 2001-02. Highest growth was in MUCO bank advances at 25.07 per cent p.a. But, this has been worked out from 1993-94 and not from 1990-91, as the data for first three years were not available. Advances of Vijaya Bank registered a growth of 23.68 per cent p.a. Among others, the advances by MRB grew at a faster rate of 17.37 per cent p.a. than any other institution. Even in case of SBI this growth was 16.43 per cent p.a. only. The SBF advances of ZIDCO also registered higher growth of 10.48 per cent than the overall growth of 8.60 per cent. On the other hand, inspite of continuous increase in MCAB advances till 1996-97, a negative growth was noticed in its advances at 4.05 per cent p.a. because of writing off of huge bad debts of Rs.10 crore approximately in 1997-98. Similarly, no growth was seen in UCO bank advances. It seems that UCO bank is shrinking in size and its business and showing no interest in development of business and industry in Mizoram. It may be concluded that SBI and MRB advances both grew steadily over the period, besides maintaining scaling difference.

Overall Financing of Small-Scale Industries

Financial institutions have a prominent role in financing of industries all over the world. The financial assistance provided by these institutions from 1986-87 to 2001-02 under various schemes in Mizoram is given in Table 4.26 and Figure 4.2.

The analysis of Table 4.26 and Figure 4.2 revealed the following:

1. The relative share of different institutions in Rs.100/- advanced to small-scale industries in Mizoram, on the average ZIDCO provided Rs.55/-, MKVIB contributed Rs.28/-, SBI gave Rs.11/-, MRB lend Rs.2/-, NEDFi, MCAB, Vijaya Bank, and UCO Bank shared Rs.1/- each. The MUCO bank did not share the responsibility of SSI credit in Mizoram. The department of industries earlier gave SSI loans under a scheme from Central Government, but later stopped financing SSI units owing to the closure of the scheme by Government of India. The relative share of MKVIB increased from 9 per cent in 1990-91 to 46 per cent in 2001-02. The relative share of MRB did not change, but in case of ZIDCO, SBI, and Vijaya Bank despite increase in total advances in absolute terms their relative share in total advances declined over the period. The decline in relative share of ZIDCO was sharp from 89 per cent in 1986-87 to 38 per cent in 2001-02. Similarly, SBI's share also came down from 12 per cent in

Table 4.26: Composition of Small-Scale Industry Financing in Mizoram from 1990-91 to 2001-02 (*Rs. in lakh*)

Year	*SBI*	*MRB*	*VB*	*UCO*	*MCAB*	*MUCO*	*ZIDCO*	*NEDFi*	*MKVIB*	*Total*
1990-91	315.88	66.84	32.67	47.88	N.A.	N.A.	1973.98	Nil	234.62	2671.87
Share (%)	(12)	(3)	(1)	(2)			(74)		(9)	(100)
1991-92	291.74	71.05	25	58.1	N.A.	N.A.	2216.84	Nil	252.56	2915.29
Share (%)	(10)	(2)	(1)	(2)			(76)		(9)	(100)
1992-93	365.64	84.68	25	63.72	4.99	N.A.	2203.41	Nil	414.25	3161.69
Share (%)	(12)	(3)	(1)	(2)	(0)		(70)		(13)	(100)
1993-94	407.97	90.21	N. A.	60.51	25.91	N.A.	2302.06	Nil	516.71	3403.37
Share (%)	(12)	(3)		(2)	(1)		(68)		(15)	(100)
1994-95	371.40	100.29	26.45	62.50	N.A.	6.43	2324.76	Nil	685.23	3577.06
Share (%)	(10)	(3)	(1)	(2)		(0)	(65)		(19)	(100)
1995-96	485.84	125.61	31.95	59.93	N.A.	10.38	2568.20	Nil	760.25	4042.16
Share (%)	(12)	(3)	(1)	(1)		(0)	(64)		(19)	(100)
1996-97	521.59	118.07	30.94	30.49	N.A.	10.07	2566.06	Nil	2110.17	5387.39
Share (%)	(10)	(2)	(1)	(1)		(0)	(48)		(39)	(100)
1997-98	584.48	143.74	28.86	17.94	22.46	10.07	2662.46	25.00	2301.89	5796.90
Share (%)	(10)	(2)	(0)	(0)	(0)	(0)	(46)	(0)	(40)	(100)
1998-99	720.32	146.68	26.89	13.36	63.71	9.82	2844.36	88.10	2863.84	6777.08
Share (%)	(11)	(2)	(0)	(0)	(1)	(0)	(42)	(1)	(42)	(100)
1999-00	781.15	169.46	21.85	11.21	63.33	14.70	3009.59	278.80	3262.76	7612.85
Share (%)	(10)	(2)	(0)	(0)	(1)	(0)	(40)	(4)	(43)	(100)
2000-01	837.01	179.80	32.25	18.30	107.22	19.56	3097.60	427.70	3781.44	8500.88
Share (%)	(10)	(2)	(0)	(0)	(1)	(0)	(36)	(5)	(44)	(100)
2001-02	781.30	216.50	32.86	14.15	206.41	22.87	3131.46	472.75	3781.44	8659.74
Share (%)	(9)	(3)	(0)	(0)	(2)	(0)	(36)	(5)	(44)	(100)
Average (%)	(11)	(2)	(1)	(1)	(1)	(0)	(55)	(1)	(28)	(100)
C.V.	35	35	13	56	90	40	14	69	78	41
Growth (%)	10.69	10.90	0.54	-15.43	64.16	16.96	4.19	110.84	36.28	12.58

Legend: SBI = State Bank of India, MRB = Mizoram Rural Bank, VB = Vijaya Bank, UCO = United Commercial Bank, MCAB = Mizoram Cooperative Apex Bank, MUCO = Mizoram Urban Cooperative Bank, ZIDCO = Zoram Industrial Development Corporation Ltd., NEDFi = Northeastern Development Finance Corporation, and MKVIB = Mizoram Khadi & Village Industries Board.

Source: Data from respective Organizations.

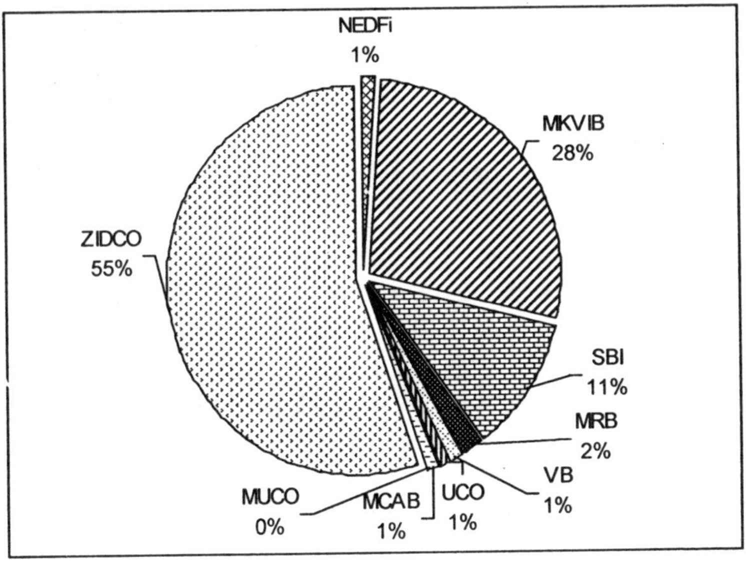

SBI = State Bank of India
ZIDCO = Zoram Industrial Development Corporation
VB = Vijaya Bank
MKVIB = Mizoram Khadi & Village Industries Board
MRB = Mizoram Rural Bank
UCO = United Commercial Bank
MCAB = Mizoram Cooperative Apex Bank
MRB = Mizoram Rural Bank
MUCO = Mizoram Urban Cooperative Bank
NEDFi = North-Eastern Development Finance Corporation (*Note: Rupes in lakh*)

Figure 4.2: Average Share of Financial Institutions in Small-Scale Industry Financing in Mizoram from 1990-91 to 2001-02

1990-91 to 9 per cent in 2001-02. In case of UCO bank though the relative share was nearly 1 per cent, its SSI advances reduced in absolute terms over the period.

2. Further, the total SSI advances in Mizoram increased 3.24 times over the period from 1990-91 to 2001-02 and marked an average annual growth of 12.58 per cent. Highest growth was in NEDFi advances (18.91 times) at an average rate of 110.84 per cent p.a., but this has been worked out from 1997-98 and not from

1990-91 as the Corporation was setup only in August 1995 and started disbursing loans from 1996-97 only and in that year SSI advance for Mizoram was 'Nil'. Next highest growth was in MCAB advances that registered a growth of 64.16 per cent p.a. but, this has been worked out from 1997-98 and not from 1990-91, as the figures for earlier years were not available. Among others, MKVIB advances grew at 36.28 per cent p.a. which was higher than the overall growth at 12.58 per cent p.a. In case of SBI the growth was at 10.69 per cent p.a. SBI though existed in Mizoram since 1971, the growth was computed from 1990-91 only owing to non-availability of figures for earlier years as the regional office in Mizoram came in existence only in 1990. ZIDCO, though played a prominent role as it financed nearly 55 per cent of total SSI advances registered least growth of 4.19 per cent p.a. MUCO and MRB recorded growth of 16.96 and 10.90 per cent p.a. respectively. However, there was no growth in Vijaya Bank SSI advances, while UCO Bank marked a negative growth 15.43 per cent p.a. It seemed that UCO and Vijaya Bank did not show any interest in economic development of Mizoram particularly on the industrial front.

3. Coefficient of variation in overall SSI advances was 41 per cent. The largest variation was in advances of MCAB (90%) and MKVIB (78%), followed by NEDFi (69%) and UCO Bank (56%). This inconsistency was less in all other cases. The least fluctuation was noticed in case of ZIDCO (14%) and Vijaya Bank (13%).
4. It may be observed from the above analysis that ZIDCO, MKVIB, and SBI played the major role in financing the industries in the State contributing 55 per cent, 28 per cent and 11 per cent respectively in funds provided over the period. However, the relative role of MKVIB increased, while of ZIDCO declined and SBI remained static. Further, over the period while the role of SBI and MRB grew at around 10 per cent that of Vijaya Bank remained static and of UCO Bank declined at 15.43 per cent. NEDFi (110.84%) though active only lately shown increasing interest.

It may be concluded from the above that SBI and MRB both are going side by side in the race. However, the declining role of ZIDCO, the institution meant for ensuring industrial development in Mizoram is a cause of worry. MKVIB as compared to others performed satisfactorily.

Target-wise Performance of Banks

To show how far the banks in Mizoram achieved their targets while advancing loans, the percentage of targets attained by different banks in Mizoram over the period 1999 to 2004 are presented in Table 4.27.

It is clear from Table 4.27 that in most of the quarters the targets were not achieved. Overall on the average 88 per cent targets could be achieved. Among them Vijaya Bank crossed the targets more than 3 times and State Bank of India stood second by attaining 1.18 times but it lagged behind 1/3rd in case of SSI targets. This indicated that either the bank did not received viable SSI projects from prospective entrepreneurs or discouraged them as it found better scope of lending in other segments. All other banks have not achieved the desired results as planned. Coming to SSI sector all the banks except Vijaya Bank lagged in attaining their respective targets. Their performance was much below the planned targets. The performance of Vijaya Bank can not be regarded important as its targets were small and it had one branch only. Lowest (4.70%) targets were attained by UCO Bank. This was conformed in a letter from the Reserve Bank of India to Zonal Manager, United Commercial Bank, Guwahati on the subject as regards poor performance of UCO Bank, Aizawl under ACP *vide* No. RPCD.Guwa/03.06.02/99-2000 dated 27th September 1999. In case of Mizoram Rural Bank the SSI targets achieved on the average at 34.63 per cent as against 59.93 per cent overall performance. This may indicate that there was no demand for loans in general and SSIs in particular from rural areas. The bank was having no viable proposals on hand on regular basis, neither from SSI segment nor from SBF and other segments.

One reason responsible for non-spread of credit in rural areas of Mizoram may be that the inhabitants of interior rural areas did not need loan/credit from a financial institution. It is evident from the fact that the area under organic manure in Mizoram was 2.2 per cent of cropped area as against the national average of 63.8 per cent in 1991-92[10]. In 1993-94, the fertilizer consumption in Mizoram was 8.69 kg/ha as against the national average of 66.34 kg/ha and in 1999-00, it was 24.84 kg/ha as against the national average of 95.23 kg/ha. When compared with Punjab

Table 4.27: Advances Disbursed by Banks in Mizoram as Compared to their Targets During 1999 to 2004

(*Figures in Percentage*)

	SSI Advances as Percentage of Targets						All Advances as Percentage of Targets					
Bank	*SBI*	*UCO*	*VB*	*MCAB*	*MRB*	*Total*	*SBI*	*UCO*	*VB*	*MCAB*	*MRB*	*Total*
30.6.1999	20.10	Nil	Nil	8.70	13.70	16.70	26.69	Nil	69.89	29.24	16.16	24.54
30.9.1999	45.30	11.70	Nil	86.90	25.40	42.70	79.33	6.74	100.00	51.01	37.19	59.16
31.12.1999	139.00	16.50	58.10	60.60	42.50	103.00	128.40	18.10	207.30	66.30	70.70	94.60
31.12.2001	49.40	0.00	968.00	26.70	56.10	52.30	130.90	13.89	627.00	71.30	65.32	94.74
31.3.2002	82.00	0.00	968.00	95.00	66.30	86.00	221.50	14.92	627.00	93.91	145.50	159.90
30.9.2004	51.73	0.00	69.23	157.00	3.79	80.23	122.90	49.62	157.00	70.58	24.72	94.63
Average	64.67	4.70	343.89	72.48	34.63	**63.49**	118.29	17.21	298.03	63.72	59.93	**87.93**
C.V.	58.	144.	129	67	65	46	50	91	79	31	72	47

Legend: SBI = State Bank of India, MRB = Mizoram Rural Bank, UCO = United Commercial Bank, VB = Vijaya Bank, MCAB = Mizoram Cooperative Apex Bank, and MUCO = Mizoram Urban Cooperative Bank, C.V. = Coefficient of Variation.

Source: Various reports of State Level Bankers' Committee Meeting for Mizoram, State Bank of India, Lead Bank Office, Aizawl (Dt: 22nd November 1999, 13th March 2000, 7th May 2002, and 3rd December 2004).

average of 175 kg/ha, it was ignorable[11]. Similarly, the consumption of pesticides and insecticides in Mizoram was low at 0.91 per cent of cropped area, as against the national average of 21.35 per cent[12]. Further, more than 77 per cent of agricultural land was under *jhum* cultivation and is not fit for mechanized application. This composition has changed a little bit in the recent past making no significant impact.

This implied that extra emphasis should be given to the creation of demand for credit from rural sectors. It further revealed that in urban locations there existed competition between SBI and Vijaya Bank. At the same time it is brought out that the UCO Bank lost its market due to not putting efforts for retaining its market. Another feature was that though MCAB did not attain the targets but it showed signs of reaching very close to the targets as compared to all other banks operating in Mizoram. As far as relative performance is concerned, the MCAB stood at forefront leaving all other banks behind. Individual bank-wise variations were more than that of overall variation both in case of SSI advances and total advances. However, it was comparatively higher in UCO Bank and Vijaya Bank.

Recovery-wise Performance of Banks

Data relating to recovery of bank finance from 1999 to 2004 are given in Table 4.28, which reveals that on the average overall recovery rate of all commercial banks was at 34.86 per cent of dues, which indicated that on the average 1/3rd of total advances received back within the same year and the length of cycle was three years. It was higher in case of Vijaya Bank at 60.47 per cent and year to year variation in its total recovery was just equal to overall variation (21%). The second highest recovery was at 45.41 per cent in case of Mizoram Rural Bank. In case of State Bank of India it was just above the overall recovery rate. The least recovery (15.41 per cent) was in case of UCO Bank. The highest variation was in UCO Bank, followed by MCAB.

On the other hand, the recovery of SSI advances was almost half of overall recovery, but it did show an increasing trend over the years, which was a good sign. In case of UCO Bank and MCAB the SSI recovery rate was below the average at 18.92 per cent. In all other cases it was higher than the average. Variation in Vijaya Bank was highest among all others. In case of SBI, there was least variation both in SSI recovery and over all recovery of advances.

Table 4.28: Recovery of Bank Finance in Mizoram During 1999 to 2004

(Figures in Percentage)

Bank	Recovery of SSI Advances						Recovery of Overall Advances					
	SBI	UCO	VB	MCAB	MRB	Total	SBI	UCO	VB	MCAB	MRB	Total
30.6.1999	19.65	4.54	2.42	5.60	N.A.	12.30	34.81	7.95	52.72	7.12	N.A.	23.22
30.9.1999	23.79	5.24	2.42	6.92	N.A.	14.47	37.36	22.70	52.72	10.63	63.23	40.09
31.12.1999	21.24	0.38	1.34	12.79	21.11	17.22	34.43	2.56	65.00	13.14	33.02	29.90
31.12.2001	21.88	5.07	11.39	7.21	29.77	19.58	40.36	13.52	49.67	22.09	35.66	35.32
31.3.2002	19.23	5.06	74.57	14.95	20.09	19.07	39.24	14.05	56.60	27.21	33.64	34.14
30.9.2004	22.15	10.40	80.00	44.38	22.53	30.85	42.39	31.66	86.08	35.60	61.52	46.48
Average	21.32	5.12	28.69	15.31	23.38	**18.92**	38.10	15.41	60.47	19.30	45.41	**34.86**
C.V.	7	57	120	88	16	31	8	62	21	52	31	21

Legend: SBI = State Bank of India, MRB = Mizoram Rural Bank, UCO = United Commercial Bank, VB = Vijaya Bank, MCAB = Mizoram Cooperative Apex Bank, and MUCO = Mizoram Urban Cooperative Bank, C.V. = Coefficient of Variation, and N.A. = Not Available.

Source: Various reports of State Level Bankers' Committee Meeting for Mizoram, State Bank of India, Lead Bank Office, Aizawl (Dated : 22nd November 1999, 13th March 2000, 7th May 2002, and 3rd December 2004).

Credit-Deposit recovery Ratio-wise Performance of Banks

The ratio of credit to deposits is an important indicator of absorptive capacity of a region on the one hand and the level of response on the other. If the average is to be taken to gauge the performance, the performances of leading banks SBI and MRB, those really counts as major players would be more meaningful. Other banks also play an important role, but cannot be taken as representative because of their very few branches and their non-average of entire region (state). Further, it is possible for one bank branch to achieve drastic (200%) increase as fall in credit-deposit (CD) ratio and may turn the analysis a misleading exercise.

The position regarding credit-deposit ratio in the banking sector in Mizoram is given in Table 4.29.

Table 4.29: Bank Credit-Deposit Ratio in Mizoram from 1998 to 2002 as on 31st March

(Figures in percentage)

Banks	1998	1999	2000	2001	2002	Average
SBI	21.62	22.33	44.97	46.80	41.38	35.42
UCO	28.99	13.42	12.57	14.87	13.21	16.61
VIJAYA	15.19	11.12	11.93	13.37	13.74	13.07
MCAB	59.02	35.40	28.22	31.94	38.69	38.65
MRB	33.45	28.48	34.84	33.67	32.90	32.67
Overall	29.29	23.40	35.30	37.84	35.71	32.31

Source: Status Paper on Banking Scenario in Mizoram, SBI, Regional Office, Aizawl.

The Table 4.29 revealed that low credit-deposit ratio in Mizoram is an indicative of more deposits than the demand for loans. It also implies that the bank branches in Mizoram were mobilizing household savings and investing the same outside the State. Nearly 68 per cent of deposits mobilized by these banks could not be put to an economic advantage of Mizoram. This fact further strengthens the perception that the demand for new loans coming from public was less which indicated that if the same had been invested in Mizoram only, its economy would have been totally different. On an average 32.31 per cent deposit mobilization were diverted to loans. In case of MCAB, SBI and MRB this ratio was higher than the average. In other two cases, this ratio was far below the average. Again, in case of UCO Bank this ratio was continuously declining over the period from 1997-98 to 2001-02. In all these years and in case of all the banks, the average Credit-Deposit (CD) ratio was half of the national policy of 60 per cent.

Comparison of CD Ratio in Mizoram with Northeastern Region

The credit-deposit ratio of Northeastern region from 1995 to 2002 is given in Table 4.30.

Table 4.30: State-wise Credit-Deposit Ratio of Commercial Banks in Northeastern Region from 1995 to 2002 (As on 31st March)

(Figures in percentage)

State	1995	1996	1997	1998	1999	2000	2001	2002	Average
Arunachal Pradesh	12.4	10.4	10.7	13.1	14.6	16.6	17.3	15.7	13.9
Assam	38.7	39.3	35.2	32.9	32.0	31.5	32.4	31.4	34.2
Manipur	58.2	53.7	57.5	58.8	47.8	36.4	38.9	25.5	47.1
Meghalaya	17.0	14.4	14.3	15.2	18.1	15.7	16.8	18.0	16.2
Mizoram	16.5	16.2	14.0	23.2	20.8	24.3	25.5	25.9	20.8
Nagaland	37.8	27.4	24.0	18.3	15.9	15.4	13.9	12.5	20.7
Tripura	47.5	42.1	37.7	34.0	30.3	25.8	23.0	22.3	32.8
N.E. Region	35.6	34.5	31.2	29.9	28.9	27.7	28.1	26.9	30.4
All India	55.6	61.9	57.3	55.5	N.A.	N.A.	N.A.	N.A.	57.6

Source: Basic Statistics of NER, 2002, Northeastern Council, Government of India, Shillong, p.263.

The Table 4.30 revealed that credit-deposit ratio in Mizoram was about 25.9 per cent in March 2002, as against the regional average of 26.9 per cent, and Assam 31.4 per cent. On the average from 1995 to 2002, the CD ratio in Mizoram (20.8%) was lower than that of Manipur (47.1%), Tripura (32.8%), Assam (34.2%), regional average (30.4%) and national average (57.6%). The lower credit-deposit ratio in Mizoram and also the northeast as compared to the national average clearly indicated outflow of bank deposits to other developed states. It was against the national policy of 60 per cent investment of mobilized deposits within the same state. The banks in the region in general and Mizoram in particular were far behind in this respect because of lack of economic activity in the Northeastern region in general and Mizoram in particular.

Public Sector in Financing

Historically, public sector has played a very important role in the development of India. This has been so in finance also. To improve growth of industry, business, service sector, etc. a variety of financial institutions were set up which included development banks as well as commercial banks in the public sector. The role expected to be played by them is a factor of their financial health/status. They, if in a bad shape, cannot be expected to contribute significantly. With this in view the status of Zoram Industrial Development Corporation (ZIDCO) has been examined here.

Zoram Industrial Development Corporation Limited (ZIDCO)

Zoram Industrial Development Corporation Limited (ZIDCO) was incorporated on 19th February 1978 with an objective of industrial development of this economically backward state, Mizoram. It is a public sector Corporation owned by the Government of Mizoram, which had subscribed 69.82 per cent shares and IDBI retained 30.18 per cent shares together making a total paid up share capital of Rs.1528.10 lakh as on 31st March 2003. The activities of ZIDCO broadly comprehend distribution of funds from NMDFC, obtaining refinance from IDBI/SIDBI in respect of funds distributed to industry, undertaking establishment of Export Promotion Industrial Park, Pukpuii. The Corporation had considered various measures for its rejuvenation and improvement. The fiscal reform programmes and restructuring efforts of ZIDCO in nutshell[13] included (a) No more recruitment (b) Reduction of over all administrative expenditure (c) One time settlement package (OTS) (d) Setting up of industrial development project (e) Settlement of outstanding dues with IDBI/SIDBI (f) Loan recovery drive and (g) Empowerment of ZIDCO by SFC Act 1951.

The financial statements of ZIDCO for the period from 1990-91 to 2001-02 were compiled, analyzed and are shown in Table 4.31.

The analysis of the Table 4.31 revealed as under:

1. Till 1996-97, the Return on Investment was small but positive. Since then it had turned negative and registered a decline and as a result, on the average, for Rs.100/- invested in the Corporation could generate Rs.1.28 as operational surplus. Though, it ranged between 6.40 per cent in 1993-94 to (–) 2.04 per cent in 1999-2000, it was too less by all standards.
2. Average Operating Profit to Operating Revenue was 73.53 per cent in 1993-94 but declined and turned negative at 88.56 per cent in 1999-00. However, the margin after tax as percent of operating revenue on the average at (–) 104.02 per cent ranged

Table 4.31: Abridged Annual Accounts and Important Financial Ratios of the Zoram Industrial Development Corporation Ltd. (ZIDCO) from 1990-91 to 2001-02

(*Rs. in lakh*)

S. No.	Position Statement	as on 31st March												Growth (%)
	Year	1991	1992	1993	1994	1995	1996	1997	1998	1999	2000	2001	2002	
	Sources of Funds													
1.	Share Capital	871.10	933.10	983.10	1103.10	1103.10	1103.10	1103.10	1103.10	1103.10	1103.10	1103.10	1103.10	1.71
2.	Share Capital Contribution	30.00	45.00	60.00	Nil	51.00	111.00	184.50	184.50	232.50	232.50	337.50	425.00	26.59
3.	Reserves & Surplus	Nil	Nil	10.00	28.10	28.10	35.10	38.10	38.10	38.10	38.10	38.10	38.10	10.14
4.	Misc. Exp.	184.41	320.53	385.27	363.01	402.68	463.66	517.05	655.64	813.17	963.49	966.21	609.49	13.06
5.	Retained Earnings (3-4)	-184.41	-320.53	-375.27	-334.91	-374.58	-428.56	-478.95	-617.54	-775.07	-925.39	-928.11	-571.39	-41.43
6.	Owner's Equity (1+2+5)	716.69	662.57	667.83	768.19	779.52	785.54	808.65	670.06	560.53	410.21	512.49	956.71	-1.58
7.	Debt	1433.31	1515.51	1531.94	1376.61	1390.01	1457.79	1518.93	1632.39	1862.05	2082.92	2582.96	2000.03	4.52
8.	Total Funds Received (6+7)	2150.00	2178.08	2199.77	2144.80	2169.53	2243.33	2327.58	2302.45	2422.58	2493.13	3095.45	2956.74	2.97
	Application of Funds													
9.	Fixed Assets	22.30	32.22	32.58	31.54	35.17	33.88	41.26	50.97	47.71	45.54	46.48	50.38	6.49
10.	Depreciation	8.01	8.34	12.50	16.14	19.35	21.33	24.43	27.06	26.96	29.48	33.09	36.67	14.55
11.	Net Block (9-10)	14.29	23.88	20.08	15.40	15.82	12.55	16.83	23.91	20.75	16.06	13.39	13.71	-1.46
12.	CWIP	5.01	3.03	3.04	3.04	3.04	3.04	3.04	3.04	3.04	3.04	3.04	2.95	-2.01
13.	Total Fixed Assets (11+12)	19.30	26.91	23.12	18.44	18.86	15.59	19.87	26.95	23.79	19.10	16.43	16.66	-1.67
14.	Investments	1.50	1.50	11.50	11.95	11.95	11.95	11.95	11.95	49.95	53.95	117.95	80.13	42.36
15.	Cash & Bank Balances	2.44	11.46	22.40	15.45	17.96	59.95	168.45	119.01	108.13	70.56	623.88	112.46	43.14
16.	Other Advances	10.17	13.63	20.47	24.76	26.54	31.31	33.40	36.20	43.35	44.07	41.25	54.59	14.06
17.	Liquid Assets (15+16)	12.61	25.09	42.87	40.21	44.50	91.26	201.85	155.21	151.48	114.63	665.13	167.05	30.43
18.	Loans & Advances	2124.27	2172.10	2167.78	2136.32	2133.47	2155.41	2131.97	2143.58	2219.19	2349.90	2337.20	2723.66	1.46
19.	Current Liabilities	7.68	47.52	45.50	62.12	39.25	30.88	38.06	35.24	21.83	44.45	41.26	30.76	3.01
20.	Working Capital (17-19)	4.93	-22.43	-2.63	-21.91	5.25	60.38	163.79	119.97	129.65	70.18	623.87	136.29	77.33
21.	Funds Employed (13+14+18+20)	2150.00	2178.08	2199.77	2144.80	2169.53	2243.33	2327.58	2302.45	2422.58	2493.13	3095.45	2956.74	2.97

(*Contd.*)

(Contd.)

S. No.	Income Statement / Year	1991	1992	1993	1994	1995	1996	1997	1998	1999	2000	2001	2002	Growth (%)
		for the year ended 31st March												
1.	Operating Revenue/Intt on Loans	106.10	89.34	110.05	188.98	127.85	118.88	133.23	85.93	75.69	57.81	79.70	81.56	-4.80
2.	Interest Tax	Nil	4.11	Nil	Nil	Nil	Nil	Nil	16.65	1.53	1.16	Nil	Nil	
3.	Net Operating Revenue (1-2)	106.10	85.23	110.05	188.98	127.85	118.88	133.23	69.28	74.16	56.65	79.70	81.56	-4.96
4.	Administrative Expenses	12.70	10.09	10.80	14.69	16.82	20.30	23.68	21.48	24.83	23.11	20.44	22.91	7.88
5.	Personnel Cost	23.26	28.26	28.08	30.77	33.78	41.99	51.41	60.42	57.98	79.03	87.53	87.25	13.84
6.	OPBD [3-(4+5)]	70.14	46.88	71.17	143.52	77.25	56.59	58.14	-12.62	-8.65	-45.49	-28.27	-28.60	-32.86
7.	Depreciation	1.45	2.89	4.15	4.57	4.01	3.35	3.10	4.38	5.97	4.68	3.62	3.58	5.14
8.	Operating Profit (OP) (6-7)	68.69	43.99	67.02	138.95	73.24	53.24	55.04	-17.00	-14.62	-50.17	-31.89	-32.18	-32.73
9.	Other Income	0.60	0.64	0.75	1.21	0.82	0.86	11.80	10.89	6.02	14.55	22.46	23.23	47.62
10.	Profit(+)/Loss(-) on Sale of F A	Nil	0.61	Nil	0.31	-0.22	-0.56	Nil	0.08	0.37	0.08	Nil	-3.04	
11.	PBIT (8+9+10)	69.29	45.24	67.77	140.47	73.84	53.54	66.84	-6.03	-8.23	-35.54	-9.43	-11.99	-30.58
12.	Interest	104.62	141.78	132.45	118.13	113.38	114.42	120.23	132.56	149.30	114.78	110.57	72.94	-1.91
13.	Profit Before Tax (PBT) (11-12)	-35.33	-96.54	-64.68	22.34	-39.54	-60.88	-53.39	-138.59	-157.53	-150.32	-120.00	-84.93	-25.03
14.	Tax	Nil	Nil	Nil	Nil	Nil	Nil	Nil	Nil	Nil	Nil	Nil	Nil	
15.	Profit After Tax (PAT) (13-14)	-35.33	-96.54	-64.68	22.34	-39.54	-60.88	-53.39	-138.59	-157.53	-150.32	-120.00	-84.93	-25.03
16.	Accumulated Losses of P.Y.	149.08	184.41	320.53	385.27	363.01	402.68	463.66	517.05	655.64	813.17	963.49	966.21	17.37
17.	Prior Period Expenses	Nil	39.58	0.06	0.08	0.13	0.10	Nil	Nil	Nil	Nil	-117.28	-441.65	
18.	Accumulated Profits (15-16-17)	-184.41	-320.53	-385.27	-363.01	-402.68	-463.66	-517.05	-655.64	-813.17	-963.49	-966.21	-609.49	-41.76

(Contd.)

(*Contd.*)

S. No.	Important Ratios / Year	1991	1992	1993	1994	1995	1996	1997	1998	1999	2000	2001	2002	Average
1.	Return on Investments (ROI)	N.A.	2.03	3.06	6.40	3.40	2.41	2.41	-0.73	-0.62	-2.04	-1.14	-1.06	1.28
2.	Admn. Exp. to Operating Revenue	11.97	11.84	9.81	7.77	13.16	17.08	17.77	31.00	33.48	40.79	25.65	28.09	20.70
3.	Personnel Cost to Operating Revenue	21.92	33.16	25.52	16.28	26.42	35.32	38.59	87.21	78.18	139.51	109.82	106.98	59.91
4.	Operating Profit to Operating Revenue	64.74	51.61	60.90	73.53	57.29	44.78	41.31	-24.54	-19.71	-88.56	-40.01	-39.46	15.16
5.	Net Profit to Operating Revenue	-33.30	-113.27	-58.77	11.82	-30.93	-51.21	-40.07	-200.04	-212.42	-265.35	-150.56	-104.13	-104.02
6.	Capital Turnover Ratio	N.A.	0.04	0.05	0.09	0.06	0.05	0.06	0.03	0.03	0.02	0.03	0.03	0.04
7.	Fixed Assets Turnover Ratio	7.42	3.57	5.48	12.27	8.08	9.47	7.92	2.90	3.57	3.53	5.95	5.95	6.34
8.	Current Ratio/Acid Test Ratio	1.64	0.53	0.94	0.65	1.13	2.96	5.30	4.40	6.94	2.58	16.12	5.43	4.05
9.	Super Quick Ratio	0.32	0.24	0.49	0.25	0.46	1.94	4.43	3.38	4.95	1.59	15.12	3.66	3.07
10.	Interest Coverage Ratio	0.66	0.32	0.51	1.19	0.65	0.47	0.56	-0.05	-0.06	-0.31	-0.09	-0.16	0.31
11.	Debt Equity Ratio	2.00	2.29	2.29	1.79	1.78	1.86	1.88	2.44	3.32	5.08	5.04	2.09	2.65
12.	Fixed Assets to Net Tangible Worth	0.01	0.01	0.01	0.01	0.01	0.01	0.01	0.01	0.01	0.01	0.01	0.01	0.01
13.	L & A to Net Tangible Worth	0.99	1.00	0.99	1.00	0.98	0.96	0.92	0.93	0.92	0.94	0.76	0.92	0.94
14.	PBIT to Operating Revenue Ratio	64.74	51.61	60.90	73.53	57.29	44.78	41.31	-24.54	-19.71	-88.56	-40.01	-39.46	15.16

Legend: OPBD = Operating Profit before Depreciation, OP = Operating Profit, PBIT = Profit before Interest & Tax, PBT = Profit before Tax, PAT = Profit after Tax.

Source: Compiled from Annual Accounts of Zoram Industrial Development Corporation Ltd. from 1990-91 to 2001-02.

between 11.82 per cent in 1993-94 to (–) 265.35 per cent in 1999-00 showed heavy loss situation. The average percentage of administrative expenses and personnel cost at 20.07 per cent and 59.91 per cent respectively were major factors for operating loss. The major cause of negative margin after tax was heavy interest burden on the organization.

3. Over the years its operating revenue declined sharply, while at the same time the operating cost registered a remarkable increase. Cost of personnel to operating revenue at 16.28 per cent in 1993-94 increased to 139.51 per cent in 1999-2000, partly because of the Fifth Pay Commission's pay revision.
4. The activity position as depicted by the average operating revenue to capital employed at 0.04 times was poor. The average operating revenue to fixed asset employed at 6.34 times appeared to be reasonable. This was so, because it is a service organization and not manufacturing and does not require huge investment in plant and machinery (fixed assets to net tangible) worth 0.01 times for generating operating income. The major component of capital investment i.e., loans and advances (0.94 times of net tangible worth) had shown sluggish activity. There was a possibility of the Loans and Advances becoming non-performing.
5. The auditors' reports for the duration had also time and again pointed out this feature commenting, "It has been observed that in a number of cases mortgage of the loan belonging to other than the borrower is taken as security. The mortgage deed was executed by the borrower on the strength of affidavit by the owner of the land to the effect that the borrower can mortgage the land to the Corporation. Thus, the owner of the land was not made a party to the mortgage deed and the borrower executed the document as owner of the same. Legal opinion was not obtained by the Corporation in this regard."[14] "Considering the faulty documentation, non-renewal of insurance, doubt about applicability of Limitations Act coupled with non-renewal/non-revival of documents, non-balance confirmation, huge overdue, non provision of bad and doubtful debts, non-reconciliation of balance with subsidiary ledger, we are of the opinion that a thorough scrutiny of entire loan part was required to assess the quantum of bad and doubtful debts and to rectify the documentary defects and to identify the borrowers etc. In order to protect the interest of the Corporation the whole of loans and

advances portfolio be reassessed and quantum of bad and doubtful debts be assessed afresh."[15] Further that "The entire loan outstanding was classified by the Corporation as secured and considered good. The Corporation holding securities in all cases were doubtful of recovery. As per the guidelines issued by the RBI to all financial institutions, provision of NPA was to be done. Hence in our opinion classifying the interest loan as secured was wrong and does not represent a true and fair view."[16] And that "It appears from the scrutiny of the records that loan as per Schedule IX included so many overdue, bad and doubtful amounts for which no provision was made in the account in this year also... No provision was made in this year also in respect of old, unidentified and unliked balances."[17]

6. The short-term solvency position of the organization appeared to be satisfactory as indicated by the average current ratio at 4.05:1 and average super quick ratio at 3.07:1. However, the quality of current assets in terms of liquidity as revealed by the average super quick ratio at 3.07:1 indicated huge accumulation of cash (liquid) resources. Current ratio and super quick ratio were abnormally high in 2000-01, which affected their respective averages. Trend in working capital, particularly in the later part of the period reported a galloping rise. Looking into the components of working capital showed that during this period cash and bank balances indicated huge accumulation. Auditors' also many times commented in their audit reports that cash and bank balances were not only accumulated to make huge amounts but the same practice was consistently noticed through out the financial years.[18] This signifies unsatisfactory cash management of the organization.
7. The trends in total funds employed showed moderate increase till 1997-98. Thereafter, it was comparatively sharper. Operating revenue on the other hand had shown an upsurge up to 1996-97, but thereafter a sharp decline. The Debt-Equity ratio on the average at 2.65:1 combined with average interest coverage ratio at 0.31 times indicated a gloomy long-term solvency position, particularly during the second half period when the interest coverage ratio was negative showing Corporation's operating revenue not sufficient enough to cover its the annual interest liability on debt. The debt-equity ratio was too low for a financial Corporation entrusted with the responsibility of inculcating

industrial culture in the State. More funds should have been channelised. An overview of financial statements revealed of accumulation of liquid funds since 1996, which remained unutilized may be because of, either the people of the State were not aware of the ZIDCO's role and did not put fresh demand for loans with new proposals or the corporation has packed up its industrial vision.

8. The ZIDCO was however not covered by Sick Industries Companies Act, 1985[19] as there was regular flow of capital contribution by the Government of Mizoram sufficient enough to compensate the loss incurred by the Corporation.
9. Several points were raised by auditors' in their report on the accounts of ZIDCO. Some of these are summarized below:

(A) Management Related Points

(i) Installments overdue for more than three years' have increased sharply, but no provision for bad and doubtful debts was made. These overdue accounts, showed locking up of funds (advances) reflecting an unproductive application of resources (loans and advances) by borrower industrial units. This is an indication of weak business in the State on the part of entrepreneurs who are supposed to lead the industrial development and make inroads for new investment.

(ii) In some cases of SRTO and Building loans documents were not made. Loan documents were not placed in safe custody. Documents executed do not contain clause for penal interest. Principal and interest were overdue even for more than 8 years. In many cases even normal interest was also waived along with penal interest because of its no definite policy on interest waiving.

(iii) In number of cases primary security was lacking and only land as collateral security was obtained. Executed documents were not revalidated even after 10 years of their expiry. In many cases the borrower has pledged land of other person as collateral security. Provisions of State Finance Corporation Act (SFC Act) and Bengal Recovery Act (Bakijai) could not be applied. The Corporation did not implement credit guarantee scheme.

(iv) Annual General Meeting book was not maintained. Directors' register was also not maintained. Physical verification of cash balance was not done by the management at any time. Further, it exceeded the limit many times. Some projects found economically unviable were also undertaken without ascertaining/undertaking their preliminary viability study.

(B) Accounting Related Points

(i) Abnormally high cash balance was being maintained since 1996 implying that the Corporation failed in utilizing cash resources properly. It ignored opportunity cost dimension and showed stagnation in the flow of funds to industrial sector of the state economy. Amount actually received on later date was credited in advance in the books of accounts.

(ii) Fixed assets register was not maintained properly. Physical verification of fixed assets was not done.

(iii) Bank reconciliation was not done in some cases.

(iv) There were some contingent assets shown in financial statements but no detail was made available.

(v) Neither gratuity nor pension liability nor interest tax etc. were provided in the books of accounts.

(vi) Interest tax return was not filed. No provision was made for various fines and penalties for statutory defaults under different Acts and Statutes.

(vii) Expenditure on development of computer software charged to revenue expenses. Pre-paid expenses not recorded according to accounting principles.

(ix) In some cases neither the terms nor conditions of the loans taken from Government of Mizoram were known, nor was the interest provided.

(x) The Corporation was lagging in documentary evidences as regards to receipts and payments of loans.

(xi) Loan assets were not classified into standard, sub-standard and doubtful as required by the RBI[20]. Classifying them as secured and good was wrong and did not represent true picture.

(xii) Faulty documentation, non renewal of insurance, doubt about the applicability of Limitation Act coupled with non-renewal of documents, non-balance confirmation, huge overdue, non-reconciliation of balances with subsidiary ledgers and non-provision of bad and doubtful debts were the main reasons demanding reassessment of entire on portfolio loans and advances.

(xiii) Loans and advances include balance of suspense account which was of a big amount in lakh. Difference in trial balance was shown as bank adjustment which was also a big amount in lakh. Cash burglary loss was shown as loans and advances. Legal expenses for filing suit against borrowers need to be debited to his/her loan account or a separate account till the case is decided but the Corporation has treated them as expenses.

(xiv) Advances for expenses were pending for adjustment for a long time and were doubtful of recovery.

The recovery position on the average was around 5.9 per cent of previous year's outstanding. This in any case cannot be regarded appropriate and because of this the interest accumulation had become equal to original sum advanced. This poor recovery was a serious problem, which encouraged the management either not to advance or advance less, which ultimately resulted in low gross operating revenue and at the same time resulted into huge accumulation of liquid resources. Moreover, additional funds contributed by the Government of Mizoram by way of additional share capital year after year were either eaten up causing loss or allowed to accumulate in the form of liquid resources, which were idle or were booked against bank deposit. Ultimately these funds were not utilized for the purpose of industrial development.

To conclude Corporation's recovery drive was on paper only. It has not fetched any concrete results. Action was required in this direction. In recent past the Corporation had launched special recovery drive all over the State and also introduced One Time Settlement (OTS) scheme for the year 2000-01.[21] ZIDCO's efforts may be honest in spirit but the repayment culture among the entrepreneurs might be absent, as is indicative from operational highlights for the year 2000-01.[22] The executives and employees should feel the existence of Corporation rather than having mind set of Government department.

NOTES

1. IBM: World Book — Dictionary, 1997.
2. Hansaria, B. L., *VI Schedule to the Constitution of India: A Study*, Ashok Publishing House, Guwahati, p.44.
3. Status Paper on Banking Scenario in Mizoram as on 31st March 2002, State Bank of India, Regional Office, Aizawl, p. 1.
4. Annual Report, 2000-01, Zoram Industrial Development Corporation Ltd. (ZIDCO), Aizawl.

5. State Presentation to the Twelfth Finance Commission, Government of Mizoram, 1st June 2004, p. 26.
6. Annual Report, ZIDCO, 2000-01, *op. cit.*
7. Directors' Report contained in Annual Report, ZIDCO, 2000-01.
8. Annual Report, MKVIB, 2000-01.
9. Auditor's Report on Annual Accounts, 1997-98, Mizoram Cooperative Apex Bank Ltd. p. 1.
10. All India Report on Input Survey, 1991-92, p. 15.
11. Economic Intelligence Service, CMIE Agriculture, February 2004, p. 45.
12. All India Report on Input Survey, *op. cit.* 1991-92, p. 15.
13. Memorandum to the Twelfth Finance Commission, Government of Mizoram, February 2004, p. 30.
14. Auditors' Report on Annual Accounts of ZIDCO, 1994-95, p. 4.
15. *Ibid*, p. 5.
16. *Ibid*, p. 4.
17. *Ibid*, 2001-02, p. 4.
18. *Ibid*, p. 3.
19. *Ibid*, p. 2.
20. Reserve Bank of India circular No. FIC-No. 841/01-02-00/'93-94 dated 28.3.1994.
21. Annual Report on Accounts of ZIDCO, 2000-01, *op. cit.*, p. 3.
22. *Ibid*, p. 7.

5

TAXATION OF BUSINESS AND INDUSTRY IN MIZORAM

Introduction

Taxes are an important source of government revenue and also a mechanism for improvement of country's economy. For people taxes are the price paid for the cost of development[1] . Developmental schemes and projects are drawn up based on the expected revenue that may be raised within a particular period.

In total revenue, both from tax and non-tax sources of Government of India, the share of contribution from taxes in the year 1994-95 was 71.04 percent[2]. Over-all tax revenue contribution is about two-thirds of total revenue. Among the state governments' revenue sources in India sales tax (new VAT) has come to occupy the most productive role and contributed 50.87 per cent in 1970-71[3] and 60.04 per cent in 1994-95[4]. Kautilya's Arthashastra, a study in details of the art and science of governance, conceived of two goals of state administration; one, to make the State financially sound, and two, to help people realize the goals of life[5]. Of these, it attached greater importance to *Artha* or wealth, for on this depended the welfare of the people[6]. Only that State could be stable, which was financially sound. For this management of state finances was of crucial importance. Budgeting and taxation formed the core of financial administration[7]. It is also established that the prosperity of business and economy leads to prosperity of government. Among the various departments mentioned in *Arthashastra*, 'the finance department and other departments dealing with business and economic activities formed vital part of the Kautilyan administrative machinery.'[8] Highest importance was attached to finance as it was the Chief mechanism of control and guided all activities of the government. *Arthashastra* classified state revenue according to source from which they were derived, such as capital, mines, public works, forests, pasture lands, and trade. Similarly, the heads of expenditure of state were described as 'sacrifices, worship of ancestors, charity, expenses of the royal household, charges of civil departments, expenses in connection with the maintenance of foreign missions, expenses of army and army supply services, public works expenditure and expenses for the preservation of forests.'[9]

In accordance with the concept of welfare state Kautilya laid down certain guiding principles of taxation in a welfare society; such as, the king was not free to levy taxes as he liked, he had to issue a proclamation of his intention to levy certain taxes, and if people approved he could levy taxes. Further, Kautilya stated that the king should levy taxes only on such enterprises, as were well-established and not new enterprises or industries[10]. He advocated a gradual system of taxation. According to him "A king should endeavour to gather the revenue from his subjects in the same way as the fruits of a garden are gathered, and as often as they become ripe. Just as the gardener would abandon the unripe fruits, lest their source should be disturbed, so the State should abandon the unripe sources of the kingdom lest they should cause anger to the people."[11]

Kautilya's theory of taxation was more like the modern theory of prices, which are charged by public authority for specific services rendered and commodities supplied[12]. It satisfied the canons of welfare. The tax was certain and not arbitrary. Land revenue was fixed at one-sixth of produce; import and export duties were fixed on *ad-valorem* basis. The general rate of import duty on foreign goods was 20 per cent of their value. Kautilya strongly recommended taxes to be not collected in a painful way. Kautilya also recommended remissions and exemptions from taxes in certain cases in accordance with the basic approach of welfare[13]. He emphasized on equity and justice in taxation, and the requirement that the citizens of the State should contribute and support the government as nearly as possible in proportion to their respective abilities[14]. He advocated that the taxation policy should be so framed that it puts an end to exploitation of man by man. He advocated that the State should encourage production of such scarce articles as were essential. He advocated a very wide role of the State in the economic activities.

An appropriate tax policy should be adopted by the State so that the prosperity is shared with those who are unfortunately placed, and are leading hard existence. By taxing the rich the government can ensure narrowing down the growing income disparities by taking excess money from the rich, investment of this money in raising the income of the poor, which would help poor households to emerge from poverty trap, and reduce dependence of the State on public debt for financing development programmes.

Objectives of Taxation

Taxes should be levied on people with great care and rationality. The taxation agency must follow a code of conduct in the form of principles of taxation. Every tax imposes additional burden on the taxpayer. Tax is a compulsory payment, which cannot be refused without attracting punishment by the government and for which the government does not promise any direct benefit to the taxpayer. Thus, it becomes essential that the burden of tax is divided fairly and appropriately. Government is responsible for providing certain facilities to the citizens, which it cannot leave to voluntary payment by citizen. It has to adopt certain principles and methods, apply principles while imposing, collecting and utilizing the money thus collected[15].

Canons of Taxation

Adam Smith had given a set of criteria known as Canons of taxation. They are still widely accepted as providing a good basis for taxation. Smith's four canons of taxation are: the cost of collection must be low relative to the yield, the timing and amount to be paid must be certain to the payer, the means and timing of payment must be convenient to the payer, and taxes should be levied according to the ability to pay. Modern economists have added three more canons to these four to update them. These are the tax must not hinder efficiency or should involve least loss of efficiency, the tax should be compatible with foreign tax systems, and tax should be automatically adjusted to changes in the rate of inflation. Other canons are canon of productivity, canon of elasticity, canon of diversity, canon of simplicity, canon of expediency, and canon of co-ordination. The best tax is one that meets all these and the worst that meets none.

The basic principles of taxation have remained more or less unchanged for the past two centuries. Juxtaposing the principles proposed by Adam Smith in 1776 and those enunciated by Stiglitz in 1980 this can be seen. Adam Smith wrote, "*Before I enter upon the examination of particular taxes, it is necessary to premise the four following maxims with regard to taxes in general.* The subjects of every State ought to contribute towards the support of the government, as nearly as possible, in proportion to their respective abilities; that is, in proportion to the revenue which they respectively enjoy under the protection of the State. The tax which each individual is bound to pay ought to be certain, and not arbitrary. Every tax ought to be levied at the time, or in the manner, in which it is most likely to be convenient for the contributor to pay it. Every tax ought to be so contrived as both to take out and to keep out of the pockets of the people as little as possible over and above what it brings into the public treasury of the State"[16].

Stiglitz's characteristics of good taxes can be summarized as *economic efficiency*—the tax should not prevent efficient allocation of resources, *administrative simplicity*—the tax should be easy and inexpensive to administer, *flexibility*—the tax system should respond easily to changes in economic conditions, *transparency*—individuals should be able to ascertain their tax burdens so that burdens can be politically tailored to what society considers desirable, *fairness*—the tax system should be fair in its treatment of different individuals, *Horizontal Equity*—individuals who are the same in all relevant aspects should be treated equally, and *Vertical Equity*—individuals who are better able to pay higher taxes should bear a higher share of total taxes (except in the case of *benefit taxes* where individuals are charged taxes in accordance with the benefit they derive from a public good or service)[17].

Every finance minister while presenting new tax proposals to parliament or assembly in his budget keeps three motives in mind *viz*., to provide certain public services in order of preference along with catering to an ever-increasing number of services in the community, create positive effect on the balance of payment. However, no taxation should be imposed beyond the tax paying capacity of the individuals, new proposal of tax should be indiscriminatory in nature and affect all people without making any distinction between the citizens, because the principle of equality before law emphatically demands it[18].

Efficiency and equity are the two basic principles of all public policies relating to economic operations. No policy of mass welfare and distributive justice can be sustained in the long run if the principle of efficiency is grossly violated. This is because of the fact that the laws of economics are inexorable and every policy has a cost, which must be defrayed by mobilizing resources[19]. The violation of efficiency criteria may give birth to distorted notion of equity and may accentuate inequality rather than reduce it. The principle of efficiency has not been strictly followed in the State finances in the North-East[20]. The North-Eastern

States provide an illustration of the conflict between principles of equity and efficiency and resultant distortion of equity principle[21].

Types of Taxes

Taxes are generally classified as direct taxes, and indirect taxes. *Direct taxes* are the taxes on income from land, and the tax on buildings; the tax on intangibles or movable property, which falls on income from investments as well as on that arising from business and professional activity; and finally the tax on total individual income. These taxes strike citizens' income at the moment of its production. *Indirect taxes* are those, which strike the private consumption of citizens and also transfer of property. They strike the income at the moment when the citizen spends it to acquire other goods[22]. The impact (immediate burden) and the incidence (ultimate burden) of direct tax fall on the same person. As against this the impact and incidence of indirect tax falls on different persons. Direct taxes create civic consciousness and are economical, equitable reducing inequalities of income and wealth, certain and elastic. On the other hand, indirect taxes are convenient, productive, and elastic, lead to social welfare, and cannot be evaded.

The incidence of a tax refers to the final or ultimate burden of tax. "When a tax is imposed without any change in the expenditure side of government account it is termed as specific incidence, and when a tax is levied as a substitute for another tax it is called as differential incidence, and when the government finances its expenditure by the yield of tax it is called the balanced budget incidence." [23] The incidence of taxes may be categorized into formal incidence and effective incidence.

A tax is always undesirable and cumbersome for a taxpayer. It reduces taxpayer's purchasing power and affects the economic life of the producer. Everyone tries to shift his burden of tax to someone else in order to save himself from the burden of tax. The implications of taxation refers to the consequences which fall on the persons directly or indirectly due to the levy of a certain tax, whereas incidence is only the reduction of money income due to the payment made in the form of a tax. The responses from the taxpayers and the economy when a tax is imposed may be of great variety and can profoundly influence the working of the economy in terms of production, growth, saving, investment, choice of techniques of production, regional imbalances, inequalities of income and wealth etc. These responses and their results are collectively called the effect of tax. The minimum effects of a tax, when imposed, will be a reduction in the disposable income of the taxpayers and if the tax is shifted, at least some price increase will occur.[24]

It must be observed that in every tax the time of payment, the manner of payment, the quantity to be paid, ought all to be clear and plain to the contributor otherwise the person subject to tax is put in the power of the tax-gatherer, which can either aggravate the tax upon an obnoxious contributor or extort by the terror of such aggravation some present or perquisite to himself. The uncertainty of taxation encourages insolence and favours corruption. The certainty of what each individual ought to pay in taxation is a matter of great importance. A tax should be levied at the time when it is most likely to be convenient for the contributor to pay; or, when he is most likely to have wherewithal to pay. A tax should neither take out nor keep out of the pockets of the people more than what it brings into the public treasury.

Taxation in India

India has adopted a taxation system that is based on the British system. However, after independence, following the philosophy of a socialistic pattern of society and democratic set-up with Federal Structure, the tax structure was designed. This has undergone many changes thereafter. Under the present arrangement as per the devolution of powers under the Constitution, taxes are levied by the Central Government as well as the State Governments both, direct as well as indirect in nature. The major taxes levied by the Central Government are direct taxes *viz.*, income tax, wealth tax, gift tax, corporate tax and surcharge thereon, while the indirect taxes include excise duty, customs duty, service tax, central sales tax (being phased out and replaced by value added tax – VAT), profession tax, service tax, state excise duty, vehicle tax, passengers and goods tax, service tax, stamp duty, registration fee, etc. Under devolution of powers some taxes are also levied by local governments, like municipalities, *panchayats*, village councils, etc., within their jurisdiction.

Taxation in Mizoram

Taxes have existed during all times and under all conditions in Mizoram, though the form and content has changed to take care of the specific requirements of the situation. It may be interesting to trace the growth of taxation regime in Mizoram during different phases of its history.

Pre-British Era (Before 1871)

The practice of taxation in an unrefined form and its origin as a measure of forced levy collected by the Chiefs from their subjects in the early history of Mizo may be regarded as the evolution of modern system of taxation in Mizoram. The actual system of levy imposed on subjects by the village Chiefs, method of collection and interval/regularity of the contribution, as well as the form of payment may not be similar to the present day practice. Mizo thus, had adopted the tax culture prior to the advent of the British by paying what they called *buh chhun*, and *sachhiah*[25]. Undeniably, the object of the imposition by whatever name called was to involve the citizens in running the governance and working for the welfare of the whole area or village, where the Chief could perform his basic responsibility of providing security to his subjects. It was a form of contribution by the subjects to the rulers, but the payment was made compulsory and enforced by the authority of the rulers for the welfare of all the inhabitants of the village. Mizo were, therefore, from their ancestors, tax-paying community and their compliance to the payment had never been in question.

During early days Lushai Chiefs received tribute or revenue from their subjects either in kind or by labour. Each family of a village paid *Fathawng* or a basket full of paddy to the Chief for the services rendered by the latter. The Chief was entitled to a substantial share of all the collections made from salt as well known as *Chikhurs*. The villagers were bound to obey and render help to their respective Chiefs in all possible ways. This system continued even after the British annexed the District.[26]

British Era (1872-1947)

In 1898, Col. J. Shakespeare, the then Superintendent of Mizo District, had formulated a land settlement policy for the District, which envisaged that each Chief would get certain area within which his people could move about and cultivate land as they liked. In doing so the area under each Chief with his people was clearly demarcated. All revenue assessments and collections were regulated by executive orders only[27]. The Chiefs and his officials were the authorized collectors of taxes and fines. The collection of tax in kind, i.e. rice was profitable to the administration for it directly helped to meet the demand of military posts and thus, saved lot of amount on account of constant change in prices of rice in the trade marts because of the difficulties of transport. British introduced the house tax and land holding tax to meet the expenditure on governance in Mizoram.

House Tax

With the inclusion and annexation of Mizoram into British Empire in the last part of the 19th Century, House tax also known as *leiman*, which formed an important source of revenue was introduced by the British *Raj* not purely for revenue but to exert their authority and to make the people subordinate and subservient to their authority. Annual cash payment of Rs. 2/- was fixed for every household as *leiman* which was a heavy burden for most of the Mizo, as till then the economic activities through money-transactions had not made inroad in the region and means of earning this much of cash was hard to find. It proved unbearable and for this reason *Chalruma*, father of *Darkhami* (a gifted and an exceptional singer of the early revival period), had moved his family in 1914 from Samtlang village (near Aizawl) to the neighbouring Tripura just to avoid "heavy taxation"[28]. Misconception held by the British regarding the object of taxation and subsequent impression of the community that it had to pay tax as "fine", may be attributed partly to the wrong spirit with which *leiman* was levied from the poor peasants by British rulers regardless of their ability to pay it. B.C. Carey's Chin Hills Regulation 1890 ironed out the multiplicity of land tenure of different tribes in the Chin Hills but because of it being deficit in rice production, Carey did not fix any fixed tribute towards house tax as was in Lushai Hills or Manipur.[29]

The local authorities realized that the Lushai Hills District suffered from economic disability. Though there might be resources of manpower and staple crops, which militated against starvation, yet there was no means of transforming the resources into currency. The local authorities adopted to a system of labour instead of currency levy as a part of dweller's reasonable contribution to the government in return for services rendered by it. The Superintendent of Lushai Hills and his assistants were authorized to levy tribute and exact labour from the Lushai which could be paid either in rice or rupees. When paid in rice, the rate was twenty seers of cleaned rice or one *maund* of un-husked rice per house per year and when paid in cash, it was Rs.2/- per house per year. Besides, each house was liable to supply one coolie (labour) to work for ten days in a year (irrespective of the days required for coming and going) but only when the Superintendent considered its enforcement absolutely necessary.

The payment of tribute in kind proved an extra burden on the people[30] and consequently, in 1904-05, the system of realizing house-tax in kind was discontinued specially in view of increased supply of currency and payment in cash was no longer a problem.

The details of house tax collection in the Lushai Hills from 1892-93 and 1932-33 is given in Table 5.1.

Table 5.1: House Tax Collected in Lushai Hills during British Period From 1892-93 to 1932-33

Year	*Total Number of Houses*	*Number of houses taxed*	*Demand (Rs.)*	*Actual Collection (Rs)*
1892-93				11,964.5
1896-97				17,098.0
1897-98				18,333.0
1904-05	16,271	14,631	29,423	28,051.8
1905-06	16,549	14,729	29,598	26,593.0
1908-09				32,371.0
1932-33				37,999.0

Source: 1. Chatterjee, Dr. Suhas: *A History of Mizo Economy*, Vol.-1, Printwell Publishers & Distributors, Jaipur, 1999, p. 184.

2. Lalrimawia, *Mizoram – History and Cultural Identity*, Spectrum Publications, Guwahati, 1995, p. 92.

In 1904-05, in Aizawl sub-division alone, 25 houses of *Gurkha* from nearby Aizawl and 47 houses of cultivators from North Vanlaiphai were taxed at Rs.3/-, each and rest 31 were assessed at Re.1/- only because of bad harvest. In 1905-06, the house tax at the rate of Rs.3/- per house was realized from 36 foreigners in Aizawl and 104 in Lunglei, and at Rs.2/- only per house from the rest.[31] In 1907-08, the house tax was raised on all foreigners to Rs.5/- per house, the rate applied in Kohima. As a result the assessment stood at Rs.32,371/- in 1908-09[32] and Rs.37,999/- in 1932-33. The increase was partly due to increase in population and partly due to certain amount of land revenue being taken to house tax by mistake.

Certain persons, like cripples; widows and old men having none to look after them were exempted from payment of house tax, if the total number of inmates of the house in aggregate were not able to pay the small tax of Rs.2/- per year. Besides, the exemption was also given to village *Khawchhiar*, men of the Lushai Labour Corps, Army Bearer Corps (who served in war) and the wives of Lushai serving Burma Rifles[33].

Land Holding Tax

No party in Lushai Hills could exclusively own land. Land belonged to the Government and the Chiefs had no right in the land[34]. Revenue derived from land (other than house tax) was land holding tax. In

1898-99, the rate of land revenue was Rs.3/- in cash or 20 Seers of rice in kind[35]. The land revenue paying bodies were the Welsh Mission at Aizawl, London Baptist Mission at Lunglei and Lakher Pioneer Mission at Serkawn in the south Lushai Hills[36]. In 1902-03, Rs.33 was realized from 33 acres and 17 poles of land leased to the Welsh Mission[37]. The land revenue from Missionaries and shopkeepers decreased in 1932-33, due to certain amount of land revenue being taken to house tax by mistake.

Opening of new shops was not permitted, except in very special cases because these proved a failure and provided larger houses for non-trading inmates. As from the very beginning it had been the policy of the government to prohibit outsiders settling in the District. Shakespeare, the then Superintendent of Lushai Hills, was of the view that settlement of undesirable aliens from the plains should be discouraged. Accordingly, foreign settlers were restricted within five miles radius[38]. But from early part of 20th century there was a rapid increase in the number of non-Lushai settlers in the vicinity of Aizawl. The Government permitted traders to open shops in the areas where demand existed. Occupants were assessed according to the area they occupied, but subject to a maximum ceiling. Shops established within the Aizawl and Lunglei town areas were assessed at higher rate than those in the interior[39]. Circle Interpreter concerned did the assessment of shops. The Chief was to for the correctness of the assessment sign before signed and carefully, the Circle Interpreter finally send the same to the Superintendent usually not later than December annually[40]. On receipt of the list a *Tauzi* (amount to be paid) would be made in the office in exact detail. The Chief concerned was to realise the money due as land revenue from the assesses, and remit the same into the office of House Tax clerk showing details of the assessees for whom the payment was made[41]. Besides, Grazing tax was also realized from Nepali grazers which amounted to Rs.420/- by the year 1932-33[42].

Tax in the Form of Labour

Government exacted impressed labour from the inhabitants of the Lushai Hills as part payment of taxes. The scale of impressed labour was maximum of ten days per year per house. It was a heavy imposition as this seriously affected the crop out-turn, because villagers were called away during important periods of *jhum* work[43].

Taxation by Chiefs

Till the abolition of the Chieftainship in 1955-56 in pursuance of the Assam Lushai Hills District (Acquisition of Chief's Right) Act, 1954, the land tenure system was basically traditional. There was, however, one important exception. During pre-annexation period the Chief's area of cultivable land depended upon what he and his followers could cover by force. After annexation, however, the area was clearly demarcated. The entire area that formed the domain of the Chief was known as "*Ram*"[44]. The entire community owned the land. The Chief was there in each village; but not as a landowner. None had heritable or transferable right over the land. For the same reason, nobody had the right of compensation when land was acquired for public purposes such as construction of roads, schools, etc. The right of user accrued over the plot allotted to him for *jhum* cultivation and that too for a brief period of cultivation. For *Jhum* cultivation the entire community took up one or two hill slopes and the land was distributed among its members.

The land settlement for the Chiefs was introduced in 1898 and "the hereditary right of the Chief to the *Ram* was strengthened in 1937 by recognizing the law of primogeniture"[45]. For cultivating the land of the Chief the villagers had to pay six tins of paddy per household per annum. However, if any household was not in a position to pay the tax in paddy they had the option of paying Rs.2/- in cash[46]. This was known as *Fathawng*. *Fathawng* has been defined as dues payable to a Chief by a cultivator in kind or cash[47]. Till 1953, the *Fathawng* never exceeded 24 gallons of unwind paddy per household per year, but in 1953, it was reduced drastically[48]. In 1955 with the abolition of Chieftainship, the payment of *Fathawng* was discontinued, but a villager was under obligation to pay house tax and to render free labour for community works taken up for the benefit of the village, such as path making, line cutting, construction and repair of the Chief's house[49]. The Chief also habitually received share of every animal shot or trapped in his area by any of his villagers. This was called *Sachhiah*[50]. Some Chiefs had salt wells on their land, which was collected for use and sale. The Chief was entitled to a due on all salt collected by the villagers. This was known as *Chichhia.*[51] "For services rendered by the Chief as a village judicial officer he received a portion of the fine imposed on villagers in judicial proceedings"[52]. This was known as *Salam.* Slavery known as *Bawi* was an exclusive privilege of the Chief. There were three types of slaves, *viz.*,

Inpui Chhung Bawis (orphans and widows in distress), *Chemson Bawis* (criminals who took shelter under the Chief to evade punishment) and *Tuklut Bawis* (who in war deserted the loser and joined the victor)[53]. Although the slaves were generally well treated by the Chief in return for their labour, they had to surrender all personal liberty and were not allowed to own any property[54]. However, they were sold out to traders against high payment[55]. The slaves could earn freedom by paying Rs.40/- to the Chief. "The Chief and *Upas* were guided entirely by Lushai customs. A Chief who disregarded customs and oppressed the villagers speedily lost the bulk of his subjects. Lushai were accustomed to migrate freely from village to village, and this custom afforded a very salutary check on too arbitrary use of power by Chiefs."[56]

With gradual refinement over time and the coming into being of the Lushai Hills District Council (later renamed as 'Mizo District Council' in the beginning of the 1950s) the levy of taxes through authorization by laws began to take its modern form. Revenue so derived were assigned and credited to the accounts of the District Council, and in this way it took the form of municipal taxes. The revenue yield of these taxes was minimal in as much as the Council's requirement were insignificant. No income tax was realized in the District in 1902-03, with the exception of deductions from the salaries of government officers[57].

Post-Independence

On 19th September 1951 the institutions of *Ramhuals* and *Zalens* were abolished without compensation and the Chieftainship was abolished in March 1954[33]. Thus a new era was ushered in Mizoram. After the abolition of the institution of Chieftainship, all lands of the Chiefs were brought under the jurisdiction of District Council, which gradually passed on to the Government after the abolition of the District Councils consequent upon the emergence of Mizoram as a Union Territory in 1972. In pursuance of the "Land-use Policy" the Government took measures and adopted operational procedures since the beginning of the Plan period which became evident that it opted for privatization of land.

However, the authority of taxation was passed on to the District Council some of the taxes levied earlier during British period were continued such as 'house tax' and '*Zoram Chhiah*'. Every house including shops, but excluding stalls, were assessed to a tax of Rs.2/- per house per year *vide* Section 3(4) of the Lushai Hills District (Revenue Assessment) Regulations, 1953. A personal levy at Rs.3/- per year which was introduced during pre-Independence period was replaced in 1953, when *Zoram Chhiah,* a tax payable by tribal was enforced[58]. Surtax (tolls on persons) at Rs. 2.50 per family per year was levyed *vide* Section 4 of the Lushai Hill District (Revenue Assessment) Regulation, 1953.[59]

The Government of India exempted Mizo living in Mizo Hills' District from the purview of Central Acts like Estate Duty Act, Excise Act, Income Tax Act, etc., unlike Manipur and Tripura, which also had tribal background but, people there had to pay Central taxes. These people resented the exemption from taxation given to the Mizo[60].

The position regarding revenue from various taxes levied and collected in Mizoram from 1951-52 to 1960-61 is given in Table 5.2.

Table 5.2: Revenue from Various Taxes Levied and Collected in Mizoram from 1951-52 to 1960-61

(*Rs. in lakh*)

Year	*Sales Tax on POL Products*	*Profession tax*	*Passengers and Goods Tax*	*Entertainment Tax*	*State Excise*	*Stamp and Registration*	*Land Revenue*	*Total*
1951-52	0.03	0.00	N.A.	0.00	N.A.	0.02	N.A.	0.06
1952-53	0.17	0.00	N.A.	0.02	N.A.	0.03	N.A.	0.22
1953-54	0.14	0.00	N.A.	0.02	N.A.	0.03	N.A.	0.18
1954-55	0.03	0.00	N.A.	0.12	N.A.	0.04	N.A.	0.18
1955-56	0.18	0.01	N.A.	0.13	N.A.	0.04	N.A.	0.36
1956-57	0.03	0.00	N.A.	0.16	N.A.	0.05	N.A.	0.24
1957-58	0.21	0.01	N.A.	0.15	N.A.	0.05	N.A.	0.42
1958-59	0.28	0.01	N.A.	0.15	N.A.	0.07	N.A.	0.51
1959-60	0.42	N.A.	N.A.	0.13	N.A.	0.08	N.A.	0.63
1960-61	0.63	N.A.	N.A.	0.14	N.A.	0.09	N.A.	0.86

Source: Census Report, 1961, (Table 6.4).

The analysis of various taxes collected from people in the then Lushai Hills District later renamed as Mizo District of Assam during post-independence period from 1951-52 to 1960-61 as shown in Table 5.2 makes it clear that neither state excise, nor land revenue, nor passengers and goods tax existed in the District. Revenue was being raised from some of the taxes applicable in the State of Assam, such as Sales tax on petroleum products, Profession tax. The total collection from all the taxes taken together was small.

The share of profession tax was hardly worth mentioning. Major contribution to State revenue was from sales tax on sale of petroleum products under Taxation Act, 1956 that was in force in the erstwhile Mizo District of Assam. Though, the sales tax revenue remained fluctuating widely, it increased from Rs.3000/- in 1951-52 to Rs.63000/- in 1961-62. Entertainment tax was levied under the Assam Amusement and Betting Tax Act, 1939[61], though, fluctuated in a narrow range showed a rising trend. The peak rise in it from Rs.2000/- in 1953-54 to Rs.12000/- in 1954-55, and then stabilized thereafter indicated that it was imposed in the district in spirit from 1954-55 and onwards. Stamps and Registration Duties formed the other important source of revenue. Though it was levied only from non-Mizo residing in the area, it recorded a continuous rising trend from Rs.2000/- in 1951-52 to Rs.9000/- in 1960-61.

Union Territory Period

The insurgency that broke out in 1966 destroyed the entire rural economy of the District. The major change brought there after was re-grouping of villages by bringing the insurgency-stricken people to new sites linked by road. A backward district without economic base struggling for life under the insurgency was converted into a Union Territory administration with effect from 21st January 1972. The Administration had neither tax nor non-tax revenue receipts worth mention. The Union Territory Government made efforts for raising internal revenues through taxation. Fresh legislations were enacted and existing laws in force were made applicable with certain modifications by Adaptation of Laws Orders. Taxation re-emerged in the form of Sales Tax on Petroleum products, Entertainment tax, and Profession tax. The operation of the Central Sales Tax Act, 1956 was also extended to Mizoram[62] by virtue of notification issued by Government of India *vide* Department of Revenue and Insurance's letter No. G.28/21/72-st dated 15th September 1972.

Department of Revenue

Consequent upon the formation of Union Territory of Mizoram, a separate Department was created for overall administrative control of revenue. In 1977, taxation was also allocated to it and soon after it was named Revenue, Excise and Taxation Department. The Revenue Department was entrusted with matters connected with land revenue, land settlement, land records, land reforms and survey, excise, money lending and money lenders, regulation of trade by non-tribals, and compensation on account of crops/private properties damaged by security forces.

For land revenue administration, the legislations enacted by the erstwhile Mizo District Council were adopted. These included[63]—The Lushai Hills District (House Site) Act, 1953, The Mizo District (Land and Revenue) Act, 1953, The Mizo District (Agricultural Land) Act, 1953, The Mizo District (Transfer of Land) Act, 1953, The Lushai Hill (Revenue Assessment) Regulation, 1953, The Lushai Hills (Taxes) Regulation, 1954, The Mizo District (Market) Regulation, 1964, The Mizo District (Professions, Trades, Callings and Employment Taxation) Regulation, 1953, The Mizo District (Agricultural Land) Rules, 1971, The Lushai Hills District (Trading by non-Tribals) Regulation, 1956, The Mizoram (Sale of Petroleum Products including Motor Spirits and Lubricants) Taxation Act, 1973. The Government made some amendments to the Acts and Rules. To evolve a working procedure between Directorate and District level offices the Department was reorganized. The revenue administration was changed and powers were delegated to the Deputy Commissioner, Aizawl and Lunglei within their respective jurisdictions.

State Excise Duty

After the formation of Union Territory, excise administration was passed on to the Revenue Department, which was earlier being by the Deputy Commissioner. Permits were issued to some individuals for importing Indian Made Foreign Liquor (IMFL) from outside, and pass fee was collected as in Assam. However, in the absence of Excise Act, no excise duty was collected on excisable articles. Later issue of liquor import permit was stopped except armed forces including Assam Rifles, CRPF and Home Guard where monthly fee was charged at Rs.1.50 per bottle on IMFL (150 ml) and 40 paise per bottle on beer[64].

With a view of augmenting whatever revenue receipts it had, the Mizoram Excise Act, 1972 was promulgated in 1973 that, however, remained dormant for some years and came into force from 10th October 1984. The Act regulated import, export, transport, manufacture, possession and sale of IMFL in Mizoram. At that time, the rate of excise duty on IMFL was Rs.101.25 per London proof gallon and on beer was Rs.5.85 per London proof gallon and pass fee on beer was Rs.18.00 per London proof gallon. These rates were about half of the existing excise duties[65].

Entertainment Tax

The Assam Amusement and Betting Tax Act, 1939 as extended by the Assam Autonomous District (Amusement and Betting) Regulation, 1952 was operative in Mizoram[66]. Entertainment Tax was charged in respect of any person admitted on payment for the purpose of entertainment and amusement, games and sports, theatre and cinematograph etc.

Licence Fee on Trading by Non-Tribals

Under the Lushai Hills (Trading by Non-Tribals) Regulation, 1954, licence fee was realized from non-tribals engaged in commerce. Non-tribals who possessed permanent trade licence were liable to pay a licence fee of Rs.50/- per annum, and those who possessed temporary trade licence were liable to pay a fee of Rs.50/- for each term for which the licence was issued[67].

With a view to promote economic growth and in the interest of public in general a new law to regulate trading by non-tribals in Mizoram and for matters connected therewith, the Mizoram Trading by Non-Tribals (Regulation) Act, 1974 was passed. The Act received the assent of the President of India on 2nd January 1975 for ten years which retained the maximum licence fee at Rs.50/- per annum. Other taxes on non-tribals were, Boat tax at Rs.2/- per trip made from outside Mizoram to any place inside Mizoram, and animal tax at Re 0.50 each animal from persons having five or more animals not below the age of three years such as buffalo, bull, bullock, pony, horse, donkey, mule and ass.[68]

Profession Tax

A tax was charged in respect of profession, trades, callings or employment etc. under the Mizo District (Profession, Trades, Callings and Employment Taxation) Regulation, 1953.[69] As amended in 1978-79, the tax in case of every person other than a Hindu undivided family (HUF) was, where the total gross income not exceeded Rs.6,000/- Rs. Nil, exceeded Rs.6,000/- but not exceeded Rs.10,000/- Rs.30/-, exceeded Rs.10,000/- but not exceeded Rs.15,000/- Rs.50/-, exceeded Rs.15,000/- but not exceeded Rs.20,000/- Rs.75/-, exceeded Rs.20,000/- but not exceeded Rs.25,000/- Rs.100/-, exceeded Rs.25,000/- but not exceeded Rs.30,000/- Rs.150/-, exceeded Rs.30,000/- but not exceeded Rs.35,000/- Rs.200/-, and exceeded Rs.35,000/- Rs.250/-. In case of every Hindu undivided family (HUF) it was, where the total gross income not exceeded Rs.10,000/-

Rs. Nil, exceeded Rs.10,000/- but not exceeded Rs.15,000/- Rs.60/-, exceeded Rs.15,000/- but not exceeded Rs.20,000/- Rs.80/-, exceeded Rs.20,000/- but not exceeded Rs.25,000/- Rs.100/-, exceeded Rs.25,000/- but not exceeded Rs.30,000/- Rs.150/-, exceeded Rs.30,000/- but not exceeded Rs.35,000/- Rs.200/-, and exceeded Rs.35,000/- Rs.250/-.

Taxation of Petroleum and Petroleum Products

Government of Mizoram did not promulgate a separate sales tax other than the Mizoram (Sales of Petroleum and Petroleum Products including Motor Spirits and Lubricants) Act. The only sales tax imposed by Government of Mizoram was on sale of petroleum and its products including motor spirit and lubricants under Taxation Act, 1956 that was in force in the erstwhile Mizo District of Assam. The aforesaid Act continued to be in force in Mizoram under the provisions of section 77 of the North-Eastern Area Reorganization Act, 1971. The Government of Mizoram passed a new Act during Union Territory period known as the Mizoram (Sale of Petroleum and Petroleum Products including Motor Spirits and Lubricants) Taxation Act, 1973, which came into effect from 1st December 1974[70]. The rates of sales tax on Motor Spirits (except diesel oil and internal combustion oils other than petrol) was 7 paise per litre, on lubricants was 8 paise per litre, on diesel oil and other internal combustion oils other than petrol was 5 paise per litre, and on crude oil no tax.

Other Taxes and Fees

Other taxes levied in Mizoram were[71] *Zoram Chhiah* (Tolls on Persons) at Re.0.50 per family p.a. except on the non-tribal government servant staying in government quarters; Stall Tax on every stall within Aizawl town at Rs.12/- p.a., and for all other stalls at Rs.5/- p.a.; Fish Pond Tax on every fishpond at Rs.15/- p.a.; and fee for issue of house tax payee's certificate at Rs.3.75 per certificate; for issue of profession tax clearance certificate at Re.1/- per certificate; for issue of income certificate at Re. 1/- per certificate; and for Land Revenue (L.S.C.) within Aizawl town for Grade-IA Rs.18/- per bigha, for Grade-IB Rs.15/- per bigha, for Grade-IIA Rs.12/- per bigha, for Grade-IIB Rs.10/- per bigha, for Grade-III Rs.6/- per bigha and for Champhai town area for Grade-IA Rs.12/- per bigha, for Grade-IB Rs.10/- per bigha, for Grade-IIA Rs.10/- per bigha, for Grade-IIB Rs.8/- per bigha, and for Grade-III Rs.6/- per bigha. Land lease rate payable per annum was fixed in accordance with areawise land valuation.

The position regarding revenue from various taxes levied and collected in Mizoram from 1972-73 to 1989-90 is presented in Table 5.3.

Table 5.3: Revenue from Various Taxes Levied and Collected in Mizoram From 1972-73 to 1989-90

(*Rs. in lakh*)

Year	*Sales Tax on POL Products*	*Profession Tax*	*Passengers and Goods Tax*	*Entertainment Tax*	*State Excise*	*Stamp and Registration Fee*	*Land Revenue*	*Total*
1972-73	N.A.	0.41	N.A.	0.29	N.A.	N.A.	2.85	3.55
1973-74	N.A.	0.52	N.A.	0.34	1.80	N.A.	3.67	6.33
1974-75	0.70	1.52	N.A.	0.40	1.85	N.A.	3.48	7.95
1975-76	0.96	2.79	N.A.	0.44	4.23	N.A.	4.36	12.78
1976-77	2.67	1.70	N.A.	0.53	13.58	N.A.	2.75	21.23
1977-78	2.48	1.57	N.A.	0.08	10.02	N.A.	3.04	17.19
1978-79	N.A.	N.A.	N.A.	N.A.	N.A.	N.A.	N.A.	N.A.
1979-80	0.93	1.18	N.A.	0.46	2.82	N.A.	1.45	6.84
1980-81	N.A.	N.A.	N.A.	2.86	12.53	N.A.	4.50	19.89
1981-82	N.A.	N.A.	5.97	4.86	10.25	N.A.	3.35	24.43
1982-83	N.A.	N.A.	6.36	4.31	15.89	N.A.	4.42	30.98
1983-84	N.A.	N.A.	N.A.	N.A.	N.A.	N.A.	1.97	1.97
1984-85	N.A.	N.A.	N.A.	N.A.	N.A.	N.A.	3.43	3.43
1985-86	4.58	12.73	N.A.	7.53	111.74	N.A.	14.29	150.87
1986-87	6.07	1.80	N.A.	8.00	271.00	N.A.	14.42	301.29
1987-88	6.54	22.84	N.A.	7.29	295.34	N.A.	N.A.	332.01
1988-89	4.47	4.79	2.69	88.56	40.14	N.A.	N.A.	140.65
1989-90	11.65	N.A.	26.68	8.62	78.64	N.A.	38.08	163.67

Source: Mizoram District Gazetteers, 1989, pp.246-250 for data upto 1977-78 and for rest of the period data compiled from various Statistical Handbooks of Mizoram.

The analysis of Table 5.3 relating to various tax receipts during Union Territory period reveals that most of the taxes were small in value till 1984-85. Since 1985-86 all tax receipts grew in size and volume. It also showed that business and industry started penetrating in Mizoram's economy from 1985-86. Before that trading activities only flourished in Mizoram. The collection of entertainment tax was less during 1977-78 as Zodin Cinema, which was the only assesse unit for entertainment tax in Aizawl Town, stopped payment of entertainment tax, when the hall was demolished on 30th June 1977[72]. The share of Stamps and Registration fee in total taxes over the entire period has been Nil, for the obvious reason that the provisions of The Registration Act, 1905 as were in force being part of Assam before the Union Territory status had lost jurisdiction and Mizo were exempted from paying Stamps and Registration duty. The U.T. Government realizing no revenue did not feel inclined to bring a similar Act enabling it to realize the same from non-Mizo residing in the area.

Post-Statehood

Statehood brought a change in the outlook of the Government. It took measures to enhance State revenue. In 1988, the "Passengers and Goods Tax" was introduced and tax collection was started from 1st April 1990. The Sales Tax was introduced in 1989. But, owing to unresolved issue involving grant of registration to non-resident traders of non-tribal community, the business community protested against the implementation of "The Mizoram Sales Tax Act, 1989" that led to its intermittent suspension first and later finally lifted with effect from 1st April 1993.[73]

Taxation of Petroleum and Petroleum Products

Under the Mizoram (Sales of Petroleum and Petroleum Products including Motor Spirits and Lubricants) Taxation Act, 1973, every dealer is required to pay sales tax, (commonly known as POL tax) at first point of sale in a financial year within Mizoram. A dealer is also subject to this tax on sales in the course of import-export outside India, and sales in the course of inter-state trade and commerce. The Act requires mandatory registration of every person or dealer who is subject to tax under the Act with the Commissioner of Taxation in the State. No unregistered dealer can realize/ collect any sales tax under the Act. The net tax payable by a dealer is to be determined at: Tax = (Rate of Tax × Taxable Turnover) ÷ (100 + Rate of Tax).

The section 3 provides that the rates of tax and items of goods taxable under the Act may be enhanced, added or modified by the State Government through notification in the official Gazette. The Section 4 authorises the State Government to grant exemption to any dealer in public interest. However, no exemption has so far been granted to any dealer. No turnover limit is yet prescribed under the Act.

Sale of petroleum and petroleum products are taxed at first point of sale in the State as Motor Spirit at 20 per cent, H.S.D. at 12 per cent, Lubricants at 8 per cent, and Liquefied Petroleum Gas at 8 per cent[74].

The provisions of the Act require a dealer to file a quarterly return of sales in prescribed form within a period of one month following the end of concerned quarter. Further, there are usual provisions of assessment, appeal, recovery of sales tax, and other penal provisions of penalty etc.

The position regarding dealers registered under the Act is given in Table 5.4.

Table 5.4: Dealers Registered under Mizoram (Sale of Petroleum and Petroleum Products including Motor Spirits and Lubricants) Taxation Act, 1973 during 2001 to 2002
(As on 31st March)

District	*Number of Registered Dealers*	
	2001	*2002*
Aizawl	19	20
Champhai	NIL	NIL
Kolasib	1	1
Mamit	NIL	NIL
Serchhip	2	3
Lunglei	4	4
Lawngtlai	NIL	NIL
Saiha	1	1
Total	27	29

Source: Statistical Handbook, Mizoram, 2002, Directorate of Economics and Statistics, Aizawl, p.38.

Table 5.4 revealed that on the whole there were very few dealers registered under the Act and there was no registered dealer in Champhai, Mamit and Lawngtlai districts. However, there was only 1 dealer each in Kolasib and Saiha districts.

State Excise Duty

Owing to the enforcement of 'The Mizoram Liquor (Total Prohibition) Act, 1995', which came into force from 20th February 1997, import, transport, manufacture, possession, sale and consumption of any kind of alcoholic liquor in the State is prohibited,[75] except in the areas of the three Autonomous District Councils *viz.*, Lai, Mara and Chakma. As a result, the Government has nothing to do with manufacturing, distribution and pricing of liquor. There existed neither a distillery nor a commercial liquor shop in Mizoram.

Under Section 30 of the Mizoram Liquor (Total Prohibition) Act, 1995 the State Government may, on receipt of application from licensee in form No. VIII, grant a licence to the armed forces deployed in Mizoram for import of IMFL for sale and consumption in their messes and canteens on payment of excise duty through treasury challan. However, the Government may prescribe pass fee from time to time. There were 11 such units of military/Para-Military forces in Mizoram whom liquor licences have been issued.

The existing rates of excise duty and pass fee prescribed by the Government[76] are (i) on IMFL: Rum/Whisky/Brandy/Gin @ Rs.52/- per proof litre, Wine @ Rs.30/- per proof litre, Beer @ Rs.8/- per proof litre, and (ii) Pass Fee on: All kinds of IMFL @ Rs. 2/- per bulk litre, Beer @ Rs.1/- per bulk litre, and All kinds of imported liquor @ Rs.5/- per bulk litre.

Sales Tax

The Mizoram Sales Tax Act was passed by the State Assembly (Act No. 8 of 1989) in 1989, which is extended to the whole of Mizoram. However, the provisions of the tax did not apply to goods taxable under Mizoram (Sale of Petroleum and Petroleum Products etc. including Motor Spirit and Lubricants) Taxation Act 1973. Under the Sales Tax Act all goods have been divided into four categories, *viz.*, (i) Goods as are included in Schedule-I that are exempted from levy of sales tax, (ii) Goods as are mentioned in Schedule-II that are subject to sales tax at *first point of sale,* (iii) Goods as are included in Schedule-III that are taxable *at last point of sale*, (However, as on now no goods/items have been included in this category), and (iv) Items/goods as are classified in Schedule-IV that are taxable on transfer of their right to use for any purpose. However, as on now no goods/items have been included in this category. Besides, some contract works whether measurement of value addition made can be known or not are also taxable under the Act.

Registration of every person or dealer, who is subject to tax under the Act, is mandatory with Commissioner of Taxation in the State. A person once found liable to be taxed continues to be an assessee for a minimum period of next 3 financial years, even if his quantum of taxable turnover is below the limit mentioned herein. But no unregistered dealer can realize/collect any sales tax under the Act. *Annual Turnover Limits*: Under Section 3 of the Act, every dealer whose turnover has once exceeded the prescribed turnover limit is liable to pay sales tax since the year in which his turnover has exceeded the limit for the first time and onwards. The annual turnover limits as has been fixed for dealers are, [78] (i) for those making first point (stage) sale Rs. Nil, (ii) for those making last point sale Rs.1 lakh, and (iii) for those executing contract works Rs. 2 lakh. It is important to note that 'no items' have been notified yet under Schedule-III to be taxed on last point of sale. It may be understood that presently sales tax in Mizoram is being levied on first point sale only. Besides every dealer is liable to pay sales tax on sale of goods outside Mizoram in the course of import or export outside India, and in the course of inter-state trade or commerce.

While determining the tax liability of a dealer his turnover as regards to exempted goods as specified in Schedule-I and goods consumed in the performance of any work-contract as specified in Schedule-IV and the turnover of the goods sold for resale purpose, which are taxable at last point of sale are subtracted from his total gross turnover. The net tax payable by a dealer is determined as follows:

Tax = (Taxable Turnover × Rate of Tax) ÷ (100 + Rate of Tax).

There has been a provision for deduction of tax at source at 2 per cent from payment to a dealer by the government, local authority, corporation, company, co-operative society, educational institution, or a promoter in respect of works-contract. Further, no contract can be awarded or order of purchase can be placed to any dealer by these organizations or bodies without obtaining tax clearance certificate from the dealer issued by the Commissioner of Taxes. The provisions of the Act require that a dealer have to file a quarterly return of sales in the prescribed form within a period of one month following the end of concerned quarter. However, a dealer may submit the same voluntarily on monthly basis within 30 days from the end of calendar month. Yet there are usual provisions of assessment, appeal, recovery of sales tax, and other penal provisions of penalty, etc.

The tax rates, as effective from 1st October 2001, are (i) Iron and Steel, Tractors, Power Tillers, Computers and Information Technology products etc. at 4 per cent; (ii) Gold, Silver and Precious Stones etc. at 5 per cent; (iii) Two Wheelers and their Spare parts, Spare parts of Motor Vehicles, Tyres, Building Materials, Tinned Packed Edibles, Drinks, Milk Products, Hospital Equipments, Bulldozers, Excavators, Earthmovers and their parts, etc. at 8 per cent; and (iv) Air-conditioners, Refrigerators, Cooling Appliances, Geysers, TV, VCD, VCP, Washing Machines, Vacuum Cleaners, Voltage Stabilizers, CVT, Fax Machines, Wireless, Xerox Machines, and all other machines, Rifles, Revolvers, Cosmetics, Toilet goods, Tooth Paste, Hair Oil, Cream, Motor Vehicles etc. at 12 per cent.

The Act, which was suspended on 1st April 1993 and since kept in abeyance was re-introduced on 1st November 1999 has widened the tax base by making it operative throughout the State. Though the system of sales tax in the State is designed for levy of tax at the first and last point of sale, it presently being levied at first point of sale only. Under Section 4(2) of the Act the State Government may specify items of goods and the rates of tax to be levied on sale of goods. Further, the State Government may, by notification in official Gazette, add to or omit any item in the Schedule or change or modify rate to be levied on sale of goods[77]. Goods exempted are set out in Schedule-I of the Act. Under Section 7(3), the State Government may add, amend or modify the exemption schedule. Further, under Section 7(4), the State Government may make a scheme or schemes for grant of incentive/relief to any class of industries.

Various goods exempted from sales tax are all cereals and pulses, milk and its products including dairy products, sago, vegetables (all except when sold in sealed container), books, slates, pencils, paper, ink, scale, colour box, drawing book, exercise book, school map, school uniform (all subject to production of certificate from the head of the institution), school bag, flour, *atta*, *maida*, *suji*, biscuits, bakery products, agricultural inputs and implements, news papers, news prints (when sold to small and medium news papers of Mizoram), periodicals, printing paper for university/board (on production of certificate from book committee), Government of India publications, vegetable seeds, fresh fruits, betel nuts and betel leaves, *gur*, sugar and sugarcane, mustard oil, salt, baby food, ice, agro-horticultural products, flowers, saplings, sericulture products, cotton and cotton textiles, handloom cloth, locally made ready-made garments, silk and silk yarn, handspun cotton yarn, mill made cotton yarn, condom and contraceptives, medicines, vaccine, anti malaria drugs, ayurvedic medicine, wheel chair, book binding cotton fabric, KVI products, potteries, cattle fodder and grass, pig feed, poultry feed, green tea leaves, fire wood and charcoal, gobar gas plants, furnace oil, electrical energy appliances, tobacco and all its products, etc. Besides, goods donated to armed forces, and goods sold to defence services (when sold at Government of India prices), Indian Aid Mission, United Nations International Children Emergency Funds (UNICEF), and arms and ammunitions sold to Mizoram police are also exempted. It is important to notice that tobacco and its products, generally covered under the purview of heavy sales tax by majority of Indian states, are exempted in Mizoram.

Though the Central Sales Tax (CST) is made operative in Mizoram and many dealers have sought registration under it but virtually it did not fetch any tax revenue in the name of CST as the inter-state trade flow was one sided only. Except agro-horticultural products (which are exempt under CST) of Mizoram nothing is sold outside the State where CST can be realized on inter-state sale. The dealers obtain registration under CST just to buy goods from outside the State.

The position regarding number of dealers registered as on 31st March 2002 under the Mizoram Sales Tax Act (MST) and Central Sales Tax Act (CST) is given in Table 5.5.

Table 5.5: Number of Registered Dealers under MST Act and CST Act in Mizoram during 2001 to 2003 (As on 31st March)

District	*No. of Registered Dealers*			
	2001		*2002*	
	Under MST Act	*Under CST Act*	*Under MST Act*	*Under CST Act*
Aizawl	206	1276	325	1445
Champhai	13	77	16	82
Kolasib	14	85	19	87
Mamit	3	14	3	14
Serchhip	5	36	5	39
Lunglei	53	88	67	103
Lawngtlai	2	30	2	31
Saiha	11	23	14	25
Total	271	1629	452	1826

Source: Statistical Handbook, Mizoram, 2002, Directorate of Economics and Statistics, Aizawl, pp.38-39.

Table 5.5 revealed that the number of registered dealers under CST was more than that of MST. The number of dealers who contributed to State revenue in the form of sales tax (MST) was much below the number of dealers who procured goods from inter-state trade. It is interesting to noted that once goods purchased under CST after paying 4 per cent CST at the point of purchase and on brining it to State border it becomes taxable under MST Act at full rate applicable. Following this, the number of dealers registered under MST Act should not be less than the number of dealers registered under CST Act (1826) as on 31st March 2002 as all these dealers are liable to pay MST on their first sale of such goods within Mizoram. However, the number of registered dealers under MST was 452 only as on 31st March 2002. It may be assumed that some dealers might be dealing in exempted goods, but not all. The big gap between these two numbers indicated that the remaining 1374 dealers though liable to be assessed under MST Act were not remitting sales tax to the Government on their sale, rather they were trading scot-free and need to be registered under MST Act as according to the provisions no unregistered dealer can realize sales tax. This indicated that all the dealers registered under CST were not paying MST on the goods they purchased in the course of inter-state trade.

Value Added Tax

Value Added Tax (VAT) is a new indirect tax levied with effect from 1st April 2005. The basis of taxation is 'Value Addition' at a point of transfer of goods. The scope of sales tax, at present is limited to first point sale on notified goods. The revenue collected from sales tax during the past years on the average was around Rs.10/- crore p.a. Value Added Tax on the other hand is likely to have a comprehensive effect on the revenue of the State, if levied on a wider base and services are brought under the VAT net.

"The Mizoram Value Added Tax Bill, 2003" was drafted on the lines of model proposed by Shri B.R. Atre, Legal Consultant, Government of India, Ministry of Finance, after it was vetted by Law Department of the State Government and approved by the Ministry of Home Affairs, Government of India for introduction in the State Legislature. As the calculation of Revenue Neutral Rate (RNR) in respect of State of Mizoram could not be made accurately due to adoption and implementation of sales tax recently, non-availability of data on turnover, item-wise sales tax levied, etc. However, an attempt was made to determine it on the basis of Shri Pawan Agarwal's method of calculation and that is arrived at 6.75 per cent[79].

Entertainment Tax

Entertainment Tax is levied under the Assam Amusement and Betting Tax Act, 1939 adopted in Mizoram on all payments for admission to any theatre, cinematograph, exhibition, circus, etc.[80] The rates of tax (i) in case of games, sports, music or dramatic performance is 12.5 per cent, (ii) in case of entertainment provided through cable T.V. 20 per cent, (iii) in any other case, where the payment for admission is Rs. 2/- or less, 50 per cent; more than Rs. 2/- and upto Rs. 3/-, 75 per cent, and more than Rs. 3/-, 100 per cent, and (iv) additional tax on cinematograph exhibition is levied per show at the rate of 10 per cent of the total payment received for admission including tax, or Rs.10/- whichever is less.

Profession Tax

The Mizoram Professions, Trades, Callings, and Employment Taxation Act, 1995 was passed by the State Assembly [Act. No.7 of 1995] in 1995, received the Governor's accent on 6th November 1995 and came into force from 1st April 1997. It is extended to whole of Mizoram, excluding the areas of Lai, Mara, and Chakma Autonomous District Councils in Chhimtuipui and Lawngtlai districts. In accordance with the provisions, every person who carries on a trade either by himself or by an agent or through representative or who follows a profession or calling or who is in employment either wholly or in part within the State is liable to pay a tax that is determined every year with reference to his total gross income or total gross turnover or total contract amount or total gross business during previous financial year from his profession, trades, calling or employment or with reference to his standing in the profession, trades, calling or employment as the case may be. This tax is in addition to any other tax he or she might be paying. However, it is not applicable to members of armed forces of India, and registered cooperative societies.

For the purpose of realization of tax, all the professions and employment as described above have been grouped into 14 categories and different rates of tax have been prescribed for them in Schedule-IV. Mizoram being the 6th Schedule area at national level, the annual upper limit of profession tax is fixed by the Indian Constitution at Rs. 2500/- only. Presently the profession tax in Mizoram is being levied from individuals (salaried persons) earning annually below Rs.10000/- at Rs. nil, between Rs.10000/- to Rs.15000/- at Rs.100/-, between Rs.15000/- to Rs. 20000/- at Rs. 150/-, between Rs. 20000/- to Rs. 25000/- at Rs. 200/-, between Rs. 25000/- to 35000/- at Rs. 250/-, between Rs. 35000/- to Rs. 50000/- at Rs. 300/-, between Rs. 50000/- to Rs. 75000/- at Rs. 500/-, between Rs. 75000/- to Rs. 1 lakh at Rs. 750/-, between Rs. 1 lakh to Rs. 1.5 lakh at Rs. 1000/-, between Rs. 1.5 lakh to Rs. 2 lakh at Rs. 1500/-, between Rs. 2 lakh to Rs. 2.5 lakh at Rs. 2000/- and above Rs. 2.5 lakh at Rs. 2500/-.

The tax for legal/medical/technical/professional practitioners below 3 years standing is at Rs. 350/-, between 3 to 5 years standing at Rs. 500/-, between 5 to 10 years standing at Rs. 750/-, and above 10 years standing at Rs. 1000/-. For agents other than estate and commission agents below 3 years standing it is at Rs. *nil*, between 3 to 5 years standing at Rs. 250/-, between 5 to 10 years standing at Rs. 500/-, and above 10 years standing at Rs. 1000/-. However, it is at Rs. 300/- for owners of taxies (LMV), at

Rs. 500/- for owners of trucks/buses, video parlors and libraries, restaurants and hotels (where food is served), owners of rice/atta/flour/oil mills, at Rs. 1200/- for owners of distilleries, breweries, bottling plant, petrol and diesel outlets, at Rs. 1500/- for cinema houses, theatres, partnership firms, etc. For director of a company, estate agents, commission agents, chit funds and lotteries, for owners of cold storage, meat processing unit, and residential hotels below 3 stories the tax is at Rs. 1000/- and for hotels above 3 stories and vendors of IMFL the tax is at Rs. 2000/-, for partnership firms, banks, and companies the rate of profession tax is at Rs. 2500/- with effect from 26th March 1997 (before that it was Rs. 2000/- for banks and companies and Rs. 1500/- for partnership firms). No profession tax is levied from dealers with annual turnover below Rs. 20000/-. While for dealers with annual turnover above Rs. 20000/-, and for owners of mechanical/ electrical/electronic repair works, fabrications, and furniture works, suppliers and contractors it is levied at 0.5 per cent of their annual turnover/ gross business/contract amount subject to the maximum limit.

It may be understood that the profession tax coverage is limited and does not cover vast services such as couriers, laundries, bakeries, automobile workshops, Xerox, lamination, STD-PCOs, knitting, tailoring, photo services, industries, etc. It may also be understood that the profession tax levied from owners of truck or bus Rs. 500/- p.a., distilleries/breweries/bottling plants Rs. 1200/- p.a., and cinema theatres Rs. 1500/- p.a. seemed small.

Stamps and Registration Fee

The Indian Stamp (Mizoram Amendment) Act, 1995 was implemented in Mizoram on 22nd April 1997, which contains description of various instruments (documents) framed after amending the Indian Stamp Act, 1899.[81]

The stamp duty for instruments relating to residential premises consisting of building unit where the value does not exceed Rs. 1 lakh is Rs. 100/-, exceeding Rs. 1 lakh but not exceeding Rs. 2.5 lakh is 1 per cent of the value, exceeding Rs. 2.5 lakh but not exceeding Rs. 5 lakh is Rs. 2,500/- plus 4 per cent of the value above Rs. 2.50 lakh, exceeding Rs. 5 lakh but not exceeding Rs. 7.5 lakh is Rs. 12,500/- plus 6 per cent of the value above Rs. 5 lakh, exceeding Rs. 7.5 lakh but not exceeding Rs. 10 lakh is Rs. 27,500/- plus 10 per cent of the value above Rs. 7.5 lakh, and exceeding Rs. 10 lakh is Rs. 47,500/- plus 10 per cent of the value above Rs. 10 lakh.

The Registration Act, 1905 (Act XVI of 1908) was introduced in Mizoram with effect from 22nd April 1997[82]. The rate of fee for registration of documents is regulated on *ad volerem* scale of 1 per cent subject to maximum of Rs. 5000/- based on the value of the right, title and interest affected. As such, fees charged for registration of documents varies from one to another.

The fee for registration of a new instrument enclosed with proof of payment of money is calculated according to the amount involved and on the basis of scale prescribed in the Act, subject to an instrument referring to the same transaction already registered earlier where the fee is limited to Rs. 15/-. The fee to be paid for deposit of a sealed cover containing a 'will' is Rs. 30/-, for opening of such cover besides the cost of copying the contents tha is charged according to the scale laid down in the table for granting of certified copies Rs. 30/-, for registration of a 'will' when opened Rs. 50/-, and for withdrawal of any sealed cover containing 'will' Rs. 30/-. When a 'will' is forwarded to any court under section 46 of the Act, it is to be accompanied by a memorandum as to fee for opening the cover and as to charges for copying.

Fee to be paid for registration of (i) certified copy of a decree or order of a court is Rs. 20/-, (ii) agreement for personal service is Rs. 10/-, (iii) any document whether rent, remuneration or hire paid partly in money and partly in kind, and the money value of the portion payable in kind not expressed is Rs. 10/-, and (iv) any document of a description not covered above is Rs. 10/-.

Fee for registration of documents such as re-lease, surrender of lease, revocation of trust and settlement deed of partnership, divorce, agreement deed of re-conveyance, dissolution of partnership and deed of cancellation (other than cancellation of 'will') may vary from Rs. 5/- to Rs. 200/-, depending upon the nature and value of the document.

Besides, the Act contains usual provision of checking or inspection or searching the documents like registers etc., with or without payment of requisite fee depending upon the nature of inspection.

Local Tax on Land and Buildings (House Tax)

The Lushai Hills District (Revenue Assessment) Regulation, 1953, as amended from time to time, provided for collection of annual tax on land and buildings/houses in the notified towns and house tax in rural areas. The Mizoram Revenue Assessment Regulation (Amendment) Act, 1994[83] provided for collection of annual tax with or without surcharge from every building in the notified town area. The rate of such tax for Assam-type residential building is Rs. 20/-, Assam-type residential building with independent flat or apartment is Rs. 20/- with surcharge of Rs. 10/- per flat or apartment, and for residential building of reinforced cement concrete or partly reinforced cement concrete is Rs. 30/- with surcharge of Rs. 20/- per flat or apartment. However, this is not applicable on buildings belonging to Government, public undertaking and institutions and such other buildings as the State Government may, by an order, exempt.

Taxes on Motor Vehicles including Passengers and Goods Tax

Taxes on motor vehicles are assessed and collected in accordance with the provisions of the Mizoram Motor Vehicles (Taxation) Act, 1996 using the rates fixed from time to time. Under Rule 90(6) of Mizoram Motor Vehicle Rules 1995, an entry fee of Rs. 500/- p.m. per vehicle is levied from vehicles entering Mizoram without National Permit or Tourist Permit. Road Toll is not levied in Mizoram. The prevailing rates of annual road tax on (i) private vehicles such as 2-wheeler below 90 kg weight is Rs. 80/-, 2-wheeler above 90 kg weight is Rs. 150/-, 3-wheeler is Rs. 250/-, light motor vehicle (LMV) below 14 HP is Rs. 500/-, above 14 HP is Rs. 600/-, light trailer is Rs. 100/-, medium trailer is Rs. 250/- and heavy trailer is Rs. 300/-, tractors below 2 MT is Rs. 125/-, tractor within 2 to 3 MT is Rs. 250/- and tractor above 3 MT is Rs. 700/-, vehicles used in transportation of goods is Rs. 840/- below 1 MT and additional Rs. 205/- for every additional ½ MT, for light crane Rs. 150/-, for medium crane Rs. 250/-, and for heavy crane Rs. 500/-, (ii) vehicles used as hired conveyance such as auto rickshaw Rs. 500/-, taxi cab (5 seater) Rs. 700/-, tourist taxi (5 seater) Rs. 2000/-, tourist bus at Rs. 300/- for every seat authorized, town bus and bazaar bus Rs. 100/- for every seat authorized, night bus at Rs. 150/- for every seat authorized, crane below 3 MT is Rs. 150/-, between 3 to 5 MT is Rs. 250/- and above 5 MT Rs. 500/-, prime earth mover in the range of Rs. 12000/- to Rs. 30000/-, (iii) composite tax on tourist taxi and tourist bus such as motor cab (6 seater) Rs. 300/- per quarter, maxi cab (7 to 13 seater) Rs. 3000/- per quarter, and omni bus (14 to 35 seater) Rs. 12000/- per quarter.

The annual tax rates on vehicles used for goods transport, depending on their carrying capacity in MT, below 8 years existence (plying inter-state) ranges between Rs. 800/- to Rs. 2900/-, above 8 years existence ranges between Rs. 600/- to Rs. 2600/-, below 8 years (plying within the State) ranges between Rs. 700/- to Rs. 2900/-, and above 8 years existence ranges between Rs. 500/- to Rs. 2600/-.

The annual tax rates on motor vehicles used for passenger transport such as auto rickshaw is Rs. 500/- for inter-state, and is Rs. 400/- for within the State, 4 seater vehicle is Rs. 800/- for inter-state, and is Rs. 600/- for within the State, and for more than 4 seater vehicle is Rs. 900/- for inter-state, and is Rs. 800/- for within the State. Similarly, the annual tax for a state carriage and bus plying on route below 40 km length is Rs. 1400/- and above 40 km length is Rs. 1800/-.

Land Revenue

Assessment and fixation of land revenue for land in rural area is done as per the provisions contained in para 3(1), 3(2), 3(11) and 3(12) of the Lushai Hills District (Revenue Assessment) Regulation, 1953 and also rule 29, 30 and 32 of the Mizo District (Agriculture Land) Rules, 1971 as promulgated by erstwhile Mizo District Council and amended from time to time. For assessment and fixation of annual land revenue, the land has been classified into five different grades based on their connectivity to road system, suitability of area, commercial use, and commercial crops grown. Land Ceiling Law is not enforced in the State. However, the standard economic holding of land in Mizoram is fixed at 30 bighas (4.00 Hectares) only and no exemption is given from payment of land revenue with reference to the size of holding.

The per bigha rate of annual land revenue for permanent settlement of agricultural land has been fixed for Grade-I at Rs. 25/-, for Grade-II at Rs. 20/-, for Grade-III at Rs. 15/-, and for Grade-IV and V at Rs. 10/-. However, for temporary settlement it has been fixed for Grade-I at Rs. 10/-, for Grade-II Rs. 8/-, for Grade-III at Rs. 7/-, and for Grade-IV at Rs. 5/-.

The assessment and fixation of land revenue for land in notified town area (Urban Land) is done as per the provisions contained in Rules 26, 27, 29 and 30 of the Mizo District (Land and Revenue) Rules, 1967. For this purpose the urban land has been divided into three categories based on their connectivity to road system, suitability of area for commercial centre, and location.

The per bigha rate of annual land revenue for permanent settlement land in notified town area has been fixed for Grade-I at Rs. 80/-, for Grade-II at Rs. 60/- and for Grade-III at Rs. 40/-.

The premium for conversion of agricultural land to non-agricultural uses[84] such as for shop and stall is raised at Rs. 200/- per site for Aizawl, Lunglei, Champhai and Kolasib towns, and at Rs. 100/- per site for other Sub-towns, and similarly, the premium for conversion of agricultural land to non-agricultural uses, such as residential house site is raised at Rs. 100/- per site for Aizawl, Lunglei, Champhai and Kolasib towns, and at Rs. 50/- per site for other sub-towns.

Other Taxes

Apart from the taxes discussed above some other taxes are also levied. Among these Shop tax[85] is levied at Rs. 150/- per shop p.a. for every shop in Aizawl town, and at Rs. 100/- per shop p.a. for every shop in other notified towns and in rural areas. Stall tax[86] is levied at Rs. 100/- per stall p.a. for every tea stall in Aizawl town, at Rs. 50/- per stall p.a. for tea stall in other notified towns and in rural areas. House tax[87] is levied at Rs. 2/- per house p.a. *Zoram Chhiah* tax[88] is levied at Rs. 50/- per family p.a. and Fish Pond tax[89] is levied at Rs. 50/- per holding p.a.

Tax Revenue

The position regarding collection of revenue from various taxes levied in Mizoram from 1990-91 to 2002-03 is given in Table 5.6. Figures 5.1 and 5.2, which revealed the following:

1. On the average over the years the relative share of sales tax was at 33 per cent, followed by profession tax 22 per cent, vehicle tax 14 per cent, state excise 13 per cent, land revenue 10 per cent, passenger and goods tax 5 per cent, entertainment tax 2 per cent and stamp and registration fee 1 per cent. The average share of different taxes is shown in Figure 5.1 as also the trend in various taxes has been shown in Figure 5.2.
2. It is satisfying to note that over the years the revenue from all the taxes and also over all has grown. Further while relative share of profession tax and land revenue has gone down, the sales tax has gone up. Other taxes remained more or less at the same level.
3. In 1990-91, the share of sales tax, profession tax and vehicle tax was more or less the same. But in 2002-03 the growth in sales tax being highest at 29.42 per cent crossed the growth of all other taxes and contributed more than half of State tax revenue for last two years. Profession tax, vehicle tax, state excise, and land revenue were next in order. Passenger and goods tax, entertainment tax, stamps and registration fee made little contribution. On the average total State around tax revenue grew at 18.25 per cent p.a. Further, it may be noted that growth in sales tax and entertainment tax was higher than the overall growth in State tax revenue. Similarly, growth in stamp and registration tax, vehicle tax, profession tax and land revenue was more or

Table 5.6: Revenue from Various Taxes Levied and Collected in Mizoram from 1990-91 to 2002-03 (*Rs. in lakh*)

Year	Profession tax	Land Revenue	Stamp and Registration	State Excise	Sales Tax	Vehicle Tax	Goods and Passenger Tax	Entertainment Tax	Total	Share in Central Taxes	Grand Total
1990-91	63.33 (18)	34.19 (10)	0.92 (0)	80.47(23)	67.52 (20)	61.17 (18)	28.77 (8)	6.71 (2)	343.08	301.00	644.08
1991-92	91.76 (27)	39.91 (12)	2.31 (1)	73.74 (22)	34.16 (10)	57.45 (17)	30.57 (9)	4.47 (1)	334.37	368.23	702.60
1992-93	94.63 (21)	32.43 (7)	1.19 (0)	76.62 (17)	152.17 (34)	57.05 (13)	27.59 (6)	3.51 (1)	445.19	437.18	882.37
1993-94	97.27 (22)	30.69 (7)	4.60 (1)	71.57 (16)	142.94 (32)	57.00 (13)	30.33 (7)	5.84 (1)	440.24	N.A.	440.24
1994-95	120.78 (26)	58.07 (13)	8.01 (2)	49.18 (11)	123.67 (27)	62.73 (14)	28.59 (6)	7.24 (2)	458.27	625.00	1083.27
1995-96	132.95 (23)	79.26 (14)	4.23 (1)	82.84 (14)	159.51 (28)	78.90 (14)	31.31 (5)	9.41 (2)	578.41	1650.49	2228.90
1996-97	159.69 (24)	79.57 (12)	2.38 (0)	88.99 (13)	198.72 (30)	92.52 (14)	30.60 (5)	14.44 (2)	666.91	2019.00	2685.91
1997-98	185.42 (24)	67.68 (9)	6.07 (1)	91.27 (12)	250.75 (32)	133.26 (17)	33.06 (4)	19.49 (2)	787.00	3145.00	3932.00
1998-99	213.47 (23)	103.67 (11)	9.22 (1)	90.08 (10)	286.66 (31)	153.02 (17)	34.38 (4)	29.05 (3)	919.55	2160.00	3079.55
1999-00	238.57 (22)	126.24 (12)	7.54 (1)	92.93 (9)	360.57 (34)	183.46 (17)	38.62 (4)	25.11 (2)	1073.04	2466.00	3539.04
2000-01	331.84 (23)	115.76 (8)	6.68 (0)	96.00 (7)	605.88 (42)	201.84 (14)	51.41 (4)	31.88 (2)	1441.29	N.A.	1441.29
2001-02	362.56 (19)	123.88 (6)	8.21 (0)	135.59 (7)	984.86 (52)	209.88 (11)	52.85 (3)	33.92 (2)	1911.75	N.A.	1911.75
2002-03	375.00 (13)	150.00 (5)	8.00 (0)	136.00 (5)	1800.00 (63)	300.00 (11)	50.00 (2)	35.00 (1)	2854.00	N.A.	2854.00
Average	189.79 (22)	80.10 (10)	5.34 (1)	89.64 (13)	397.49 (33)	126.79 (14)	36.01 (5)	17.39 (2)	942.55	1463.54	1955.77
Growth (%)	15.82	14.64	16.85	5.18	29.42	15.92	5.47	22.38	18.25	—	—
C. V.	55	49	52	26	119	59	25	67	75	—	—

Legend: S. D. = Standard Deviation, C. V. = Coefficient of Variation.

Note: Figures in parenthesis represent percentage of total.

Source: 1. Department of Finance, Government of Mizoram, Aizawl.

2. State Representation to the Twelfth Finance Commission on 1st June 2004, Government of Mizoram, p. 4.

3. Notes on various topics submitted to the Twelfth Finance Commission, March 2004, GOM, pp. 88-89.

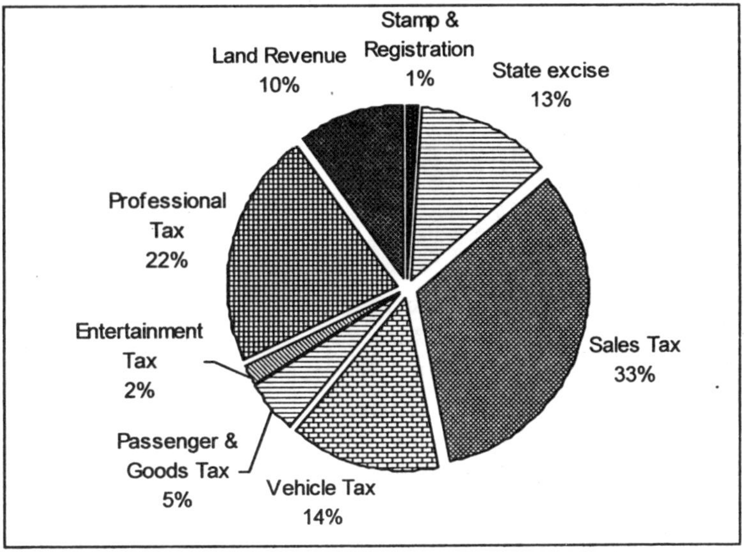

Figure 5.1: Average Share of Taxes in Mizoram from 1990-91 to 2002-03

less near to overall growth in state tex revenue. On the other hand, the growth in state excise, and passengers and goods tax was less. Variation in sales tax revenue (C.V. = 119) was higher than the variation in total tax revenue and the variation in other taxes was less than the variation in total tax revenue (C.V. = 75).

4. The increase in state excise revenue was not in tune with increase in total tax revenue. The slow growth in state excise may be attributed to State's policy of total prohibition since 20th February 1997 and as a result the State was deprived of a large chunk of excise revenue. Presently excise is levied only on liquor supplied to Army and Para military forces and in the areas of Autonomous District Councils *viz.*, Lai, Mara and Chakma.
5. Slow growth in passenger and goods tax, which is also an indicative of the status of goods transport business in the State is definitely a cause of worry. There were only 488 MMV trucks and 1182 HMV trucks in the State as on 31st March 2002[90].
6. Vehicle tax has increased to five fold while passenger and goods tax has increased by two fold. This shows that private (non-commercial) vehicles are increasing at faster pace. This again confirms that people of Mizoram possesses adequate purchasing

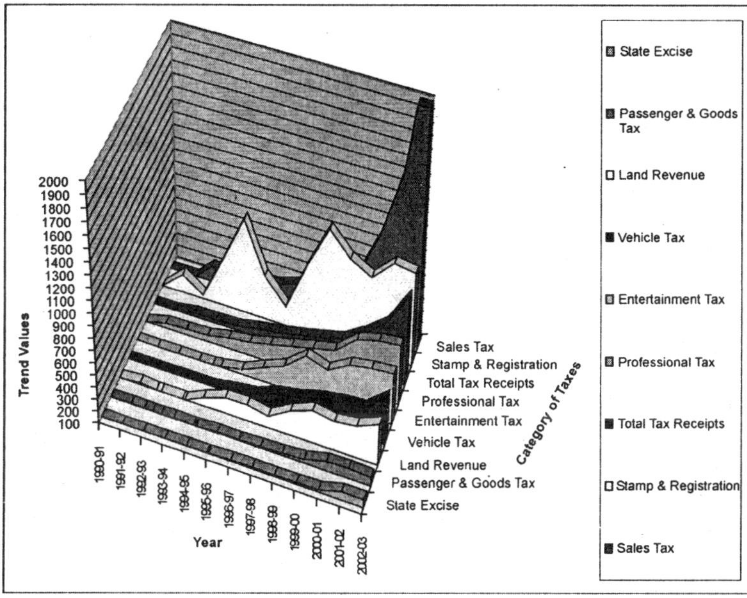

Figure 5.2: Trends in Various Taxes in Mizoram from 1990-91 to 2002-03

power. But growth in economy especially business and industry field has not grown well. They did not discount the opportunities that were available/existed in the State.

7. The size of entertainment industry in Mizoram was almost negligible.
8. Revenue from stamps and registration fee as a source of state revenue increased only after 1997-98 as the Registration Act, 1905 (Act XVI of 1908) was extended to Mizoram for the first time on 22nd April 1997. Earlier Mizo were exempted from payment of stamps and registration duty. Till 22nd April 1997 it was being realized from non-Mizo residing in the State. Similarly the provisions of Indian Stamp Act, 1899 were also made applicable on Mizo in Mizoram through the Indian Stamp (Mizoram Amendment) Act, 1995 with effect from 22nd April 1997.

Profession Tax and GSDP

Comparison of profession tax receipts and its contribution to GSDP (industry, construction, transport, trade, hotel and restaurants, banking and real estate and public administration) is shown in Table 5.7. and Figure 5.3.

Table 5.7: Growth in Profession Tax and Contribution to GSDP (Share of Industry, Construction, Transport, Trade, Hotel & Restaurants, Banking, Real Estate and Public Administration) from 1990-91 to 2002-03 (As on 31st March)

(Rs. in Lakh)

Year	Profession Tax Receipts			Share of Industry, Construction, Transport, Trade, Hotel & Restaurants, Banking, Real Estate, & Public Administration in GSDP		
	Amount	Indices	% of total tax	Amount	Indices	% of GSDP
1990-91	68.33	100	18	20681	100	61
1991-92	91.76	145	27	25151	122	54
1992-93	94.63	149	21	30300	147	57
1993-94	97.27	154	22	37402	181	53
1994-95	120.78	191	26	42683	206	58
1995-96	132.95	210	23	53646	259	57
1996-97	159.69	252	24	61381	297	57
1997-98	185.42	293	24	65103	315	58
1998-99	213.47	337	23	69699	337	56
1999-00	238.57	377	22	82114	397	58
2000-01	331.84	524	23	102064	494	58
2001-02	362.56	572	19	113970	551	59
2002-03	375.00	592	13	N. A.	N. A.	N.A.
Growth	15.82 %	Average	22	16.17 %	Average	57

Note: For indices the year 1990-91 is taken as base year.

Source: 1. Department of Finance, Government of Mizoram, Aizawl.
2. State Domestic Product of Mizoram-New Series, Directorate of Economics & Statistics, Aizawl.

The overall contribution of industry, construction, transport, trade, hotel and restaurants, banking, real estate, and public administration (derivatives to profession tax) at nearly 57 per cent of GSDP was high over the years from 1990-91 to 2001-02. All this indicated that the income level of the people of the State has increased. Table 5.7 and Figure 5.3 revealed that the growth in profession tax at 15.82 per cent and its derivative to GSDP at 16.17 per cent was more or less the same. Figure 5.3 also revealed that the growth in profession tax was above the corresponding growth in its derivative since the upward revision of profession tax rates with effect from 1st April 1997.

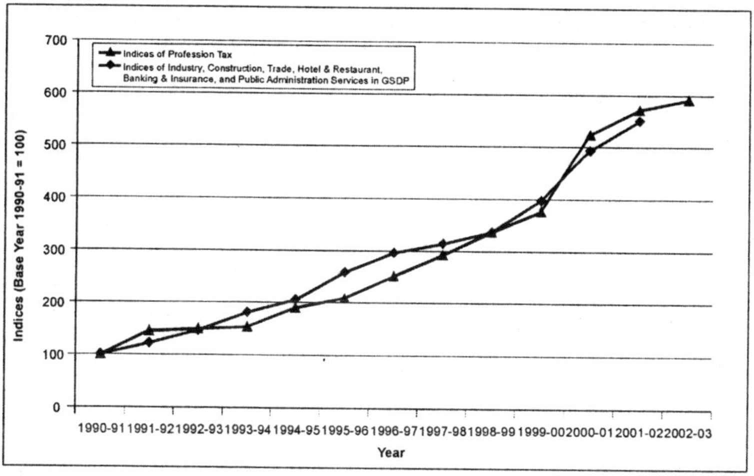

Figure 5.3: Growth in Profession Tax Receipts and Share of Industry, Construction, Trade, Hotel & Restaurant Services from 1990-91 to 2002-03

The industry, construction, transport, trade, hotel and restaurants, banking, real estate, and public administration being the major contributor to employment, the burden of profession tax has increased on it, which in the long run may adversely affect the growth of business and service sector as in the long-run upward revision of tax rates cannot be considered helpful in balanced growth of state economy. It is in this sense, the profession tax policy of the state is faulty and needs to be rationalized in the light of State's long term tax policy to ensure progressive tax collection with growing economy.

Sales Tax and GSDP

Comparison of sales tax with its contribution to GSDP (industry, construction, trade, hotel and restaurants) from 1990-91 to 2002-03 is given in Table 5.8 and Figure 5.4.

Among different sources of tax, sales tax registered highest increase, which was significant in size and volume, and had dominated over other sources of revenue since 1992-93. Though industry and trade are the major contributors of sales tax directly and construction indirectly, these are also important contributors to State GSDP. The relative share of industry in State GSDP had declined over the years from 6 per cent in 1990-91 to 1 per cent in 2001-02 [Appendix-5(A)]. The contribution

Table 5.8: Growth in Sales Tax and Contribution to GSDP (Share of Industry, Construction, Trade, Hotel & Restaurants) from 1990-91 to 2002-03 (As on 31st March)

(*Rs. in Lakh*)

Year	*Sales Tax Receipts*			*Share of Industry, Construction, Trade, Hotel & Restaurants in GSDP*		
	Amount	*Indices*	*% of total tax*	*Amount*	*Indices*	*% of GSDP*
1990-91	67.52	100	20	8757	100	26
1991-92	34.16	51	10	10457	120	23
1992-93	152.17	225	34	14123	161	27
1993-94	142.94	212	32	17027	194	24
1994-95	123.67	183	27	20142	230	27
1995-96	159.51	236	28	26969	308	29
1996-97	198.72	294	30	29957	342	28
1997-98	250.75	371	32	29738	340	26
1998-99	286.66	425	31	30221	345	24
1999-00	360.57	534	34	31698	362	22
2000-01	605.88	897	42	37367	427	21
2001-02	984.86	1459	52	41506	474	22
2002-03	1800.00	2666	63	N. A.	N. A.	N.A.
Growth	29.42%	Average	33	14.33 %	Average	25

Note: For indices the year 1990-91 is taken as base year.

Source: 1. Department of Finance, Government of Mizoram, Aizawl.

2. State Domestic Product of Mizoram—New Series, Directorate of Economics & Statistics, Aizawl.

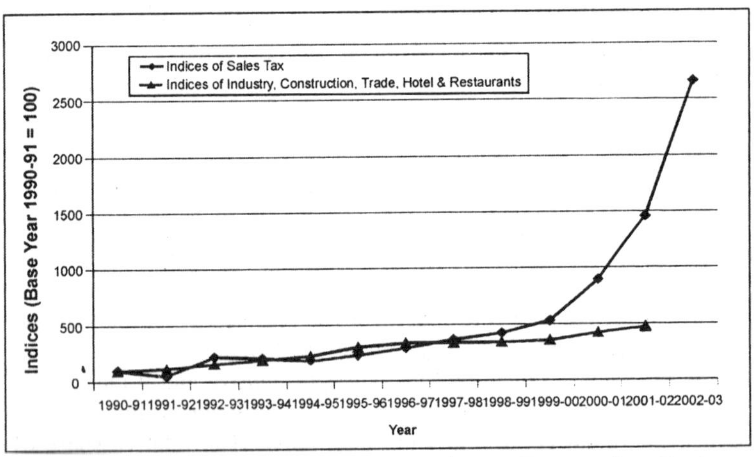

Figure 5.4: Growth in Sales Tax and Industry, Construction, Trade, Hotel and Restaurant Services from 1990-01 to 2002-03

of trade, hotel and restaurants in State GSDP consistently increased from 5 per cent in 1990-91 to 10 per cent in 2001-02 [Appendix-5(A)].

However, the growth in construction activity with respect to State GSDP fluctuated averaging at 11 per cent [Appendix-5(A)]. Till 1st November 1999, these sectors contributed nothing towards the growth in sales tax as the Mizoram Sales Tax Act 1989 could be implemented properly from 1st November 1999 only and before that it was under intermittent suspension since 1st April 1993. During this period sales tax only on POL products was realized. Further, there was an upward revision of sales tax rates effective from 1st October 2001 and the tax base was also widened bringing some more items in its ambit. Earlier hardware and building materials were being taxed at 4 per cent, i.e. below the level in other neighbouring states. It was revised upward to 8 per cent. Increase in sales tax and fall in the share of construction in GSDP may partly be attributed to this upward revision in sales tax rates.

Automobiles a fast growing trade had remained under taxed till 1st October 2001, when the sales tax rate was raised from 6 per cent to 12 per cent. Similarly, all types of machines were brought under the tax net at 8 per cent. The upward revision of sales tax rates may not be viewed as faulty, but frequent upward revision from long-term perspective cannot be considered fair.

Tax Receipts and GSDP

Comparison of tax receipts and GSDP from 1990-91 to 2002-03 has been presented in Table 5.9 and Figure 5.5, which revealed the following:

From 1990-91 to 2001-02, the State's tax revenue and GSDP increased 5.57 times and 5.65 times respectively. It may be observed from Figure 5.5 that the increase in tax revenue was always less than the increase in GSDP for all the years. However, both tend to converge; the increase in GSDP was more consistent (C.V. = 47 %) from year to year while the tax revenue fluctuated more (C.V. = 75 %) [Appendix-5(A)]. Increase in tax revenue was more than the increase in GSDP mainly due to upward revision of various tax rates during the period.

Mizoram Taxation Policy *vis-à-vis* Other Northeastern States

The position of per capita tax revenue to per capita NSDP in Mizoram from 1990-91 to 2001-02 is given in Table 5.10.

The Table 5.10 revealed that per capita tax to per capita NSDP on the average was 0.74 per cent. When compared to other Northeastern states, it

Table 5.9: Growth in Tax Revenue and GSDP from 1990-91 to 2002-03 (As on 31st March)

(*Rs. in Lakh*)

Year	*Total Tax Receipts*		*Total GSDP*	
	Amount	*Indices*	*Amount*	*Indices*
1990-91	343.08	100	34084	100
1991-92	334.37	97	46511	136
1992-93	445.19	130	53276	156
1993-94	440.24	128	71146	209
1994-95	458.27	134	73877	217
1995-96	578.41	169	93654	275
1996-97	666.91	194	107234	315
1997-98	787.00	229	112317	330
1998-99	919.55	268	124590	366
1999-00	1073.00	313	140939	414
2000-01	1441.30	420	176872	519
2001-02	1911.80	557	192417	565
2002-03	2854.00	832	N. A.	N. A.
Growth (%)	18.28		15.84	

Note: For indices the year 1990-91 is taken as base year.

Source: 1. Department of Finance, Government of Mizoram, Aizawl.

2. State Domestic Product of Mizoram-New Series, Directorate of Economics & Statistics, Aizawl.

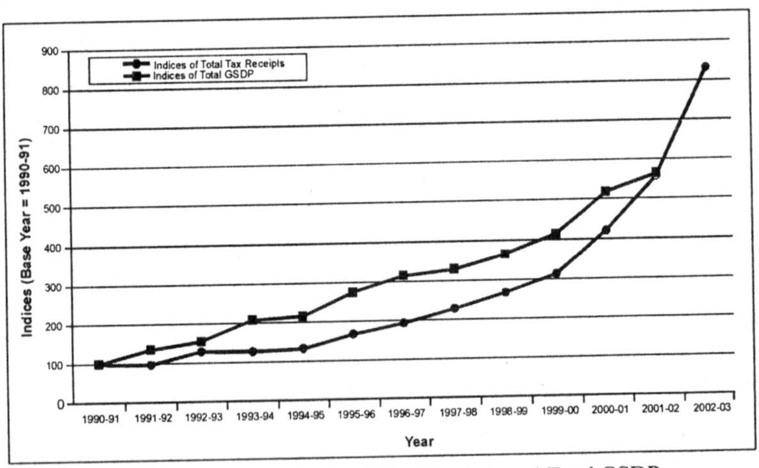

Figure 5.5: Growth in Total Tax Receipts and Total GSDP from 1990-91 to 2002-03

was the lowest. For Meghalaya the ratio was 6.9 per cent, Assam 6.5 per cent, Tripura 5.4 per cent, Nagaland 3.6 per cent, and Manipur 3 per cent for the year 1999-2000[91]. The annual average growth was 1.06 per cent. It may be understood that there was no growth in per capita tax payment in Mizoram. The people in Mizoram contributed least towards state's development among Northeastern region. This also indicated that there exists scope for raising revenue in the state. This confirmed the view expressed earlier that inspite of the introduction of new taxes and enforcement measures, the per capita tax revenue remained low signifying that though the people of Mizoram had adopted to tax culture even prior to the advent of British, presently they are under taxed both in terms of direct taxes as well as indirect taxes. This also indicated that there is an ample scope to tax them now. It may be explained partly by the State's desire to provide goods and services at lower rate as they are loaded with high transportation costs. On ideological ground the government does not favour giving sales tax number to non-Mizo as they may claim residency in the State. It may be recalled that the implementation of "the Mizoram Sales Tax Act, 1989," was opposed by business community in Mizoram and its intermittent suspension was due to unresolved issue involving grant of registration under the Act to the non-Mizo traders and the tax was finally lifted with effect from 1st April 1993[92].

Table 5.10: Per Capita Tax Revenue to Per Capita NSDP of Mizoram from 1990-91 to 2001-02

Year	*Per capita*		*Tax to NSDP*
	Tax (Rs.)	*NSDP (Rs.)*	*(percentage)*
1990-91	50.23	4474	1.12
1991-92	47.60	5941	0.80
1992-93	61.45	6599	0.93
1993-94	40.05	8318	0.48
1994-95	40.40	8793	0.46
1995-96	48.12	10953	0.44
1996-97	58.23	12210	0.48
1997-98	71.10	12393	0.57
1998-99	108.82	13479	0.81
1999-00	124.19	14909	0.83
2000-01	163.04	18491	0.88
2001-02	211.95	19704	1.08
Average			0.74
Growth (%)			1.06
Coefficient of Variation			0.32

Source: Compiled from State Domestic Product of Mizoram, Directorate of Economics and Statistics, 2004.

High Independence on Centre

The per capita devolution from Centre to Mizoram at 94 per cent as against for Nagaland 81 per cent, Tripura 76 per cent, Manipur 67 per cent, Meghalaya 66 per cent, and Assam 65 per cent for the year 1999-2000 was highest among the Northeastern States and for the whole country.

Table 5.11: Central Assistance as Proportion to North-Eastern States' Total Receipts from 1997-98 to 2001-02

(*Rs. in crores*)

Year	*Total Receipts*	*Central Assistance*	*Central Assistance to Total Receipts (%)*
1997-98	679.89	626.27	92
1998-99	773.08	727.70	94
1999-00	860.84	808.76	94
2000-01	828.22	773.42	93
2001-02	867.79	803.80	93

Source: Notes on Various Topics Submitted to Twelfth Finance Commission, Government of Mizoram, March 2004, pp. 88-89.

Shukla Commission Report (Transforming the North-East: High Level Commission Report, 1997) commented: "The performance of the North-East states in mobilizing additional resources for development has been poor". Efforts should be made to reduce this dependence by raising the rates of tax and through effective tax management.

Administration of Taxes

The desired objectives of a tax can be achieved only when it is properly administered. No amount of fineness of a tax law or refining its economic attributes can help if it is not adequately administered. Poor administration of tax laws leads to widening the gap between intention and implementation and the net results remain unproductive if not counter productive, and tax evasion and mass avoidance may ensue. In this sense, it could be rightly argued that tax administration is tax policy in practice. It is important to realize that failure to properly administer a tax defeats its very purpose and threatens the canon of equity, because full payment of tax is made only by those who cannot or do not want to avoid it. Thus, a badly administered tax further increases or encourages evasion of tax affecting adversely the morale of honest taxpayers. Good and efficient administration of tax law is, therefore, of paramount importance.

The Government of Mizoram has appointed Commissioner of Taxes as the overall authority for tax administration in the State. Commissioner is assisted by Deputy Commissioners of Taxes, Appellate Commissioners of Taxes, Assistant Commissioners of Taxes, Superintendents of Taxes, and Inspectors of Taxes to facilitate the assessment and realization of taxes.

Enforcement of the tax in the field is done by Superintendents of Taxes with area or territorial jurisdiction, which may vary according to trade/business concentration. All areas under Lunglei district and Chhimtuipui district are placed under the jurisdiction of one Superintendent of Taxes with headquarters at Lunglei and other areas presently under the districts of Aizawl, Aizawl "E" and Aizawl "W" are divided into two tax administrative circles with headquarters at Aizawl. Two unit offices at Serchhip and Saiha headed by Inspector of Taxes have been put into operation with a view to reduce the workload of the administrative circles and to relieve the public of the problems of paying taxes from areas far from the tax district headquarters. A border check gate at Vairengte has been setup with a view to preventing evasion of taxes. The rationale for establishing check post lies in the need of monitoring the flow of goods into the Sate through the main artery of Aizawl-Silchar road for ensuring the recovery of sales tax and other taxes. In addition to sales tax work, the check gate is required to ensure payment of passengers and goods tax by owners of taxable vehicles plying in and out of the State through border.

Every person who is liable to pay the tax is required to submit to the assessing authority a return in the prescribed form by 30th June, following the end of financial year (due date). However, in case of profession tax payable by a person, who is in the employment of Government or Local Authority or Firm or Company or Association of Persons, need not file a return separately. In this case, the employer is under obligation to make deduction of tax at source from employee's salary, and remit the same to treasury along with a consolidated return.

Failure on the part of an assessee without having reasonable cause to submit any return required under the law in due time, or submit a false return, or neglect of compliance without giving reasonable cause, or evading payment of tax, or concealing the tax, is liable to penalty.

Any person aggrieved by an order of the assessing authority may appeal in prescribed manner to the Appellate Commissioner of Taxes within 60 days from the date of service of said order. The Commissioner of Taxes is the highest administrative authority on the matter and can call for examination of records of any proceedings that has taken place under the Act against an assessee by any officer subordinate to him and may revise after enquiry by passing an appropriate order after giving reasonable opportunity of being heard to the party concerned. In cases of escaped tax, an assessing authority at any time within three years from the end of financial year for which the assessee is liable to tax under the Act may serve a notice of demand. Either party may initiate rectification of mistake at any time within 3 years from the date of assessment order.

There is a provision of penalty u/s 22 of the Mizoram Sales Tax Act as regards concealment of turnover and evasion of tax. But, it has been observed that majority of dealers do not keep carbon copy or second copy of invoices/sale bills except for goods of high value. This creates doubt as to correct realization of sales tax. Further, majority of dealers do not keep proper accounting and in absence of relevant accounting records how precisely an assessment can be made to ensure that the tax so realized is accurate is in question. Here it is worth mentioning that there were only 392 regular assesses against a total registration of 452 dealers under Mizoram Sales Tax Act 1989 and 1826 dealers under Central Sales Tax Act, 1956 as on 31st March 2002. Further, under Rule 94 of Mizoram Sales Tax Rules, 1990, every dealer is required to list in writing the items being dealt that are exempted from sales tax in Schedule-I, and display the same at sales counter. But, in practice this provision has not been followed.

In Mizoram, it may be expressed with regret, that administration of tax laws has not been given due importance. The collection agency had its roots in the Land Revenue and Settlement Department set up soon after the inception of Union Territory status, and the arrangement continued until a separate department was established in 1983. While the functional activities of the Department were bifurcated at the Commissioner level, the institutional activities relating to the pattern of internal organization at the administrative level received no change. The organizational leadership of the Taxation Department in Mizoram at the Commissioner level is from the beginning occupied by officers drawn from the IAS or other central services officers in ex-officio capacity. The arrangement of holding the post on ex-officio basis was unavoidable because of the absence of a regular post of Commissioner in the Department. In short, the entire administration of the tax laws is placed under the direct supervision of the Commissioner who, in addition to other works under his charge, holds it in ex-officio capacity. Moreover, as the officer is from other service cadre, there are functional problems in administering the tax laws, at least initially. For it takes some time for the officer to know the working of the Department. Experience during the past gave an indication of inadequate attention given to the administration of tax-laws in the State.

Tax Compliance in Business and Industry

To determine the status of tax compliance in business and industry the entrepreneurs were asked to give information about tax registration, tax payment, etc. in the survey. It was observed from the replies that nearly 54 per cent (70 out of 130) industrial entrepreneurs were registered under Mizoram Sales Tax Act and 46 per cent (60 out of 130) of them were registered under Central Sales Tax Act. About 46 per cent (60 out of 130) entrepreneurs paid sales tax in time but the rest did not clear the sales tax liability in time. It is interesting to note that only 31 per cent (40 out of 130) were registered under both, MST Act and CST Act. Thus about 15 per cent entrepreneurs though registered under CST Act for the purpose of inter-state trade did not pay any sales tax neither under CST Act nor under MST Act. It may be concluded from the above that sales tax administration in Mizoram was lax.

Nearly 46 per cent (60 out of 130) industrial entrepreneurs were registered for profession tax. However, none deducted profession tax from the salaries and wages of their employees and did not remit; perhaps they were not aware of their responsibility as employer in this respect.

NOTES

1 Fiscal Management through Tax Measures, *Interim Report on Administrative Reforms*, Government of Mizoram, 1998, p. 245.
2. Computations are based on the revenue figures, *Interim Report on Administrative Reforms*, *Ibid*, p. 245.
3. Compiled by Public Finance Statistics, *Interim Report on Administrative Reforms*, *Ibid*, p. 245.
4. Government of India figure, *Interim Report on Administrative Reforms*, *Ibid*, p. 245.
5. Kohli, Ritu, *Kautilya's Political Theory*, Deep and Deep Publications, New Delhi, 1995, p. 102.
6. Dikshitar, V.R.R., *The Mauryan Polity*, Motilal Banarsidas, Delhi, 1932, p. 141.
7. Kohli, Ritu, *Kautilya's Political Theory*, *op. cit.*, p. 113.
8. Prasad, D. Ravindra, Prasad, V.S., Satyanarayana, P., *Administrative Thinkers*, Sterling Publishers, Delhi, 1989, p. 24.

9. Banerjee, Parmarthanath, *Public Administration in Ancient India*, Uppal Publishing House, Delhi, 1985, p. 181.
10. Kohli, Ritu: *Kautilya's Political Theory*, *op. cit.*, p. 108.
11. Dikshitar, V.R.R., *The Mauryan Polity*, *op. cit.*, pp. 147-48.
12. Rao, M.V. Krishna, *Studies in Kautilya*, Munshi Ram Manoharlal, Delhi, 1958, p. 213.
13. Kohli, Ritu, *Kautilya's Political Theory*, *op. cit.*, p. 108.
14. Rao, M.V. Krishna, *Studies in Kautilya*, *op. cit.*, 1958, p. 214.
15. Vaish, M.C., *Money, Banking, Trade and Public Finance*, New Age International (P) Ltd., Publishers, New Delhi, 3rd edition, 1997, p. 707.
16. Smith, Adam, *The Wealth of Nations*, Book V, Chapter-II, 1776 (http://www.bized.ac.uk/virtual/economy/library/economist/smith.htm)
17. *Ibid.*
18. Vaish, M.C., *Money, Banking, Trade and Public Finance*, *op. cit.*, p. 706.
19. Bhattacharjee ,P.R., *The Problem of Ensuring Financial Efficiency in the North-Eastern States*, Dialogue, Vol. 4, No. 1, p. 59.
20. *Ibid*, p. 65.
21. *Ibid*, p. 60.
22. Antonio De Viti De Macro: *First Principles of Public Finance*, reprinted 1950, p. 130.
23. Musgrave, Richard A., *The Theory of Public Finance*, 1959, pp. 211-13.
24. Vaish M.C., *Money, Banking, Trade and Public Finance*, *op. cit.*, p. 707.
25. Fiscal Management through Tax Measures, Interim Report on Administrative Reforms, *op. cit.*, p. 245.
26. Parry, N.E., *A Monograph on Lushai Custom and Ceremonies*, Reprint Aizawl, 1976, Ch. I, p. 3. Quoted in Lalrimawia, *Mizoram-History and Cultural Identity*, Spectrum Publications, Guwahati, 1995, p. 91.
27. Art and Culture Department, *Mizoram District Gazetteers*, Government of Mizoram, 1989, p. 239.
28. Rev. Lalsawma, '*Revival—The Mizo Way*,' p. 109.
29. Carey, B.C., The Chin Hills Regulation—1890. Quoted in Chatterjee, Dr. Suhas, *A History of Mizo Economy*, Vol. 1, *op. cit.*, p. 184.
30. A.S. Home B., July, 1905, Nos. 1601-16. Quoted in Lalrimawia, *Mizoram-History and Cultural Identity*, *op. cit.*, p. 92.
31. *Ibid*, August, 1906, Nos. 452-74, File No. 1G/1G, Genl B. quoted in Lalrimawia, *Ibid.*
32. *Ibid*, October, 1909, Nos. 36-37, File No. 1G/1G, Genl Misc. B. Quoted in Lalrimawia, *Ibid.*
33. McCall, A.G., District Cover (Lushai Hills), pp. 98-99. Quoted in Lalrimawia: *Mizoram-History and Cultural Identity*, p. 93.
34. A.S., Pol. B, December 1930, Nos. 651-662; *Rules regarding succession of Sailo chiefs and clans in the Lushai Hills* (*Notes and Orders*). Quoted in Lalrimawia, *Mizoram: History and Cultural Identity*, *op. cit.*, p. 93.
35. Chatterjee, Dr. Suhas, *A History of Mizo Economy*, Vol. 1, *op. cit.*, p. 183.

36. McCall, A.G., District Cover (Lushai Hills), p. 101. Quoted in Lalrimawia, *Mizoram: History and Cultural Identity, op. cit.* p. 93.
37. A.S. Home B, August 1903, Nos. 351-370, File No. G. Quoted in Lalrimawia: *Mizoram-History and Cultural Identity, op. cit.* p. 93.
38. *Ibid*, July, 1905, Nos. 1601-16. Quoted in Lalrimawia, *Ibid,* p. 92.
39. McCall, A. G., *op. cit.* quoted in Lalrimawia, *Mizoram-History and Cultural Identity, op. cit.* p. 93.
40. *Ibid.*
41. *Ibid.*
42. A.S., Pol B, September 1933, Nos. 862-74. Quoted in Lalrimawia, *Mizoram-History and Cultural Identity, op. cit.*, p. 94.
43. A.S., Pol B, August 1921, Nos. 15-16, XIV, *Impressed Coolies*. Quoted in Lalrimawia, *Mizoram: History and Cultural Identity, op. cit.*, p. 94.
44. Art and Culture Department, *Mizoram District Gazetteers, op. cit.*, p. 239.
45. Goswami, B.B., *Social and Political Institution of the Mizo,* Seminar on Social and Political Institutions of the Hill People of NE India, ASI and NEICSSR, Shillong, 4th-5th July, 1977, p. xiii. Quoted in Dutta, P.S., *India's North-East: A Study in Transition*, Har-Anand Publications, New Delhi, 1992, p. 101.
46. *Ibid*, p. 12. Quoted in Dutta, P.S., *Ibid.*, p. 101.
47. The Lushai Hills District (Reduction of Fathang) Act, 1953.
48. *Ibid.*
49. Art and Culture Department, *Mizoram District Gazetteers, op. cit.*, p. 240.
50. Goswami, B.B., *Social and Political Institution of the Mizo*, Seminar on Social and Political Institutions of the Hill People of NE India, *op. cit.*, pp. xiii and 5. Quoted in Dutta, P.S., *op. cit.*, p. 101.
51. *Ibid*, p. 5. Quoted in Dutta, P.S., *Ibid.*
52. *Ibid*, p. xxiv. Quoted in Dutta, P.S., *Ibid*, p. 102.
53. Sen, D., Early History of the Lushai with Special Reference to Lushai Chiefs, *Social Research*, Vol. 4, No. 3-4, 1984, pp. 14-15.
54. Dutta, P.S., *India's North-East: A Study in Transition*, Har-Anand Publications, New Delhi, 1992, p. 102.
55. Lalrimawia, Historic Migration of the Mizo, Proceedings to the NEI History Association, 1981, pp. 23-31.
56. Dutta, P.S., *India's North-East: A Study in Transition, op. cit.*, p.102.
57. A.S. Home B., August, 1903, Nos. 351-370, File No. G. Quoted in Lalrimawia, *Mizoram-History and Cultural Identity, op. cit.*, p. 92.
58. Art and Culture Department, *Mizoram District Gazetteers, op. cit.*, p. 242.
59. Notes on Various Topics submitted to Twelfth Finance Commission, Government of Mizoram, March 2004, p. 10.
60. Chatterjee, Dr. Suhas, *Mizoram: Encyclopedia*, Vol. II, Jaico Publishing House, Mumbai, 1990, p. 419.
61. Art and Culture Department, *Mizoram District Gazetteers, op. cit.*, p. 249.

62. Fiscal Management through Tax Measures, *Interim Report on Administrative Reforms, op. cit.*, pp. 246-47.
63. Art and Culture Department, *Mizoram District Gazetteers, op. cit.*, p. 243.
64. *Ibid*, pp. 245-46.
65. Notes on Various Topics submitted to Twelfth Finance Commission, *op. cit.*, p. 24.
66. Art and Culture Department, *Mizoram District Gazetteers, op. cit.*, p. 249.
67. *Ibid*, p. 246.
68. *Ibid.*
69. *Ibid*, p. 247.
70. *Ibid*, p. 248.
71. *Ibid*, pp. 247-48.
72. *Ibid*, p. 249.
73. Notes on Various Topics submitted to Twelfth Finance Commission, *op. cit.*, p. 17.
74. *Ibid.*, p. 16.
75. *Ibid*, pp. 23-24.
76. *Ibid*, p. 25.
77. Department of Taxation, "*The Mizoram Sales Tax Act, 1989*," Government of Mizoram, p. 13.
78. Notes on Various Topics submitted to TFC, *op. cit.*, p. 22.
79. *Ibid*, p. 23.
80. *Ibid*, p. 30.
81. *Ibid*, p. 15.
82. *Ibid*, p. 11.
83. *Ibid*, p. 9.
84. *Ibid.*
85. *Ibid*, p. 3.
86. *Ibid.*
87. *Ibid.*
88. *Ibid.*
89. *Ibid.*
90. Directorate of Economics and Statistics, *Statistical Handbook, Mizoram, 2002*, Government of Mizoram, p. 104.
91. Jayanta, Madhab, *Commentary on the Fiscal Situation of the North-Eastern States*, Dialogue, Vol. 4, No. 1, July-September 2002, p. 56.
92. Notes on Various Topics submitted to TFC, *op. cit.*, p. 17.

6

PROBLEMS OF BUSINESS AND INDUSTRY IN MIZORAM

The Scenario

Planned economic development of Mizoram began from 1972 when it became a Union Territory. In 1971-72, total plan outlay for Mizoram was Rs.2.05 crore, which increased more than seven times in 1973-74. Since then, the State's plan outlay in absolute terms has kept rising at a rapid stride outdoing other States to reach a maximum level of per capita revenue receipts at Rs. 8399 in 1995-96 as against the national average of Rs. 1494[1].

Estimate of Gross State Domestic Product (GSDP) is one of the most important single economic indicator to measure the over all economic development of a State. It is the estimate of value of all goods and services produced within the State during a reference period of one year. The per capita State Domestic Product (SDP) is used to determine both the absolute and relative performance of economy in a State. It facilitates the work of policy makers, planners and administrators. The Net State Domestic Product (NSDP) at factor cost includes all factor incomes originating within the boundaries of a State. As per the Directorate of Economics and Statistics (DES), Government of Mizoram, estimates of GSDP and NSDP with the new base year 1993-94 on the lines, concept, coverage and methodology as recommended by Central Statistical Organization (CSO), Government of India, could not be estimated at constant price due to some technical deficiencies for Mizoram. Hence, SDP reported is related to current prices only.

The relative share of primary, secondary and tertiary sector in the State NSDP and per capita income at current prices in Mizoram for the period from 1980-81 to 2001-02 are given in Table 6.1 which revealed the following:

It may be seen from Table 6.1 that the NSDP at factor cost at current price in 2001-02 was estimated at Rs. 1,77,730 lakh as against Rs. 6,218 lakh in 1980-81, which had increased nearly 28.6 times over the years, marking average annual growth of 17.75 per cent. The per capita NSDP at factor cost and at current price was estimated at Rs. 19704 in 2001-02 as against Rs. 1289 in 1980-81, which also registered an average annual growth of 14.40 per cent.

The share of primary sector in State NSDP was highest in 1991-92 and the same was the trend in its components also in 2001-02, but, then declined continuously. It contributed in State NSDP on the average at 32.41 per cent from 1980-81 to 2001-02 recording an increase of 16.74 per cent p.a.

The secondary sector, which include manufacturing, construction, electricity, gas and water supply achieved an annual growth of 15.77 per cent p.a. and made an overall contribution of 13.82 per cent in State NSDP. The relative share of construction was always higher than that of manufacturing. Both the registered and unregistered manufacturing contributed to the State NSDP on the average at 3.10 per cent. But, the share came down significantly since 1997-98 in spite of increase in the number of registered and unregistered SSIs in the State, because the so called growth in number of industries was on paper only. All the State PSUs incurred huge loss year after year and more specially MIFCO, which ultimately produced nothing. Further, the units registered as SSIs were actually engaged in trading, as is indicated by poor per unit investment in fixed assets (Rs. 1.02 lakh) lower than the normal investment by a trading concern.[2]

The tertiary sector included transport, storage, communication, trade, hotel and restaurant, banking, insurance, real estate, traveling, business services, public administration and other services, registered a growth of 18.78 per cent p.a. and contributed in the State NSDP on the average at 53.77 per cent over the years.

However, Mizoram continued to remain an industrially least developed State due to persistent inhibiting factors. Due to the absence of any large industry, small scale and tiny industries played a key role in the economy of the State. Upto March 2002 the total number of registered small-scale industrial units (SIDO) was 4,770 with a total employment of 26,629 persons and investment in fixed assets Rs. 6,110 lakh[3]. These industries had attained annual production of Rs. 14,950 lakh. The total number of units registered under Khadi and Village industries were 5772 upto March 2001.[4]

Table 6.1: Relative Share of Primary, Secondary and Tertiary Sector in State NSDP from 1980-81 to 2001-02

(Figures in Percentage)

Year	Primary Sector					Secondary Sector				Tertiary Sector							Total NSDP (Rs. in lakh)	Per Capita Income (Rs.)
	Agriculture	Forestry	Fishing	Mining & Quarrying	Total of Primary Sector	Manufac-turing	Construc-tion	Electricity, Gas & Water	Total of Secondary Sector	Transport, & Storage	Trade, Hotel & Restaurant	Banking & Insurance	Real Estate, & Business Services	Public Administ-ration	Other Service	Total of Tertiary sector		
1980-81	24.38	4.39	3.57	0.00	32.34	2.52	16.92	-2.43	17.02	1.67	7.08-	0.53	13.77	15.47	12.13	50.64	6218	1289
1981-82	21.41	5.02	3.78	0.00	30.22	2.94	16.92	-3.48	16.37	1.91	8.38	0.77	14.26	15.89	12.19	53.40	7005	1383
1982-83	19.61	4.03	4.03	0.00	27.67	2.43	15.85	-5.65	12.63	2.14	8.11	0.93	15.16	17.50	15.86	59.70	7765	1471
1983-84	19.49	3.85	5.04	1.05	29.43	2.81	14.95	-4.24	13.51	2.03	8.64	1.01	13.91	17.08	14.39	57.06	9471	1724
1984-85	22.22	4.42	3.93	1.78	32.36	2.94	14.12	-3.78	13.28	2.00	9.68	0.94	12.03	16.40	13.31	54.37	12199	2139
1985-86	27.18	4.15	3.54	2.04	36.92	1.12	15.97	-3.83	13.26	2.20	10.96	1.16	10.52	13.65	11.33	49.83	15725	2658
1986-87	32.99	3.32	1.63	2.01	39.96	3.26	15.01	-4.25	14.01	1.08	9.62	1.26	9.83	15.12	9.11	46.03	19413	3165
1987-88	28.44	9.25	2.70	1.69	42.08	3.04	15.65	-4.76	13.93	2.11	8.79	1.26	8.32	14.46	9.06	43.99	25886	4077
1988-89	26.55	3.30	2.98	1.62	34.44	4.85	16.94	-4.53	17.26	2.91	8.21	1.36	9.59	14.27	11.95	48.29	26007	4026
1989-90	29.90	2.94	3.01	0.05	35.90	5.65	14.19	-2.37	17.46	4.13	5.74	1.72	9.83	14.24	10.98	46.64	28076	4135
1990-91	23.85	3.17	2.88	2.30	32.21	5.78	14.93	-2.79	17.93	5.80	5.39	1.81	10.52	15.87	10.47	49.87	30560	4474
1991-92	32.21	3.84	2.57	2.14	40.77	6.25	11.26	-3.22	14.30	4.04	5.49	1.30	8.81	16.43	8.87	44.93	41733	5941
1992-93	29.75	2.20	2.30	0.44	34.68	6.34	13.93	-2.56	17.71	4.02	7.06	1.34	8.93	15.13	11.12	47.61	47810	6599
1993-94	27.73	3.71	1.66	0.12	33.23	2.74	7.09	-0.39	9.45	1.13	16.47	1.06	11.33	15.22	12.10	57.32	61809	8318
1994-95	29.38	1.02	1.15	0.24	31.79	3.16	10.92	-0.56	13.52	1.09	14.41	1.07	11.59	15.39	11.13	54.69	67178	8793
1995-96	24.65	4.31	1.13	0.24	30.34	3.13	10.83	-0.40	13.56	1.18	16.08	1.07	10.29	14.55	12.94	56.10	85874	10953
1996-97	27.45	1.27	1.25	0.24	30.21	3.14	11.36	-0.53	13.98	1.31	14.61	1.15	10.29	15.19	13.26	55.81	98293	12210
1997-98	27.50	0.67	1.27	0.45	29.89	1.59	10.62	-1.08	11.13	1.52	15.36	1.29	11.50	15.89	13.42	58.98	102239	12393
1998-99	27.25	0.80	1.23	0.11	29.39	1.23	10.50	-0.23	11.51	1.34	13.39	1.48	12.68	15.08	15.14	59.10	113896	13479
1999-00	21.63	0.60	1.02	0.52	23.78	1.22	11.53	0.71	13.46	1.37	10.50	1.48	14.28	17.78	17.36	62.76	128818	14909
2000-01	27.29	0.55	0.97	0.12	28.93	1.06	8.29	-1.59	7.77	1.77	12.39	1.78	14.07	17.93	15.36	63.31	163461	18491
2001-02	24.55	0.49	1.28	0.21	26.52	0.96	10.87	-0.81	11.02	1.87	10.37	2.01	14.59	18.66	14.96	62.45	177730	19704
Average	26.16	3.06	2.41	0.79	32.41	3.10	13.12	-2.40	13.82	2.21	10.31	1.26	11.64	15.78	12.56	53.77	58053	7379
Growth	18.6	5.5	9.3	1.87	16.74	14	14.4	-8.2	15.77	15.7	20.97	21.57	17.81	18.15	18.9	18.78	17.75	14.40

Source: Compiled from State Domestic Product of Mizoram, Directorate of Economics & Statistics, Government of Mizoram, Aizawl, 2004 (New-Series), pp.16-18.

Problems of Business and Industry in Mizoram

The overall position of business and industry in Mizoram cannot be regarded as satisfactory. Actually, there were no industries in the State worth mentioning. There are no medium or large-scale industries. Only small, tiny, cottage and village industrial units existed. The Directorate of Industries, Directorate of Sericulture, Zoram Industrial Development Corporation Ltd. (ZIDCO), North-Eastern Development Finance Corporation Ltd. (NEDFi), Small Industries Service Institute (SISI), North-Eastern Industrial Consultancy Ltd. (NECON), Industrial Development Bank of India (IDBI), Small Industries Development Bank of India (SIDBI), Mizoram Khadi and Village Industries Board (MKVIB), and Commercial Banks share the responsibility of promotion and development of industries in Mizoram.

However, none of the sectors of economy was trouble free. A State of nearly 9 lakh people spread over 21087 sq. km. area, out of which about 75 per cent is forest lacked proper environment for industrialization. Generally, places with high density of population and with means of livelihood other than agriculture and government jobs are conducive for industrial development. But, the problem of sparse population with low density was compounded by the absence of proper roads and transport system. These problems combined together did not encourage the growth of industries. The same was the case with various forms of modern business.

The problems of business and industry in the State may conveniently be divided under seven headings *viz.*, (i) Problems relating to business, (ii) Problems relating to industries, (iii) Problems relating to business finance, (iv) Problems relating to taxation, (v) Problems relating to entrepreneurship, (vi) Problems relating to infrastructure, and (vii) Problems general in nature.

These problems are discussed here in the above order.

(i) Problems Relating to Business

Business like all other economic activities in the State is in nascent stage. State being small the overall size of market is small, and the size of most enterprises is also small. Business is in the hands of Mizo, as there is no provision in existing Regulations for non-local outside people to operate business in their own name. Except for food items there is no local production, as such most of the items are procured from outside mostly from Silchar, Guwahati and Kolkata. Some foreign goods are also sold, which are procured through non-formal channels.

In the above environment business in Mizoram faces a number of problems that can be divided into two parts, *viz.*, problems of internal trade and problems of external trade, which are discussed below:

Problems of Internal Trade

The problems of internal trade are as follows:

1. *Small Sized Markets*: Compared to other States the markets in Mizoram are small, as the group of users of goods and services (working group of population) is small. This comes in the way of expansion of trade and business.
2. *Low Purchasing Power*: Though the propensity to spend and consume is more in Mizoram, the purchasing power of customers is low because of their relatively low level of savings. The benefit of calculative spending is lacking among people in general. While money is available in their hands, they do not defer the needs, no matter be it a spending on necessity or transport (hiring taxi) or capital or luxury or consumer durables or otherwise. They live in present and not in future. They are not induced to save even under section 88 of Income Tax Act, 1961, as Mizo are not subject to it.
3. *Problems of Marketing*: People are not aware about the use of products as they hardly care for the instructions/directions about the use of product written on its wrapper in English. They feel that these instructions should better be written in Mizo if necessary. Customers are ignorant about better quality products and run after one particular brand only. Any change in fashion may lead to accumulation of obsolete goods. Due to small sized markets in the State middlemen collect agricultural produce at the doorstep of producer at substantial discount. Poor scope of marketing affected the economic activity in the state and caused a substantial portion of the produce to be directed for family consumption[5].
4. *Competition from Foreign Goods*: The imported goods from Myanmar and Nepal under 'informal channel,' which leads to saving in duties and taxes that make them cheap, results into high cost of Indian goods. Foreign goods are the obvious choice of consumers in such cases. However, this hurts domestic trade.

5. *Sellers' Market*: Marketing plays a vital role in the development and growth of an enterprise. Marketing involves creation of customers and their orientation backed by integrated and long run customer welfare, which are key to success in achieving organizational goals. Marketing has been accepted as a means for the betterment of society. From economic and social angle taken together, one would agree with Paul Mazur that marketing is the delivery of standard of living. Nevertheless, the marketing practices in Mizoram have no such conceptual base. The Mizoram market is a seller's market. The gulf between buyer and seller continues to be significantly wide. This is an alarming situation, which needs to be addressed systematically by bringing in the concept of marketing, which ultimately may revamp the whole scenario of business, trade and industry. This problem can be solved with increased competition among market players.
6. *Benami Trade*: *Benami trade* practice exists in Mizoram as there are no rules governing trade in the State, more specially trade by Non-Tribals. This showed that the State had no clear policy as regards trade by Non-Tribals. The inner-line regulations also do not provide enough scope for them. Moreover, the Indian Partnership Act, 1932 is yet to extend to Mizoram. In view of the above a Non-Tribal can trade under *Benami* arrangements only, because formally he/she cannot enter into a contract of partnership. Mizo in general are not exposed to company form of organization and partnership is not possible. This is the reason why the number of proprietorship firms is more. Even though a partnership in reality among two Mizo also being carried either as proprietorship or cooperative society (wherever formal registration is required).
7. *Higher Profit Margin*: The vendors in Mizoram generally charge higher price for a product they deal. To an extent, this is due to higher transportation cost involved. However, this is not a valid reason in case of goods bought from neighbouring countries, as the physical distance is not much. As an illustration, it may be cited that China made pencil battery (cells) in Delhi are available at almost half the prices of Mizoram. Similarly, Korean blankets are available in Mizoram at almost the same price as elsewhere in the country. One fails to understand the well-knitted theory behind higher prices charged in Mizoram. Perhaps this is the reason that is why the

goods from Mizoram, except for handloom, handicrafts, and horticulture products like ginger, chillies, etc., do not find market outside the state. Owing to this, the trucks coming to Mizoram from different parts of the country often return empty and charge two-way fare for a single load. If return load can be provided then the transportation cost can come down. Mizoram market basically is a consumption market. To make Mizoram business economy sustainable two-way exchange of surplus is necessary. The businesspersons of Mizoram should revamp the concept of business to make this a reality. This may provide a boost to border trade through Mizoram also.

Problems of External Trade

External trade in Mizoram is limited to exchange of some items by people living on the two sides of border under the traditional 'head load' system. Some items are also brought through informal channels, though mostly for local consumption. Formal trade is yet to take shape. Some of the problems of border trade in Mizoram are as follows:

1. *Lack of Credit Arrangement*: The Memorandum of Understanding concerning banking service for border trade with neighbouring countries has not yet been finalized. As a result the business enterprises undertaking import and export and service providers find it difficult in obtaining credit from financial institutions.
2. *Unaffordable Import Duties*: The rates of tax such as 45 per cent import duty on Soyabean, *Katha*, Resin, etc., make foreign trade unprofitable activity for a number of items.
3. *Under Billing and Avoidance of Customs Duty*: Many Myanmari and Bangladeshi businesspersons insist on payment for the items supplied in Indian currency and not in their respective currencies, as the value of Indian currency (*Rupee)* tends to be higher than that of the respective currencies. Further, as some of the items of trade attract tax, some business people resort to under-billing of consignments to reduce the incidence of customs duty and other taxes. This adversely affects the long-term trade prospect.
4. *No Service after Sales*: Foreign goods sold in Aizawl market the traders do not provide 'service after sales' to the customers. The customers hesitate to buy such goods, as the risk is high and service after sales is not available. If the border trade is to

be chanalized through Mizoram, local entrepreneurs need to provide service after sales.

5. *Sustainability and Transportation Cost*: There have been difficulties in exports and imports through land routes of Mizoram, say, long distance, high cost of transportation, inner-line restrictions, etc. Further, for such a trader from outside the state, there are other short and cheap options available. The economic viability of the foreign trade infrastructure that is being developed is dependent upon the export-import potential of Mizoram with its neighbouring countries. The experience of people presently engaged in this business in Manipur suggests that transportation of goods from Dimapur to Moreh is very expensive, costs high and makes the business unprofitable. The same holds true in case of Mizoram. Bangladesh has direct border with Myanmar and Bangladeshi entrepreneurs may not like to use Mizoram route for sending their goods to Myanmar and *vice versa*. Even Indian goods can be transported to Myanmar through other land routes or alternatively through sea routes from Howrah, Visakhapatnam, Chennai, etc. Thus, the border points of Mizoram could be utilized by the entrepreneurs of Mizoram for exchange of whatever they can produce profitably at local level.
6. *Instability of Exchange Rates*: Although considerable overland trade takes place regularly through Champhai-Rih and Demagiri-Marpara, the divergence in the exchange rate of Indian rupee-Burmese Kyat between official and non-official channels restrict such a trade on banking channel and a major volume moves on non-banking channels.
7. *Loss of Exchequer*: At present a major part of border trade is being carried on through illegal channels. This causes loss of tax revenue all through. Once a consignment is allowed to pass through the check gate under *'poilo'* system with/without paying duties, it is not recorded anywhere in Mizoram. There is no pressure on traders for maintaining records of business transactions. The enforcement authorities do not check invoices at a later date to determine whether the consignment was recorded properly in the books of the firm and sales tax has been paid or not. Moreover, the benefit of taxation is not passed on to the customers. Rather, it goes in enhancing the traders' margin.

8. *Restrictive Policies of Neighbouring Countries*: The Confederation of Indian Industry (CII) had expressed certain apprehensions about the policies of neighbouring countries. For instance in Myanmar the economic reform process, which started in 1990, has been rolled back. Several restrictions including the provision that from export earnings 60 per cent has to be used for import of essential commodities and 40 per cent can be used for non-essential/luxury items have been reintroduced. Sale of certain commodities including rice is in the hands of Government in Myanmar. Repatriation of profits, which was earlier allowed, has come under severe restrictions. The repatriation limit has been set at US $ 50,000 a month. Severe restrictions have been imposed on border trade. All trades through border has to be through 'Letters of Credit' and that too in US dollar ($). Myanmar faces foreign exchange crises, there is no stability and repatriation of profits is difficult. Investments are mainly in hydrocarbon sector. Investment in tourism and hotels has turned non-viable, as tourism did not take off as expected.

   Bangladesh Government has laid the condition of at least 10 per cent value addition to be ensured in giving passage to Indian goods through its territory. Apparently, it may seem all right, but in reality the result brings no value to Bangladesh Government, which otherwise it would have received, while the Mizoram trade is hurt.

9. *Illegal Trade in Drugs*: Mizoram faces the problem of inflow of drugs from Myanmar. Due to this, drug addiction is spreading among youths. Mizoram has emerged as one of the hotspots of narcotics traffic with drug traffickers operating from Myanmar and China away from the vigil of enforcement agencies due to Mizoram's proximity to the Golden Triangle, the tri junction of Myanmar, Thailand, and Laos, that account for over 60 per cent of the narcotics trade across the globe. The area under poppy cultivation in Myanmar has increased nearly three-fold. It was 2,10,039 hectares in 1996[6]. During last decade alone, the Golden Triangle produced at least 2,000 MT of heroin. The entry of narcotics into Mizoram is through Lungbung, Nagarchhip and Champhai. Consignments usually originate at *Bhoken* near *Khampat* in Myanmar.

   Drug running is risky and involves hard physical labour, but with the opening up of border for trade it has become easy.

Official statistics reveal that, in 1996-97 over 1992, though Indian trade with Myanmar grew by a mere 0.3 per cent, the narcotics traffic shot up five-fold. Acetic anhydride, a chemical essential for making fine grade heroin, is smuggled from India to 42 heroin conversion laboratories in Myanmar. There are no checkpoints between border towns over 270 km. long stretch, which makes it almost impossible for Myanmar and Indian security forces to guard the border and check smuggling. Though India and Myanmar have signed three major agreements to tackle the problem, these have had little effect.[7]

Involvement of government agencies and security forces in smuggling in border area cannot be ruled out. To prevent drug trafficking along the border improvement in intelligence network is needed. Further, once formal trade is allowed, less illegal trade shall take place.

10. *Other Problems*: High to very high cost of transportation, frequent disruption of communication due to natural calamities, lack of awareness of export formalities, absence of information on marketing strategies, etc. are some other major problems in the way of exports and imports from Mizoram. Taxes and customs duty also make foreign goods costlier. Currency exchange and Visa problem often takes toll of time. Moreover foreign suppliers do not provide credit facility.

(ii) Problems of Industry

There are a number of factors that come in the way of industrialization of the State. Among them some are natural and some are man made. Natural hurdles may be set right just by re-aligning the system, but, the man made hurdles cannot be solved so easily. It takes generations to bring change in social outlook. These factors may broadly be divided into exogenous and endogenous. The exogenous factors hindering industrialization include lack of marketing support, absence of data bank to help entrepreneurs, communication gap leading to lack of information on technology and market development, restricted entry of non-tribals due to inner line permit system, disturbed socio-political conditions, inducement to large trading profits not making the region attractive for industry, non-adaptation of technology to suit local needs, ineffective entrepreneurial development through promotional agencies and lack of follow-up programme to develop trained personnel, etc. Except for forests and agricultural products, there are no enough raw materials for medium and large-scale industries. No big industry can run without proper skilled labour. The endogenous factors that restricted industrialization included defective capital base and operational plans, shortage of working capital, obsolete techniques of production, lack of understanding for productive and preventive maintenance, etc. The industrial development programme suffered from lack of efficient management, especially in personnel and financial areas. Control and supervision along with co-ordination in the matter of design and training is essential for improvement of production. Apart from the above some specific problems of industrialization are discussed here:

1. *Lack of Concern*: There is a general lack of concern for industrial development of State among entrepreneurs. Entrepreneurs receiving assistance from government in the form of incentives and finance do not increase investment in plant and machinery[8] to increase production, rather they are known for diverting the funds for some other purposes.
2. *No Inducement to Outside Investment*: The majority of businessmen in Mizoram are local. Outside participation is almost negligible because of such restrictive regulations are in force. For instance, the provisions as regards the establishment of industries by non-Mizo in the State are not encouraging, rather they are discouraging. A non-Mizo cannot establish any small-scale industry. If the proposed investment in plant and machines exceeds Rs. 50 lakh, then a non-tribal may establish SSI in thrust areas and that too in joint venture with local entrepreneur only. However, this is subject to fulfilment of other conditions also. A non-Mizo may set-up medium scale or large-scale industry in joint venture with the State Government and subject to fulfilment of certain conditions. Further, the provisions of Inner-line Regulations do not provide for issue of permanent 'inner-line pass' except to those who hold permanent trade licence from the former Mizo District Council.
3. *Protected Market*: The State Government in spite of political changes have continued to play safe by protecting the so called interest of Mizo and provided them with a safety cover of *'no competition'* from outsiders as well as maintained ethnicity, at least sentimentally. Due to non-participation of outside entrepreneurs, the market has remained confined to the State of Mizoram only.

4. *High Manufacturing Cost*: Manufacturing cost in Mizoram has been higher than that in the neighbouring States. The industrial units incur about 10-20 per cent extra cost as compared to units in other States owing to high cost of transportation, industry in general being material intensive, etc. The project cost is also higher by 20-25 per cent. Moreover, the critical inputs that mostly come from outside are neither available in adequate quantity nor in time.
5. *Higher Cost of Skilled Labour*: Cost of skilled labour is relatively high in the State due to scarcity of skilled workers in general. Further, the average annual productivity per employee is very low. As a result the value addition per person employed and profitability is low.
6. *Lack of Trained Manpower*: The Industrial development programme in Mizoram also suffered due to non-availability of trained and experienced personnel. There existed no proper institutional setup for the development of technical and managerial talent. Due to lack of adequate supervision the worker's efficiency is below the expected level and resulted in higher operational cost.

   There are some unemployed engineering graduates in the State, but not adequately trained and oriented for running industries. These persons do not constitute the need-based skilled manpower required for industry. Moreover, the State does not have enough professional and technical institutions to develop appropriate manpower base.
7. *Absence of Industrial Environment*: Though there existed five state owned corporations to pursue various production/promotional/financing activities in Mizoram, there could not be developed any high-value public sector enterprise which in turn may lead to development of ancillarisation[9]. In absence of any mechanical engineering industry in the region, the SSIs have to procure even small spare parts and accessories from outside causing undue delay in repair and replacement work, which in turn hampers production. Supply of spurious spare parts and non-availability of experienced trained mechanics also add to industries problems.
8. *Inappropriate Tax Incentives*: As Mizo are not subject to income tax and other central taxes, the prospective entrepreneurs fail to realize the value of most of the tax benefits as provided in

Industrial Policy of Mizoram, 2000 associated with setting up of export oriented enterprises, SSI units, etc. These provisions did not work as motivating factors to Mizo entrepreneurs.

9. *Entry Restrictions*: The inner line restriction on the entry of outsiders into the State and provisions of Industrial Policy of Mizoram, 2000 as regards to non-tribals also created hindrance in the growth of industries in the State. High cost of production, heavy transportation cost, higher wage rates, absence of bargaining, high cost of living, extortion, etc. are some other issues responsible for not attracting investment from out side the State. Antipathy of the State to non-local traders prevented and discouraged potential industrialists to invest in the State.

10. *Inadequate Financial Incentives*: Financial incentives for industries when compared to other neighbouring states were inadequate. To give a specific example, compared one by one with that of Tripura, it is observed that Capital Investment Subsidy is less by 15 per cent and the maximum ceiling is less by Rs. 15.00 lakh; Additional Capital Investment Subsidy in case of 100 per cent Export-Oriented Units (EOU) is less by 10 per cent and the maximum ceiling is less by Rs. 10.00 lakh; no incentive is provided to Information Technology (IT) industry, Transport subsidy is given only on transportation of plant and machinery and not on movement of raw materials and finished goods within the Northeastern region, which is @ 90 per cent and 50 per cent respectively, no Air Freight Subsidy from Aizawl to Kolkata on transport of fruits/fruit products for export, which is at 75 per cent, no comprehensive insurance coverage for 10 years from the date of commercial production is given, and no grants-in-aid on setting up horticulture-based industries, especially fruit processing up to Rs. 4 crore, i.e., 50 per cent of total capital cost and on other food processing industries up to Rs. 75 lakh i.e., $33^1/_3$ per cent of total capital cost is provided.

11. *Lack of Demand for Local Products*: Mizo society is now passing through a phase with two extremes, *viz*., traditional and western. While the western has greater influence on their life style, the traditional influences the work ethics. The industrial structure in Mizoram has failed to expand sufficiently to provide a forward shift to an agricultural economy towards industrialization. A long heritage in weaving has not stopped the use of mill-made modern fabric by people. The emergence of neo-rich class of indigenous

people and growing number of government servants created demand for factory made goods. Due to the absence of taxes and accountability for hoarded money among neo-rich and government officers, demand for luxury items, and electronic goods is growing to maintain a higher standard of living. People prefer to spend money on construction of multi-storied buildings for rent, but lack enthusiasm to set-up new ventures that are risky in nature and offer low profit margin.

12. *Improper Utilization of Natural Resources*: The natural resources of the State are not being used for industrialization. For instance, Mizoram has about 15935 sq. km. area under forests, of which 7127 sq. km. is reserved forest; 3568 sq. km. is under control of District/Village Councils, and 5240 sq. km. is non-classed state forest. Firewood, bamboo and valuable timber is found in abundance but the steepness of the ranges and transport bottleneck are the main constraints in the way of scientific forestry. Further, none of the industry except construction is based on produce of these natural resources. Only one ply factory is being established.
13. *Role of State Government*: The State Government is expected to play a leading role in promoting the industries. In actual practice, it appears to have not taken initiative to the desired extent. The meagre outlay in the State Plans for industries is one indication of the fact. Late formulation of Industrial Policy is another indication. It declared industrial policy for the first time during VII Five Year Plan (1989) followed by the second in 2000. Its most of the provisions remained unimplemented.

    It is often announced that legislative changes are expected, certain bills are to be introduced and some dynamic changes in the Government shall be made. But the Government cannot be expected to come up with legislations, pass bills and make changes in a short time. It has to be a gradual process. The fundamental change that is expected from the Government is to facilitate the economic development of the State for which it should come forward and make the situation more comfortable for entrepreneurs.
14. *Sickness in Industry*: The performance of existing industrial units cannot be regulated satisfactory. Nearly 43.91 per cent units (1972 out of 4490) were sick units as on 18th June 2001. Although proprietors cite lack of adequate funding as the main reason for

dismal performance the real cause was poor management of respective units. Actually, most entrepreneurs are ignorant about the basic principles of management. They do not know the system of maintaining their books of accounts. They do not invest total funds received from funding agency for setting up the industry, diverting a part thereof for personal expenditure. Even though training programmes are arranged periodically for the entrepreneurs few turn up to take advantage. Even among those who complete the training programme not many set up their own enterprises. An important reason for such a situation was the background of entrepreneurs. A study revealed that whereas in the North-East region about 60 per cent of the entrepreneurs come from business community, 20.3 per cent from artisan families, 17 per cent from the farming families and only 3.9 per cent from service class, in Mizoram 92.1 per cent entrepreneurs come from farming families.[10]

(iii) Problems of Finance for Business and Industry

Finance constitutes the life line of business and industry. Over the last two decades a variety of institutions including commercial banks and cooperative banks have been setup in the State to take care of the needs of business and industry, the basic problem remained unaddressed. The problems in financing of business and industry in Mizoram may be summarized as follows:

1. *Inadequate Security*: Due to lack of adequate security for funds advanced and poor recovery, financial institutions in the State are hesitant to advance loan to private entrepreneurs. Generally, banks advance loan against security of land among other guarantees. But, in Mizoram, as there is no permanent land settlement the land belongs to community. Village Councils lease the land on annual basis. From banks' point of view, this is not a trust worthy security. The guarantors are not reliable.
2. *Absence of Valuation Services*: Valuation services for the valuation of immovable properties to be taken as security are not available in the State. Procurement of such a service from outside the State is neither feasible nor viable.
3. *Lack of Competition among Financial Institutions*: The number of banks operating in the State and their branch network

continues to be small. There are no non-nationalized private banks and as a result the coverage is also low.

4. *Lack of Cooperation from Government Officials*: The recovery position of bank advances in Mizoram is poor. The banks have reservations to finance freely for all economic activities, as a large proportion of firms failed to make repayment. The drawing and disbursing officers of the State Government also do not make deduction of loan installments at source from salary of employees concerned, who had availed bank loan for some purposes[11]. On request from bank, instead of effecting recovery by deduction at source they issue a general notification to employees for clearing their dues in time.
5. *Low Demand of Credit from Rural Area*: As is seen from the analysis of financing in Mizoram loan proposals received from rural areas were less. One reason responsible for such a situation is that in view of meagre allocation of budgetary funds by government for promotion of industries in the State, the spread of infrastructure development did not cover the rural areas of the State in its ambit. Infact most of the budget allocations are spent only in Aizawl district. Another reason is that rural population is yet to be oriented about various entrepreneurial activities. They have to be given some kind of exposure. Programmes, therefore, need to be designed that are suitable of implementation in village economy. To bring this change is not an easy task. It may take years together.
6. *Shortage of Loanable Funds*: The imbalance between resource use and resource availability is slowly asserting itself creating a number of problems in the State. The crisis in the finances of Northeastern states has been accentuated by new economic policy since 1991. The IDBI stopped subscribing to the ZIDCO's share capital under new economic policy. The new policy assigned greater role to market forces and undermined interventionist steps. The states in the Northeast have suddenly awakened to the rude reality that they can no longer be relied on the continued largesse of the Centre in their pursuit of expansion of the administrative infrastructure in the name of promoting development and mass welfare.
7. *Creation of Equitable Mortgage*: Creation of equitable mortgage in the State has been rendered difficult, as all centres of business and industry have not been declared by the State Government as Notified Centres.

8. *Bankers' Least Preference for SSI Advances*: The recovery position in personal loans and SBF segment is better and the banks are more inclined to advance to these two categories, which indirectly helps business and industry by boosting demand for products. But, this failed to generate demand for the local products. Bankers' favour does not extended to industry of the State. Though trading benefited but not industry. This resulted in out flow of funds from Mizoram and deprived the State of multiplier effect, increased scale of operations, etc. As the size of most agricultural, industrial and business enterprises in the State was small, credit demand was also low and the quantum of bank finance absorbed was low.
9. *Poor Recovery*: Most dissuading factor in bank finance is poor recovery. At the same time the recovery from SSIs is far less than over all recovery. Only 23.38 per cent of banks' annual disbursement could be recovered from industrial sector. Even in some cases the recovery was as low as 2.42 per cent. However, overall recovery position of all the banks may be considered satisfactory as nearly 34.86 per cent of annual disbursement were received back by way of recovery. In case of ZIDCO, in spite of special recovery drive and one time settlement scheme launched in recent past, the overall recovery rate could not be improved beyond 5.91 per cent. In case of MAMCO, the recovery rate of farmers' loans was 'zero' per cent over last 10 years.

   As the enactment for revenue recovery proceedings against bank defaulters for government sponsored loans has not yet been adopted in the State, the recovery rate of bank loans had remained depressed. The poor loan recovery by financial institutions hampered the process of sanctioning fresh loans. Bankers feel that "money flow is a one-way traffic and little comes back. This hurts the bankers and it cuts at the root of the banking system. The bankers feel uncomfortable at the time of annual closing, when they are compelled to make huge provisions for bad debts. This is the point where the government comes in. The government should introduce new legislations to make bankers feel more comfortable in disbursing loans. It should also enforce certain discipline on the borrowers and they should feel obliged not only to borrow money but also to repay what has been borrowed. The borrower has to understand that the money he has borrowed is public money. Both bankers and the government functionaries have the responsibility to spread public awareness towards loan repayment"[12].

Reasons for poor recovery can broadly be classified as socio-economic factors, beneficiary factors and organizational factors:

(a) *Socio-Economic Factors*: The overdues are the consequence of the negative response of borrowing entrepreneurs. It is well known that entrepreneurs who are illiterate and uneducated are prone to commit more default than others; people belonging to backward castes are prone to commit more default than those belonging to forward castes; people whose primary occupation is non-agriculture commit more default than those whose primary occupation is agriculture; and people borrowing large amount commit more default than those who borrow small amount.[13] The same is applicable to Mizoram.

(b) *Beneficiary Factors*: The factors that contribute directly to the increase in overdues of banks are at the borrowers' level. The causes of poor recovery at the beneficiary level may be classified into Controllable causes; and Uncontrollable causes. Controllable causes include wilful default by the borrower, diversion of credit, and lack of solvency of the borrower. Uncontrollable causes include failures due to flood, draught and famine, and other natural calamities.

Another reason for the poor recovery of bank credit is the lack of credit worthiness of the borrower, due to un-remunerative prices of their products, large sized families; and chronic indebtedness. Market factors in the form of fluctuation in demand and prices of their products also affect the economic strength of borrowers. The regulated markets, which are supposed to provide infrastructure for marketing of products, have not been functioning efficiently in Mizoram. Many small and medium producers dispose of their produce at village level itself.[14] Agricultural marketing infrastructure is very important for providing better prices to the farmers of Mizoram. Most of the farmers are compelled to resort to distress sales immediately after harvest. Majority of the farmers faced the problem of transportation etc.[15]

(c) *Organizational Factors*: The lending policy should be such that the right amount of money at right point of time is made available to a genuine borrower. It seemed that banks in Mizoram did not follow a rational lending policy and financed least to industry and were more inclined to small business financing, where the amount of lending was small. Reasons for this irrational financing by banks were ceiling limit, unrealistic scale of finance, inadequate security, procedural bottlenecks, mode of disbursement of credit and improper repayment period, etc.[16]

Serving periodical notices, visiting the borrower have been the routine recovery efforts. However, in Mizoram these did not yield the desired results, cases pending in courts are piling up year after year, and the trend is moving upward. In a court of law, banks are treated as ordinary litigants. No special treatment is given to them. Further, Bengal Recovery Act, 1913 is yet to introduce in Mizoram.[17] In case of ZIDCO, doubt about the application of Limitation Act to Mizoram prevailed.

The systems and procedures were also not simplified to the extent desirable to make these easy to follow by the villagers. A complaint often made was that the projects submitted to the banks were not up to the mark as per banking procedures and thereby not considered bankable. The same was returned with no note how to remove the deficiency. Though the banking sector had expanded in rural areas deterioration in the efficiency of banking system and poor quality of services to the clientele were evident.

(10) *Inadequacies of Banking System*: While the commercial banks spread their network in rural areas, adequate attention was not paid to strengthening the organization and structure of rural branches. In fact some of the rural branches were manned with skeleton staff comprising one passing official, one clerk-*cum*-cashier and one sub-staff, and the banks did not have adequate staff. Thus, the rural areas to go around. Moreover, quality of staff posted in rural areas was not always suitable, particularly from the view point of their expertise and willingness to work in rural areas. Training and other staff welfare facilities with banks for orienting the urban staff to rural conditions and motivating them to agriculture and other rural pursuits were generally inadequate.

The systems and procedures were also not simplified to the extent desirable to make there easy to follow by the villagers. A complaint often made was not the projects submitted to the banks were not up to the mark as per banking procedures and thereby not considered bankable. The same was returned with no note how to remove the deficiency. Though the banking sector had expanded in rural areas deterioration in the efficiency of banking system and poor quality of services to the clientele were evident.

(iv) Taxation Related Problems of Business and Industry

Taxation is the mechanism through which the State raises its revenue to meet the expenditure. It is the duty of every citizen including business entities to pay tax. However, to be mutually beneficial the system need be well thought out and planned. In this light the taxation related problems of business and industry in Mizoram are discussed here:

1. *Poor State of Tax Revenue*: Most of the Northeastern States in India have paid inadequate attention[18] to the development of their financial resources. The ratio of State tax revenue to revenue expenditure is very low in the region. Most Northeastern states in general and Mizoram in particular, being special category states were given a time limit to build up their own revenue base and till then the Centre had promised to support. However, instead of building the required base they preferred waiting till expiry of time limit to take maximum advantage of liberal funding from Centre. On the expiry of the period, realizing weak political authority at Centre they further took advantage of the situation and moved proposals for extending the time period of liberal funding as they could not built-up the base needed for sustenance. Owing to this a common man including those in business in Mizoram carried the impression that taxation is not for 'Mizo' but for outsiders ('Vaipa') only.
2. *Sluggish Growth in Business and Industry*: There are no manufacturing units in Mizoram worth mentioning that may be making articles for sale on which tax may be levied. Mizoram, a small State with a small area and small population with inadequate resources of economic significance and having no economic infrastructure cannot be expected to have high tax revenue and a strong tax base. Manufactured goods are brought to Mizoram from other states after paying tax. Sales tax can be

imposed on some items only. Sales tax is directly levied on certain notified goods. Such goods are also brought from outside the State for resale in the State. It was observed that the dealers while selling goods, except in case of some branded items, hardly keep carbon copy of the invoices issued to the consumers. This puts a question mark on the accuracy to their books of accounts and settlement of their tax liability. Consumers might be paying sales tax on goods purchased by them but how much of it reaches to State government account cannot be stated.

3. *Violation of Efficiency and Equity*: Efficiency and equity are two basic principles of public policy relating to economic operations. No welfare policy and distributive justice can be sustained in the long run if the principle of efficiency is grossly violated, as the laws of economics are inexorable and every policy has a cost, which must be defrayed by mobilizing resources[19]. The violation of efficiency criteria may give birth to distorted notion of equity and may accentuate inequality rather than reduce it. The principle of efficiency has not been strictly followed in State finances in North-East.[20] in general and in Mizoram in particular and provides an illustration of the conflict between principles of equity and efficiency.

   One conspicuous deviation from the national pattern of proportional share is the low contribution of the state excise. Though sales tax occupied a position of primacy in the percentage share, only seven selected items such as petroleum products and consumer durables are taxed[22]. Recently some more items have been added to it and tax rates were also revised upward. Still scope exists to increase tax base by including some more items. Now VAT has replaced sales tax with effect from 1st April 2005. State's own revenue is far too inadequate and can hardly meet 5 per cent of the revenue expenditure. Tax revenue increased from Rs. 6.67 crore in 1996-97 to Rs. 14.43 crore in 2000-01, but its share in revenue receipts stood at 2 per cent. A pertinent issue in this connection is the test of financial viability, for which the tax receipt is an index. Similarly, the ratio of tax receipts to GSDP suggests the policy flexibility. While a low ratio implies that the government can tax more by introducing a more flexible system, a high ratio shows that a good deal of efforts for approaching the limit of flexibility has been made. In case of Mizoram, this ratio has declined from

1.01 in 1990-91 to 0.99 in 2001-02. On the other hand, the ratio of sales tax receipts to GSDP has increased from 0.20 per cent in 1990-91 to 0.51 per cent in 2001-02 and this change itself suggest the capability of the State to raise more resource through taxation. It would therefore be prudent for the Government to plan its taxation policy appropriately.

4. *Inadequate Taxation Efforts*: The State tax revenue to revenue expenditure in the year 1996-97 was as low as 1.2 per cent, whereas the national average stood at 43 per cent[21]. It showed that the State's own tax revenue was comparatively low. In 2000-01, out of the total (own-sources) revenue receipts of Rs. 54.80 crore, the share of non-tax revenue was Rs. 40.37 crore (73.6 per cent). This reflected a sordid state of the State's finance. For 2000-01, the percentage share of tax revenue in the internal sources of total revenue receipts was 26.4 per cent and its main sources were sales tax (42 per cent), tax on vehicles (14 per cent), land revenue (8 per cent), state excise (7 per cent), and other taxes (29 per cent). This showed that serious efforts have not been made for augmenting the resources of the State through effective tax administration.

One conspicuous deviation from the national pattern of proportional share is the low contribution of the state excise. Though sales tax occupied a position of primacy in the percentage share, only seven selected items such as petroleum products and consumer durables are taxed[22]. Recently some more items have been added to it and tax rates were also revised upward. Still scope exists to increase tax base by including some more items. Now VAT has replaced sales tax with effect from 1st April 2005. State's own revenue is far too inadequate and can hardly meet 5 per cent of the revenue expenditure. Tax revenue increased from Rs. 6.67 crore in 1996-97 to Rs. 14.43 crore in 2000-01, but its share in revenue receipts stood at 2 per cent. A pertinent issue in this connection is the test of financial viability, for which the tax receipt is an index. Similarly, the ratio of tax receipts to GSDP suggests the policy flexibility. While a low ratio implies that the government can tax more by introducing a more flexible system, a high ratio shows that a good deal of efforts for approaching the limit of flexibility has been made. In case of Mizoram, this ratio has declined from 1.01 in 1990-91 to 0.99 in 2001-02. On the other hand, the ratio of sales tax receipts to GSDP has increased from 0.20 per cent in 1990-91 to 0.51 per cent in 2001-02 and this change itself suggest the capability of the State to raise more resource through taxation. It would therefore, be prudent for the Government to plan its taxation policy appropriately.

(v) Problems Related to Infrastructure Development

Infrastructure is *sine qua non* of development in general and business and industry's development in particular. Some of the problems related to infrastructure development in Mizoram are as follows:

1. *Inadequate Power Supply*: Power and electricity are basic infrastructure for economic development of a country. The degree of economic growth is highly correlated with the consumption of electricity. Power being a basic infrastructure; its regular and uninterrupted supply is essential for the growth of industries. But in Mizoram, power has been always in short supply. Mizoram is still to have a good network of power lines and sources of supply. Presently, under arrangement with Government of Assam, hydro electric power is being purchased and brought to Mizoram through a 66 KV high tension line. Besides, some power is also generated from its own hydel power plant project and diesel sets. But still there remains a wide gap between supply and demand.

   Although Mizoram possesses hydel potential the progress in this sector has been slow, creating a huge gap between demand and supply of electricity. Installation and generation could not keep pace with the fast growing demand for power. Consequently, power supply situation in the State continues to remain unsatisfactory. During 2001-02, the total consumption was 132.88 MW, as against the production of 9.12 MW, though the total installed capacity was 39.766 MW. Of the total consumption the share of domestic consumption was largest at 93.02 MW (70 per cent), whereas the share of SSIs was least at 1.99 MW (1.50 per cent). There was no addition to the installed capacity of power during 2001-02. The actual production of electricity declined from 11.97 MW in 2000-01 to 9.12 MW in 2001-02.
2. *Irregular Water Supply*: Scarcity of water is another problem in the growth of industry. For industries such as agro-based, forest-based, and chemical industries, there is a need for regular supply of water. But, the situation is that its supply even for domestic consumption is not made on regular basis.

3. *Weak Communication System, Bad Road Conditions and Infrastructure*: The total road length in the State was 5485.82 km in 2001-02 of which 3513.61 km was surfaced road (64.05 per cent) and 1972.21 km unsurfaced road (35.95 per cent). The number of vehicles on road in Mizoram had increased from 30,659 in 2000-01 to 33,876 in 2001-02 showing an increase of 10.49 per cent over the year. Out of the total 732 (2001 census) inhabited villages in the State, all weather roads connected 360 villages only, while fair weather roads connected 342 villages. The total number of Post Offices at the end of 2000-01 stood at 397, out of which 329 were in rural areas and 68 in urban areas. By the end of 2000-01 there were 62 Telephone Exchanges in the State, and 5 towns/cities had telegraph facilities. The number of working telephone connections by 2000-01 stood at 37,718, as against 34,615 in 1999-2000.

   Roads in Mizoram are in bad shape, which caused frequent damage to goods-in-transit while the reimbursement of damaged goods from supplier/transporter/insurer is a tough task. Lack of proper communication to and from the State created serious problems. Even though there has been improvement in road conditions in recent past, still it may take time for people to identify themselves with the national mainstream. Materially also, better communication is essential for industrial development. Poor communication also caused hindrances to business in Mizoram.

4. Without a variety of other infrastructure, it may not be possible to setup and operate industry. At present in this respect facility like warehouses, telecommunication system, post and telegraph services, banking, export-import facilities, credit arrangement, customs clearance, business centres, civic facilities, training institutes etc. available in the State are not up to the requirement.

(vi) Problems Related with Entrepreneurship

Entrepreneurship is a driving force for business and industry. However, other facilities may be provided externally entrepreneurship has to be nurtured through a systematic process over a long period of time. Some of the problems related with entrepreneurship development in Mizoram are as follow:

1. *Low Risk Taking Ability*: The entrepreneurs in Mizoram lack risk taking ability besides the problems involved in providing capital, skilled workforce, raw material supply, quality,

marketing of products, etc. Over the time people in Mizoram have found ways of earning easy money through contracts, etc., and have developed antipathy to soil hands by undertaking new ventures in agricultural production, manufacturing, trade and commerce. They fail to accept the challenges of business. Rather the local people have developed dependence on government to come to their rescue through sponsored programmes, which remain confined within narrow limits.

Higher literacy coupled with essential skills like carpentry, repairs and maintenance work etc., possessed by local people have not helped much in creating industrial climate in the State. Young people possessing requisite technical education prefer to go for government jobs. They hesitate to setup their own enterprise. The prevalent high prices of goods and high profit margin charged by traders have failed to generate adequate demand for indigenously produced goods.

2. *First Generation Entrepreneurs*: Majority of the entrepreneurs in business and industry are from first generation and do not have adequate knowledge of management practices and control techniques for business. There are no management institutes to train new manpower in the State. The entrepreneurs in general are unaware of management skills.
3. *Failure of Entrepreneurship Development Programmes*: Various agencies conduct entrepreneurship development programmes from time to time on regular basis or otherwise in the State. But the problems that come in the success of these programmes were lack of response from public in general and many times a scheduled programme had to be deferred time and again for want of adequate number of participants, no interaction by the participants with resource persons indicated lack of keenness or interest or the programme meant for them is not liked by them, high absenteeism of participants, and many a times these programmes were mere a formality on papers and their quality as well as contents may be questioned.

Although the Government of Mizoram provided training and subsidy support to willing persons entrepreneurship could not be developed sufficiently in the State enabling entrepreneurs to undertake high-value projects. With the initiation of development activity in the State the government has become the biggest employer employing more than 24 thousand persons (1986) in different jobs from a set of population of about 6 lakh. The position as on 31st March 2002 was 41484 jobs from a population of 891058. Local entrepreneurs have been shy and they lack motivation. Like other less developed countries, one factor responsible for lack of development in Mizoram is inadequacy of motivated entrepreneurs. People are not motivated to take up business. They mostly are interested in government jobs. Entrepreneurial career is chosen either by compulsion or by chance, but, not by choice.

These problems are to be investigated further in depth and if needed the programmes should be redesigned in the light of findings so as to make them concrete, realistic, appealing, and interesting.

(vii) General Problems

Apart from the specific problems discussed above some problems of general nature were also observed. Few of them are as follows:

1. *Long Period of Isolation*: A long period of isolation and neglect that the region faced had its impact on the development of the State. While industries had their foothold in the county during pre-Independence period and proliferated smoothly after independence, this part of the country remained untouched by the process of development. While it was part of Assam and a Union territory, no serious efforts were made for development. For a long time people of this region were not allowed to take active part in decision making and development process as they were given no representation in the State assembly. Identity of the region as Mizoram could emerge only after the Statehood was granted.
2. *Remoteness of the State*: Remoteness of the State is another important impediment in industrial development. Being located at the remotest periphery of country, people of Mizoram have developed a sense of alienation from national mainstream. They faced continual isolation since British period. For British, the cost of administering the region was more important than the likely benefits. Keeping this in view, the British classified it as 'excluded area'. The partition of India in 1947 increased the distance to Kolkata more than three fold, without building an

alternative mode of quick transport. This further threw this part of India into isolation.

3. *Lack of Business Orientation*: It is observed that the people in general lack business orientation and basic entrepreneurial knowledge. Lack of proper knowledge of business management is a serious lacuna for the promotion of industrial environment in Mizoram. There is neither a management training institution in the State nor the educated youth prefer to go for such training elsewhere outside the State. Industry will be a myth without properly trained technical and managerial personnel. Modern form of business and industry is of recent origin in Mizoram and may be traced to recent past near statehood.
4. *Absence of Minerals*:. The Geological Survey of State revealed that there are no reserves of minerals of specific economic value. This made the State dry in mineral resources. According to the Survey and Planning Report on Industrial Development in Mizo Hill District (now Mizoram), 1963 coalmines were reported in Chawngte, Bairabi and Billikhawthlir. Salt springs were in existence for many years in western, eastern and northern side of the State. In the absence of minerals of any specific value, people had to depend on agriculture and its allied activities such as forestry, pisciculture, and weaving.
5. *Difficult Hilly Terrain*: As preponderant portion of the State is hilly, availability of flat land is scarce and this has rendered modern agriculture, business and even transportation inwards and outwards more expensive.
6. *Lack of Multiplier Effect*: The multiplier effect of government expenditure backed by Central transfers is extremely poor in the Northeastern States including Mizoram.[23] If things go this way, in the long run the State cannot be expected to acquire dynamism and is bound to remain permanent financial liability of the nation.
7. *Long Supply Line*: As the suppliers of various items of trade are from far off places, the supply lines are long. Due to frequent landslides and natural calamities there are delays in supplies. This frequently leads to 'no stock' situation. Recently Amul Taaza Milk remained in short supply for about 6 months. For two years before 2004, petrol and diesel were under rationing. Only once in a week the supply was made open for public.
8. *Lack of Trade Related Research*: Research is important for development of business and industry. There has been complete

lack of research on various aspects of business and industry in Mizoram, which may contribute to better understanding of the need and problems of business and industry including border trade, and above all the sustainable development. To explore the problems and prospects of all-round development of business and industry in Mizoram including border trade, research relating to all aspects should not only be encouraged but be undertaken from time to time by all agencies concerned.

NOTES

1. Thangchungnunga, Fiscal Management in Mizoram, *Dialogue*, Vol. 4, No. 1, July-September, 2004, p. 141.
2. Table 3.5, p. 106, Compiled from data obtained from Directorate of Industries, Government of Mizoram, Aizawl.
3. Table 3.5, *op. cit.*
4. Table 3.13, p.120, Compiled from Annual Report, MKVIB, 2000-01.
5. Report of the Sub-Committee of State Level Banker's Committee for Mizoram on Credit-Deposit Ratio, Dated 15th November 1996, State Bank of India, Regional Office, Aizawl, pp. 1-2.
6. Mahapatra, A.B., *Border Trade with Myanmar brings Drugs, HIV*, Inter Press News Service, 25th May 1997.
7. *Ibid.*
8. Lalhniangi F.C., *Role of Forestry in Socio-Economic Development of Mizoram*, Lallianpari, 1990, p. 129.
9. Report of the Sub-Committee of State Level Banker's Committee for Mizoram on Credit-Deposit Ratio, *op. cit.*, pp. 1-2.
10. Banerjee, Amalesh & Kar, Biman, *Economic Planning and Development of North-Eastern States*, Kanishka Publishers, Distributors, New Delhi, 1999, p. 432.
11. Report of the Sub-Committee of State Level Banker's Committee for Mizoram on Credit-Deposit Ratio, *op. cit.*, pp. 1-2.
12. State Level Bankers' Committee Meeting for Mizoram, Dt: 28th June 1999, State Bank of India, Lead Bank Office, Aizawl, pp. 1-2.
13. Rajashekar, H., "*Commercial Banking and Finance*," Mangal Deep Publications, Jaipur, 2000, pp. 53-75.
14. *Ibid*, pp. 76-91.
15. Lalthanthuami Deputy Manager (Finance & Accounts) MAMCO: "*Agricultural Marketing in Mizoram*" (Unpublished Ph. D. work).
16. Rajashekar, H., "*Commercial Banking and Finance*," *op. cit.*, pp. 118-33.
17. State Level Bankers' Committee Meeting for Mizoram, 28th June 1999, *op. cit.*, p. 3.
18. Bhattacharjee, P.R., *The Problem of Ensuring Financial Efficiency in the North-Eastern States*, Dialogue, Vol. 4, No. 1, p. 63

19. *Ibid*, p. 59.
20. *Ibid*, p. 65.
21. Report on 'Economic Situation in the North East' by Dr. Gulshan Sachdeva submitted to the North Eastern Council
22. Thangchungnunga, *Fiscal Management in Mizoram, op. cit.*, p. 144.
23. Bhattacharjee, P.R., *The Problem of Ensuring Financial Efficiency in the North-Eastern States*, *Op. cit.*, p. 63.

7

SUGGESTIONS TO PROMOTE GROWTH OF BUSINESS AND INDUSTRY

Mizoram is yet to develop a suitable base for large and medium scale industries due to geographical disadvantages, lack of proper communication, paucity of raw materials, non-availability of adequate skilled labour, absence of large market, absence of notable mineral wealth, non-viability from the viewpoint of cost effectiveness, etc. There existed scope for bamboo and bamboo based industries, paper and pulp industries, flour mills, wooden and plywood industries in the State provided enough power supply, improved road conditions; good communication, subsidies and encouragement from the State government are provided. Of course, there exists scope for small-scale industries and the Government of Mizoram has identified certain priority areas *viz*., fruit processing, agro based industry, tourism, agriculture, horticulture, sericulture, forests, textiles, handloom and handicrafts, electronics and information technology. Besides scope for wood and wooden based industries, animal feed, pork and poultry processing, food processing, automobile workshop, fabrication, tinsmithy, etc. also existed. The problems discussed earlier need to be tackled to promote growth of business and industry in the State and ensure all round economic development. In this respect the following suggestions may be put forth:

(I) Suggestions as Regards to Internal Trade

Most of the problems discussed under internal trade are basically consumer driven. If consumers are educated properly maximum problems may be solved.

1. *Consumer Awareness Education*: Consumers in Mizoram are in general ignorant of their rights. They hardly bother while paying a price higher than the MRP and hardly ask for the features and

uses of products they buy. This is at the root of Mizoram's market being a 'Seller's Market'. Few dealers provide service after sales. If buyers (consumers) are educated about their rights perhaps the situation may change gradually. For this purpose a separate paper on 'consumer protection' and related laws may be introduced in the course curriculum at degree level by the University and for the time being some consumer awareness camps may be organized.

2. *Removal of Entry Restrictions*: As a level playing field is not made available to outsiders, the markets of Mizoram have remained protected. Once the markets are made open for non-tribals, it will lead to healthy competition and benefits will go to the consumers.
3. *Insurance Services*: Entrepreneurs may be educated through awareness camp about increasing use of insurance services for their goods-in-transit so as to reduce hardship and loss on account of damages owing to bad road conditions as also inappropriate handling of goods by transporters.

(II) Suggestions as Regards to External Trade

The problems of external trade are mostly concerned with border trade of Mizoram where familiarity with export-import formalities is required. If entrepreneurs are educated about these formalities the problem shall remain no longer.

1. *Border Trade Credit*: Border trade credit problem is a short term problem as the border trade through Mizoram has not been opened formally. Credit facility for border trade transactions though announced has yet not been made operative by the designated branch of State Bank of India, Champhai as it is governed and regulated by the RBI. According to banks export finance can be promoted if the exchange rate is also suitably pegged.
2. *Check on Illegal Trade in Drugs*: Vigilance authorities should tighten security in border area. Rather they should work in coordinated manner with their counterpart agencies in neighbouring countries to check illegal drug trade. Further, the present '*poilo*' system should be done away with at check posts.
3. *Stability in Exchange Rates*: It has been noticed that greater the instability in exchange rates greater the trade routes through

informal channel and especially in case of Myanmar and Bangladesh where Indian currency is freely accepted by people like in Nepal. Controlling agencies like RBI should therefore, attempt to stabilize the exchange rates between Rupee-Kyat and Rupee-Taka. The official exchange rate of Rupee-Kyat may be suitably adjusted by the Reserve Bank of India to bring about parity with the unofficial rates.

4. *Review of Bilateral Agreement/Joint Committee Meeting*: Policies which are against the national interest of one country should be discussed at joint committee meetings which should be held regularly as bilateral agreements are governed by international law on one to one basis.
5. *Export-Import Formality Awareness Camps*: The University may offer a separate paper on 'border trade/international trade' as a part of degree course curriculum. Alternatively the university may offer a separate diploma course on 'border trade'. For the time being to educate present entrepreneurs engaged in border trade, awareness campaigns may be conducted for making them familiar with export-import formalities.
6. *Check on Informal Border Trade*: Informal border trade of goods not covered by Border Trade Agreement (BTA) with Myanmar should be checked more rigorously. Border trade formally should be opened, which will augment revenue in the form of custom duty that is presently being evaded.
7. *Local Resource Base Border Trade*: Various studies have estimated volume of border trade in their own way. Its actual volume will always be in question. Owing to of Mizoram's topography, the entrepreneurs from rest of India may not find it economical in undertaking border trade through Mizoram owing to long physical distance that causing high transportation cost, difficult terrain, entry restrictions, etc. In view of this the built-in infrastructure in the form of LCS may remain under utilized or will remain limited to entrepreneurs of Mizoram only. To prosper from in-built LCS infrastructure and to make LCS economically viable in the long-run, the entrepreneurs and promotional agencies should promote export of products of local resource based industries. As has been discussed earlier Mizoram has some scope for export of food/ fruit processed items, aluminium utensils, match box, cutting and polishing of granite and precious stones, etc. Here trade specific research may prove helpful.

(III) Suggestions as Regards to Industry

Industrialization is necessary for the economic development and ways and means have also been suggested to attract increasing investment, technology, etc. here.

1. *Promotion of Tourism*: Mizoram offers attraction for tourists from across the country and world. The topography, climate and culture are the attractions. Mizoram's pleasant climate is an added advantage to boost tourism. It can be ideal place for summer resorts. In this direction, the government may ease out entry restrictions, and may advertise in print and electronic media to attract tourists. Alternatively, ILPs may be issued round the clock on the spot at border promptly. This will result neither in loss of revenue to the Government nor additional costs, as the office at ILP check gate already in operation round the clock can take up this job easily. Though the geographical limits of markets cannot be extended and number of buyers in market also cannot be increased all of a sudden but it is known that the boom in tourism industry leads to boost in domestic market, as tourists are generally tempted to buy certain unique but distinct indigenous products. For Mizoram this may be handloom and handicrafts segment. It will also lead to development of service industry say hospitality, transport, etc. Development of adequate infrastructure for the Reiek Tourist Complex, Palak Lake, Dampa´ Sanctuary and Thenzawl/ Vantawng is the need of the hour.
2. *Inducement to Save*: People of the State owing to their life style live in present and are not motivated to save for future needs. They may be educated through mass awareness camps about the need, use and benefits of saving for future. This will add to their purchasing power and also will lead to increased capital formation at first and investment at second.
3. *Indian Partnership Act, 1932*: Presently the Indian Partnership Act, 1932 does not apply to Mizoram and consequently the form of business enterprises is proprietorship, capital investment is less, managerial manpower is limited. If this Act is extended to Mizoram many entrepreneurs may join hands formally with others and can expand their business, and increase capital base. This shall also lead to increase in their credit worthiness and supervisory manpower problem shall be solved to [illegible]ficant

extent. They shall benefit from increased scale of operation and that will result in curbing '*Benami Trade*' practices.

4. *Outside Investment*: For speedier economic development through industrialization more investment is needed, irrespective of the fact that who is investing. In this process both public and private investments have a vital role. Government alone cannot afford huge investment for various reasons, but it being a facilitator the policies should be investment oriented, encouraging private investment without any pre-conditions. Private investment, a critical component in the new economic policy needs investor friendly ambience. The need is to attract and increase investment in the State, whether in thrust area or otherwise. It will have increased money multiplier effect, which is important. Further it will lead to increase in employment, import of new technology, etc. Industrially advanced States could develop because of their openness to private investment without prejudice of ethnicity. For speedy economic development retaining ethnicity is not desirable as both do not go together. Even Multinationals (MNCs), MRTP and FERA companies may be requested to setup units in Mizoram[1]. It will not only generate employment opportunities but also will be an eye-opener for local entrepreneurs. People of the State in general and Government in particular have to make a choice among ethnicity and economic development. A businessperson, whether Mizo or otherwise is guided by profits, safety, and security and not by ethnicity while making decision about investment.

Attracting outside State Investment by removing restrictive provisions may not be a difficult task but the willingness of society may not come, due to deep-rooted phobia. During survey only 15 per cent (20 out of 130) entrepreneurs agreed and the remaining 85 per cent (100 out of 130) entrepreneurs rejected the idea of throwing the field open for non-locals giving arguments like 'outsiders will dominate the scenario in Mizoram as the Mizo do not have that much knowledge, exposure and professionalism'. The Industrial Policy of Mizoram, 2000 welcomed outside investment 'with caution keeping in view the interest of the tribal population of Mizoram to safeguard the socio-cultural identity of the indigenous people of Mizoram,' which is a hurdle. According to it, a non-tribal may invest through joint venture with a local in a SSI in thrust areas with a minimum investment in plant and machinery of Rs. 50 lakh.

Thus the constraints are both natural and man-made. In order to develop industrial environment and bring about general prosperity in the State the natural constraints can be overcome by adjusting the system, but, to overcome man-made hurdles, individuals, society and political system need to reorient their approach.

5. *Large-Scale Production*: Owing to low level of operation and absence of technological benefits of large scale operations the manufacturing cost is high in Mizoram. To bring down manufacturing cost large scale production is necessary, but then there shall be problem of marketing for which entrepreneurs may explore markets outside the State and neighbouring countries. It will also lead to reduction in transportation cost, as the inward trucks, which are at present returning empty will carry return load.
6. *Technology Upgradation*: The methods of production in use in industries of Mizoram are outmoded and as a result the productivity is low. Technological investment is necessary to raise the level of production to bring down labour cost as well as over all manufacturing cost.
7. *Trained Manpower*: Presently Industries of Mizoram lack professional outlook. Even in public sector, professional management concepts and practices are far away. In general the organizational setup and level of investment do not permit them to afford professionally qualified managers. With increase in scale of operation and technological upgradation need of professionally qualified persons shall arise. The University may start offering specialized management courses along with other technical courses like engineering, etc. to meet this requirement. The proposed Institute of Forestry may produce qualified graduates in forest engineering and resource management.
8. *Taxes and Incentives*: Incentives, subsidies in terms of tax relief are necessary to invite new investment. Tax cuts, incentives and subsidies play a vital role in developing an area industrially. But this policy did not work well in Mizoram, as the entrepreneurs failed to realize its value as Mizo are not subject to central taxes. Sales tax in its real sense was enforced in Mizoram from 1st November 1999 only. These incentives are expected to go well with non-tribals, but they hesitate while investing owing to safety, security, extortion, ILP, restrictive

provisions of Industrial Policy, etc. It is, therefore, necessary to provide tax incentives and also relax the restrictions.

9. *Standardization of Local Products*: The local products should be standardized and branded like others to make them compatible with other branded products. The industrial policy of Mizoram, 2000 provided special incentive to entrepreneurs for obtaining ISO 9000/ISI certificate for their products. Adequate publicity should be given to this aspect so that entrepreneurs may take advantage of it.

10. *Re-organization of PSUs*: The PSUs should be revived and their management should be made rational and efficient. Their management should be made accountable for operational performance. The State Government should give them freedom to raise capital from market and allow them to avail bank finance for their projects. This will lead to dropping of non-feasible and non-viable projects and bring cost consciousness among them. MIFCO should take up lead role in the development of agro-base industries in the State and work as role model. It should revive its activities to flourish agro-base industries in private sector in the State and credit may be obtained from co-operative banks for the purpose.[2]

    There exists good scope for fruit processing industry but owing to the absence of marketing support no bank is prepared to finance any fruit-processing units. MAMCO should provide marketing support to such industries rather than just fixing floor prices of agricultural produces, so that bank credit may reach the fruit growers of the State in general and Mamit district in particular.

11. *Promotion to Local Resource Based Industries*: Industrialization is based on either availability of raw materials or market for finished goods. Mizoram has a market for many things but non-availability of raw materials puts barriers in the production. A better option of industrialization is, therefore, to concentrate on the development of locally available raw materials based industries. Among these bamboo based industries, timber based industries, medicinal plant based industries, agro-horticulture and agro based industries such as food and fruit processing, animal feed, tea, coffee, rubber and tung plantations, orchid cultivation, floriculture based industries, etc. are prominent. According to Forest Survey of India (State of Forest Report,

2001), Mizoram with forest cover of 82.98 per cent of State's geographical area ranked third[3] after Lakshadweep (89.91 per cent) and Andaman & Nicobar (84.01per cent) in India. In terms of economic value of goods (i.e. timber, fuel wood, etc.) and service (income and employment) annual contribution of forest is estimated at Rs. 100 crore.[4] Considering the local resource base the branch SISI, Aizawl through Industrial Potential Survey, 1996 had identified industries having scope in Mizoram. This included[5] wooden furniture, wooden handicrafts, wooden doors and windows, wooden rulers, graduated scale, handmade pencils, cane furniture, bamboo craft, baskets, wooden packing boxes, etc., tent poles, bamboo ladders, agarbatti sticks, artistic photo frames, trays etc., umbrella handles, walking sticks, canes for police, handles for sports goods, ginger processing, and dehydration, potato chips, mushroom processing, fruit juice, jams, jellies, banana chips and processing, corn flakes, papaya processing, starch from tapioca, oils extraction, meat, fishes, vegetables and fruits, animal, cattle and poultry feed, handmade paper from wooden waste, agro waste, plastic recycling, waste particle board from wooden shavings, fuel briquettes from charcoal dust, wooden waste country type bricks and clay tiles. A brief description of some of these industries is given here.

(i) *Food Processing Industries*: Ginger, banana, orange, pineapple, sugarcane, chilly, bamboo shoots, passion fruits etc. are produced in large quantity and are in excess of domestic consumption in the State. Ginger is available between Rs. 5/- to Rs. 10/- per kilogram. When pickle is made it becomes worth Rs. 175/- per kg. Similarly, passion fruit a rare variety in the country is available in Mizoram in plenty. It may be exploited profitably and may become a monopoly item if squash or juice or powder is made. Recently, the MIFCO's has installed an Integrated Fruit Juice Concentrate Plant at Chhingchhip, which needs regular supply of various types of fruits for further processing. This may lead to ancillarisation for packing material from plastic, polythene and glass, spices (masala), label printing, etc.

(ii) *Fruit Processing*: In view of high quality of banana of Mizoram, scope exists for its processing into banana slices (chips). Similarly, concentrated fruits squash may be converted into powdered form and after packing on the lines of Kissan/Maggi Tomato Soup pouch or milk powder may be sold in the country and outside. There is a need for making these products value added at competitive cost, which can be achieved by applying management techniques, improving production technology, etc.

(iii) *Agro-Based Industries*: The National Sugar Research Institute, Kanpur had conducted a study on feasibility of establishing a Mini-Sugar Plant during V^{th} Five Year Plan period and had recommended that a plant with an installed capacity to crush 50 MT of cane can be setup. During the year 1978-79, it was contemplated to make it operative. However it remained on paper. It may be taken up again in the light of annual sugarcane production of 9360 MT.[6]

(iv) *Coffee Plantation*: Coffee is cultivated in the State without any core and maintenance with practically no technical inputs being applied. The Coffee Board has identified 4,000 hectare of land having potential for coffee cultivation, while presently 300 hectare of land only is being used for the purpose. According to MS Swaminathan Report about 10,000 hectare may be used for coffee plantation in seven blocks. Black pepper and orange may be sown as companion crops. This source may earn an income of Rs. 15,000/- per hectare from fourth year that may be raised to Rs. 88,000/- from eighth year. It may promote allied services of pulping machines and drying yards. It is important to note that the Coffee Board is presently meeting 50 per cent of the cost of coffee cultivation. Further, several incentives are given by the Coffee Board. It is suggested that necessary inputs, and requisite technology may be extended to coffee growers by introducing "coffee grower card". This in turn is expected to discourage *jhoom* cultivation.

(v) *Tea Industry*: Land measuring 10,000 hectare has been identified as ideal for tea growing and it is estimated that this can earn a net income of Rs. 13,000/- per hectare from fourth year, which may raise to Rs. 82,000/- in eighth year and onwards. It may promote allied services needed for processing the green tea leaves such as pruning knives, trailer basket, tea sample containers, wire fencing nails, nuts, bolts, aprons, rain coats, umbrella, pesticides, fertilizers, weedicides, polythene bags, soaps, detergents, phenyl, dettol, bandage, cotton, drugs, pharmaceuticals, tea chests with polythene lining and aluminium lining etc. Further, the Tea board also offers benefits and incentives that may be availed by the entrepreneurs.

(vi) *Rubber Plantation*: Rubber Plantation need to be resumed as this source has a potential for raising Rs. 13,000/- per hectare from seventh year onwards. The literature on Mizoram shows that rubber plants existed in plenty during pre-British time. This indicated that the land is fit for rubber plantation. It was estimated that about 5,000 hectare of land is presently suitable for rubber plantation near the Western border, which may produce/extract rubber 1,000 kg p.a. from seventh year to 1500 kg p.a. in the tenth year and onwards. At the same time banana and pineapple may be grown during gestation period.

(vii) *Tung Plantation*: Mizoram's land is suitable for tung plantation. Tung is an important input for paint and wax industries. Mizoram is the only state/place in India where tung trees are grown on large scale. Technical estimates revealed that about 275 trees per hectare may be raised and tung seeds after shelling and drying may be sold to the oil extraction companies at Rs. 10/- per kg ex-factory price. This source may earn a net income from one hectare of tung plantation in the fifth year at Rs. 1000/-, which may raise to Rs. 13,000/- from the tenth year and onwards. Mushroom cultivation may be also promoted as the land and climate is congenial to its production. Commercial orange farming on large scale in Mamit District may be encouraged.

(viii) *Orchid Cultivation*: Mizoram has rich diversity of natural orchids, which have domestic and international potential in cut flowers and medicinal market. More than 200 varieties of orchids are found in Mizoram. Mizoram is the only natural home of *Vanda Coerules* (Blue Vanda), *Renanthera Imschootiana* (Red Vanda) among the Northeastern States. *Cymbidium* variety may be cultivated for sale as cut flowers in Delhi/Kolkata markets with the assistance of forest department. Cultivation of 1000 plants of *cymbidium* hybrid may earn an income of Rs. 67,000/- from third year that may go upto Rs. 1,21,000/- from fifth year onwards. However, these natural orchids are not properly conserved and developed to a sustainable level of utilization due to lack of eco-scientific management in Mizoram. In order to conserve and attain sustainable utilization of natural orchids certain measures such as 'survey and demarcation of orchid rich areas' within the state, framing of proper rules and regulation to stop illegal collection and export of wild orchids, establishment of proper orchid research and development centre, providing latest technology for breeding, multiplication, cultivation and management etc., establishment of an orchid farming society, etc. are necessary. This is expected to generate employment of local youth, and commercialization of orchids may be adopted.[7]

(ix) *Rural Nurseries*: There exists scope for establishment of nurseries in Kolasib district to produce quality-planting material for cash crops. This source may earn an annual income of Rs. 2.37 lakh each nursery. There is a scope for growing new crops *viz*., mango, cashew, banana, cinnamon, clove, areca nut, geranium, mint, etc.

(x) *Bamboo-Based Industries*: While bamboo resource is depleting in other parts of the country Mizoram has abundant natural bamboo resource. Around 57 per cent of the geographical area of Mizoram ranging from 400 - 1500 metre above the mean sea level is under bamboo cover. There are twenty species of bamboo in Mizoram of which Melocanna baccifera is dominating variety of the State, which fetches Government a revenue of Rs. 80 lakh annually[8]. The Government receives a sum of Rs. 66 lakh per year as royalty on bamboo. Annual availability from the total growing in the State is 5.83 million MT, but aggregate annual consumption of bamboo including paper mills supply stands at 28315 MT only. Bamboo-based products such as fibre-board, mat-ply, bamboo pens, umbrella handles, wall hangers, traditional hats, water piping, broomsticks, ceiling cleaners, decorative and household items, etc., can be manufactured without much investment. Bamboos grow up to 8-10 metre height and are widely used for construction of *Kaccha* houses, furniture, weaving, pulping, and fencing. The shoots are eaten on large scale during rainy season and constitute a dominant food item. There is no proper management of the bamboo resources of the State. The Government has recently framed a bamboo policy for ensuring optimum utilization of this resource. A Bamboo Institute may be opened in the State to train young entrepreneurs in producing different products and caring for its varieties.

In view of the vast potential of bamboo resource, a paper mill was set up at Panchagram in Cachar district, under the ownership of M/s. Hindustan Paper Mills Ltd., a public sector undertaking. Bulk of the raw material to this mill is sent from Mizoram. During 1976-77, the Government had initiated for another paper mill within Mizoram. The feasibility study suggested for a plant at Bairabi with capacity of 200 MT per day of printing and writing paper. But it could not materialize. There might have been some flaws in the project, which can be removed by redesigning the same and it may be taken up again to turn the vast untapped bamboo resource known as 'green gold' of the State into 'cash gold'. Paper and pulp projects may encourage ancillarisation of alum, salt cake, starch, lime, sulphuric acid, resin, paper cones, telecom powder, gum taps, wooden plugs and sodium chloride.

(xi) *Timber-Based Industries*: Mizoram receives 778 cm rainfall annually. It is a home for a great variety of ever green as well as deciduous timber species. Among these *Michelia champaca* is a big evergreen tree with high quality timber. Its timber is graded as A-II class, which is the highest grade among the indigenous species in Mizoram. It is a fast growing variety with a long, clean and cylindrical bole. Artificial regeneration of the variety is found to be quite successful and widely tried in the State. *Terminalia myriocarpa* is the second highest graded timber in the State, next to *Michelia* variety. It is a big tree found in almost all parts of Mizoram. Its timber is widely used and is moderately hard and moderately refractory and durable. *Artocarpus chaplasha* is one of the best timbers for manufacturing motor bodies and country boats. It is indigenous to the State and graded as A-II class. Artificial regeneration has been largely tried with good success. *Tectona grandis* teak is exotic to

Mizoram but due to its high demand in quality furniture making, it is widely planted both by private and government agencies. Majority of the government plantations are teak plantations in pure form as well as mixed with *Gmelina arborea*. Plantations of economic tree species on abandoned *jhum* land and degraded forest area is the best alternative. Timber-based industries have good scope in the State. Mizo carpenters manufacture good quality furniture. To make it commercially viable and export oriented, industrial units may be set up with efficient managerial skill. However, deforestation due to timber-based industry should be accompanied by afforestation to prevent environmental hazards. In view of Supreme Court order dated 15th January 1998, which banned fresh felling of forest trees except in accordance with the working plan of State Government, there is a need to frame such a plan at an early date.

(xii) *Medicines*: Mizoram is rich in bio-diversity. Work on botanical collection and botanical research started in 1990 and by now more than 400 medicinal plants have been identified in Mizoram, of which 62 are recorded as new medicinal plants. Further, it was reported that existence of estimated 90 per cent of India's medicinal plant diversity in forests and 10 per cent in non-forests habitat suits Mizoram conditions[9]. Entrepreneurs with exposure and training in forestry should be encouraged to undertake medicine extraction.

12. *Promotion to Demand Based Industries*: An alternative approach to industrialization can be to produce goods for which there is a ready demand in the market. Considering this, the SISI branch, Aizawl in its Industrial Potential Survey, 1996 identified demand based industries having scope in Mizoram. This included[10] plastic injected molded components, polythene carry bags, poly-packs etc., hawai chappals, detergent powder, washing soap, vim powder, vessel cleaning chemicals, paper bags, envelopes, exercise notebooks, bags for school children, paper pins, stapler pins, gum and pastes, office file covers, file pads, tags etc., ready mixed paints, varnish, thinner, wood polish, fence polish, biscuits, breads, noodles and vermicelli, chalk, crayons, teaching aids, Montessori school equipment, steel furniture, almirah, steel

rack etc., rolling shutter, gates and grills, wire nails, panel pins, wood screw, aluminium utensils, containers, ready made garments, wax candles and decorative festive candles, plastic molded switches, plugs, pins, wooden/fabricated switch boards, ceiling, etc., phenyl, deodorant, aerated water and soft drinks, hair oil, hair dyes etc. light roofing sheets, mosaic flooring tiles, chemical porcelain wares, tile, glass mirror, polishing unit, glazed pipes, printing ink, ball pen ink.

Besides, it also found some industries having considerable market potential that are hollow cement blocks, cement bricks, RCC spun pipes, water pipes etc., aluminium furniture, office partitions; blue metal and stone crushing; cone ice creams, popcorn, paint brushes, domestic brushes, knitting woollen socks, hosiery items; ladies bags, purses and novelties; electrical accessories like choke, starter etc.; plastic extruded items, agricultural tools and equipments; fans, hardware, tower bolts, hinges etc.; bolts and nuts, mechanized wire-cut bricks, automobile components, cables, clutch wire, non-ferrous items like brushes, pins, barbed wires, steel expanded metal for fencing, bee keeping-*cum*-honey processing, caffeine from tea waste, pineapple processing, vinegar from fruit waste, frozen fish cutlets, hatchery and poultry farm, meat processing and preservation, sports goods (wood, cane and bamboo), paper pulp from wood waste[11]. Among the above the industries having ready demand are as follows:

(i) *Poultry and Pork Processing Industry*: Looking into the eating habits of people, eggs, chicken, and pork are important items of daily menu. Presently, around 80 per cent of eggs are procured from distant places (Andhra Pradesh), while there is a chronic shortage for chicken and pork. To meet the demand for meat, on the average 1000-1200 pigs, 1100-1300 cattles, buffaloes, 300-600 goats are slaughtered monthly[12]. Mizoram Food & Allied Industries Corporation Ltd. (MIFCO), a State owned PSU has set up a pork and poultry processing plant with a capacity to process 15,000 pigs and 4,50,000 poultry birds p.a. All this indicated that the State presently has acute shortage of poultry and pork products. The entrepreneurs may, therefore, be encouraged to set up industrial units to support MIFCO's

'Pork and Poultry Processing plant' or set up their own farms for poultry and piggery, birds, boiler, etc.

(ii) *Inland Fisheries*: Inland Fisheries projects are employment oriented. Domestic fish production stood at 3154 quintals as on 31st March 2002 as against corresponding demand of 7830 quintals.[13] Tata Economic Consultancy Services Study had projected that 10,000 new ponds may be dug as against existing 5082 fishponds as on 31st March 2002. In the light of this, allied industries like cold storage and ice plants have good potential where entrepreneurs need to be encouraged.

(iii) *Animal Feed Industry*: Around 70,000 tons of feed is required annually for cattle, poultry and piggery in Mizoram. The existing animal feed mills are unable to meet the requirement and presently, the State's requirement is met from inter-state trade. Further, the State has sizeable production of maize 16645 MT[14] every year. This makes it clear that animal feed plants in private sector have good scope and new entrepreneurs need to be motivated to undertake such venture.

(iv) *Handloom and Handicraft Industries*: Besides increasing the income of the poor artisans, these traditional units preserve craftsmanship and art heritage. Such units enable a large number of people to earn a descent living and thus pave the way for social justice. However, considering the scarce capital, low level of technical know how, inadequate managerial experience and absence of huge mineral reserves the small scale sector of traditional pattern has better potential in Mizoram. The traditional handloom and handicraft industry should be taken up for modernization by induction of improved designs and technology. Power looms may be set up to increase production, reduce production cost and develop varieties with computer aided designs. Presently, though the quality handloom and handicraft products available in market do not attract (appeal) customers owing to high price. In order to make these products export oriented and competitive in other markets, these industries need to be modernized and production needs to be rationalized so as to fit in 'cost theory' and 'theory of consumer'. The handloom and handicraft weavers should diversify their product range from '*puan*' to other dress materials such as cloth for *saree*, skirt, top, shirt etc. This may attract more customers from outside Mizoram.

(v) *Information Technology*: Information technology offers accelerated employment opportunity. Mizoram with its high literacy has good potential in this line. TECS had suggested that establishment of a software development centre can ensure optimum utilization of qualified engineering manpower currently available in the State. This should be taken up on priority basis.

(vi) *Electronics*: High literacy, intricate capabilities of local women workforce and pleasant and agreeable climate of Mizoram are conducive to the development of electronics. The setting up of a Mizo Technical Service Centre, to cater to the needs of training in consumer electronics, computers and general electrical and electronics is desirable. It may lead to ancillarisation of services, components, assembling, etc.

(*iv*) Suggestions as Regards to Finance

Financial institutions contribute to economic development. However, as discussed earlier they faced a number of problems and are not able to play their role in the development process. The following steps should be taken to reinforce their contribution:

1. *Private Banks*: Private Banks may be allowed to operate in Mizoram. This is expected to inculcate healthy competition among different banking institutions.
2. *Promotion of Banking in Rural Areas*: Loan proposals from rural areas many times contain certain flaws. Instead of rejecting the proposals the entrepreneurs may be advised to remove the defects. They may be suggested ways of removing flaws in their project report. Bank personnel in rural branches besides their normal banking business may help giving consultancy to rural entrepreneurs for preparation of project reports. Some awareness programmes from time to time may be undertaken to make people familiar with project report preparation. The University may also offer a paper on entrepreneurship development and project report preparation should be taught. Awareness camps of short duration do not bring expected results and an entrepreneur cannot be

trained within a short period. These programmes many a times fail in opening their horizons. The duration and depth of training may, therefore, be increased.

3. *Increase in Capital Base of ZIDCO*: The government may authorize ZIDCO to mobilize household savings in Mizoram in the form of public deposit to raise its capital base.
4. *Waiving of Stamp Duty*: Stamp Duty may be waived for loans up to Rs. 2 lakh for the creation of registered mortgage, wherever equitable mortgage is not feasible.
5. *Valuation Service*: As there are no approved valuers in the State, the State Government may constitute departmental committee for certification of market value of immovable property offered as security to banks.
6. *Joint Recovery Drives*: In order to simplify the recovery of Government sponsored loans a law should be passed by the State Government so as to empower its officials to adjudicate recoveries from bank loan defaulters. Government departments may be involved in the joint recovery drives of the banks to step up recoveries and to enable recycling of funds. State Government may instruct its departments to authorize Salary Disbursing Officers to recover bank loan installments from the salary of Government personnel who have availed bank loans. The people of the State also need to bring a change their outlook from 'social banking' to 'economic banking'.
7. *Relaxation of Norms*: It was observed that financial institutions in Mizoram in general are not able to achieve their loan targets. In this regard it may be suggested that norms for lending in rural and remote areas may particularly be relaxed. In view of land mortgage problem in Mizoram, some alternative solution may be evolved as a substitute, which may pave the way for easy and quick lending. The problem may be discussed at the State level bankers' committee meeting to work out an alternative. Other lending norms such as margin money, security, etc. may also be relaxed.
8. *Supervisory Credit*: It is the duty of the lending institution to ensure that the money lent is not mis-utilized.[15] Credit provided by an institutional agency has to be properly supervised in order to ensure that it is used for the purpose for which it was granted and in approved manner. The RBI sponsored Expert Group on State Enactments had made it clear in 1971 that "in the absence

of a link between credit and marketing, it is very difficult to ensure recovery of loans through sale proceeds[16]. In case of trade and industrial advances, the term "supervisory credit" denotes periodic visit to premises of industrial unit of the borrowers specially to ensure the existence of assets hypothecated to bank as security.[17] This practice should be adopted by all banks.

(V) Suggestions as Regards to Taxation

Taxation is necessary for a State to fulfil its role and the business and industry have a prominent role in it. In the light of problems discussed earlier some possible alternatives which may lead to widening and strengthening of tax base in the State have been enumerated here:

1. *Widening the Base of Sales Tax*: The base of Sales tax needs to be widened by bringing in a variety of commodities in its ambit and rates of sales tax need to be revised to the extent possible, so as to bring uniform floor rates of sales tax. It is desirable that the tax rate should not be below the level what has been prevailing in the neighbouring States. For example, petroleum tax levied by the State is perhaps lowest among the Northeastern States. This may be brought at par with other neighbouring states. However, frequent upward revision of tax rates should be avoided. Sales tax has been replaced by Value Added Tax and this suggestion holds good for VAT also.
2. *Widening of Profession Tax Base*: Profession Tax Policy should be revised so that tax collection could be raised as the economy is growing. The government servants are important contributor to the tax and progressive tax collection from the growing size of economy should be ensured. Employers and drawing and disbursing officers may be explained about their role in the development of the State and their cooperation should be sought.
3. *Surprise Inspection of Accounting Records*: Once a consignment is passed from border check point the enforcement agencies (sales tax) may visit entrepreneurs' premises and inspect accounting records to ensure that the same has been recorded properly and proper sales tax is realized and remitted to government account.
4. *Review of Total Prohibition Policy*: To increase the tax base total prohibition policy owing to which the State government is

presently deprived of a large chunk of State tax revenue need be reviewed.

5. *Reorganization of Tax Administration*: To bring about efficiency in tax administration, the Taxation Department need be strengthened and reorganized. A full-fledged commissioner, a statutory requirement with professional expertise in tax matters need be appointed. For organizing departmental set-up, districts and circles may be rearranged and the whole state need be divided into zones and circles according to the need of the region. State Government may review the existing arrangement of making different departments severally responsible for the collection of taxes with a view to bringing down the cost of tax collection. It may be more practicable to have one collection agency for all taxes and the existing taxation department may be appropriate for the work.
6. *Computerization of Commercial Taxes Information System*: Computerization of Commercial Tax Information System is need of the hour to meet the objectives[18] of improving tax revenue collections and proper management of accounting procedures, providing concise and concrete databases of all vital information regarding the dealers and taxes and also assessing authorities and their units, ensuring a smooth flow of works and eliminating unnecessary delays in the process, keeping top management well informed about all activities taking place within units by generating timely reports, introducing state of art technologies to improve not only the efficiency of the department as a whole but also the quality of life of the commercial tax personnel, facilitating better monitoring and controlling of tax assessment, collection and enforcement throughout the State, improving the efficiency and effectiveness of tax administration, and providing management with reliable and accurate information in time so as to assist them in tax planning and in decision-making.

   There is also a need to setup communication links between different offices of Taxation Department and five check gates using VSAT Technology with centralized database system centre at Aizawl for online processing and authentication as well as retrieval of dealers' details.
7. *Tax Education*: A dealers' (registered and non-registered) meet may be organized to make them aware of the benefits of getting

registered, to appraise them of benefits of voluntary compliance, and their role play in the development of the State. The University may include in its course curriculum at degree level various tax laws in force in the State, the procedure of determining tax liability, assessment procedure, etc. future entrepreneurs. The University may also offer diploma courses in State Taxes.

8. *Imposition of Direct Taxes*: The indigenous residents of Mizoram are exempted from Income Tax. As the Income Tax is applicable only to persons whose income exceeded a certain limit, and this way, it does not affect poorer sections of the society. The State Government may accept Shukla Commission's report in principal and may make a request to Central Government to introduce income tax with certain special arrangement such as, (i) initially, 100 per cent tax proceeds from the State may be given for State's development, or (ii) grant some special deductions, or (iii) fixing lower tax rates, or (iv) fix minimum income chargeable to tax at higher level, etc. This will do away with a big anomaly as presently there is discrimination amongst people in the State service; some pay income tax while others do not pay. Shukla Commission Report had commented that "The performance of the North-East states in mobilizing additional resources for development has been poor. Clearly for accelerated development of the region, it is imperative that the State governments in the region rein in non-plan expenditure and substantially step up additional resource mobilization....All Northeastern states or those segments of tribal population hitherto exempt from income tax should voluntarily accept the principle of taxation in accordance with the ability to pay, subject to the proviso that the net proceeds or additionality be credited to a special development fund for the concerned State/district council for a stipulated period say 15 years. The rates of tax would be marginally lower than the all India rates in all the states for an initial period"[19]. It would be equitable and just if the suggestion is implemented.

(VI) Suggestions as Regards to Entrepreneurship Development

People in general including those in business lack in business orientation and entrepreneurship. The following suggestions may be put forth in this respect:

1. *Redesigning the EDPs/MDPs/SDPs*: The aim of entrepreneurship development programmes is to open entrepreneurs' horizons. Considering this in future the EDPs, the MDPs etc. need be made trade specific and selection of trade may be from local resource based industries first and consumer based industries next instead of general. There is an urgent need to make these programmes more attractive and content-wise qualitative, so as to ensure increasing participation of willing persons, rather than just completing the target. For ensuring this some suitable scrutiny measures need be adopted.

   The agencies concerned need be deeply involved into the task of entrepreneurship development. Wide publicity of the programmes with their utility should be done. Prospective entrepreneurs need be given an exposure to unemployment situation outside the State, which may perhaps motivate them to remain participative throughout the programme. Follow-up statistics may be compiled by each agency. Some kind of undertaking may be obtained from the participants and prospective entrepreneurs on completion of the programme that they will undertake the venture for which training was given to them.
2. *Coordination*: The entrepreneurs need a package of services at different points of time like stimulatory incentives, supportive services and sustaining measures. These services are to be provided by different organizations and institutions in a coordinated and integrated manner with due monitoring and proper follow-up. What is actually needed is effective co-ordination among all these organizations and institutions involved in entrepreneurship development to ensure better results of the programmes.[20] The promotional agencies in Mizoram such as SISI, Directorate of Industries, DICs, ZIDCO, NECON, MKVIB, etc. concerned with SSI development in the State need to act as catalysts for growth and development of SSI sector and not merely as infrastructure agencies.
3. *Management and Technical Institutes*: At present there are no technical and management institutes in the State except for the ITI and CEDIT. Since there technical institutes and training centres need to be established. Some periodic training programmes need be conducted to acquaint the present and future entrepreneurs as well as workers about the latest developments

in the field of management and technology. The State Government may launch campaign to motivate people to take up entrepreneurship, rather than seeking jobs. Programmes for awareness and enlightenment may be conducted frequently to generate industrial atmosphere in the State.

4. *Education*: The education need be such that the future entrepreneurs become job providers and not job seekers and should be able to motivate them to lead hard life.

(VII) Suggestion as Regards to Infrastructure Development

The process of industrialization goes side by side with availability and development of infrastructural facilities. Industrialization and development can be ensured only with better infrastructure facilities like road, power, communication etc. In this respect the following may be suggested:

1. *Power Sector*: Availability of power itself is a major problem in the State. Two big projects, namely Tuivai (120 MW) project (a central project) and the Kolodyne phase-I (100MW) project, waiting for clearance at appropriate levels, need be implemented on top priority basis. Besides, the State may try for more grid power from neighboring states. Power sector may lead to ancillarisation and industries such as lighting arrestor, PVC cables, switch and fuse, KWH power meter, strap fitting for sickle insulator, hand wire fitting and accessories, rubber gloves, insulators, conductors, GI standard wire, ground materials etc. may be set up.
2. *Road Network*: The total length of roads in Mizoram was 5486 km on 1st April 2002. This consisted of 3514 km surfaced and 1972 km unsurfaced roads. There is a need for development of road and transport system not only within the State but also with other states of the region to provide connectivity.
3. *Water Supply*: Water supply once in a week for domestic consumption may be alright, but for industries and more specially for growth of chemical based industries, etc. water supply needs to be augmented. For this new water supply system need be developed.
4. *Water ways*: The State had in past water links with Chittagong and Arakan hills. Since partition these routes are artificially closed. These may be resumed under international arrangement. This

alternative will render the region easy access to Kolkata and other cities of India. This need be taken up on priority basis.

5. *Railways*: Mizoram is connected with rest of India through one single road only, and even this road remains interrupted owing to landslides, etc. Alternative road approaches are yet to develop. With a view to make available cheaper and easy mode of transport railway connectivity may be developed at least up to Aizawl.
6. *Communication*: Though the telephone facility in the State has improved to a great extent in recent past, still it need to be improved and strengthened further by allowing private telephone companies that are yet to enter Mizoram to bring in a healthy competition in the field of communication.

The Government is expected to act as facilitator in development process. Its main responsibility is to create an environment that is conducive to faster growth of business and industry. It should undertake a study in depth to investigate into the reasons of high sickness and slow growth of industries. The legal and administrative framework need be upgraded to promote business and industry. The DIC may be given the responsibility of providing training in a variety of trade skills suited to the business environment and preparing and floating viable proposals to potential entrepreneurs. The Directorate of Industries may prepare and provide a list of proposed industries having good potential in the State and provide all round support to the entrepreneurs on Single Window approach.

NOTES

1. Sarma, B.K., *Industrial Land-Scape of North-East India*, Mittal Publications, New Delhi, 1993, pp. 251-53.
2. Report of the Sub-Committee of State Level Bankers' Committee for Mizoram on Credit-Deposit Ratio, 15th November 1996, State Bank of India, Regional Office, Aizawl, p. 4.
3. Department of Environment & Forests, *Mizoram Forest, 2003*, Government of Mizoram, Aizawl, p. 4.
4. *Ibid.*
5. Assistant Director-in-charge, Small Industries Service Institute, Aizawl, July 1996.
6. Department of Environment & Forests, *Mizoram Forest*, 2003, *Op. cit.*, p. 3.

7. *Ibid*, p. 46.
8. *Ibid*, p. 15.
9. *Ibid*, p. 22.
10. Assistant Director-in-charge, Small Industries Service Institute, *op. cit.*, July 1996.
11. *Ibid.*
12. *Ibid.*
13. Directorate of Economics and Statistics, *Statistical Handbook*, 2002, Government of Mizoram, Aizawl, pp. 23-24.
14. Department of Forests, Mizoram Forests, 2003, *op. cit.*, p. 3.
15. Kemani, C.L., *Concept of Supervision in Rural Credit*, An Article published in *SBI Bulletin*, March 1981, p. 140.
16. Reserve Bank of India, *Report of the Expert Group of State Enactments having a Bearing on the Commercial Banks Lending to Agriculture*, Bombay 1971, Chapter VII, p. 31.
17. Kemani, C.L., *Objectives of Field Visits in Agricultural Banking, op. cit.*, February 1986.
18. Supplementary Memorandum on Upgradation of Standard of Administration and Special Problem Scheme submitted to TFC, GOM, May 2004, pp. 36-40.
19. Madhab, Jayanta, Commentary on the Fiscal Situation of the North-Eastern States, *Dialogue*, Vol. 4, No. 1, July-September 2002, pp. 56.
20. Gupta, A.D. and Singha, R.K.P.G.: New Economic Policy, Human Resource Development and Entrepreneurship—A Case Study of Northeast India, *Kangleipak Business Review*, Vol. I, Department of Commerce, Manipur University, Imphal, 1996, p. 65.

APPENDIX-5(A)

Major Components of GSDP from Secondary and Tertiary Sector in Mizoram

From 1990-91 to 2001-02 (As on 31st March)

Year	*1991*	*1992*	*1993*	*1994*	*1995*	*1996*	*1997*	*1998*	*1999*	*2000*	*2001*	*2002*	*2003*	*Mean*	*C.V.*
Industry	2047	2953	3428	2088	2594	3215	3650	2386	2208	2438	2534	2577	N.A.	2677	18
	(6)	(6)	(6)	(3)	(4)	(3)	(3)	(2)	(2)	(2)	(1)	(1)	—	(3)	
	100	144	167	102	127	157	178	117	108	119	124	126	—	-0.37	
Construction	4890	5091	7075	4597	7680	9725	11688	11354	12460	15394	14207	20103	N.A.	10355	42
	(14)	(11)	(13)	(6)	(10)	(10)	(11)	(10)	(10)	(11)	(8)	(10)	—	(11)	
	100	104	145	94	157	199	239	232	255	315	291	411	—	13.64	
Transport	2179	2171	2499	1440	1592	2000	2419	2782	2878	3253	4395	4607	N.A.	2685	34
	(6)	(5)	(5)	(2)	(2)	(2)	(2)	(2)	(2)	(2)	(2)	(2)	—	(3)	
	100	100	115	66	73	92	111	128	132	149	202	211	—	7.90	
Trade, Hotel & Restaurants	1820	2503	3620	10342	9868	14029	14619	15998	15553	13866	20626	18826	N.A.	11806	49
	(5)	(5)	(7)	(15)	(13)	(15)	(14)	(14)	(12)	(10)	(12)	(10)	—	(11)	
	100	138	199	568	542	771	803	879	855	762	1133	1034	—	22.32	
Banking & Insurance	571	564	669	785	849	1042	1284	1497	1849	2075	3103	3784	N.A.	1506	63
	(2)	(1)	(1)	(1)	(1)	(1)	(1)	(1)	(1)	(1)	(2)	(2)	—	(1)	
	100	99	117	137	149	182	225	262	324	363	543	663	—	19.21	
Real Estate	3441	3939	4560	7407	8234	9345	10663	12387	15176	19209	23911	26962	N.A.	12103	59
	(10)	(8)	(9)	(10)	(11)	(10)	(10)	(11)	(12)	(14)	(14)	(14)	—	(11)	
	100	114	133	215	239	272	310	360	441	558	695	784	—	20.73	
Public Administration	5733	7930	8449	10743	11866	14290	17065	18699	19575	25879	33288	37111	N.A.	17552	53
	(17)	(17)	(16)	(15)	(16)	(15)	(16)	(17)	(16)	(18)	(19)	(19)	—	(17)	
	100	138	147	187	207	249	298	326	341	451	581	647	—	17.38	
Other Services	3271	3785	5411	7596	7611	11263	13207	13916	17464	22619	25394	26955	N.A.	13208	58
	(10)	(8)	(10)	(11)	(10)	(12)	(12)	(12)	(14)	(16)	(14)	(14)	—	(12)	
	100	116	165	232	233	344	404	425	534	692	776	824	—	21.83	
Total GSDP	34084	46511	53276	71146	73877	93654	107234	112317	124590	140939	176872	192417	N.A.	102243	45
	100	136	156	209	217	275	315	330	366	414	519	565	—	15.84	

(Contd.)

(*Contd.*)

Year	1991	1992	1993	1994	1995	1996	1997	1998	1999	2000	2001	2002	2003	Mean	C.V.
State Tax Revenue to Total GSDP (%)	1.01	0.72	0.84	0.62	0.62	0.62	0.62	0.70	0.74	0.76	0.81	0.99	—	0.75	0.17
Industry, Construction, Transport, Trade, Hotel & Restaurants, Banking, Estate & Public Admn.	20681	25151	30300	37402	42683	53646	61388	65103	69699	82114	102064	113970	N.A.	58683	0.47
	(31)	(54)	(57)	(53)	(58)	(57)	(57)	(58)	(56)	(58)	(58)	(59)	—	(57)	
	100	*122*	*147*	*181*	*206*	*259*	*297*	*315*	*337*	*397*	*494*	*551*	—	*16.17*	
Industry, Construction, Trade, Hotel & Restaurants	8757	10547	14123	17027	20142	26969	29957	29738	30221	31698	37367	41506	N.A.	24838	0.39
	(26)	(23)	(27)	(24)	(27)	(29)	(28)	(26)	(24)	(22)	(21)	(22)	—	(25)	
	100	*120*	*161*	*194*	*230*	*308*	*342*	*340*	*345*	*362*	*427*	*474*	—	*14.33*	

Note:
1. Figures in parenthesis represent the relative share of respective total in percentage.
2. Figures in Italics represent indices.
3. Figures in Italics of Mean Column represent average annual growth rate.
4. For indices the year 1990-91 is taken as base year.

Legend: C. V. = Coefficient of Variation

Source:
1. Department of Finance, Government of Mizoram, Aizawl.
2. State Representation to the Twelfth Finance Commission on 1st June 2004, Government of Mizoram, Aizawl.
3. Notes on Various topics submitted to the Twelfth Finance Commission, March 2004, Government of Mizoram, Aizawl.
4. Compiled from State Domestic Product of Mizoram, New-Series, 2004, Directorate of Economics & Statistics, Government of Mizoram, Aizawl.

BIBLIOGRAPHY

A.S., Home B (1933): Nos. 351-370, File No. G, August.

A.S., Pol B (1933): Nos. 862-74, September.

Acharya, N.N. (1984): '*Modernisation of Mizoram*,' Proceedings of the N.E.H.A., Aizawl.

Agarwal, A.K. (1985): '*North East India—An Economic Perspective*,' Chugh Publications, Allahabad.

Agarwal, A.K. (1987): '*Economic Problems and Planning in North-East India*,' Sterling Publishers, New Delhi.

Agarwal, A.N. and Singh, S.P. (1982): '*The Economics of Underdevelopment*,' Oxford University Press, Delhi, 1958, reprint.

Allen, B.C.: '*Assam District Gazetteers*,' Vol. X, Part-III, Lushai Hills District.

Anon (1873): Bengal Eastern Frontier Regulation (Inner Line Pass Regulations).

Anon (1873-74): Report on Frontier Tribes of Assam.

Anon (1949): Constituent Assembly Debates, Vol. X No. 27, 6th September.

Anon (1953): The Lushai Hills District (Money Lending by Non-Tribals) Regulation.

Anon (1953): The Lushai Hills District (Reduction of Fathang) Act.

Anon (1953): The Lushai Hills District (Trading by Non-Tribals) Regulation.

Anon (1954): The Lushai Hills District (Trading by Non-Tribals) Rules.

Anon (1973): The Mizoram (Sales of Petroleum and Petroleum Products including Motor Spirit and Lubricants) Taxation Act.

Anon (1974): The Mizoram Trading by Non-Tribals (Regulation) Act.

Anon (1978): '*The Lushais (1878—1889)*,' Firma Klm Pvt. Ltd., Kolkatta on behalf of Tribal Research Institute, Aizawl (Mizoram), Indian reprint.

Anon (1981-82 to 2003-04): Annual Accounts, Mizoram State Cooperative Marketing & Consumers' Federation Ltd.

Anon (1984): Administration Report, Government of Mizoram.

Anon (1985-86 to 2000-01): Annual Reports of Mizoram Khadi & Village Industries Board.

Anon (1987): A.R. File No. S-13/8/97, Draft Notification, 1st October.

Anon (1989): '*Mizoram District Gazetteers*,' Directorate Art & Culture, Government of Mizoram, Aizawl.

Anon (1989): The Industrial Policy of Mizoram.

Anon (1989): The Mizoram (Sales of Petroleum and Petroleum Products including Motor Spirit and Lubricants) Taxation Rules.

Anon (1989): The Mizoram Sales Tax Act.

Anon (1989-90 to 2001-02): Annual Accounts, Mizoram Handloom & Handicrafts Development Corporation Ltd.

Anon (1990): The Mizoram Sales Tax Rules.

Anon (1990-91 to 2001-02): Annual Accounts, Zoram Industrial Development Corporation Ltd.

Anon (1990-91 to 2001-02): Auditors' Report on Annual Accounts, Zoram Industrial Development Corporation Ltd.

Anon (1990-91 to 2003-04): Annual Accounts, Mizoram Food & Allied Industries Corporation Ltd.

Anon (1990-91 to 2003-04): Annual Accounts, Zoram Electronics Development Corporation Ltd.

Anon (1990-91 to 2003-04): Auditors' Report on Annual Accounts, Zoram Electronics Development Corporation Ltd.

Anon (1991-92): All India Report on Input Survey.

Anon (1993-94 to 2002-03): Annual Accounts, Mizoram Agricultural Marketing Corporation Ltd.

Anon (1993-94 to 2002-03): Auditors' Report on Annual Accounts, Mizoram Agricultural Marketing Corporation Ltd.

Anon (1993-94 to 2003-04): Annual Accounts, Mizoram Multi-Commodity Producers' Cooperative Union Ltd.

Anon (1994-95 to 1997-98): Annual Accounts, Mizoram Co-operative Apex Bank Ltd.

Anon (1995): The Mizoram Professions, Trades, Callings and Employments Taxation Act.

Anon (1996): The Mizoram Professions, Trades, Callings and Employments Taxation Rules.

Anon (1996): The Mizoram State Agricultural Produce Marketing Regulation (General) Rules.

Anon (1997-98): Auditors' Report on Annual Accounts, Mizoram Co-operative Apex Bank Ltd.

Anon (1998): A Blue Print for Sustainable Agricultural and Rural development for Mizoram State, The M.S. Swaminathan Research Foundation, Chennai.

Anon (1998): Interim Report on Administrative Reforms, Government of Mizoram.

Anon (1998-2002): Mizoram—A Perspective Plan, Tata Economic Consultancy Services, Mumbai.

Anon (1998-99 to 2001-02): Audited Annual Accounts of Mizoram Rural Bank.

Anon (1999): Study on Scope to Increase Trade and Investment in Myanmar, Exim Bank, Mumbai, July.

Anon (2000): The Industrial Policy of Mizoram.

Anon (2000-01): Auditors' Report on Annual Accounts, Mizoram Food & Allied Industries Corporation Ltd.

Anon (2000-01): Directors' Report on Annual Accounts, Zoram Industrial Development Corporation Ltd.

Anon (2001-02): Auditors' Report on Annual Accounts, Mizoram Handloom & Handicrafts Development Corporation Ltd.

Anon (2004): Memorandum to the Twelfth Finance Commission (TFC), Government of Mizoram, February.

Anon (2004): Notes on Various Topics submitted to Twelfth Finance Commission (TFC), Government of Mizoram, March.

Anon (2004): State Presentation to the Twelfth Finance Commission (TFC), Government of Mizoram, 1st June.

Anon (2004): Supplementary Memorandum on Upgradation of Standard of Administration & Special Problem Scheme submitted to Twelfth Finance Commission (TFC), Government of Mizoram, May.

Antonio De Viti De Macro (1950): '*First Principles of Public Finance*'.

Anuradha, A & Rao A. V. V. S. K. (1995): 'An analysis of Inter-State Industrial Disparities in India,' *Indian Journal of Regional Science*, Vol. XXVII, No. 1 & 2.

Assistant Director-in-charge (1996): '*Potential Industries of Mizoram*,' Small Industries Service Institute, Govt. of India, Ministry of Industries, Aizawl. July.

Banerjee, Amalesh & Kar, Biman (1999): '*Economic Planning and Development of Northeastern States*,' Kanishka Publishers-Distributors, New Delhi.

Banerjee, Parmarthanath (1985): '*Public Administration in Ancient India*,' Uppal Publishing House, Delhi.

Bhattacharjee, P.R. (2002): 'The Problem of Ensuring Financial Efficiency in the North-Eastern States,' *Dialogue*, Vol.-4, No. 1, July-September.

Bhattacharya, Hrishikes (1995): '*Total Management by Ratios—An Integrated Approach*,' Sage Publications, New Delhi.

Carey, B.C. (1890): '*The Chin Hills Regulation*'.

Carey, Bertram S. & Tuck, H. N. (1976): '*The Chin Hills*,' Vol.-1, Firma KLM P. Ltd., Kolkata for Tribal Research Institute, Aizawl, 1932, republished.

Chatterjee, Suhas (1990): '*Mizoram—Encyclopaedia*,' Vol.-1, Jaico Publishing House, Mumbai.

Chatterjee, Suhas (1990): '*Mizoram—Encyclopaedia*,' Vol.-2, Jaico Publishing House, Mumbai.

Chartterjee, Suhas (1990): '*Mizoram-Encyclopedia*,' Vol.-3, Jaico Publishing House, Mumbai.

Chatterjee, Suhas (1999): '*A History of Mizo Economy*,' Vol.-1, Printwell Publishers Distributors, Jaipur.

Colney, Rualkhunga (1997): 'Small Scale and Cottage Industries in Mizoram' Ph. D. thesis, North-Eastern Hill University, Shillong.

Das, Gurudas & Purkayastha, R.K. (2000): '*Border Trade—North East India and Neighbouring Countries*,' Akansha Publishing House, New Delhi.

Das, Gurudas (2000): 'Trade between the Northeastern Region and Neighbouring Countries: Structures & Implications for Development,' in edited volume "*Border Trade: Northeast India & Neighbouring Countries*," by Das, Gurudas & Purkayastha, R.K., Akansha Publishing House, New Delhi.

Das, Gurudas (2001): 'Trade between Northeastern Region and Bangladesh: Nature, Trends and Implications for Development Cooperation,' *Dialogue*, Vol. 2, No. 4, April-June.

Deb, Ranabijoy (1993): '*Small Scale Industries in India*,' Mittal Publications, New Delhi.

Deogaonkar, S.G. (1980): '*Problems of Development of Tribal Areas*,' Leela Devi Publications, Delhi.

Department of Environment & Forests (2003): 'Mizoram Forest,' Government of Mizoram, Aizawl.

Dikshitar, V.R.R. (1932): '*The Mauryan Polity*,' Motilal Banarsidas, Delhi.

Directorate of Economics & Statistics (1976 to 2002): Statistical Handbooks of Mizoram, Government of Mizoram.

Directorate of Economics & Statistics (1977, 1990 and 1998): Economic Census of Mizoram, Government of Mizoram.

Directorate of Economics & Statistics (1979-80 and 2000-01): Socio-Economic Review of Mizoram, Government of Mizoram.

Directorate of Economics & Statistics (1990-91): Economic Survey of Mizoram, Government of Mizoram, Aizawl.

Directorate of Trade & Commerce (2001): Current Status Note on Border-Trade with Bangladesh and Myanmar, Government of Mizoram, Aizawl, December.

Dutta, P.S. (1992): '*India's Northeast—A Study in Transition*,' Har-Anand Publications in association with Vikas Publishing House Pvt. Ltd., New Delhi.

Eastern Panorama (2003): Vol. XIII, No. 7, May.

Economic Intelligence Service (1998): Foreign Trade, CMIE, August.

Economic Intelligence Service (2004): Agriculture, CMIE, February.

Editorial Perspective (2002): 'India's Northeast,' *Dialogue*, Vol.-4, No.1, July-September.

Ghosh, S.K. (1983): '*Development Scenario: India*,' World Press, Kolkatta.

Gopalakrishnan, R. (1991): '*North-East India: Land, Economy and People*,' Har—Anand Publications, New Delhi.

Goswami, B.B. (1977): '*Social & Political Institution of the Mizos*,' Seminar on Social & Political Institutions of the Hill People of NE India, ASI & NEICSSR, Shillong, 4th -5th July.

Gupta, A.D. and Singha, R.K.P.G. (1996): '*New Economic Policy, Human Resource Development and Entrepreneurship - a case study of N-E India*,' Kangleipak Business Review, Vol.-1, Department of Commerce, Manipur University, Imphal.

Gupta, Ashis (1994): '*Indian Entrepreneurial Culture*,' Wishwa Prakashan, New Delhi.

Hornby, A.S. (1985): '*Oxford Advanced Learner's Dictionary of Current English*,' 9th ed.

Hunter, W.W. (1879): '*Statistical Account of Assam*,' Vol.-2, Kolkata.

IBM (1997): '*Encyclopedia,*' World Book (on CD).

IIFT (1995): Study on Promotion of Border Trade between India and Myanmar, Indian Institute of Foreign Trade, New Delhi, November.

J. Knox Wight (1884): I. F. Est. A, (Report), No. 380, October.

Kabra, K C. & Singha, R.K.P.G. (2003): '*Border Trade of Mizoram,*' a research paper presented at the National Seminar of "Challenges of Development in North-East India" organized by the ICSSR Regional Centre, Shillong, held on 21-23rd October.

Kabra, K.C. & Singh, Bhartendu (2004): '*Cooperative Financing in Mizoram (A case study of Mizoram Cooperative Apex Bank),*' a research paper presented at the 57th All India Commerce Conference of the Indian Commerce Association organized by MKHS Gujarati Girls College, Indore, held on 26th—28th December.

Kemani, C.L. (1981): 'Concept of Supervision in Rural Credit,' *State Bank of India (SBI) Bulletin*, March.

Kemani, C.L. (1986): '*Objectives of Field Visits in Agricultural Banking,*' State Bank of India (SBI) Bulletin, February.

Khanka, Prof. S.S. (1998): '*Making the Entrepreneurial Society,*' *Journal of NEC,* Vol.-18, No. 4.

Khanka, S.S. (2004): '*Entrepreneurial Development,*' S. Chand & Co. Ltd., New Delhi.

Kohli, Ritu (1995): '*Kautilya's Political Theory,*' Deep & Deep Publications, New Delhi.

Kuchhal, S.C. (1989): '*Financial Management,*' Chaitanya Publishing House, Allahabad.

Lalhniangi, F.C. (1990): '*Role of Forestry in Socio Economic Development of Mizoram,*' Lallianpari, Aizawl.

Lalrimawia (1981): '*Historic Migration of the Mizos,*' Proceedings to the NEI History Association.

Lalrimawia (1995): '*Mizoram: History and Cultural Identity,*' Spectrum Publications, Guwahati.

Lalrinchhana (2004): 'Agricultural Input-Output Analysis of Mizoram,' (Unpublished Ph.D.).

Lalthanthuami (2005): 'Agricultural Marketing in Mizoram,' (Unpublished Ph.D. thesis).

Lewis, W.A. (1965): '*The Theory of Economic Growth,*' London.

Lianzela (1993): 'Economic Development of Mizoram' Ph.D. thesis, Gauhati University, Guwahati (Assam).

Lianzela (1994): '*Economic Development of Mizoram,*' Spectrum Publications, Guwahati.

Lianzela (1995): '*Four Decades of Planning in Mizoram,*' Khuangkungi, Aizawl.

Lianzela (1998): '*Economy of Mizoram,*' Mizoram Publication Board, Aizawl.

Machiraju, H.R. (1999): '*Indian Financial System,*' Vikas Publishing House P. Ltd., New Delhi.

Mackenzie, Alexander (1999): '*The North East Frontier of India,*' Mittal Publications, New Delhi, 1884 republished in 1979 and reprint.

Madhab Jayanta (2002): 'Commentary on the Fiscal Situation of the Northeastern States,' *Dialogue*, Vol.-4, No.1, July-September.

Mali, D.D. (2002): 'Entrepreneurship & Socio-Cultural Ethos and Values in the in Northeast Region,' *Kangleipak Business Review*, Vol.-2, No. 1, Department of Commerce, Manipur University, Imphal.

Mathew, T. (1980): '*Tribal Economy of North-Eastern Region,*' Spectrum Publications, Guwahati.

McCall, A.G. (1972): '*District Cover (Lushai Hills).*'

Murty, (Mrs.) S. (1999): '*Market Economy and Economic Growth,*' RBSA Publishers, Jaipur.

Musgrave, Richard A. (1959): '*The Theory of Public Finance*'.

Nair, Sukumaran (1987): '*Tribal Economy in Transition,*' Inter-India Publications, New Delhi.

Narasaiah, M. Lakshmi (2001): '*Small-Scale Entrepreneurship,*' Discovery Publishing House, New Delhi.

NEC Secretariat (1980): '*Basic Statistics of NE Region,*' Government of India, Shillong.

NEC Secretariat (2002): '*Basic Statistics of NE Region,*' Government of India, Shillong.

Northeast Trade Line (2003): '*Indo-Myanmar Border Trade,*' Vol.-1, No. 3, February.

Perry, N.E. (1932): '*The Lakhers,*' Macmillan & Co. Ltd., London.

Parry, N.E. (1976): '*A Monograph on Lushai Custom & Ceremonies,*' Aizawl Reprint.

Patrick, Martin (1999): '*Self-Employment and Successful Entrepreneurship,*' Kanishka Publishers-Distributors, New Delhi.

Prasad, D. Ravindra, Prasad, V.S., Satyanarayana, P. (1989): '*Administrative Thinkers,*' Sterling Publishers, Delhi.

Prasad, R.N. & Agarwal, A.K. (2003): '*Modernisation of the Mizo Society,*' Mittal Publications, New Delhi.

Prasad, R.N. and Agarwal, A.K. (1991): '*Political and Economic Development of Mizoram,*' Mittal Publications, New Delhi.

Prasad, R.N. and Agarwal, A.K. (1995): '*Landmarks: A Study of Public Administration in Mizoram,*' Indian Institute of Public Administration, Aizawl Branch, Mizoram.

Rajashekar, H. (2000): '*Commercial Banking and Finance,*' Mangal Deep Publications, Jaipur.

Rao, M.V. Krishna (1958): '*Studies in Kautilya,*' Munshi Ram Manoharlal, Delhi.

Ray, Animesh (1972): '*Mizoram,*' Pearl Publishers, Kolkata.

Ray, Animesh (1982): '*Mizoram - Dynamics of Change,*' Pearl Publishers, Kolkata.

Ray, B. Dutta (1987): '*North-East India 2000 A.D.: Perspective for Futurology,*' Deep & Deep Publications, New Delhi.

Reserve Bank of India (1971): "Report of the Expert Group of State Enactments having a Bearing on the Commercial Banks Lending to Agriculture", Bombay.

Reserve Bank of India (1994): Circular No. FIC-No. 841/01-02-00/'93-94 Dt: 28th March.

Reserve Bank of India (2000): *A.P. (DIR Series) Circular* No. 17, Dt: 18th October.

Roy Burman, B.R. (1970): '*Demographic and Socio Economic Profiles of the Hill areas of Northeast India,*' Department of Publication, Delhi.

Sarma, B.K. (1993): '*Industrial Landscape of North-East India,*' Mittal Publications, New Delhi.

Sen, D. (1984): '*Early Histroy of the Lushais with Special Reference to Lushai Chiefs,*' Social Research, Vol. 4, No. 3-4.

Shakespear, H. (1975): '*The Lushai Kuki Clans,*' Part-I, Thangruma Printing Press, Aizawl.

Sharma, B.D. (1978): '*Tribal Development: The Concept and Frame,*' A.K. Dash, New Delhi.

Sharma, B.D. (1984): '*Planning for Tribal Development: The Concept and the Frame,*' A.K. Dash, New Delhi.

Sharma, K.R. (2004): '*Research Methodology,*' National Publishing House, New Delhi.

Sikidar, Sujit (1992): '*Rural Banking—An Infrastructural Input for Hill Area Development,*' Anmol Publications, New Delhi.

Singh, S.K. (1982): '*Economics of the Tribes and their Transformation,*' Concept Publishing Co., New Delhi.

Singh, S.N. (1994): '*Mizoram: Historical, Geographical, Social, Economic, Political and Administrative,*' Mittal Publications, New Delhi.

Singha, R.K.P.G. & Gupta, A.D. (2003): 'Industrial Development in Mizoram—Towards Sustainable Development,' in edited volume "*Modernisation of the Mizo Society*" by Prasad, R.N. & Agarwal, A.K., Mittal Publications, New Delhi.

Small Industries Development Organisation (1971): Report on Development of Industries in Mizo Hills, Ministry of Industrial Development and Internal Trade, New Delhi.

Smith, Adam (1776): '*The Wealth of Nations,*' Book—V. (http://www.bized.ac.uk/virtual/economy/library/economist/smith.htm).

Srinath, Baruah (2000): 'Certain Observation on Informal Border Trade with Neighbouring Countries & Economic Prospects of Northeastern Region,' in edited volume "*Border Trade: Northeast India & Neighbouring Countries,*" by Das, Gurudas & Purkayastha, R.K., Akansha Publishing House, New Delhi.

Srivastava, R.M. (2000): '*Financial Management*', Pragati Prakashan, Meerut.

State Bank of India (1996): Report of the Sub-Committee of State Level Banker's Committee for Mizoram on Credit-Deposit Ratio, Lead Bank Office, Aizawl, Dt: 15th November.

State Bank of India (1999): State Level Bankers' Committee Meeting for Mizoram, Lead Bank Office, Aizawl, Dt: 28th June.

Thangchungnunga (2004): 'Fiscal Management in Mizoram,' *Dialogue*, Vol.-4, No.1, July-September.

UN-ESCAP (1996): Study on India's Border Trade with Select Neighbouring Countries, Research and Information System for Non-Aligned and Developing Countries, New Delhi.

Upadhyaya, K.K. (1986): '*Development Problems and Prospects of Mizoram*,' Inter-India Publications, New Delhi.

Vaish, M.C. (1997): '*Money, Banking, Trade and Public Finance*,' New Age International (P) Ltd., Publishers, New Delhi, 3rd ed.

Vargheese, Brigadier C.G. and Thanzawna, R.L. (1997): '*A History of the Mizos*,' Vol. 1, Vikas Publishing House Pvt. Ltd., New Delhi.

Viswanathan, R. and Talwar, R.K. (1982): '*Industrial Finance*,' S. Chand & Co. Ltd., New Delhi.

Yogi A.K. (1991): '*Development of the Northeast Region: Problems and Prospects*,' Spectrum Publications, Guwahati.

Zahid Hussain (2000): 'The Nature of Border and Border Trade of Northeast India,' in edited volume *"Border Trade—North East India and Neighbouring Countries,"* by Das, Gurudas & Purkayastha, R.K., Akansha Publishing House, New Delhi.

INDEX